SHARED GOVERNMENT IN
EMPLOYMENT SECURITY

Shared Government in Employment Security

A STUDY OF ADVISORY COUNCILS

Joseph M. Becker, S.J.

COLUMBIA UNIVERSITY PRESS

New York, 1959

COPYRIGHT © 1959 COLUMBIA UNIVERSITY PRESS, NEW YORK

PUBLISHED IN GREAT BRITAIN, CANADA, INDIA, AND PAKISTAN
BY THE OXFORD UNIVERSITY PRESS
LONDON, TORONTO, BOMBAY, AND KARACHI

LIBRARY OF CONGRESS CATALOG CARD NUMBER: 59-7384
MANUFACTURED IN THE UNITED STATES OF AMERICA

TO MY FATHER
JOHN WILLIAM BECKER
MY LEADING EXEMPLAR
OF SHARED GOVERNMENT

CONTENTS

PART FOUR. EXPERIENCE WITH OTHER ADVISORY COUNCILS

PART FIVE. SUMMARY AND ANALYSIS

APPENDIXES

PREFACE

THE general concern of this book is the problem of how to maintain popular control over modern—which means big and growing—government. The problem extends into nearly every area of social life, but this book is concerned with only the area of industrial relations. Labor and management are easily the two most powerful private groups in modern society, and the relationships they establish between themselves and government go far to determine the relationships between society as a whole and government.

Within the broad area of labor-management relations I have concentrated on a single sub-area, that encompassed by the program of employment security. For reasons explained in Chapters 1 and 2, I was interested in the institution of the advisory council, and the program of employment security provided a wealth of experience in the use of advisory councils. It was a body of experience that was twenty years deep and sufficiently broad to include states of various sizes and of varied industrial and political complexion. This variegated experience presented a better opportunity than is usually available to the social scientist—deprived as he is of the natural scientist's control over the conditions of his experiment—to investigate correlations between variations in council effectiveness and possible factors of effectiveness.

The goal of the investigation was therefore a qualitative one, to find out what makes an effective advisory council effective. The means to the goal consisted of one researcher free to travel for a year or more. The qualitative nature of the goal and the limited nature of the means together determined the research method.

The qualitative nature of the goal ruled out the use of mailed questionnaires. The Bureau of Employment Security in 1941 and again in 1945 and Rhode Island in 1951 had used questionnaires to compile information on advisory councils, but the results were very inadequate as a measure of council effectiveness. Only on-the-spot investigation could produce the kind of information that was needed. The limited nature of the means precluded the investigation of all the councils; a selection had to be made. The study of why effective councils were effective promised more rewards than a study of why other councils were not; so only those councils were chosen which a preliminary investigation had established as having some promise of effectiveness. (It was clear at this early stage that even in a sample so chosen there would be no lack of examples of relatively ineffective councils.) This procedure produced a sample of nineteen councils.

I decided to make my own curiosity the norm of the investigation and to adapt my method at each successive stage to the changing requirements of that norm. My plan was simple: I would begin with those states which seemed to have the most promise, and move on to the rest in turn; in each state I would seek out those persons and ask those questions which my growing knowledge and my consequently changing curiosity dictated; I would stay as long as my inquiries continued to produce fruit, and when the law of diminishing returns began to manifest itself I would move on to the next state.

I expected that this procedure would result in my "doing" many states partially rather than a few completely. And since the emphasis of the inquiry would be a function of both the peculiar characteristics of each state and my own changing knowledge, I expected that the procedure would result in my varying the emphasis of the inquiry from state to state. And so it turned out. I went into eighteen states and the District of Columbia and in each followed a somewhat different line of inquiry.

This method was not adapted (nor was it intended) to produce balanced histories of the individual councils, and the sixteen narrative chapters are not offered as such. They are offered only as a collection of council experiences selected for their usefulness in answering the central question: What makes an effective council effective? The narrative chapters should be read, not as self-contained units each having its own significance, but as parts of a whole, and therefore as deriving their significance from that whole.

It is important that this point be quite clear. The narrative chapters should be read as partial accounts affected by limitations that operated at the stages of both investigation and reporting. I have already explained how selective and variable was my method of investigation. It could and did result in my studying Problem X intensively in State A, for example, and omitting it entirely in State B, not necessarily because Problem X was less important in State B than in State A, but because having already satisfied my curiosity with regard to Problem X in State A I preferred to use what time I had in State B to investigate Problem Y, for example, which was perhaps unique to State B.

At the stage of reporting, a further limitation came into play. Many council experiences that were recorded could not be reported even in this overlarge book. In selecting the experiences to be reported, I was again influenced by the goal of the book, which was to present, not a balanced history of the individual councils, but evidence—as much as one researcher could unearth and one book hold—on what makes an effective council effective. The reporting, consequently, was as selective as the recording. Experience X of State B might be minimized or omitted, for example, and Experience Y emphasized, not because Y was a more significant part of B's history, but because X had already been sufficiently exemplified in the reported experiences of State A, and it seemed best to use the space available for State B to illuminate some other facet of the central problem of the book.

It follows that caution must be used in basing interstate comparisons on the narrative chapters. The argument from silence, always tricky, is quite unreliable in these chapters. No conclusion can be drawn from the bare fact that Experience X is recounted in the history of State A but not in the history of State B. The narrative chapters were not written with a view to making detailed interstate comparisons, and they can be used for that purpose only within narrow limits.

Although the narrative chapters are not complete histories of the individual councils, they are not positively distorted histories. What is reported as having happened did happen. More important, the conclusions that have been drawn from the selected experiences of each council would not be changed significantly by a fuller history of the councils.

The study will have different interests for different groups. The administrators of employment security will find it a useful handbook on the care and nurture of advisory councils. The administrators of many other programs have problems sufficiently like those in employment security to profit from the experiences narrated here. Perhaps the book will help administrators keep alive their perception that the quintessence of good government is so to administer their programs as to encourage political democracy.

Students of industrial relations, including the leaders of labor and management, will be interested in the process of producing agreed bills. Most collective bargaining situations involve single firms and unions, or at most all the firms and unions in a single industry, and the bargaining takes place under threat of a strike. But here the bargaining takes place between all of labor and all of management in the state, and the pressure on the two parties to reach agreement is the threat, not of a strike, but of compulsory arbitration (by the legislature). This is an interesting situation in its own right; it has, moreover, a close affinity to the "emergency dispute" situation, which threatens to become a characteristic problem of our era.

Finally, students of government will find this a recent investigation of an ever-contemporary political problem—what Ernest Barker calls the "permanent tension between the authority of the State and the voluntary play of freely formed and freely acting groups or societies." Students of government will also welcome the additional historical material provided here relating to those most neglected of political divisions, the states in our federal system.

The book is constructed like a sandwich, with two slices of theory and analysis surrounding a center of history. One slice consists of a pair of introductory chapters on the theory of advisory councils. The other slice consists of four analytical chapters of summary and conclusions. In between is a substantial filling of sixteen chapters that narrate some of the experiences of selected councils. (Of nineteen councils studied, three had to be omitted from the narrative because of space limitations.)

Today's reader, facing a torrent of printed matter that threatens to overwhelm him, has a right to know how he can, if he needs to, get the gist of a given book without reading the whole of it. Chapter 1 may be skipped by anyone who recognizes that the great growth of centralized government in the United States presents problems for liberty and efficiency and that a prime factor in the solution of those problems is furnished by the existence of voluntary groups intermediate between the state and the individual. The entire middle part, consisting of Chapters 3–18, may be skipped by anyone who is not primarily interested in the employment security program and who is willing to accept the author's summary in Chapter 19. Even Chapter 19 may be skipped by those who merely want conclusions. But everyone who wishes to understand the book at all must read at least Chapters 2, 20, and 21.

I wish to express my appreciation to the Rockefeller Foundation and to various groups in labor and industry for their financial assistance in carrying through this study. I am indebted to the many federal and state administrators of employment security and to the still more numerous members of advisory councils whose cooperation provided the "stuff" of the study: I wish that I could acknowledge my indebtedness to each by name. The Institute of Social Order and St. Louis University provided indispensable facilities for the work.

JOSEPH M. BECKER, S.J.

Institute of Social Order
Saint Louis University
October, 1958

Part One

FUNCTIONS OF ADVISORY COUNCILS

1

SHARED GOVERNMENT

PHILOSOPHICAL PRESUPPOSITIONS

THE problem of organizing society is ultimately, like most problems, an aspect of the One-Many dichotomy. To achieve the ends of society men must choose to act as individuals, and therefore as Many, or to act as a group, and therefore as One. This basic choice recurs on three levels, which in logic represent successive choices but which in practice are often simultaneous.

The first choice is whether to make use of the group technique at all, that is, whether to allocate a given function of society to a group or to leave it to individuals. If the function is to be allocated to a group, the next choice is whether to use a private group or the public group called the state.[1] The third choice is whether to have much or little democracy within whatever group is used, that is, whether to give the members of the group much or little participation in the decision-making processes of the group.

Although all three choices are intimately connected, this study is concerned only with the second and third. It is concerned with these two precisely in so far as they overlap, that is, in so far as one method of promoting democracy within the state is to give private groups some share in the government of the state.

[1] By the state is meant here the organization whose jurisdiction is *universal* (extends to all who belong in a given geographical area), *supreme* (recognizes no legal superior), and *coercive*. If its jurisdiction extends to all the functions of society, the state is also *absolute*.

PRINCIPLE OF SUBSIDIARITY

The proper criterion for making these decisions is the "common good." [2] But how this "good" is to be defined, and how after being defined it is to be determined (by the philosopher-king? by the expert? by majority vote?) are profound questions of political philosophy which this chapter wisely does not attempt to answer. The aim of this chapter is simply to set out certain basic presuppositions which underlie much of the analysis that follows and which explain many of its emphases. These presuppositions can be gathered together under one heading and stated as a preference —a preference for the principle of subsidiarity. The principle of subsidiarity states that a higher unit of society should not undertake to perform functions which can be handled as well by a lower unit but rather should offer help (*subsidium*) where necessary to enable the lower unit to function at full capacity. The principle carries the crucial implication that decision making should be shared as widely as possible.

A preference for the principle of subsidiarity is thus seen to be equivalent to a preference for what is called political democracy. Democracy has been defined in scores of different ways, but the definitions generally fall into one of two categories: they emphasize either what people get from government or what people do in government. Democracy in the first sense is sometimes called "economic" and in the second sense "political." Economic democracy is said to exist when certain substantive criteria are met; for example, when there exists a certain degree of equality of income. This is the sense in which democracy is generally used in the Communist world.[3] That this view of democracy has significance for the Western world as well was recognized by the

[2] In practice, of course, the decisions are often made according to simpler norms: precedent, the press of events, or even personal interest. *Quantula regitur mundus sapientia!*

[3] For the different meanings given to "democracy" by Russia and the West, see "The UNESCO Questionnaire on Ideological Conflicts concerning Democracy," in *Main Currents of Western Thought,* ed. Franklin L. E. VanBaumer (New York: Alfred A. Knopf, 1952), pp. 653–58. Edward S. Corwin uses much the same distinction in defining "liberty." See his *Liberty against Government* (Baton Rouge: Louisiana State University Press, 1948), pp. 3–7.

President's Committee on Administrative Management: "Without results we know that democracy means nothing and ceases to be alive in the minds and hearts of men." [4] When Lincoln spoke of "this government *for* the people," he probably had something like economic democracy in mind.

Political democracy exists when the governed participate in the decision-making processes of government. Lincoln was describing political democracy when he spoke of "this government *of* the people, *by* the people." This is the traditional definition of democracy and the one used generally in the West.[5] At its minimum political democracy means freedom of speech and association for all the members of the group, so that every member is free to praise or blame the ruler(s) of the group and to organize a party of support or opposition. At its maximum political democracy means full and direct participation by every member in every decision the group makes. The maximum is usually an impossibility in most groups and always an impossibility in the state, but according to the democratic principle the closer this maximum can be approached, the better—other things being equal.

BASIS OF THE PRINCIPLE

The basic justification for the principle of subsidiarity is that the units of human society are *persons,* that is, beings possessed of intellect and free will. From this basic fact flow three practical conclusions, one derived from a perfection in those who are ruled, and two derived from imperfections in those who rule.

When the Many have the perfection of persons, they can never make One as the many parts of a machine make one machine, nor even as the many parts of a tree make one tree.[6] Because the

---

[4] Report of the President's Committee on Administrative Management, *Administrative Management in the Government of the United States* (Washington: Government Printing Office, 1937), p. 1.

[5] See, for example: James Bryce, *Modern Democracies* (New York: Macmillan Co., 1924), II, 595; and R. M. MacIver, *The Web of Government* (New York: Macmillan Co., 1945), pp. 206-7.

[6] This is where the metaphor of organism as applied to the state—the *body* politic —breaks down and has to be used warily.

ruled are persons they can be one only in a unity of purpose, that is, in a unity forged by the activity of their own intellects and wills. The unity of persons can thus never be a purely passive thing; it must be the result of activity on the part of the persons involved. In the literal sense of the phrase it must be a result of personal activity. A person may properly devote himself to achieving the ends of the larger social whole of which he is a part, but he must do so in accordance with his own nature—that is, he must understand those ends and will them. In thus subordinating himself to society he does not surrender his selfhood; rather he fulfills his selfhood in intelligent and free service rendered to the common good.[7]

The perfection of personality leads to a preference for the principle of subsidiarity in an additional way. Persons seem to have an inexhaustible capacity for variation. They are not like potatoes in a row, all of which will prosper under the same sort of treatment, but exhibit the greatest variety in their needs and still more in their desires.[8] Whenever persons become parts of a group, unless the group limits its goals to those in respect to which the members are perfectly homogeneous—an almost impossible condition—there will always be some loss of individual satisfaction incurred by group action. To keep this loss to a minimum the group should be kept as small as possible, so as to make it as homogeneous as possible; but if the group must be large—as in the case of the state—then its goals should be limited to those which are common to all its members and other goals should be left to be attained by other, more specialized groups.

Whereas the first justification for the principle of subsidiarity was founded on a perfection of those who are ruled in human society, the second is founded on an imperfection of those who rule. The will does not always act according to the light of the intellect. For this reason the ruler(s) of a group cannot be entirely

[7] In this connection see "The Person and the Common Good," Ch. 8 of *The Social and Political Philosophy of Jacques Maritain: Selected Readings*, ed. Joseph W. Evans and Leo R. Ward (New York: Charles Scribner's Sons, 1955), pp. 82–88.

[8] The reason is, according to traditional Aristotelian-Thomistic philosophy, that persons are spiritual beings. But whatever the reason, the fact is unmistakable.

trusted. In the Acton formula, all power corrupts, and absolute power corrupts absolutely. In the Michels formula, there is an iron law of oligarchy whereby once a group has established its rulers, those rulers gradually substitute their own particular good for the general good of the group as the norm of group action.[9] Granted that Michels exaggerates the "iron" quality of his law, it is literally true that no type of organization has managed to escape entirely from the law's operation—not the church, not labor unions,[10] not the state. The threat, at least, of the iron law is always present.

Of the various defenses against the iron law the most effective has proved to be competition. The individual is safest from the operation of the law when power is divided between a number of groups, each of which is in competition with the others for the individual's loyalty. A woman is never so safe from the greater strength of men as when she has a number of suitors. The application of the principle of subsidiarity normally results in a plurality of groups. By playing one against the other, the individual can check the growth of onerous power in any one. That this defense is needed most urgently against the state follows from the fact that the state is the group with the greatest power, but a balanced view should note that the reverse is frequently true and that the state may be needed as a defense against the onerous power of private groups. The state may be needed, for example, to protect the individual members of a group from the tyranny of a father who beats his wife and denies education to his children, or from the tyranny of a medical society that imposes unrealis-

[9] James Bryce ruminates: "It [democracy] will have to go on trying, for Nature is always tending to throw Power into the hands of the Few, and the Few always tend by a like natural process to solidify into a Class, as the vapours rising from the earth gather into clouds." *Modern Democracies,* II, 549. David Truman has an enlightening discussion of the relationship between the "active minority" in a group and the rest of the group; see *The Governmental Process* (New York: Alfred A. Knopf, 1955), pp. 139–55.

[10] A striking recognition of the iron law was the establishment by the UAW in 1957 of a Public Review Board, composed of seven distinguished citizens not connected with the union, with power to hear appeals of rank-and-file unionists against their leaders and to investigate any alleged violation by union leaders of the ethical practice codes of the AFL-CIO. See *Monthly Labor Review,* LXXX (June, 1957), 699.

tic standards, or from the tyranny of a corporation that will not allow its employees to organize, or from the tyranny of a labor union that is dominated by criminals.

The third justification for the principle of subsidiarity is likewise founded on an imperfection of human nature. The human intellect is limited. As the size and scope of any organization grow, those who manage the organization find themselves increasingly unable to know what is happening in all its parts and to make decisions that accord with the facts. The larger the organization and the greater its scope, the more it suffers, in the phrase of Lamennais, from apoplexy at the center and anemia at the extremities. Other things being equal, it is easier to manage a small organization than a large one. The application of the principle of subsidiarity prevents organizations from growing unnecessarily large in either size or scope.

As applied to the state, this limitation is especially apt and especially important. It is apt because the state's task of overall governance is more complex than that of any other organization. It is important because the state is absolutely necessary to society; and if for no other reason than to be free to perform its essential tasks efficiently, the state should restrict itself to managing only those concerns which smaller groups cannot manage as well, or almost as well, for themselves, and leave other functions to other groups.[11]

To sum up. Society makes three major choices in allocating functions to its members: it chooses between the individual and the group, between the private and the public group, and between more and less democracy within groups. In each instance the principle of subsidiarity is a proper guide to the correct choice because the members of human society are persons, with the perfections and imperfections of persons. That is to say— taking the three justifications for the principle of subsidiarity in inverse order—rulers are not always able to do what is best for

[11] J. S. Mill's Ch. 11 in Book V of his *Principles of Political Economy* (New York: Longmans, Green & Co., new edition, 1909) is still a readable, pertinent summary of the major considerations which lead to limiting government.

their subjects; even when they are able, they are not always willing; even when they are able and willing, the members may prefer to do it for themselves, for even good government is not a substitute for self-government when the governed are persons.

HISTORICAL PERSPECTIVES

Like all particular principles, the principle of subsidiarity applies to the existential order only with the qualification "other things being equal." Because in fact "other things" vary greatly, the principle of subsidiarity must in some situations yield its preferred position to other principles. Society may prefer at times less of democracy and more of something else—more efficiency, possibly, in the collection of garbage, or more security against foreign attack. Or perhaps just less bother. One of the not unimportant reasons that members of a group designate a few of their number to be more active than the rest in the affairs of the group is to save the time and energy of the rest. No one wants to spend all his holidays auditing the accounts of his alderman. Thus it happens that the allocation of society's functions as between the individual, the private group, and the state can vary, and historically has varied, endlessly.

France and America taken at the times of their respective revolutions in the late eighteenth century illustrate almost diametrically opposite positions with respect to the place of private groups in society. If the story of all modern Europe consists largely of the "successive extrications of both individual and the State from the fetters of medieval group life," [12] in France the process of extrication was carried out with dramatic violence to its final logical conclusion. France had an *ancien régime* of which it wanted to rid itself. The roots of that regime extended into every sphere of life—economic, political, religious. Only the state, and only an omnicompetent state, could root out the regime completely and quickly. So the French Revolution produced an omnicompetent

[12] Robert A. Nisbet, *The Quest for Community* (New York: Oxford University Press, 1953), p. 80.

state based on the convenient philosophy that society and the state were coterminous and that private groups were the enemy of both.

Rousseau provided the philosophy. Rousseau brings to fruition a line of thought beginning in Bodin (confusedly and mildly) and developed by Hobbes (clearly and extravagantly) that the state alone is charged with a concern for the common good and that all private associations within the commonwealth are, in the graphic figure used by Hobbes, "so many worms in the entrails of a natural man." According to Rousseau, every citizen must be "perfectly independent of all his fellow men, and in absolute dependence on the State." [13] The full logical application of this philosophy is seen in the *Loi Chapelier,* which abolished all private groups, even the guilds and professional societies. Chapelier announced to the Constituent Assembly of 1789: "There are no longer any guilds in the state, but only the private interest of each individual and the general interest." [14]

According to Rousseau, all citizens are "absolutely dependent on the state." But they are also absolutely free, and they are free *because* they are dependent. Whatever a citizen may think to the contrary, his "true" will is identical with the General Will, which is the will of the state. The state is conceived as an organism having a distinct will of its own, which is not the same as the sum of all the particular wills of its members. When the citizen is compelled to obey the General Will of the state he is merely being "compelled to be free," much as the cell of a body is merely being compelled to fulfill itself when it is put to work for the good of the whole body. It is this subtle identification of freedom with state absolutism that constitutes Rousseau's unique contribution to the theory of totalitarianism [15] and that more than any-

---

[13] Jean Jacques Rousseau, *The Social Contract,* trans. Henry J. Tozer (London: George Allen & Unwin, 1895), p. 147.

[14] Quoted in Thomas Neil, *The Rise and Decline of Liberalism* (Milwaukee: Bruce Publishing Co., 1953), p. 71. If Von Gierke and Maitland are correct, the "reception" of Roman law in Europe toward the end of the Middle Ages contributed to the decline of private groups and the growth of the modern state by its doctrine that all associations other than the state received their existence from the state.

[15] Rousseau is anything but consistent in his various works. This has led to much controversy among scholars as to his commitment to totalitarianism. (See *The Social and Political Ideas of Some Great French Thinkers of the Age of Reason,* ed. F. J. C.

thing else accounts for his popularity with the French Communists today. Rousseau today is a fountainhead of that intellectual devotion to the state which makes so favorable a climate for the growth of political totalitarianism.[16]

Although only thirteen years separated the American Revolution from its French counterpart, the underlying philosophy of the two was very different, especially in regard to the rights of private groups as against the state. Rousseau's semideification of the state sounded an alien note in American ears. The tone of Jefferson's first inaugural address was more congenial:

A wise and frugal government, which shall restrain men from injuring one another, shall leave them otherwise free to regulate their own pursuits of industry and improvement and shall not take from the mouth of labor the bread it has earned. This is the sum of good government.

The political philosophy underlying the American Revolution was largely the philosophy of Locke, which, like that of his scholastic predecessors, kept clear the fundamental distinction between society and the state and thereby provided the principle by which to limit government. To most Americans at the time of the Declaration of Independence it was a self-evident truth that all men were endowed by their Creator with certain unalienable rights, which governments were instituted to secure and which even republican governments might not invade. To the Rousseauan argument that the "General Will" as expressed by the state is the individual's "true" will, whether the individual thinks so or not, skeptical Americans were inclined to reply that the "General Will" might often enough be highly colored by the will of the Some who happened to be in control of the apparatus of government.

This difference in political philosophies was due partly to

Hearnshaw [New York: Barnes & Noble, Inc., 1950], pp. 184, 185.) The interpretation followed here is substantially that of C. E. Vaughan as given in his edition of *The Political Writings of Jean J. Rousseau*, 2 vols. (London: Cambridge University Press, 1915).

[16] Hegel has often been charged with fathering modern totalitarianism. Currently, a reappraisal of Hegel is going forward which seeks to change that judgment. For an early instance of such reappraisal see Kung Chuan Hsiao, *Political Pluralism* (New York: Harcourt, Brace & Co., Inc., 1927), pp. 211 ff. and 256.

differences in political experience. In the American experience there was no oppressive Old Order to be rooted up. Individual independence and a large degree of self-government were the normal experience of the American people from the very beginning of the nation. The Declaration of Independence did not so much inaugurate a new social regime as give legal sanction to a preexisting one.

Since the people were always on the move from the more settled to the undeveloped regions of the country, successive generations of common men were forced to discard settled customs and fixed habits, to break with family ties and old associations, and, relying on their own initiative and common sense, to reshape social institutions and forms of governments to suit the practical needs of life in new and relatively primitive conditions. . . . It is this peculiar historical experience that has disposed the American people to emphasize the freedom and responsibility of the individual and to minimize the function and authority of the government.[17]

Although this wary attitude toward government has undergone modification with the years and although Americans have become keenly aware of the dangers to the common good inherent in the activities of private interest groups,[18] the typical American still feels much closer to Jefferson than to Rousseau.[19] It remains an American characteristic to see a greater threat of oppression coming from government than from private groups. There has been no American counterpart of the *Loi Chapelier*. On the contrary, from the beginning private associations have had the fullest freedom to operate, and they have flourished. When the Frenchman Alexis de Tocqueville visited America in 1830, he was struck

[17] Carl L. Becker, *Freedom and Responsibility in the American Way of Life* (New York: Vintage Books, 1955) pp. 15, 16. Quotation used by permission of Alfred A. Knopf, Inc.

[18] For example, the investigations of the House Select Committee on Lobbying Activities (81st Cong., 2d session), which published in 1950 ten volumes of hearings and eleven volumes of reports. In the 85th Congress a subcommittee of the House Committee on Government Operations held hearings on a bill that would set up a code governing the operations of advisory groups "as a minimum safeguard against the use of any such group to influence public policy for the benefit of private interests." And see n. 62 below.

[19] Arthur Schlesinger, Jr. is very American and very un-Rousseauan is his remark that the normal American "can take Government, like liquor, in moderation and benefit from it." "Whittaker Chambers and His Witness," *Saturday Review Reader No. 2* (New York: Bantam Books, 1953), p. 62.

by their number and vigor. In a chapter entitled "Of the Use
Which Americans Make of Public Associations in Civil Life,"
Tocqueville observed that "wherever at the head of some new
undertaking you see the government in France, or a man of rank
in England, in the United States you will be sure to find an association." [20] Indeed, it was precisely in this phenomenon that
Tocqueville saw the soundest hope for preserving the American
type of democracy, which he much favored over the Rousseauan
type.

THE PROBLEM OF GOVERNMENT
PREDICTION

The doctrine of laissez-faire as applied to government was never
more vigorous in any country at any time than in the United
States in 1830, when Tocqueville visited the young republic and
wrote his classic *Democracy in America*. In view of the popularity
of laissez-faire thought, and in view of the actually limited scope
of government at that time,[21] it is surprising that Tocqueville's
analysis was deeply concerned with the threat of a future despotism.

Tocqueville [22] predicted that government in America would
grow greatly in both scope and size and would become more centralized. He based his prediction on the nature of democracy and
on the nature of the modern economy. First of all, in a democracy
subjects are willing to grant a ruler great power because they consider that government is their creation and that when they obey
government they are in a sense only obeying themselves. Second,
in a democracy equality ranks very high in the hierarchy of social

[20] Alexis de Tocqueville, *Democracy in America* (New York: Vintage Books, 1954),
II, 114.

[21] Especially of the central government. For some of the qualifications which must
be made to this proposition in respect to the state governments, see Oscar and Mary
Handlin, *Commonwealth of Massachusetts, 1774–1861* (New York: New York University Press, 1947), p. xii and *passim*.

[22] Everything that is here illustrated by Tocqueville could be illustrated by a number of more modern political writers. But Tocqueville has certain advantages. His
position of a century and a half ago lends perspective. His presentation of the principal issues is simple, uncomplicated by controversies over details that have arisen
since his time. Yet he is modern, for the several swings in emphasis among political
writers since his time have brought us back to where he started. And, of course,
Tocqueville has the added dramatic flavor that attaches to the prophet.

values. But equality is extraordinarily difficult to achieve. To many citizens the most direct route to equality will seem to be to give everybody the same amount of influence in government (one vote) and then concentrate all power in government. Third, whether or not the first two forces are operative, competition between citizens for the favors of government will constantly augment the power of government. In Tocqueville's words:

It frequently happens that the members of the community promote the influence of the central power without intending to. . . . [They] will admit, as a general principle, that the public authority ought not to interfere in private concerns; but, by an exception to that rule, each of them craves its assistance in the particular concern on which he is engaged and seeks to draw upon the influence of the government for his own benefit, although he would restrict it on all other occasions. If a large number of men applies this particular exception to a great variety of different purposes, the sphere of the central power extends itself imperceptibly in all directions, although everyone wishes it to be circumscribed. Thus a democratic government increases its power simply by the fact of its permanence. Time is on its side; every incident befriends it; the passions of individuals unconsciously promote it; and it may be asserted that the older a democratic community is, the more centralized will its government become.[23]

Finally, Tocqueville based his expectations on the nature of the modern economy. He foresaw that the modern economy would become ever more complex and interdependent, and that as a consequence there would be greater need for central direction by government. "It is easy to foresee that the time is drawing near when man will be less and less able to produce, by himself alone, the commonest necessaries of life. The task of the governing power will therefore perpetually increase." [24]

Having thus argued to the inevitable growth of government in a democracy, Tocqueville describes the kind of despotism which might result. His last chapter but two is entitled "What Sort of Despotism Democratic Nations Have to Fear." Although written

---

[23] Tocqueville, *Democracy in America*, II, 311–12.

[24] *Ibid.*, p. 116. He adds the perspicacious observation that "the manufacturing classes require more regulation, superintendence, and restraint than the other classes of society, and it is natural that the powers of government should increase in the same proportion as those classes. . . . It would seem as if despotism lurked within them and naturally grew with their growth." (*Ibid.*, pp. 327, 329.)

so early in the modern period, it stands unsurpassed as a description of the modern brand of totalitarianism which combines absolute control with the terminology and trappings of democracy.

I had remarked during my stay in the United States that a democratic state of society, similar to that of the Americans, might offer singular facilities for the establishment of despotism. I think that the species of oppression by which democratic nations are menaced is unlike anything that ever before existed in the world; our contemporaries will find no prototype of it in their memories. I seek in vain for an expression that will accurately convey the whole of the idea that I have formed of it; the old words *despotism* and *tyranny* are inappropriate; the thing itself is new and since I cannot name it, I must attempt to define it.

The first thing that strikes the observation is an innumerable multitude of men, all equal and alike. Above this race of men stands an immense and tutelary power, which takes upon itself alone to secure their gratifications and to watch over their fate. That power is absolute, minute, regular, provident, and mild. It would be like the authority of a parent if, like that authority, its object was to prepare men for manhood; but it seeks, on the contrary, to keep them in perpetual childhood.

I have always thought that servitude of the regular, quiet, and gentle kind, which I have just described might be combined more easily than is commonly believed with some of the outward forms of freedom, and that it might even establish itself under the wing of the sovereignty of the people. Every man allows himself to be put in leading-strings, because he sees that it is not a person or a class of persons, but the people at large who hold the end of his chain. By this system the people shake off their state of dependence just long enough to select their master and then relapse into it again.[25]

FULFILLMENT

Tocqueville's prediction that the control of government over the country's life, especially over its economic life, would continuously expand and that the administration of government would continuously become more centralized has, of course, been fulfilled. In the field of collective production, that is, the direct ownership by government of the means of production (the essence

---

[25] *Ibid.*, pp. 334, 336, 337. Suspension marks have been omitted in the interest of easier reading.

of socialism), the growth of government has been modest.[26] But in the field of collective consumption and in the field of regulation (of both production and consumption) the growth has been spectacular.

In the century and a quarter separating Tocqueville's visit to the United States and the present, the proportion of gross national product passing through the hands of government was increased at least tenfold. Even between the census years 1930 and 1950 the proportion nearly doubled—from 12 percent of the GNP in 1930 to 21 percent in 1950.[27] During the same period the labor force increased by 25 percent, but the civilian employees of government increased by 91 percent, so that government employees as a proportion of the labor force increased from 6 percent to 9 percent.[28] By 1957 the proportion was averaging in the neighborhood of 11 percent.[29] Growth of government has been great on all levels,[30] but especially on the federal level. Between 1930 and 1950, while the expenditures of all government as a percentage of the GNP were almost doubling (12 percent to 21 percent), those of the federal government more than quadrupled (3 percent to 14 percent); [31] and while the civilian employees of all government were increasing 91 percent, those of the executive branch of the federal government increased 230 percent.[32] Thus the federal government has become a larger part of a larger whole and to that extent the administration of government has become more centralized.

Most of this federal growth has occurred in the administrative departments. Between 1930 and 1950 the various departments, agencies, bureaus, commissions, and so forth of the federal government increased from about 400 to over 2,000. Together they

[26] Being confined chiefly to public power developments, such as the TVA.

[27] U.S. Department of Commerce, *National Income*, 1954 edition, pp. 164, 172.

[28] U.S. Department of Commerce, *Business Statistics*, 1955 edition, pp. 56, 59, 63.

[29] Bureau of the Census, U.S. Department of Commerce, *Monthly Report on the Labor Force*, monthly estimates for 1957.

[30] Between 1900 and 1954 the employees of state governments increased five times as fast as population, and state expenditures increased four times as fast as national income. Arthur B. Langlie, Governor of Washington, presented these data in an address—to the 61st Annual Conference on Government, National Municipal League, July 25, 1955—which analyzed the shift of power from the states to the federal government.

[31] *National Income*, pp. 164, 172.

[32] *Business Statistics*, pp. 56, 59, 63.

constitute the government bureaucracy, which because of its size and influence has come to be known as the "fourth branch" of government.[33] David Truman is speaking for political scientists generally when he calls this development "the most characteristic feature of twentieth century government." [34] Its importance is put succinctly by Hyneman: "Government has enormous power over us, and most of the acts of government are put into effect by the men and women who constitute the bureaucracy." [35]

Centralization is most prominent in this "fourth branch" of government, which effectively combines what the Founding Fathers so carefully separated. The three traditional branches of government found that they themselves could not perform or even directly supervise the multitudinous new tasks imposed on them by a service-minded society in a technological world. Neither legislator nor judge nor chief executive had either the time or the competence to give continuous direction to such tasks as grading wheat, regulating the sale of securities, allocating radio frequencies and television stations, paying unemployment benefits, and all the rest. It was found necessary to set up specialized administrative agencies and to grant them wide discretion.[36] Each branch of government has been obliged, in effect, to delegate a part of its responsibility and a corresponding part of its discretionary power to each of the specialized agencies. As a result there has developed a branch of government which although narrower in extension is broader in comprehension than any of the three traditional

[33] "The rise of administrative bodies probably has been the most significant trend of the last century, and perhaps more values today are affected by their decisions than by those of all the courts. . . . They have become a veritable fourth branch of the Government, which has deranged our three-branch legal theories much as the concept of a fourth dimension unsettles our three-dimensional thinking." Justice Jackson of the U.S. Supreme Court, as quoted in Hearings on H. Res. 462 (To Establish a Committee on Administrative Procedure and Practice), Special Subcommittee of Committee on Rules, House of Representatives, 84th Cong., 2d sess., May 22, 1956, p. 3.

[34] *The Governmental Process,* p. 395.

[35] Charles H. Hyneman, *Bureaucracy in a Democracy* (New York: Harper & Brothers, 1950), p. 38.

[36] Congress has generally given to these agencies the power "to issue such regulations as it [the agency] may deem necessary or proper in order to carry out the purposes and provisions of this act." Ernest Freund has described the gradual relaxation of the detailed restraints which legislatures formerly wrote into the laws they passed; see his *Standards of American Legislation* (Chicago: University of Chicago Press, 1917), pp. 144–84, 248–70.

branches. That is, although each agency is limited to a single program, within that program the agency performs functions proper to all three branches.[37]

The growth of government influence has not been confined to the kind measurable in terms of men and money. There has been a great increase in the regulatory powers of government, and this development is not adequately reflected in terms of budgets and personnel. It would be underestimating the impact on the country's life of the Federal Communications Commission, for example, or of the Anti-Trust Division of the Justice Department to measure their influence solely by the size of their relatively small staffs.[38] It was the growth of governmental regulatory powers, as much as anything else, that caused Charles Beard to reverse himself in his *The Economic Basis of Politics.* The first edition of the book (1922) developed the thesis implied in the title. The last edition (1945) carried an additional chapter in which Beard reviewed the changes in government which had taken place since the first edition and concluded that the relationship between politics and economics had been reversed: politics now determined economics.

Among the more obvious forces which caused this great growth in government were those which Tocqueville had anticipated. A principal cause was the portfolio of new needs presented by an urbanized,[39] technological [40] society. Another major cause has been the competition among private groups for the favors of government. This source of growth is illustrated most strikingly in the establishment of the "clientele" agencies, beginning with

[37] John R. Commons refers to this phenomenon of merging functions in his *Legal Foundations of Capitalism,* first published by the Macmillan Co. in 1924 and reprinted by the University of Wisconsin Press in 1957; see p. 343 of the Wisconsin edition.

[38] It is significant that whereas in 1912 there were fifty-five letters mailed out for every federal employee, in 1953 the corresponding figure was 522 letters. See Alfred De Grazia, *The American Way of Government* (New York: John Wiley & Sons, Inc., 1957), p. 475.

[39] Eli Heckscher notes this effect of urbanization even in the Middle Ages. He describes how it was the growth of towns that brought about "the first attempt in Western Europe, after the decline of the ancient world, to regulate society on its economic side according to consistent principles." *Mercantilism* (New York: Macmillan Co., revised ed., 1955) I, 39.

[40] For a discussion of the three technological factors of interdependence, specialization, and mobility as causes of change in government, see MacIver, *The Web of Government,* pp. 289–96.

the Department of Agriculture in 1862, continuing with the Department of Commerce in 1903, the Department of Labor in 1913, and going on to the Veterans Administration in 1930, and to others subsequently. In a TNEC report Blaisdell remarked: "The competition among groups for official approval of their aims is perhaps the outstanding characteristic of the governmental process in America of the twentieth century." [41]

Wars and depressions have, of course, contributed greatly to the growth of government but their impact has been so marked primarily because they have occurred in a technological setting.[42] Moreover we expect that these phenomena will always be literally extraordinary and that the governmental activity to which they give rise will cease with their disappearance. To the extent that this expectation is not realized the growth of government will be enormously accelerated. But even if the expectation is realized, and the normal state of society proves to be one of prosperity and peace, the quiet forces to which Tocqueville pointed will remain continuously at work, and government will continue to grow.

There has been one significant cause of growth in government which Tocqueville did not anticipate, namely, increased efficiency in government. After an early period of marked inefficiency and corruption, which was exposed by the "muckrakers," there followed a long period of reform, which was at its height during the "Progressive Period" (extending roughly from 1890 to the First World War) but which has not yet ended. The reform took two paths, one leading to "efficient citizenship" and the other to "efficient administration." The first emphasized the need for an informed electorate which would participate actively in the work of government; it demanded the publication by government of relevant information and advocated the use of such devices as the short ballot, proportional representation, and the initiative, ref-

[41] Donald C. Blaisdell, *Economic Power and Political Pressures,* Temporary National Economic Committee Monograph No. 26 (Washington, D.C.: Government Printing Office, 1941), pp. 55–56. His conclusion—"To decide who shall win in this competition . . . is the government's continuing assignment"—leaves open the possibility that government itself may be the ultimate winner.

[42] It is significant that whereas the First World War at its height consumed a quarter of the nation's income, the Second World War at its height consumed a half. The increase was partly due to the expanded demands of an advanced technology.

erendum, and recall. The second emphasized, along with centralization of responsibility in the executive, a permanent, highly
trained, and professional bureaucracy protected from the corrupt-
ing influence of "politics" by the merit system.[43]

The second path proved easier to travel than the first and much
progress was made along it.[44] The efficiency of government improved steadily and had the twofold effect of making government
more capable of taking on new tasks and of making citizens more
willing that government do so. The final result was an increase in
the scope and size of government.

DANGER

The growth of government which Tocqueville foresaw has occurred and for the reasons he anticipated; what of the end he
envisioned? Has the American democracy he admired become the
benevolent despotism he feared?

It is certainly not one of the presuppositions of this study that
anything of the sort has occurred. The great growth of government we have witnessed since Tocqueville's time has not been a
misfortune. On the contrary. Modern life is unthinkable without
big government, and Americans properly count among their rich-
est blessings those that are brought to them through the instru-
mentality of government. Far from being a necessary evil, the
modern state is rather man's most ambitious attempt to live according to the noble norm of "one for all and all for one." Plato
and Rousseau, for all their general impracticality, supply a salu-
tary emphasis in their exaltation of the general good over the
particular good.

But it *is* one of the presuppositions of this study that the
United States has moved measurably further along the road whose
end Tocqueville described. In all probability, moreover, the

[43] For a review of the literature of these two movements, see Dwight Waldo, *The Administrative State* (New York: Ronald Press Co., 1948), Ch. 2.

[44] Note the implication, for example, in the following comment on one aspect of the reform: "Gradually, in the public administration movement as a whole, research and facts have come to be regarded less and less as devices of citizenship cooperation and control, and more and more as instruments of executive management." *Ibid.*, p. 33, n. 28.

country will continue to move in that direction. Since the same forces that produced the past growth of government are still operative, the extrapolation of past trends still seems the best guess for the future. This past and probable future growth of government constitutes a danger for democratic society.

The extent of the danger will be appraised differently by different persons,[45] but all who share a preference for the principle of subsidiarity will probably agree that the field of exercise for the principle is less extensive now than it was in the time of Tocqueville and that a new urgency attaches to institutional arrangements which can enlarge its scope. Certainly, there is a large and growing body of responsible opinion which exhibits an uneasiness over this apparently irreversible trend toward an ever bigger government.

It would be hard to find an economist more universally respected for integrity and balance than John Maurice Clark. Professor Clark's concern with the "problem" aspect of government is indicated by the title of his first postwar work, *Alternative to Serfdom*.[46] The concern of such a balanced scholar as Robert M. MacIver is manifested in his reserving the final paragraphs of *The Web of Government* for a warning against the encroachments of government. Harold Laski in his pre-Marxian days was much distressed by the way the new dimensions of politics tended to place the operations of government beyond the reach of the citizen.[47] Senator Paul Douglas has warned:

Few political leaders are deeply tolerant by nature. They have to be taught tolerance by the balance of political and economic power within the state. Let that balance become overwhelming or put almost complete power in their hands, then they will almost certainly use that power to coerce opposition. Russia should have taught us

[45] And differently, of course, for different areas of social life. MacIver employs a useful distinction according to "cultural," "welfare," and "economic" areas (*Web of Government*, Ch. 11).

[46] John Maurice Clark, *Alternative to Serfdom* (New York: Alfred A. Knopf, 1948).

[47] After describing "the increasing separation of the individual citizen from the source of decision," Laski concludes: "So much has to be done, so remote is the ambit of decision from his daily contacts, that he becomes, increasingly, the mere recipient of orders he has to obey—orders in the issuing of which no search has been made for his consent, no demand for his scrutiny." *Dangers of Obedience* (New York: Harper & Brothers, 1930), pp. 64, 65.

the lesson that complete collectivism is ultimately destructive of freedom.[48]

The "problem" of government is posed in its most characteristic and acute form by the "fourth branch" of government, the bureaucracy, which, although not elective, is given wide discretionary powers because it is expert. The bureaucracy's expertise is its key characteristic—the basis of its claim to power and the reason why the legislative and judicial (presumably the more responsible) branches of government cannot readily direct and control it. Granted that Max Weber exaggerates in the following passage, he is nevertheless stating a substantial truth:

Under normal conditions, the power position of a fully developed bureaucracy is always overtowering. The "political master" finds himself in the position of the "dilettante" who stands opposite the "expert," facing the trained official who stands within the management of administration. This holds whether the "master" whom the bureaucracy serves is a "people" equipped with the weapons of "legislative initiative," the "referendum," and the right to remove officials, or a parliament, elected on a more aristocratic or more "democratic" basis.[49]

The difficulty inherent in the direction and control of a bureaucracy is widely recognized.[50] The Dimocks close their text with a chapter on "Holding Administration Accountable" and declare: "To say that the concentration of power in administration might subvert popular government and democratic control seems not to be too strong a statement, and calls attention to a condition that should be watched." [51] Charles Hyneman in his careful study *Bureaucracy in Democracy* analyzes the various ways

[48] Address delivered at the Roosevelt Day dinner of Americans for Democratic Action, and printed in the *Congressional Record*, March 2, 1957, p. A1660.

[49] *From Max Weber: Essays in Sociology,* trans. and ed. H. H. Gerth and C. Wright Mills (New York: Oxford University Press, 1946), p. 232.

[50] For examples of the very critical and the very favorable approaches to the problem, see James Montgomery Beck's *Wonderland of Bureaucracy* (New York: Macmillan Co., 1932) and George Appleby's *Big Democracy* (New York: Alfred A. Knopf, 1945). For examples of more balanced analyses, see V. O. Key, Jr., "Legislative Control," in *Elements of Public Administration,* ed. Fritz Morstein Marx (New York: Prentice-Hall, Inc., 1946), pp. 339–64; Hyneman, *Bureaucracy in a Democracy,* Chs. 3, 5–10; George Galloway, *The Legislative Process in Congress* (New York: Thomas Y. Crowell Co., 1953), Ch. 4.

[51] Marshall and Gladys Dimock, *Public Administration* (New York: Rinehart & Co., Inc., 1953), p. 491.

in which a bureaucracy can "undermine the foundations of our system of popular government." [52] An authority in the field of social security, Professor Eveline M. Burns, concludes in her latest work: "The last, and perhaps the most important, of all the major administrative problems confronting countries operating extensive social security systems is how to ensure a truly democratic administration of these programs." [53] Peter Blau reminds us that the problem of democracy in bureaucracy springs from roots that pervade the whole of our society; [54] and he is supported in his contention by George Brooks with respect to labor unions.[55] In 1956 the American Bar Association conducted a vigorous campaign in Congress to restrict the quasi-judicial functions of administrative agencies.[56] But perhaps the most striking testimony comes from an English source. In a statement which was highly praised by Clement Attlee, the Socialist Union declared: "Its attainment [the good life] is now threatened by the new dangers of what has been loosely called 'the managerial society.' A managerial society is in essence one run by administrators out of reach of popular control." [57]

SOLUTION OF THE PROBLEM

The problem we have been considering is complex, and its solution is necessarily complex. Many factors interact to determine how and to what extent the principle of subsidiarity may be applied: the persons involved (how intelligent? how moral?), the environment in which they live (how much prosperity? how much peace?), and the social structure that relates persons to environ-

[52] For the various ways, see Ch. 2, pp. 20–37.

[53] *Social Security and Public Policy* (New York: McGraw-Hill Book Co., Inc., 1956), p. 262; see also p. 266.

[54] Peter Blau, *Bureaucracy in Modern Society* (New York: Random House, 1956), pp. 20, 117.

[55] George W. Brooks, "Observations on the Changing Nature of American Unions," *Monthly Labor Review*, LXXX (February, 1957), 152, 153.

[56] Hearings on H. Res. 462 (To Establish a Committee on Administrative Procedure and Practice), Committee on Rules, House of Representatives, 84th Cong., 2d sess., May, 1956.

[57] *Socialism: A New Statement of Principles,* presented by the Socialist Union (London: Lincolns-Prager, 1952), p. 55.

ment. The concern of this study is only with factors of structure. Of these, the two that commonly have been relied upon to protect democracy are the division of powers in government and the citizen's right to vote. Both are important parts of our total defense, but both also are subject to serious limitations. A consideration of their limitations will lead directly to what is the center of interest for this study, the function of private associations.

The structure of government in the United States is a complex system of checks and balances which divides power to an extent unparalleled in any major nation known to history.[58] The system has probably been an important influence in preventing the development of the monolithic governmental power feared by Tocqueville. Its effectiveness has been somewhat diminished over time, however, by several influences [59] and there has been a growing body of opinion which holds that the system is no longer appropriate to the needs of modern government. Beginning at least as early as Woodrow Wilson's famous essay [60] there has been an uninterrupted stream of criticism directed at the system of divided powers on the score that it makes not only for inefficiency [61] but also for diminished democracy. It is said to work against democracy because by offering private interest groups multiple points of access to government it facilitates government by minorities and gives rise to the evils of the "dispersive state." [62]

[58] Within the limits set by a written constitution, power is divided between federal and state governments. Within each of these, power is further divided between three branches—legislative, executive, and judicial—and within the legislative branch, between two autonomous houses. Within each house, the committee system with its custom of selecting chairmen by seniority works to obstruct the operation of the political party, on which rests the country's chief hope for unified action, but which, especially on the national level, is a weak instrument, unable to hold even a single strong committee chairman in line with party policy.

[59] For example, by the growth of the "fourth branch" of government, which brings together in one governmental organ the functions of all three of the traditional branches.

[60] "The Study of Administration," *Political Science Quarterly*, II (June, 1887), 197–222.

[61] A luxury that is too costly for a nation which has grown from a couple of million persons clustered on the eastern seaboard to 170 millions scattered over a continent and which has become the acknowledged leader of half the world.

[62] For examples of literature dealing with the danger and difficulties of the dispersive state, see: Galloway, *The Legislative Process in Congress*, Ch. 20; Truman, *The Governmental Process*, Ch. 6; Ernest S. Griffith, *Congress, Its Contemporary Role* (New York: New York University Press, 1951), pp. 106, 112; Donald C. Blaisdell

The critics would like to center more power in fewer hands in order to achieve more policy integration. Democracy, they argue, will not be impaired under such a system because responsibility will be more clearly focused and the effectiveness of the voting function thereby increased. The citizen will be better able to discern who is responsible for a given policy and at election time will be able to express approval or disapproval effectively by re-electing or defeating the responsible person.

Usually this line of argument makes much use of the distinction between policy (a choice of ends) and administration (the use of means to attain already determined ends), and relies on the rule, "Elect for representation, appoint for administration." It envisages a system in which a relatively few elected officials will make all the decisions and a multitude of appointed officials will merely carry them out. In its extreme form this leads to the conclusion that administration is neutral as between different forms of government and that the administrative structure in a democracy need be no different than in an autocracy.[63]

This solution of the problem (more integration in government) has pertinence, but its use is limited by several considerations. First, policy making and the exercise of discretion are not confined to a few top officials but extend far down the bureaucratic pyramid. Second, the elected officials find it extremely difficult, as noted previously, to exercise adequate direction and control over the administrative machine. Third, to the extent that the citizen's participation in government is restricted to the periodic selection of a few top officials, the principle of subsidiarity has been abandoned as a practical guide, and democracy has been relegated to the status of a minor value.[64] The pre-Marxian Laski

---

American Democracy under Pressure (New York: Ronald Press Co., 1957), *passim.* E. Pendleton Herring and V. O. Key have written extensively on this subject.—For a related line of thought, see analyses of the difficulties inherent in guild socialism; for example: Waldo, *The Administrative State*, Chs. 7 and 8; Hsiao, *Political Pluralism*, pp. 115–25.

[63] F. A. Cleveland and A. P. E. Buck (two of the famous "ABC powers") are quoted to this effect by Dwight Waldo in *The Administrative State*, pp. 74, 75.

[64] For a recent extreme expression of concern over the growth of the executive power, see Amaury de Riencourt, *The Coming Caesars* (New York: Coward-McCann, Inc., 1957).

described such a system as one in which "political significance comes to most . . . as a brief and pitiful moment at election time." [65] Pendleton Herring, although an advocate of more integration, voices the warning: "If contact with the governing process is confined to the periodic casting of a ballot, democracy is sterile indeed." [66]

To spell out this last limitation a bit more: Voting as an instrument of direction and control suffers from several major weaknesses. (1) Less than three fifths of the eligible voters actually vote, on the average.[67] (2) When they vote, they are using a crude instrument. For the most part voting has only a negative function. The voter can reject a candidate or a proposal, but he does not participate positively in the selection of candidates or the construction of proposals. Moreover, the voter can vote only on the basis of the whole of the candidate's record; he cannot be selective, approving this, disapproving that. (3) The average voter does not have adequate knowledge of the person or the matter on which he is invited to vote, and he lacks the time and ability to gain such knowledge.

PRIVATE ASSOCIATIONS

Yet, what greater participation can be given to the individual? What more can he do than cast his vote? The answer is—very little. The scope and complexity of modern government make it impracticable for the individual citizen to come into anything like intimate association with the operations of government.

But the individual belongs to other groups besides the governmental group. He belongs also to private associations, and his representatives in these associations possess the expertise and the time he lacks to participate in the process of government. The private association is an essential key to the problem of how to keep modern government democratic.[68]

[65] Dangers of Obedience, p. 60.

[66] Public Administration and the Public Interest (New York: McGraw-Hill Book Co., Inc., 1936), p. 19.

[67] The proportion varies with age, sex, race, education, and residence, as well as with the importance attached to a particular election.

[68] According to Sir Ernest Barker: "The problem of resistance is in actual life always a problem of groups. Theorists may set limits to the State in the name of the

This was the key, as a matter of fact, to which Tocqueville pointed. Tocqueville did not think that the historical development he described was inevitable—differing from Marx in this respect as in others—but thought it could be prevented, and he suggested as one of the chief means a system of private associations intermediary between the individual and government.

The circumstance which most contributed to secure the independence of private persons in aristocratic ages was that the supreme power did not affect to take upon itself alone the government and administration of the community. Those functions were necessarily partially left to the members of the aristocracy; so that, as the supreme power was always divided, it never weighed with its whole weight and in the same manner on each individual.

I readily admit that recourse cannot be had to the same means at the present time, but I discover certain democratic expedients that may be substituted for them. Instead of vesting in the government alone all the administrative powers of which guilds and nobles have been deprived, a portion of them may be entrusted to secondary public bodies temporarily composed of private citizens. . . . By this means many of the greatest political advantages of aristocracy would be obtained without its injustice or its dangers.[69]

Tocqueville's solution finds wide support today. There is a mounting chorus of influential voices affirming the crucial role to be played by private associations. Example could be piled on example; the following are merely representative.

Most of us are probably practicing, if not theoretical pluralists. . . . We recognize that it requires a considerable measure of power and a great deal of rule-making to operate successfully an industrial system, but that this power and this rule-making (although not ultimate sovereignty) are more safely and effectively distributed into many hands than into a few.[70]

When Robert M. MacIver comes to put down three conditions which "make possible the goal of democracy," all three turn out to relate to the functioning of private groups as plural power

---

individual; practical resistance is always a matter of group-consciousness." (*Church, State and Education* [Ann Arbor: University of Michigan Press, 1957], p. 160.) Harold Laski says simply: "The citizen who stands alone today is lost. It is as part of a group that he secures the power to fulfill himself." (*Dangers of Obedience*, p. 59.)

[69] Tocqueville, *Democracy in America*, II, 341, 342.

[70] Clark Kerr, "Industrial Relations and the Liberal Pluralist" (presidential address), *Annual Proceedings of the Industrial Relations Research Association*, December 28–30, 1954, p. 6.

centers.[71] When Barbara Ward Jackson, of the London *Economist,* came to sum up the discussions at Columbia University's bicentennial celebration, whose theme was freedom, she had occasion to ask "whether you can, in a society which recognizes no values outside society, find the *pou sto,* the place to stand in your opposition to the total claims of the state. Can you without organized institutions which are separate from the state confront an institution of such overwhelming power as that of the modern Caesar?" [72] E. Pendleton Herring writes:

The solution of the liberal democratic state must lie in establishing a working relationship between the bureaucrats and special interests —a relationship that will enable the former to carry out the purpose of the state and the latter to realize their own ends. . . . Special groups that are directly involved in the jurisdiction of certain bureaus must be brought into the administrative process.[73]

According to the Dimocks: "When interest groups work closely with government officials, the effect is to democratize administration." [74]

The degree and manner of group participation by private groups in the task of organizing society must vary with different areas of society and with the groups involved. In the industrial area, which is the particular concern of this study, the dominant groups are organized labor and management. These are the crucial groups in modern society, in the sense that the relationship of government with them goes very far toward determining the relationship of government with society as a whole. In respect to organized labor and management there is a consensus which amounts almost to unanimity that they should play a very active role in the solution of industrial problems.

[71] *The Web of Government,* pp. 108, 109.

[72] "Summing Up," *National Policies for Education, Health, and Social Services,* ed. James E. Russell (Garden City, N.Y.: Doubleday & Co., Inc., 1955), pp. 495, 496. A namesake and countrywoman, Barbara Wooton, who is a warm advocate of expanded government, in a chapter entitled "Who Is to Plan the Planners?" warned: "Every extension of government activity . . . needs, in consequence, a corresponding growth of small local organs to control officials." *Freedom under Planning* (New York: Van Rees Press, 1945), pp. 173, 174.

[73] *Public Administration and the Public Interest,* pp. 24, 25, 43. Quotation used by permission of McGraw-Hill Book Co., Inc.

[74] *Public Administration,* p. 513.

Taylor opens his work on *Government Regulation of Industrial Relations* with the statement:

One conclusion invariably emerges whenever and wherever "the labor problem" is subjected to impartial analysis. It is . . . that organized labor and management should settle their own differences by understanding, compromise, and agreement, and without government interference.[75]

He adds that with regard to that statement, "a rare unanimity of opinion exists."

Any random sampling of American writers in the field of industrial relations will turn up innumerable examples in proof of that unanimity. When the University of Pennsylvania held its conference on the subject of "Less Government in Labor-Management Relations" it posed the issue, significantly, not in terms of whether less government was desirable, but only whether it was achievable.[76] Cyrus Ching's memoir, *Review and Reflections,* has the recurring theme that labor and management should call on government as little as possible and manage their own affairs as much as possible. Labor and management themselves are in general agreement with that conclusion.[77] Examples could be multiplied; but one more must suffice:

Commons had a theme, if not a full-blown theory, as Witte has recently pointed out, that mass organizations were central to our type of society and should be accepted as such, understood, and not rejected as improper intrusions into a nicer atomistic world or as barriers to achievement of the Utopia of state socialism. . . . I once looked upon Taylor's appeal for "industrial self-government" with some suspicion for it seems to sound like an invitation to collusion, and on Slichter's arguments for the responsibility of unions to the general level of wages and prices . . . but it is probably only through

[75] George W. Taylor, *Government Regulation of Industrial Relations* (New York: Prentice-Hall, Inc., 1948), p. 1.

[76] *Proceedings of Conference: Less Government in Labor-Management Relations an Achievable Goal?* (Philadelphia: Wharton School, University of Pennsylvania, 1953).

[77] For a convenient collection of statements on this theme by leaders of labor and management in the postwar period see Warren J. Samuels, "The Concepts of Major Business and Labor Organizations on the Role of Government in the Economy" (Unpublished Ph.D. dissertation, Department of Economics, University of Wisconsin, 1957). Samuels's conclusion regarding labor: "Labor's is thus essentially a pluralistic view of human society." (*Ibid.,* p. 520.)

the effective self-government advocated by Taylor and the responsible unionism by Slichter (and responsible corporation behavior, too) that a pluralistic system can be indefinitely maintained.[78]

Private associations do not by the very fact of their existence guarantee a wide scope for the principle of subsidiarity. For that, the associations must possess two qualities: they must be independent and they must be responsible. If they lack either of these qualities they will promote rather than limit totalitarian government.

Private associations must be independent. To the extent that they are dependent on government they merely strengthen and lengthen the reach of government. Like the labor unions in Russia, they become additional instruments by which the government can impose its will more effectively on the mass of the citizens.[79]

Private associations must also be responsible, or, to use the term John R. Commons favored, reasonable. The quality of being responsible, or reasonable, is difficult to define.[80] Of its nature it is somewhat vague and variable, though certainly not unreal or uninfluential. But for our purposes responsible action can be described as action which is in accord with what MacIver calls the "firmament of law" [81] and Truman the "rules of the game" [82] —meaning those basic values which possessed in common hold a society together. If, for example, a given society has a strong preference for a certain degree of income equality (or for gradual and peaceful, rather than sudden and violent, change), it will consider any group which seriously impairs that equality (or uses violence) as "irresponsible" or "unreasonable" and will seek to curb the group. To curb irresponsible groups society generally turns to the state. In this way irresponsible group behavior has been one of the greatest forces making for an enlarged state, and

[78] Kerr, "Industrial Relations and the Liberal Pluralist," *Proceedings, IRRA*, 1954, p. 11.

[79] For an application of this line of argument to the problem of intraunion democracy, see S. M. Lipset, M. A. Trow, and J. S. Coleman, *Union Democracy* (Glencoe, Ill.: The Free Press, 1956), pp. 79, 80.

[80] Commons once defined reasonableness as "idealism limited by practicability." J. R. Commons, *Myself* (New York: Macmillan Co., 1934), p. 156.

[81] MacIver, *The Web of Government*, Ch. 4.

[82] Truman, *The Governmental Process;* see index under "rules of the game."

John Maurice Clark sees no "alternative to serfdom" if the powerful, organized groups of modern society, especially organized labor and management, do not act responsibly.[83]

[83] "Between the individual and government . . . stand great organized groups; farm federations, business corporations, and labor unions. And these are the crux of the present dilemma. In a simple economy without such groups, irresponsible self-interest is—almost—a possible organizing principle in the strictly material realm. It would merely mean the exploitation of the weak by the strong, the incapable by the capable. But organize society into groups, and irresponsible self-interest can both corrupt the groups and shatter the society." *Alternative to Serfdom*, p. 5.

2

SHARED GOVERNMENT THROUGH
ADVISORY COUNCILS

THE argument of the preceding chapter amounted to this: Because of the nature of democracy and of technological society, the scope of government in the United States has grown greatly and will probably continue to grow; this growth, whatever its effect on economic democracy, constitutes a danger for political democracy in so far as it limits the operation of the principle of subsidiarity; the preservation of political democracy requires a corresponding, balancing growth of private groups, which, if they are both independent and responsible, can share with government the task of organizing society.

WAYS OF SHARING

The activity of groups may be related to the activity of government in a variety of ways. The private group may act in place of government or with government; if with government, it may act with authority (be vested with jurisdiction) or be merely advisory; if merely advisory, it may act informally (through lobbyists) or formally (through an advisory council).

When a private group acts so as to make government action unnecessary, it in effect takes the place of government. A simple example is that of labor and management agreeing on a new contract in an industry so vital to the common welfare that government would be compelled to impose a settlement if the contestants themselves could not arrive at one. Another example is that of a county medical association establishing standards of medical practice for its district. Innumerable other examples exist in almost every area of the nation's life.

The most ambitious plans for this kind of independent group action were put forth in the pluralist literature of the first quarter of this century.[1] The plans included proposals for the establishment of "industry councils" [2] and even for separate, autonomous parliaments for "political" and "economic" matters respectively. These more ambitious plans never attracted wide support and after the depression years were largely forgotten.

Although this type of activity is very desirable (it offers the maximum scope for the principle of subsidiarity), it is limited in many ways. Most of government's tasks cannot be turned over to private groups. Some tasks, like that of providing a navy, are absolutely beyond the capability of any group; others cannot be relinquished without unduly dividing authority in our highly integrated society and thus intensifying the evils of the "dispersive state"; [3] still others could be undertaken by private groups, but will not be because the groups are unwilling to exert the necessary effort or to act with the necessary degree of responsibility. When private groups acting independently have done all they can, there will remain a very wide area of necessary governmental activity.

In the remaining forms of group activity, the group acts with government, supplementing rather than supplanting governmental action. The group may act with government in either an authoritative or advisory capacity, that is, its representatives may wield legal authority or they may merely proffer advice. A convenient illustration of both types of participation is provided by the Michigan employment security agency, which has both a governing commission and an advisory council, each consisting

[1] For a review of the major pluralist writings see Kung Chuan Hsiao, *Political Pluralism* (New York: Harcourt, Brace & Co., Inc., 1927).

[2] These were to be associations of labor and management organized to run the nation's industrial machine. For the use of the term in this sense see Harold Laski, *Dangers of Obedience* (New York: Harper & Brothers, 1930), pp. 83–86. The papal encyclical *Quadragesimo Anno,* published in 1931, may reflect this pluralistic period. The encyclical lays considerable emphasis on the *ordines*—variously translated as "vocational groups" and, in the United States, "industry councils."

[3] For references to the evils of the dispersive state see Ch. 1, n. 62.

of four representatives of labor and four representatives of management.[4]

The authoritative type of participation takes many forms according as the private interests are more or less directly represented on the governmental body and according as their representatives have more or less scope and authority.[5] But in all its forms it encounters a dilemma that is inherent in its very nature. Because the representatives of the private group are vested with legal authority, they must take on direct responsibility for the common good and relinquish some of their freedom to work for the private goals of their own group. That is, they must to some extent function like regular governmental employees. For this reason interest groups are sometimes reluctant to accept positions on governmental bodies. Moreover, in so far as they function like governmental employees, a legitimate question can be raised as to whether this kind of participation limits more than it extends governmental power.

On the other hand, if the representatives of private groups accept such positions of public authority but fail to conduct themselves with the impartiality that is expected of governmental employees, administration suffers in point of both efficiency and fairness.[6] It may be granted that every individual, whatever his office, is to some degree prejudiced in favor of his own interests, but we expect (and get) more impartiality from men in some positions than from men in others: for example, more from a judge than from a lawyer, and more from the senator of a silver mining state than from the secretary of a silver miners' association. The dilemma arises when we seek to invest the secretary with some of the public authority of the senator.

[4] Similarly in the Federal Reserve System there is both a board of governors (composed of representatives of the "financial, agricultural, industrial, and commercial interests") and an advisory council (composed of representatives of the member banks).

[5] Avery Leiserson describes a variety of such forms in his *Administrative Regulation* (Chicago: University of Chicago Press, 1942), Chs. 3, 4, 5.

[6] "Interest groups often fail to recognize that they may want fairness and impartiality in administration even more than they want a share of official responsibility for policy determination." Avery Leiserson, "Interest Groups in Administration," in *Elements of Public Administration,* ed. Fritz Morstein Marx (New York: Prentice-Hall, Inc., 1946), p. 336.

In general, this method of using private groups to help organize society is subject to the same limitation as the preceding method: it tends to augment the dangers of the "dispersive state." It is for this reason that most students of public administration have been critical of multiheaded boards composed of representatives of interest groups, and that there has been a marked trend toward replacing such boards with single, full-time executives.[7] Leiserson is substantially correct when he claims that "the overwhelming trend of opinion favors the elimination of explicit interest representation in all forms but that of advice."[8] In recent years even the use of "WOC's" (private citizens who serve in government without compensation) has come under heavy fire. The WOC system was ended in the Department of Commerce in early 1958, all WOC's in that department being replaced by career governmental employees.

The nonauthoritative or advisory type of interest representation is relatively free of this public-private dilemma and therefore has wider potentialities.[9] The advisory type is itself divisible into two subtypes, the formal and the informal—according as the interest groups operate with or without benefit of membership in an officially constituted advisory body.

The informal type is simply the institution of lobbying. Lobbying provides the essentials of private advisory participation in government, and will always have an important role to play in a democracy. It is the existence of the institution of lobbying that makes it incorrect to say that advisory councils are in any strict sense necessary to full democracy. Yet, as compared with advisory councils, lobbying labors under the same disadvantage as do the other forms of participation just discussed—it aggravates the evils of the dispersive state. Consisting as it does of the independent, uncoordinated efforts of private groups to secure private favors, it endangers the necessary unity and order of society. John R.

[7] For examples of this trend in the employment security program, see chapters on the councils of Massachusetts, Rhode Island, Ohio, California.

[8] *Administrative Regulation*, p. 12.

[9] As Harold Laski observes: "Because the system is advisory and not executive in character, it leaves simple and intelligible the ultimate institutions, and it does not make authority degenerate into anarchy by the indefinite division of power." *Dangers of Obedience*, p. 81.

Commons emphasized this drawback of lobbying when he compared it with the method of advisory councils in his famous 1916 Report on Industrial Relations:

At present there is no definite means provided whereby lobbyists can be required to come together and confer regarding measures. They appear usually as antagonists or lawyers before legislative committees, and not as the conferees of an advisory representative council. . . . There are unbridled agitators of this kind on both sides of the contest, and it is only when the two sides are brought together, and their charges, countercharges, and alleged grievances are boiled down by investigation to the residuum of facts, that mere unfounded agitation can be expected to give way to deliberations on remedies for recognized evils. This does not mean that both sides can be made to agree on remedies for all evils and grievances, even after they have agreed on the facts. It means only that there is found to be a much larger field than was supposed where they can agree, and it is worth while for legislation to provide the means for bringing both sides together for a continuous search after the common points of agreement.[10]

To sum up: Twentieth-century American society is a managerial society with two principal sets of managers, governmental and nongovernmental. From these two proceed opposite dangers —too much centralization and too much decentralization, tyranny and anarchy, the danger of the dictatorial state and the danger of the dispersive state. The chief limitation on the forms of private group activity thus far considered is that, while erecting a bulwark against the dictatorial state, they bring closer the dangers of the dispersive state.

The chief virtue of the advisory council is that it moderates both dangers simultaneously. It brings together the competing interest groups, labor and management, under circumstances best adapted to the channeling of their activities toward the common good. It is designed to make private groups not only more active but also more responsibly active. Moreover since it is completely flexible as regards both size and scope it is adaptable to almost any situation. Of the various ways open to private groups to par-

[10] U.S. Senate (64th Cong., 1st sess.), Sen. Doc. No. 415 (1916), U.S. Commission on Industrial Relations, Final Report and Testimony, I, 203, 183.

ticipate in the governmental process, the advisory council has the widest applicability.[11]

The rest of the chapter is a discussion of how in theory advisory councils function. The theory is developed with special reference to employment security in order to facilitate the application of theory to the experience of advisory councils in that program. Before beginning the discussion, it may be well for the sake of the reader unfamiliar with employment security to provide a brief sketch of the program's structure and operations.

EMPLOYMENT SECURITY

The program of employment security consists of two branches —the employment service, which supplies jobs, and unemployment compensation, which supplies benefits to those for whom there are no jobs. The employment service is much the older of the two. Some states had public employment offices before the turn of the century. The system became operative on a national scale in 1933 with the enactment of the Wagner-Peyser Act, which offered federal matching funds to states having employment offices. The Wagner-Peyser Act includes a provision for advisory councils. After describing a Federal Advisory Council,[12] the act states: "The Secretary shall also require the organization of similar State advisory councils composed of men and women representing employers and employees in equal numbers and the public."[13]

The unemployment compensation program did not begin until 1932, when Wisconsin enacted its law. The other states began to follow suit in 1935, when the Social Security Act was enacted. The Social Security Act in effect forced the states to establish some kind of unemployment compensation program and provided funds for its administration. The federal statute left the states with large freedom in the matter of determining the specific

[11] See A. W. Macmahon, "Boards, Advisory," *Encyclopaedia of the Social Sciences,* II, 609–11.
[12] See p. 362.
[13] U.S.C. Tit. 29, Sec. 49 j (a).

provisions of their laws, and as a result the individual state programs vary considerably.

The federal law did not specify an advisory council. But the "Draft Bill" which the Bureau of Employment Security sent out to the states for their guidance contained a section suggesting the establishment of a council, and many of the states followed the suggestion. Of the state laws which provided for an advisory council, the majority adopted the provisions of the "Draft Bill," but some developed provisions of their own. Over the years many states have amended their laws with respect to advisory councils so that now the provisions regulating advisory councils differ greatly.

The relationship of the employment service to unemployment compensation has varied from state to state and over time, but in general the pattern has been one of growing integration. In some states and for a few years separate advisory councils functioned for each program. But now almost all states have only one council, which is structured to meet the requirements laid down for the employment service in the Wagner-Peyser Act but is responsible for unemployment compensation activities as well.[14]

In addition to the state councils there is a Federal Advisory Council, which differs materially from the state councils and is described separately in Chapter 18.

FUNCTIONS OF ADVISORY COUNCILS

The function of an advisory council in a governmental program is to help those responsible for the program to know and to do

[14] In a few of the states the advisory council is called a "committee" and in a few others a "board," but the term "council" is used uniformly throughout this study. This is a convenient place to note several other variations in terminology. Some states call their law-making body the General Assembly or General Court; the term "legislature" is used uniformly throughout this study. Likewise states vary in the use of terminology to designate the chief executive officer of their employment security agency. In this study the term "director" is used uniformly and, except where confusion might result, is often used interchangeably with "administrator." Finally the generally applicable term "agency" is used in preference to more specific but variable terms like "division," "department," or "bureau." The selection of terminology in this study was made to simplify and clarify the picture for the general reader.

what the program requires. More specifically, the council's function is to provide government and governed with a window and a door through which they can the better control legislation and administration. This proposition obviously consists of three pairs of elements, six in all: (1) government and (2) governed; (3) window and (4) door; (5) legislation and (6) administration. Logically equal, they represent six possible coordinate divisions of council functions. The use of all six, however, would result in an overly elaborate scheme and involve much repetition. Therefore, after some general remarks on each of the three pairs, we shall discuss council functions under the two headings of legislation and administration, using the other pairs as subdivisions wherever convenient.

Government-Governed. From the viewpoint of the government and the governed, the council's functions are seen as so many desirable results to be attained through the council. Although basically both the government and the governed desire the same results (both want an efficient and democratic program), their viewpoints are not identical, and the council may reflect one viewpoint more than the other. The council may operate primarily to help government carry out governmental decisions,[15] or primarily to help government make those decisions; and in the latter case the council may merely provide information, or it may also share responsibility.

The difference in emphasis shows itself principally in the choice of council members, who may be merely men of prestige, or experts, or representatives (men who can speak authoritatively for organized interests). If the council is to be an opportunity for private participation in government decision making, its members must include either experts or representatives, and if it is to share responsibility, it must include representatives.

[15] This seems generally to have been the emphasis in the early days of the program, and it is still reflected in a 1952 paper which William Haber, a veteran of the employment security program, presented to the Interstate Conference of Employment Security Agencies on the subject of advisory councils; see the *Proceedings* of the Conference, 16th Annual Meeing (U.S. Department of Labor, Washington, D.C.), pp. 27, 28. For a comment on this emphasis see this author's paper in the *Proceedings,* 18th Annual Meeting, 1954, p. 110.

Window-Door. The advisory council provides a window for the intellect and a door for the will [16] —a window through which the government and the governed can see what is happening in the program, and a convenient door through which they can enter the program to make adjustments as needed. Together, window and door help government and governed to want what they ought and to get what they want.

The knowledge which the government and the governed obtain through the window of the advisory council will make them want what they ought only in so far as the Platonic proposition holds true, that knowledge is virtue. But how far is that? This study tries to avoid in its assumptions the extremes of both mechanism and skepticism. It recognizes that "facts" do not automatically settle issues—because all "facts" are partly subjective, because all the relevant facts are rarely available, and because malice is a real factor distinct from ignorance. Even the most thorough investigation can leave an area of dispute in which the expert has nothing more to say and peaceful settlement can come only through bargaining. (One of the most important "door" functions of an advisory council is to provide labor and management with an ideal setting for bargaining.)

On the other hand, the study recognizes that "facts" are not wholly subjective but have an existence outside the mind; that the intellect has a native bent to conform itself to this objective reality; and that the will has a native bent to follow the intellect. This is a crucial point in the theory of the advisory council, for the single most important advantage of an advisory council is that it educates the decision makers and increases the area of agreement among them.

John R. Commons, who was an indefatigable campaigner for advisory councils, provides an excellent illustration in his own person of how to avoid the extremes of both the mechanistic and the skeptical interpretations of the role of "facts." On the one hand Commons based most of his arguments for advisory coun-

---

[16] This terminology of faculty psychology does not imply that "intellect" and "will" are separate agents, but only that the soul, although simple, has two very different ways of acting.

cils on the usefulness of investigation of the "facts." Commons had found that men generally were possessed of sufficient reasonableness to achieve an acceptable compromise of their different interests. By "reasonableness" Commons meant "idealism limited by practicability." [17] He explained that "reasonable values and reasonable practices were not the subjective opinion of anybody, but were the collective opinion, expressed in action, of those whose economic interests were conflicting but who investigated together and knew by experience all of the facts." [18] If Commons had been allowed to make only one recommendation for better industrial relations and had to make it in one word, the word would probably have been "investigation."

On the other hand Commons was aware that the investigation of facts could not resolve all differences. For this reason he never subscribed to the notion of "government by experts." Speaking of his own experience as adviser to many labor, management, and government leaders, he stated what he had learned:

The place of the economist was that of advisor to the leaders, if they wanted him, and not that of propagandist to the masses. The leaders alone had the long experience of success and defeat. It was they who took the risks of defeat and deserved the credit of success. The intellectual, a doctor, lawyer, minister, economist, could find a job elsewhere. But the striker must go back to the same employer. If you furnished a worker-leader or political leader with any material he could use, he alone could tell how much of it he could use, and when and how, if it was to "get across" to his followers. Hence I always accepted philosophically what they rejected of my hard work, and stuck to them nevertheless.[19]

Legislation-Administration. The distinction between these two has been stated in many different ways. It is the distinction between decision and execution, ends and means, values and facts, discretion and instruction, skeletal policy and detailed application. All are useful ways of separating the two concepts, but none

[17] John R. Commons, *Myself* (New York: Macmillan Co., 1934), p. 156. Quotations used by permission of the Macmillan Company.

[18] *Ibid.,* p. 160.

[19] *Ibid.,* p. 88. Richard Lester's plea for a greater use of academic experts (presidential address in the *Annual Proceedings of the Industrial Relations Research Association,* December 1956, pp. 2–9) needs perhaps to be balanced by some such observation.

is adequate for distinguishing the two processes in action. Not only do they shade into each other by a continuous gradation, but they are intermingled in the concrete social agencies which are called legislative and administrative. The legislators concern themselves with many matters that can properly be called administrative, and the administrator performs many functions that can properly be called legislative.

In the case of administration it is convenient to distinguish between what is called "administrative law" and "pure administration." Administrative law is marked by a higher content of discretion in policy making. In employment security the precedent decisions of the appeal tribunals constitute the clearest examples of administrative law, but there are many others. For example, when the "guaranteed annual wage" appeared in the contracts of the automobile and steel industries, administrators had to make such crucial decisions as whether these private unemployment benefits were or were not "wages" and whether they did or did not therefore prevent the payment of regular state unemployment benefits. For another example, the author has been a firsthand witness in several states of a marked policy change (claims were paid that were denied before, and vice versa) without any change in the state law. A new administrator had simply given orders that brought about changes in "administrative law."

But even in "pure administration" there can be important elements of discretion. Scores of times a day, the employment service interviewer makes a discretionary judgment to send Jones out on a job instead of Smith, and the unemployment insurance claimstaker makes a discretionary judgment to approve Brown's claim for benefits but to hold up Black's for further investigation. This prevalence of discretion throughout the program gives the affected interests, labor and management, a strong reason for wanting to share not only in the legislative but also in the administrative processes of the program.

From the viewpoint of labor and management the legislative and administrative processes involved in a governmental program are much like the negotiation and administration of their regular industrial contracts, "administrative law" corresponding roughly to "grievance procedure." The collective bargaining techniques they use in arriving at their industrial agreements are applicable to the task of agreeing on a governmental program. There is of course this considerable difference, that in a governmental program the alternative to agreement is not a strike or lockout but compulsory arbitration; and even when labor and management agree on what they want, the government may ignore their agreement or introduce modifications. But the essential similarity between the two situations remains and carries the corollary that the development of the science and art of collective bargaining in industry strengthens the probability of successful participation by labor and management in the legislative and administrative operations of governmental programs.

"Contract negotiation" is of frequent occurrence in the employment security program. The "contract" can be opened for renegotiation every year in some states and every other year in the rest.[20] Typically, both labor and management take advantage of this opportunity and introduce many bills in the legislature, for the employment security program is very controversial,[21] and each side is always attempting to change the terms of the contract in its own favor.[22]

"Contract administration," including grievance procedure, of course involves even more continuous activity. In the employment security program administrative decisions that involve considerable discretion are made literally every day.

LEGISLATION

Viewpoint of Government

Although this study emphasizes the advantages that accrue to the governed from the operations of advisory councils, the inter-

[20] The following states have annual legislative sessions: Arizona, California, Colorado, Maryland, Massachusetts, Michigan, New Jersey, New York, Rhode Island, and South Carolina. The rest meet biennially (nearly all of them in the odd-numbered years).

[21] During the past twenty years, employment security has occasioned more continuous and more bitter labor-management controversy than has any other state program.

[22] Legislators have at times declared themselves weary of this process of continuous amendment and have asked, "Can't we set up this program so that it will stay unchanged for at least a few years?" But the answer seems fated to remain in the negative.

ests of government cannot be ignored. If governmental programs are necessary—and they are—it follows that advisory councils must function so as to assist, or at the very least not to hinder, government in the performance of its essential tasks. Even democracy cannot be allowed to interfere overmuch with efficiency. Furthermore, if government officials see some personal advantages accruing to themselves from the operation of an advisory council, they are likely to be more anxious to make the council a success. Experience has demonstrated that an advisory council will be no better than the officials of government, especially the administrator, want it to be.

Technical Aid. An advisory council can be expected to provide government with two kinds of aid, technical and political. Technical aid is the one of lesser importance for all three levels of government. It is of least use to the administrator because he and his staff are the technicians par excellence in the program. It is of minor use to the governor; he is too busy to be able to give much consideration to the technical side of any single part of government, and he can rely on the administrator, his own appointee, for whatever technical advice he needs.

The legislature is the only one of the three levels of government that has much need for the council's technical help and can make some use of it. Normally there is tension between the executive and legislative branches of government, and the legislature is disinclined to rely entirely on the technical guidance of the administrator, who is viewed as being primarily the governor's agent. Lobbyists are available to the legislators as a source of technical information, but while this can be a very competent source, it is likely to be biased. Many states now have a small staff of researchers and clerical workers generally called the "legislative reference bureau." But the limited size of this group and the vast amount of proposed legislation mean that a legislator must frequently go elsewhere if he wants a thorough analysis of a given bill.

An advisory council can render a valuable technical service to the legislature by preparing reports which set out the issues, the arguments on each side, and major relevant data. Such reports, certified by the entire council as accurate and impartial, can provide all decision makers with a firm beginning for their thinking. This is the function on which John R. Commons laid chief stress: "There can be no provision more essential than that of providing the *representative* machinery for *reliable* investigations, findings, and publicity." [23] The complexity of the task facing the modern legislature is such that anything which helps its members understand the matters on which they have to pass judgment is of prime importance.[24]

The extent to which the legislature makes use of technical information should not be exaggerated. The average state legislature meets intermittently for about half a year every other year and in that time has to consider hundreds upon hundreds of bills involving all the complex problems of a modern state's operations. The state legislators are not full-time politicians, but men who have to take the time they give to lawmaking from their usual daily pursuits. Moreover, the majority do not serve more than a few sessions. The vote of the average legislator on the hundreds of bills that are placed before him is determined more often by general norms of party or sectional loyalty, or even by personal interests, than by a clear understanding of the intrinsic merits of each bill. Sometimes even the introducer of a bill does not understand it well enough to explain or defend it in floor debate. In the case of a program like employment security one would not expect to find more than three or four members of the average state legislature who had a passable understanding of its technical aspects.

[23] U.S. Commission on Industrial Relations (1916), Final Report, I, 193. The italics are mine and are causally related. In the context from which the quotation is taken Commons was saying that the reliability necessary to engender confidence would be secured if representative advisory councils vouched for the impartiality of the investigations.

[24] "Greater stress should probably be placed on making pertinent information available to legislative committees. . . . This should be regarded as one of the paramount duties of administrative agencies. Such information should be more frequent, and more institutionalized channels should be provided for it." Murray Edelman, *Government's Balance of Power in Labor-Management Relations* (University of Illinois Institute of Industrial and Labor Relations, reprint series No. 8, January, 1951), p. 35.—The administrative agency will find an advisory council the best possible channel for getting information to legislative committees in the most acceptable form.

Political Aid. "Political" is taken here in a narrow sense and refers primarily to the business of getting or holding political office. The political aid coming from an advisory council is likely to be of very considerable importance to all three branches of government. No branch of government is immune from a concern for politics. This is obvious in the case of the governor and the legislators, who have to stand for election periodically, but it is also true in the case of the administrator.

Although it is desirable that the administrator be less enmeshed in politics than the elected officials, he can never be completely free from political pressures.[25] Since the administrator is the direct representative of the governor, and his actions affect the political fortunes of the governor, he must have a care for the political consequences of what he does.[26] Further, unless an administrator satisfies the interest groups who are immediately affected by the program he administers, they will soon apply political pressure in an effort to remove him.

A strong advisory council can protect both the administrator and his program. A strong council can be the reason that the administrator is not sacrificed to the needs of political patronage. More important, a council can be the reason that the program is not distorted by the vagaries of political logrolling. Logrolling tends to substitute the particularized view of an individual legislator for the overall view required for the good of the whole program. It is a political commonplace that the executive generally has a wider view of the common good than has the individual legislator. The administrator is the focus of pressures from all parts of the state and has to be concerned with satisfying all the different interests that are affected by his program. But the individual legislator is concerned chiefly with the effect of the program on his own constituents. An individual legislator may offer an amendment to the employment security law which is intended to satisfy a particular group, or even a particular person,

[25] And probably should not be. Administration should be professionalized and made resistant to certain sorts of outside pressures; but if these characteristics are developed too far, the result is an unresponsive, self-centered bureaucracy.

[26] This holds even for the few directors of employment security who are under civil service.

among his constituents. Such a bill often has side effects not foreseen by either the introducer of the bill or his fellow legislators. It may make administration impossibly difficult, for example, or it may open loopholes for abuse.

The administrator may find that he alone cannot persuade the legislature to abstain from the proposed measure. He is hampered not only by the ever-present tension between the legislative and executive departments of government but also by logrolling deals within the legislature. But if the representatives of labor and management on the council join with the administrator, a new political dimension is added. The legislators will be unwilling to offend these powerful blocs in their own constituencies, and even the initiating legislator can shrug his shoulders and say to the constituent who persuaded him to introduce the bill: "What can I do? Your own leaders are opposing it. Work it out with them first." A council in this situation performs a coordinating and unifying function like that of the political party and helps the administrator lessen the danger of "localitis."

The council's political aid (to all three levels of government) is at a maximum when the council can produce what is called an agreed bill, that is, a bill upon which all members of the advisory council agree. Since issues in employment security carry a high charge of controversy, the governor and the legislators run the risk of incurring intense political animosity if they act contrary to the wishes of either of the affected interests. But if the opposing interests can themselves work out a compromise agreement, government officials are saved from having to make a difficult and politically dangerous decision and need only bless the agreement. (This result follows, of course, only to the extent that the council members can speak authoritatively for the affected interests.) In this role, the council performs much the same function as the legislative committee: it reduces controversies to manageable form.

The governor and the legislature sometimes put pressure on labor and management to come to an agreement by refusing to decide the issues between them and telling them to "go off and come back with an agreement." Government's justification for this tactic is the sound principle of settling disputes at the lowest possible level of authority.[27]

From the viewpoint of the administrator, the proper relationship between himself and the advisory council is not unlike that which some writers say should exist between the executive and legislative branches of government—the one should be the active proposing power, and the other should be the consenting, supervising, criticizing power.[28]

Viewpoint of the Governed

As a source of information—a window—the council is of greater value to the governed than to any of the levels of the government. Although most council appointees presumably have some initial understanding of the program, they inevitably acquire more through their work on the council. At regular council meetings agency experts explain problems of the program and present the latest data; thus primed, the council members debate the major issues in an atmosphere of leisure and thorough study that can rarely, if ever, be duplicated in the committee rooms and corridors of the legislature. Between council meetings the members receive from the agency both oral and written reports on all major developments in the program. Because their official position as council members makes them known throughout the state, they receive complaints and requests that require them to devote still more time to the program and become still better educated in it, even in its technical aspects.

This technical knowledge is of crucial importance in the case of the governed. Only to the extent that technical competence is spread throughout the community and not concentrated in the government is there the possibility of private groups participating effectively in the decision-making processes of the government. Moreover, as the labor and management members of the council

---

[27] See George W. Taylor, *Government Regulation of Industrial Relations* (New York: Prentice-Hall, Inc., 1948), p. 371. See also Ewan Clague, "Government and Industrial Relations in a Free Economy," *Annual Proceedings of the Industrial Relations Research Association*, December, 1953, pp. 2–12.

[28] Walter Lippmann is one of the more recent propounders of this thesis. See his *Public Philosophy* (Boston: Little, Brown & Co., 1955), pp. 28–30.

grow in understanding of the program, a few of the differences that exist between them in the order of ends narrow, and many differences in the order of means disappear. The probability of agreed bills (wherein the council reaches its maximum effectiveness) is thereby strengthened.

The council serves the members not only as a window but also as a door, increasing not only their understanding of the kind of legislation the program needs but also their ability to get the kind of legislation they want. Since most legislation in the employment security program represents a compromise between the demands of labor and management, getting the kind of legislation they want usually means getting a compromise that they themselves devise. The choice which faces labor and management is either to make their own compromise, which can be tailored to fit, or accept a ready-made compromise from the legislature.

It is an axiom among arbitrators that the parties at interest know their own needs better than the most expert arbitrator—and the legislature is scarcely an expert arbitrator in the complex field of employment security. Moreover, the legislative process is full of uncertainties. It is subject to the pulls of a hundred different fluctuating forces operating within and without the legislative chambers. Even the most experienced lobbyist working out of the strongest position can never be certain what the final disposition of a bill will be, especially when, as often happens, the final decisions on the most important legislation are left to the very end of the session—when the clock is covered or stopped and the last-minute trading begins.

On the advisory council the labor and management representatives have the opportunity to avoid these legislative uncertainties by working out their own compromises. The council can begin to meet months before the start of the legislative session and can have an agreed bill on the desks of the legislators not long after the legislature convenes. Since it is almost certain that agreed bills will be enacted into law, the parties at interest can become in effect their own legislature.

It is useful to distinguish four kinds of agreed bills according to the perfection of the agreement. There is the "strict" agreed bill, in which the agreement is reached before the legislature has taken any action at all. Falling short of this perfection by increasing degrees is the agreement reached after a bill has been introduced in the legislature, after it has been studied in committee, and after it has been debated on the floor. Then there is the "full" agreed bill, which comprehends all the employment security legislation sought by members of the council or their constituents in any given legislative session. Falling short of this perfection by varying degrees is the agreement which embraces only a part of this legislation, and which leaves the interested parties free to fight for additional, though, of course, not contradictory, legislation. The perfect agreed bill is one that is both strict and full. Other agreed bills may be strict but not full, or full but not strict, or neither strict nor full.

An agreed bill normally involves collective bargaining. What the institution of the advisory council does is to provide ideal conditions for successful collective bargaining. For example, the council meetings provide the equivalent of the precollective-bargaining conference on which Taylor lays so much stress.[29] The meetings also eliminate the evils of the "tactical demand"[30] by making it unnecessary. All the information needed for intelligent bargaining is normally made available to council members in the course of their regular meetings.

As in industrial negotiations, the process of bargaining in employment security may or may not result in agreement. When the council cannot achieve an agreed bill, its direct influence is less, but its indirect influence may still be significant. For example, the council will almost inevitably influence legislation indirectly by influencing the administrator. "Probably the most effective way to make a public official act as an interest wishes him to do is to assure by institutional means that he will become thoroughly acquainted with its problems as the adherents of the interest

[29] "If understanding is to supplant tactical maneuvers in the conduct of negotiations, the precollective-bargaining conference will be given a place of great prominence." Taylor, Government Regulation of Industrial Relations, p. 360.

[30] Neil W. Chamberlain, Collective Bargaining (New York: McGraw-Hill Book Co., Inc., 1951), p. 73.

see them." [31] Any influence the council members have on the administrator normally finds its way into the recommendations that the administrator makes to the governor and to the legislature. Since the administrator is usually the single most important source of legislation, this kind of council influence can be of great value. Another important indirect influence of the council on legislation is likely to stem from the effect of the council meetings on the council members themselves. Their work on the council will probably influence the way that council members argue their case before the legislative committee, or the way they accept the legislature's final decision.

ADMINISTRATION
Viewpoint of Government

The value of advisory council participation in any activity of government varies directly with the degree of discretion exercised in the activity and with the difficulty of supervising it. In administrative law the degree of discretion involved is almost as great as in legislation itself, and the difficulty of supervising it is much greater. The difficulty is greater because the process of administrative lawmaking is continuous and its control requires continual supervision. The inability of the governer and of the legislature to maintain adequate supervision is the crux of the problem of "bureaucracy in a democracy." [32] The advisory council can help solve this problem by serving as watchdog for the governor and the legislature. The council has more technical competence and more time than either the governor or the legislature; having also an ever-open window onto the operations of the agency, the council is in an excellent position to inform the proper authorities

[31] Murray Edelman, "Governmental Organization and Public Policy," *Public Administration Review*, XII, No. 4 (Autumn, 1952), 279.

[32] Charles S. Hyneman in his book with this title describes in detail the need for such supervision and the difficulty of providing it. Although Hynemen does not mention advisory councils—his interest is in improving the competence of the legislature—the whole book is in fact an argument for councils because it makes so clear the limitations under which the legislature necessarily works in performing the task of supervision.

in good time if the administrator begins to misuse the discretionary power invested in him.

From time to time dissatisfied clients of the program complain about the administrator to their representatives in the legislature or to the governor. Lacking detailed information and not having time to investigate, the authorities are at a loss whether to believe the complainants or the administrator. If there is a functioning advisory council, the authorities will find it their best source of guidance, and if the council supports the administrator, all three levels of government will find it a useful political shield. The administrator can use it to protect himself from punitive action by the higher authorities, and the governor and the legislators can use it to protect themselves from possible retaliation by their constituents among organized labor and management. The governor and the legislators can quote the advisory council against the complainants and suggest that the complainants straighten out the matter with their own representatives on the advisory council.

The administrator will find the council a help in preventing the rise of situations that lead to complaints. The council meetings can serve as an escape valve for the tensions and dissatisfactions that inevitably build up from time to time in any administrative situation. At the council meetings the members can voice their dissatisfactions early enough, and the administrator can explain his position thoroughly enough to draw off the head of steam and prevent an explosion. The council meetings can also serve as a testing ground for contemplated policy changes. If the administrator breaks a proposed new rule on the back of the council, he will discover beforehand where the proposal might cause trouble, either because it runs counter to strong preferences of the affected parties or because it will lead to administrative complications.

In the area of "pure" administration, the council is of less use. The governor and the legislature are likely to look to the council for guidance only in situations of obvious and serious abuse. The administrator is likely to use the council somewhat more often. On occasion he will find the council useful in helping him get certain administrative aids, such as larger appropriations or better housing for the agency. More important, he can enlist the council's help in the perpetual battle to protect his staff—and himself for that matter—from the inroads of political patronage.

Viewpoint of the Governed

In the area of administrative law the governed can use the council to make their preferences known early, at the stage of policy formulation, and to police the administrator at the stage of policy execution. Resort to the courts or to the legislature is so cumbersome that it can be used only occasionally and for major matters. Adequate policing of administrative lawmaking requires what the advisory council supplies—persons who have technical competence and can give time regularly to a continuous flow of problems.

Parties with grievances and questions can go to their representatives on the council with the directness and simplicity of a phone call, and the council member, because of his official standing and familiarity with agency personnel, can go just as simply and directly to the appropriate decision-making center in the agency. The operation of an effective advisory council reduces the likelihood that abuses will continue merely because the decision makers are too far removed from the persons who are ultimately affected by their decisions.[33]

In the area of "pure" administration the governed should not expect to exert much direct influence. It would be an abuse on the part of the council if its members became busybodies and thrust themselves into purely technical administrative problems. The council will do enough if it protects the program against gross administrative incompetence either by giving early warning of such incompetence in the case of a poor administrator or by protect-

---

[33] Dwight Waldo uses the Centralia mine disaster (1947) as an example of the difficulty of correcting abuses in a complex organization. A report on the disaster reviewed the fruitless remonstrances made by the miners during a period of two years preceding the explosion and concluded: "As one strives to fix responsibility for the disaster, again and again one is confronted, as were the miners, not with any individual but with a host of individuals fused into a vast, unapproachable, insensate organism. Perhaps this immovable juggernaut is the true villain in the piece. Certainly all those in authority were too remote from the persons whose lives they controlled. And this is only to confess once more that in making our society complex we have made it unmanageable." *Ideas and Issues in Public Administration*, ed. Dwight Waldo (New York: McGraw-Hill Book Co., Inc., 1953), p. 22.

ing the efficiently functioning machine of a good administrator from outside harmful influences. The second is the more frequently needed and important function. The corrosive acids of political patronage and of the spoils system perpetually attack good administration and must be wiped away as fast as they form. An effective advisory council can supply the political strength which an administrator often lacks to resist the demands of the governor and of individual legislators that appointments in agency personnel be made to meet the needs of the political machine rather than to meet the needs of the program. John R. Commons used to lay great emphasis on this function of advisory councils.[34] It is less of a crucial function now than in Common's day because of the greater prevalence now of the civil service or merit system;[35] but any merit system may be manipulated to some extent, and the administrator himself does not usually come under the system. To protect the program from the defects of excessive political patronage is still an important function of an advisory council.[36]

Disadvantages of Advisory Councils. In the preceding discussion the functions of advisory councils have been treated as so many advantages to be expected from the operation of the council. The "gross" value of a council will consist of these advantages in so far as they are realized in practice. But the net value of a council

[34] Commons gives an example drawn from his experience with the employment office of Milwaukee, Wisconsin. The Industrial Commission had removed an appointee and had replaced him with two socialists who had been recommended by the Wisconsin Advisory Committee. A delegation went to the governor to protest the change. A meeting was arranged between this delegation and the employer members of the Advisory Committee. Commons reports: "We learned afterwards of the drubbing which the employers gave to their political fellow citizens. The political incumbent, they said, had been running merely a loafing place for 'heelers' and the employers could not take on anybody sent to them for jobs." Commons, *Myself,* pp. 104–5.

[35] All the states have merit systems in their employment security programs, for example. A state must have a merit system covering this program in order to be eligible for federal administrative funds.

[36] The following judgment of one of the pioneers in American social insurance is still sound. "In the long run, I believe, the only real protection against 'politics' and the only real stimulus to effective administration of a social insurance system will lie in the insistence of employers and wage-earners on the efficient operation of a system which will so vitally affect them both." Elizabeth Brandeis, "Economic and Administrative Criteria for a Social Insurance Program," *American Labor Legislation Review,* XXV (March, 1935), 28.

will be something less. It will be these advantages less any disadvantages that may flow from the operation of a council. Logically, then, potential disadvantages might be discussed at this point; but it will save much repetition if we postpone their discussion to a later chapter (19), where their validity in the light of experience can be discussed at the same time.

METHODS OF ADVISORY COUNCILS

Council functions are like so many ends to be achieved. Council methods are means to those ends. Methods are understood here as comprising both structure (how the machine is put together) and procedure (how it operates).

The main decisions to be made with respect to structure are decisions on the council's membership, scope, size, terms, remuneration, staff, and method of appointment. The main decisions to be made with respect to procedure are decisions on rules, meetings, minutes, reports, committees, the use of hearings, and methods of voting. A wide variety of choices is available with respect to both structure and procedure, and in the employment security program the states have as a matter of fact experimented with many combinations of methods.[37]

To develop at this point theoretical arguments for and against each alternative method would be a lengthy and not very rewarding task. The discussion of the "right" methods will be more meaningful in a later chapter, after we have examined the history of advisory councils. We can then reason from actual events rather than speculate about possible ones and can judge realistically which methods enable councils to perform their functions most effectively.

[37] The reader may have expected to find somewhere in this book a table of the structural and procedural provisions of all the state councils. It has not been provided because it would have served no other purpose than to satisfy curiosity. Some of the states whose laws provide for advisory councils do not have councils; some of those which have councils do not follow their own laws regulating the council's structure and procedures; and, finally, some councils are effective and some are not. Until the actual practices of each state are known—and they can be known only by on-the-spot investigation—a mere table of legal provisions is meaningless. The table in Appendix A is confined, therefore, to those councils which have been investigated in the course of this study.

We may make one exception, however. One element of council structure is uniquely important and warrants special mention at this point. That element is council membership. The "who" of a council largely determines its "what." That is, the quality of a council's membership goes further to determine the council's effectiveness than do all its other characteristics combined.

The appointing authority has a choice among many alternatives. One important choice is between a tripartite council, which includes public members, and a council restricted to representatives of labor and management.[38] An equally important choice is whether to give the affected interest groups much or little voice in the selection of their representatives on the council.[39] Among other choices to be made are these: Are the council members to be persons of technical competence, of social prestige, or of political influence? Are they to be professional representatives of employer and employee organizations, or "genuine" employers and workers? Shall the public members include legislators? Shall there be representatives for such "special" groups as women, veterans, farmers? for racial and religious groups?

The appointing authority will make its choices in accordance with the ideal type of advisory council it has in mind. Although the difference between the various types is chiefly a matter of emphasis, and a council which is predominantly of one type will contain elements of the others, still it is useful to distinguish five variations which may be designated briefly as the rubber-stamp, prestige, political, expert, and representative types.

For the rubber-stamp type of council, the members are chosen primarily with a view to the facility with which they can be manipulated by the administrator. In a study of this kind, whose

[38] Of the councils examined in this study only Wisconsin, Michigan, and (for a time) Minnesota have restricted membership to labor and management.

[39] Avery Leiserson distinguishes five grades of discretion in the appointing authority: "(1) No restriction upon executive choice other than political expediency, (2) a statutory provision providing that an appointment shall be made from a category of interest such as bankers, manufacturers, employees, agriculture, etc., (3) statutory provision that appointment shall be made 'after consultation with' groups representative of such groups or classes of interest, (4) statutory provision that appointments shall be made from panels suggested by groups representative of specified classes of interests, and (5) appointment of a nominee by the interest group itself." *Administrative Regulation,* p. 101.

central assumption is that the decision-making activities of government should be shared with nongovernmental agents to the greatest possible degree, this type of council necessarily rates very low.

For the prestige type, the members are chosen primarily because their standing in the community makes their support of the administrator a valuable asset. It does not differ sufficiently from the rubber-stamp type to escape the same judgment. In a program as technical as employment security, council members whose chief qualification is prestige can do little more than support what the administrator tells them they ought to support.

For the political type, the members are chosen primarily on the basis of their affiliation with political parties. This type of council also must rate low on the value scale of a study whose interest lies in precisely the opposite direction. The whole burden of the argument in Chapter 1 is that the decisions of society should *not* be all political decisions made through the political apparatus, but that plural power centers should provide the opportunity for decisions to be made under a variety of formalities.

For the expert type, the members are chosen primarily on the basis of their technical competence. The President's Council of Economic Advisers is an outstanding example of this type (as is also the French Conseil d'État). It is in accord with the assumptions of this study that the council must possess considerable expertise, for only experts can control experts. Without technical competence the advisory council would be in the same position as Weber's legislature.[40] Pendleton Herring has been a strong advocate of the expert type of council, even to the point of deprecating the representative type.[41]

However, expertise will not suffice of itself to guarantee the council a share in the decision-making activity of government un-

[40] See p. 22.

[41] "If positive recommendations are sought from an advisory committee, this body should be composed of experts rather than representatives. The individuals on these committees must be drawn directly from industry or the professions. Their fundamental purpose is to do away with that middleman, the politician. . . . The representative factor is of little consequence except as an indication of the expert qualifications of the committeeman, the breadth of his experience, and his close touch with a profession or industry. When an economic or social interest has the vitality to sustain a responsible organization, this agency should be taken into account when spokesmen for this interest are selected. This connection, however, must be taken as

less virtue is knowledge and knowledge itself is complete. If at the end of investigations conducted by experts, areas of dispute still remain between powerful interest groups, the council will need more qualifications than expertise if it is to participate effectively in the decision-making process. It will need the power to bargain, for disputes which cannot be resolved by investigation can be settled only by violence or bargaining.

For the representative type of council, the members are chosen primarily for their ability to speak authoritatively for organized interest groups. Such members have the power to settle by bargaining disputes that cannot be settled by investigation. Since such disputes occur constantly in the employment security program, the councils will need the power to bargain if they are to be fully effective. It is one of the assumptions of this study that a council to be effective needs representative members.

We have arrived at this point in our inquiry: Granted that effective [42] advisory councils are desirable in theory, have they proved to be feasible in fact? That is, have they actually performed the functions expected of them? Why or why not? The rest of our inquiry is directed to answering those questions. The history of sixteen councils is described in some detail in Chapters 3 to 18, and is summarized and analyzed in Chapter 19. The conclusions and recommendations which flow from that analysis are contained in Chapters 20 and 21.

---

indicative of the appointee's competence to advise rather than of his authority to represent." *Public Administration and the Public Interest* (New York: McGraw-Hill Book Co., Inc., 1936), pp. 359, 360. Quotation used by permission of McGraw-Hill Book Co., Inc.

[42] By an "effective" council is meant one that has an impact, an effect, on the program—simply this and nothing more. It lies outside the scope of this investigation to make a judgment as to whether that effect is good or bad by some higher standard than the standard used in Chapter 1, the principle of subsidiarity.

Part Two

EXPERIENCE WITH MORE EFFECTIVE
ADVISORY COUNCILS

3

THE WISCONSIN ADVISORY COUNCIL

IN Wisconsin the unemployment compensation and the employment service divisions of the employment security program are administered separately, each having its own administrator and its own advisory council. They have developed along such different lines that it is best to take each separately. The first and larger part of this chapter deals with unemployment compensation. The remaining part deals briefly with the employment service council and adds a few observations on the advisory council in workmen's compensation.

UNEMPLOYMENT COMPENSATION

A survey of advisory councils in unemployment compensation properly begins with Wisconsin, whose council is the oldest and has functioned the most effectively. And the story of the Wisconsin council properly begins with John R. Commons (1862–1945), who vigorously propagated the idea of advisory councils throughout most of his thirty years of activity in the state.

Commons was introduced to the essentials of the idea early.

The essential point, as I learned in 1900 at the miners' joint conference, was the elimination, as far as possible, of a third party, the arbitrator—whether King, legislature, governor or dictator, handing down rules and regulations from above—and the substitution of rules agreed upon collectively, by conciliation. It was to be, as I then learned in 1900, not Democracy in the historic meaning of a majority overruling the minority, but representation of organized voluntary but conflicting economic interests. After thirty years I attempted to work my discovery of 1900 into a system of institutional economics.[1]

When in 1911 he helped set up Wisconsin's Industrial Commission (the first in the country), he organized advisory councils as an essential part of the commission's machinery. As a member of the United States Commission on Industrial Relations in 1915, he recommended that advisory councils be established nationally on the Wisconsin model. In his last work, published posthumously in 1950, he advocated the use of the advisory council technique as an important part of our defense against fascism and communism.[2]

Throughout the 1920's Commons was a major proponent of unemployment compensation legislation for Wisconsin. He was the principal author of the unemployment compensation bills that were introduced in each session of the Wisconsin legislature from 1921 through 1929.[3] He included a provision for an advisory council in all these bills and envisaged a very broad field of action for the council. He wanted the legislature to pass a very general sort of law which would leave to the Industrial Commission and the advisory council the determination of such substantive matters as benefit levels, tax rates, and eligibility conditions. Commons was influenced by the experience of the advisory committees which had been established to draw up safety codes for industry. These committees, which Commons had helped to establish and which operated under a broad charter of delegated discretion,[4] had been very successful. Commons was probably influenced, also, by the temper of the period, during which the ambitions of the pluralists reached high tide.[5]

Commons was less active in the final campaign for unemploy-

[1] John R. Commons, *Myself* (New York: Macmillan Co., 1934), pp. 72–73. Quotation used by permission of the Macmillan Company.

[2] John R. Commons, *The Economics of Collective Action* (New York: Macmillan Co., 1950), pp. 262–63, 288–89.

[3] Commons was not the first proponent of unemployment compensation in Wisconsin. The socialists had begun to introduce unemployment compensation bills as early as 1907.

[4] The law specified little more than that the safety standards should be "reasonable." See Elizabeth Brandeis, "Labor Legislation," in *History of Labor in the United States, 1896–1932*, III (New York: Macmillan Co., 1935), 650.

[5] See p. 33.

ment compensation legislation in 1931, which was carried on mainly by some of his former students [6] and resulted in the enactment of an unemployment compensation law in January, 1932. This law contained a provision for an advisory council but did not give the council the ambitious scope envisaged by Commons. The framers of the law, including Commons's students, felt that the analogy with safety codes did not hold. Because the issues in unemployment compensation were much more controversial than in safety codes, there was less latitude for determination of substantive matters by technical experts and more need for determination by the legislature.

STRUCTURE

The law as finally enacted contained the following provision for an advisory council:

The industrial commission shall appoint advisory employment committees, by local districts or by industries or for the whole state, consisting in each case of one or more representatives each of employers, employees and the public, who shall assist the commission, without compensation but with reimbursement of necessary expenses, in administering and carrying out the purposes and provisions of this chapter.

The provision for local committees was never activated, but a state committee was set up in March, 1932, which was composed of three representatives of employers, three of employees, and one "public" member—the secretary of the Industrial Commission, Arthur Altmeyer.

From the beginning therefore, the Wisconsin advisory council was in reality bipartite, despite the apparent intention of the law to provide for a tripartite council.[7] Who made this interpretation of "public" to mean a government official? It is unfortunate that an interpretation so significant is obscure in its origin. None of

[6] Chiefly Arthur Altmeyer, Harold Groves, Elizabeth Brandeis, and Paul Raushenbush.
[7] The language of this 1932 provision was prepared by Paul Raushenbush and cleared with John R. Commons.

those who were in a position to know remembered with certainty. But the probability is that Mr. Altmeyer himself made the interpretation at the request of the labor and management members.[8]

A 1937 amendment made this interpretation official, and specified further that the director of the agency should act as the council's chairman.[9] The Wisconsin chairman has always refrained from voting, even when invited to vote by the other members of the council. The council has thus been bipartite in the fullest sense.

Another 1937 amendment provided compensation for council members. A per diem rate of $25 was established at the time and has never been changed. There is no limit to the amount which council members may be paid in the course of a year; but work done by individual members apart from council meetings is not compensated.

As amended in 1937, the law read:

The Commission shall appoint a state advisory committee on this chapter, and may appoint additional committees for industries or local districts. Each committee shall consist of a salaried commissioned employee who shall serve as chairman, and of one or more representatives of employers and an equal number of representatives of employees, who shall receive for each day of active service such reasonable compensation as the commission may determine and reimbursement of necessary expenses, and shall assist the commission in administering and carrying out the purposes of this chapter.

A 1939 and final amendment added the sentence:

The state advisory committee shall submit its recommendations with respect to amendments of this chapter to each regular session of the legislature, and shall report its views on any pending bill relating to this chapter to the proper legislative committee.

This 1939 amendment, which originated with the advisory council itself, recognized and sanctioned actual practice at the time. Its significance was twofold: it authorized the council to go directly

---

[8] For another instance of labor and management members preferring a bipartite council, see Rhode Island, p. 280.

[9] Paul Raushenbush, director of the unemployment compensation department, has been chairman since 1934, when he succeeded Arthur Altmeyer.

to the legislature rather than through the Industrial Commission and to appraise all bills rather than merely present its own. It has been customary in Wisconsin for the legislature to hold up action on all bills originating from sources other than the advisory council until the council has expressed its opinion on them.

The Wisconsin council has always been "representative" in the Commons sense. The leading labor and management organizations have always been invited to nominate their own representatives, and the Industrial Commission has proceeded to appoint the nominees. When the first members were to be appointed, the Wisconsin State Federation of Labor and the Wisconsin Manufacturers Association were unchallenged in their claim to be the "leading organizations," and the first council was composed of their nominees alone. Later, in 1948, to recognize the growth of the CIO and the state Chamber of Commerce, each of these organizations was invited to nominate a representative, and the advisory council was expanded from seven to nine members.

The terms of the members are not limited by law, and in practice members have remained on the council for long periods. The Wisconsin council had the lowest turnover rate of all the councils in the sample.[10] For the period 1932–1957, its turnover rate was 4.7 percent.

PROCEDURES

The law makes no prescription regarding meetings of the advisory council. In practice, the council meets on call by its chairman, and he has tended to call meetings only when there has been some definite work to be done. Since 1941 (when the record of meetings begins) the council has averaged about nine meetings yearly. As the following table shows, the meetings have not been evenly spaced but have tended to cluster around legislative sessions, that is, in the period from fall to spring of every other year.

[10] Turnover rate is obtained by dividing the actual number of council members by the number who could have been council members if the entire membership had been changed each year.

Period	Months	Meetings	Meetings per Month
Jan., 1941, through May, 1941	5	15	3.0
June, 1941, through Sept., 1942	16	1	0.1
Oct., 1942, through March, 1943	6	11	1.8
April, 1943, through Sept., 1944	18	1	0.1
Oct., 1944, through April, 1945	7	13	1.9
May, 1945, through Nov., 1946	19	4	0.2
Dec., 1946, through April, 1947	5	8	1.6
May, 1947, through Aug., 1948	16	7	0.4
Sept., 1948, through April, 1949	8	13	1.6
May, 1949, through Aug., 1950	16	5	0.3
Sept., 1950, through March, 1951	7	12	1.7
April, 1951, through April, 1952	13	6	0.5
May, 1952, through April, 1953	12	18	1.5
May, 1953, through Aug., 1954	16	7	0.5
Sept., 1954, through July, 1955	11	16	1.5
Aug., 1955, through Sept., 1956	14	1	0.1
Oct., 1956, through April, 1957	7	13	1.9

Three periods, 1941–1942, 1943–1944, and 1955–1956, show exceptionally few meetings. The director admitted that long periods between meetings were harmful to the spirit of an advisory council, but pointed out that two of these three instances reflected wartime conditions. Attendance at meetings for the period covered by the table averaged 83 percent. The attendance record of management was 79 percent and that of labor was 87 percent.

The meetings usually cover one day, beginning about 10:00 in the morning and ending about 4:00 in the afternoon.[11] They are conducted informally, with much give and take around the table. No minutes of any kind are kept, on the theory that discussion is freer if unrecorded. The chairman sits at the upper end of the council table, the labor and management members on opposite sides, and a number of top staff people at another table across the foot of the council table. Having the staff people present makes information immediately available to the council, educates the staff members in public policy, and emphasizes for the council the importance which the agency attaches to the meetings, since so many agency personnel are taken from their regular work to attend. At the meetings which I attended, the staff only occasionally volunteered remarks or information; for the most part

---

[11] At lunch time the three groups—labor, management, agency—separate and use the occasion for caucusing.

they waited to be called upon. There was evidence of a long-standing intimate acquaintanceship between council members and agency staff.

Although meetings are called occasionally simply to keep the advisory council members abreast of new developments and to consult them on current administrative problems, most of the meetings are focused sharply on the purpose of working out needed changes in legislation and in administrative law. Council members are provided—ideally in advance of a meeting, but sometimes at the meeting itself—with the agenda of the meeting and with sheaves of pertinent facts. The director of the agency has found that members do not always read the materials sent to them in advance of meetings and even lose them. He makes certain that all important matters are studied in the council meetings themselves.

Since the reaching of an agreed bill has been the chief activity of the Wisconsin council, it is desirable to describe the procedure of the agreed bill in detail. The council reaches agreement on its agreed bill by the usual bargaining stages. In the preliminary stages all agreements on particular items are tentative and subject to modification in the light of other concessions that may be gained or granted late. Accordingly, these tentative agreements remain confidential within the membership, except as either side may find it necessary to consult a few key people in its respective group outside the council.

The chairman plays an active and important part in the meetings. He plans them and provides materials for them. At the meetings themselves, besides guiding the general discussion, he argues positions and gives explanations of technical points or historical developments. Yet, despite his active role, he stays sufficiently clear of controversy to perform the useful role of mediator in a collective bargaining situation. As the meetings progress, a possible "package bill" begins to take shape. The chairman is in touch with and is trusted by both sides. As a result he can foresee the probable acceptable compromise and can begin to move the two sides toward that goal—prudently careful not to violate confidences.

The council's agreed bill is not left in general terms. It is reduced to exact language, usually by the chairman of the council, before final agreement is reached. The council has always supplied the legislature with a written explanation of the changes it recommended. Since 1949 the explanation, set in distinctive type, has been included as a part of the bill itself, and the innovation has found general favor with the legislators. The bill bears the statement on its face, "Introduced by request of the statutory Advisory Committee on Unemployment Compensation," and the practice has been to secure introduction of the bill by a legislative committee rather than by an individual legislator.[12]

The council may and frequently does submit more than one bill. A noncontroversial matter may be introduced early in a separate bill, especially if it requires immediate passage, as was the case in 1953 with a bill relating to benefits for veterans. Recommendations to extend coverage are usually introduced separately, so as not to endanger other recommendations.[13] But the council always has one main bill which represents the bargained conclusions reached on controversial matters.

When the main bill is up for hearing, the council members appear personally before the legislative committee. As official representatives of their respective groups they formally state their approval of the bill and remain to answer questions and objections. The chairman of the council lays great stress on this personal appearance of council members, particularly for the main bill. In the case of bills which the council has agreed to oppose, usually the chairman alone makes an appearance at the hearing in the name of the whole council. However, other council members have appeared at these hearings, when the matter was of major importance, or when a particular member could exert some special influence. Some council members are lobbyists for their organizations, and are on hand to contact legislators whenever that proves necessary—which is seldom. The chairman keeps

[12] The choice of committee has depended on the nature of the bill, the composition of committees in a particular year, and the wish of the majority leader. In 1953 the practice was adopted of introducing companion bills in the two houses to assure hearings in each and to speed up passage.

[13] See n. 14, below.

all members informed of the progress of all bills by means of frequent bulletins.

The labor and management representatives have a "gentleman's agreement" to forego independent action in the legislature and to make all action joint action. They were unable to state with exactness the theoretical limits of this agreement. In practice the limits seemed to amount to this, that each side would abstain from such independent action as would lead the other side to conclude that the advantages of an agreed bill were not worth its price. Until 1957 it meant that both sides refrained from all independent action. They supported only the agreed bill and jointly opposed all other bills, even bills which one of them might have desired very much to see enacted. At different times both labor and management have been in the position of having to oppose in a public hearing some bill which was very favorable to their own groups.

ACTIVITIES

The ambitious role which John R. Commons conceived for an advisory council was probably, as his co-workers thought, impracticable in the form in which he conceived it—as a legal blank check to be filled in by the council. But the role which the legally limited council actually played was not very different from the one Commons had envisaged. The council exercised a decisive influence on every aspect of the program throughout the program's life. In every legislative session except the last covered by this study (1957) the council produced an agreed bill which the legislature accepted and enacted into law. The only important council recommendation which the legislature rejected during more than two decades was the recommendation to extend coverage to smaller firms.[14]

[14] The council repeatedly made this recommendation, but, except during the 1937 session, the legislature as often rejected it. At first the advisory council included this recommendation with its omnibus bill; but since the bill was inevitably amended to remove this recommendation, and since the process of amendment is full of uncertainties, the council later adopted the practice of putting its recommendations relating to coverage into a bill separate from the omnibus bill so that the legislature could, if it insisted, kill the one without touching the other.

The long succession of agreed bills wrought so many changes that by 1957 the program could truly be said to be fashioned in the image of the advisory council. The extent to which the council rewrote the law is made strikingly evident by a comparison between the early law—say, before 1935—and the law as it stood in 1957. According to the early law: Coverage was limited to employers of ten or more employees; the maximum benefit was $10; the maximum duration was ten weeks, and the duration ratio (weeks of benefits per weeks of work) was one to four; there was a three-week waiting period applicable to each stretch of unemployment and to each employer in the claimant's base period; an employer was not responsible for unemployment due to an "Act of God"; reserve funds were on an individual basis, so that if an individual employer's account became exhausted his employees did not receive benefits; the maximum tax rate on employers was 2 percent; the tax rate tended to fluctuate sharply and in the same direction as changes in unemployment.

As the program stood in 1957: Coverage included employers of four or more employees (council action had extended coverage to six and federal action had carried it the rest of the way); the maximum benefit was $38; the maximum duration was twenty-six and one half weeks, and the duration ratio was one to one and one half; the waiting period was one week and was served only once in any one benefit year; reserve funds were pooled, so that the exhaustion of an individual employer's fund did not deprive his employees of benefit rights; the maximum tax rate was 4 percent, the tax mechanism was adjusted so that the changes in tax rates were less likely to aggravate the swings in employment and more likely to sustain the fund at an adequate level.

This great difference between the earlier and later programs was wrought by a multitude of small changes made session after session. In addition, many other changes were made. The major amendments made during the period 1933–1955 are given by legislative session in Appendix C. Since the council kept no minutes and made no reports, the bare facts of the amendments are all that remain. No details are known of what must have been a varied and colorful history of collective bargaining. But one who is steeped in the program will be able to use the bare facts to recreate imaginatively the long periods of study and tense sessions of bargaining that lay back of each painfully contrived agreed bill and that make of the unbroken chain of agreements a striking illustration of gradualism in action.

The tradition of agreed bills remained unbroken until 1957, but it did not always operate without friction. When the CIO joined the advisory council in 1948, a crisis of sorts developed with regard to the "gentleman's agreement" (which requires both sides to support the agreed bill against all conflicting bills). To be effective, the agreement must be binding not only on the advisory council members but on the organizations which they represent. Prior to 1949 the labor and management members of the council had been able thus to commit their organizations. But in the 1949 and 1951 legislative sessions, although the CIO representative on the council signed the agreed bill and appeared at the hearing to support it, CIO officials actively supported other bills, which were more favorable to their side, against the agreed bill. After the 1951 session the rest of the council laid down an ultimatum to the CIO: either it work within the council's traditional rules, or leave the council if it preferred independent action. The CIO elected to remain on the council. At its 1952 convention the CIO agreed to permit its representative on the council to commit it by the agreed bill, but only if he first cleared the terms of the agreement with the CIO executive council. In 1953 this meant in practice that the council representative put in a telephone call to the CIO president when the crucial point was reached in the council's final bargaining session.

Among the factors that contributed to the change in the CIO's position the most important seems to have been a growing familiarization with the process of the agreed bill and an increased esteem for its advantages. Two legislators who were also CIO members were outraged by the "gentleman's agreement" when they first discovered its existence (one of them wrote an article attacking it) but later came to approve of it as they learned more about it. They reserved to themselves as legislators the right to introduce whatever bills they wished, but did not object to the state CIO using its energies in support of the agreed bill rather than of their own bills.[15]

The Federation representatives on the council had a more secure and trusted—their critics said a more bureaucratic—relationship with their organizations than had the CIO representative.[16] Where the CIO state convention passed many detailed resolutions pertaining to unemployment compensation, the Federation state convention passed few resolutions, and those few of a general nature. The Federation representatives, therefore, were left with almost complete discretion. The *Wisconsin Federationist* for February, 1951, carried a report on Federation bills introduced in the legislature. After listing and explaining fifteen separate bills, none of which dealt with unemployment compensation or workmen's compensation, the report continued:

Changes in Workmen's Compensation and Unemployment Compensation matters wait upon the reports or action of the State Advisory Committees on those laws. The federation participates on those committees through WSFL president George A. Haberman and Mr. Nagorsne.

The situation is clear: in other fields the Federation worked through its machinery of convention resolutions and legislative representatives (lobbyists); but in the fields of unemployment compensation and workmen's compensation it worked through the established machinery of the advisory councils.

The Federation representatives on the council have had their occasional difficulties. In 1951, for example, one of them was criticized sharply by his own union for opposing a bill the union wanted. He was able, however, to explain his actions to his union

---

[15] These two legislators were manual workers who, when the legislature was in session, were on leave from their regular jobs in machine shops. Another legislator, also closely connected with the CIO, who shared office space with them, was present during the interview. He was not a manual worker and was probably a college graduate. He disagreed with his colleagues regarding the agreed bill procedure and thought the CIO should fight it. There is the temptation to explain this difference of opinion in terms of the distinction which Lenin used to make between the rank-and-file labor leader and the "intellectual" in their attitude toward revolution.

[16] There were many reasons for the difference, among them the fact that the CIO representative was not a highly placed elected official, as were the Federation representatives.

satisfactorily and to obtain its approval for future actions similar to the one for which he was criticized. When this council member has to testify on a bill his union favors but which conflicts with the agreed bill, he tells the legislative committee:

Our union is interested in getting the agreed bill passed whatever else happens. You can do what you like about this other bill, but don't let it interfere with passing the agreed bill. That is the one labor is interested in.

If there are new legislators on the committee, they usually ask why he takes this attitude toward a bill that would clearly help labor. He then explains the workings of the advisory council and its agreed bill.

In 1951 an exception occurred which was more apparent than real. The advisory council had been studying disability benefits intensively for several years and had been moving steadily closer to a program acceptable to both labor and management. In 1951 the employer members felt they could not support such a bill as yet; but the labor members were under strong pressure from their unions to "do something." To ease that pressure the employer members explicitly consented to the labor members' unilaterally supporting a bill which the unions would introduce. Lacking joint support, the bill failed to pass.

During the period immediately preceding the 1951 legislative session the council was made aware of some employer dissatisfaction with its procedures. The legislature had been receiving complaints from employers, especially small employers, that unemployment compensation was becoming a heavy burden; some of the complainants blamed the advisory council and its agreed bills. Questions were raised by legislators as to whether small employers were adequately represented on the advisory council, whether appointments to the advisory council ought not to require Senate confirmation, and in general whether the advisory-council-agreed-bill system was working satisfactorily. The Legislative Council Committee on Labor and Industry was directed to make an investigation. In addition to attending some advisory council meetings, the committee held public hearings in three cities.

The advisory council was invited to assist the committee at these hearings and did so. The legislative committee's final report was favorable to the council on all counts:

Advisory Committee Appointments

On the question of whether the advisory committee members should be confirmed by the senate, the committee is of the view that this is not necessary since advisory committees merely recommend—they do not have rule making powers. The advisory committee members are elected by certain organizations to back certain policies, and if any member fails to do so the organization can replace him, a system which would present complications if this type of organization were made subject to senate approval. Moreover, all proposals of the advisory committee are subject to approval by both houses of the legislature.

Small Employer Representation

There have been suggestions that small employers should be represented on the advisory committee. At present the smallest employer on the committee employs approximately 800 persons.

Mandatory legislation does not appear to be necessary on this since the state chamber of commerce and the manufacturers association have many small employer members and can see to it that a small business man is represented. The hearings held around the state by the committee have given the small employer an opportunity to express his viewpoint. It may be advisable for the industrial commission to have similar meetings from time to time.

Summary

The Wisconsin unemployment compensation program is basically sound; it is functioning very well, and its administration compares favorably with other states. The Wisconsin advisory committee plan contributes toward amicable working relationships between labor and management. Both the advisory committees on unemployment and workmen's compensation have set a record of performance in reaching agreement in controversial problems that is without precedent. The advisory committee idea is an effective vehicle for sifting, evaluating and reaching agreement on many questions which would be extremely time consuming and costly if handled entirely by the legislature. The experience and counsel of employer and labor members of the advisory committee has been most helpful to the committee.[17]

[17] Report of Wisconsin Legislative Council, 1950, II, 129.

Not included in the committee's formal report was its opinion that some relief should be provided for employers charged with benefits paid to employees who quit voluntarily. Although the committee indicated that it did not intend to interfere with the advisory council's usual procedures by introducing such a bill itself, the weight of its opinion is reflected in the advisory council's 1951 agreed bill, which included a noncharging provision. These 1950 events clearly reveal both the advisory council's secure and influential position and the legislature's ultimate authority.

The 1953 session passed quietly enough in unemployment compensation, and the usual agreed bill was achieved. In workmen's compensation, however, the CIO violently attacked the agreed bill produced by the advisory council. Since most of the same labor and management representatives were on the advisory councils of both programs and were accustomed in both to work through the technique of the agreed bill, this disturbance in workmen's compensation probably had its repercussions in unemployment compensation.

Employer unrest bubbled to the surface again in 1955 and showed itself stronger. The social security committee of the Wisconsin Manufacturers Association decided at one point that the freedom of its representatives on the advisory council to negotiate an agreed bill should be restricted by requiring them to check back with the committee before concluding any agreement on the council that had not previously been approved by a majority vote of the committee. The council reminded the committee that employers had criticized the CIO representative on the council for this very tactic in the 1949 and 1951 negotiations. Perhaps for this reason, perhaps because the board of directors of the Wisconsin Manufacturers Association favored the agreed bill procedure, the employer representatives on the council were left free to negotiate as before.

However, a group of employers comprising a dozen firms—some of them large—jointly opposed the advisory council's agreed bill at the legislative hearings that year. This group submitted a formal statement which objected to the steady liberalization of the program that had taken place under the advisory council's agreed bills and appealed to the legislature for protection. The statement recommended that "as of now, the Legislature take back its prerogative to initiate and pass, after full and complete debate, legislation, and once and for all put an end to this so-called super legislature operating under the fancy terminology of the 'Advisory Committee.'"[18] This group sponsored a bill to re-organize the advisory council. The bill would have limited council membership to a fixed term of four years, required appointment by the governor with confirmation by the Senate, and eliminated remuneration for council services.

This bill did not pass, but the advisory council's agreed bill did. Although the waves were rising, the advisory council was still able to surmount them.

The waves finally swamped the agreed bill procedure in 1957. The extension of coverage to employers of four or more (effective in 1956) was one cause of intensified employer opposition to the agreed bill (smaller employers were generally more suspicious of the procedure); but the main cause was the issue of supplementary unemployment benefits (SUB). An influential group of employers was determined to pass a law invalidating the simultaneous payment of unemployment compensation and SUB benefits. Because they thought that the employer members then on the council could not effectively lead a drive for such legislation (one of them was with a firm that had a SUB contract), they brought about a change in the employer representation on the council. The new employer members on the council refused to discuss increased benefits or any other changes in the law except as a return for labor's acceptance of the proposed SUB amendment. Labor refused this ultimatum[19] and for the first time in its history the council failed to achieve an agreed bill.

Both sides introduced legislation independently of the other.

[18] Statement of Gilbert L. Klein on 64-S in behalf of Globe-Union, Sivyer Steel, Norberg Mfg., Falk Corp., Lakeside Bridge & Stl., Harnischfeger, Heil Co., Dings Magnetic Separator, Chain Belt and Grede Foundries: to the Committee on Labor and Taxation, February 22, 1955.

[19] The proposed SUB amendment would have had only a minor effect on AFL workers in Wisconsin, but the just-completed amalgamation of the AFL with the CIO and Reuther's great personal interest in the SUB program made negotiation on this issue impossible.

The employers' SUB bill failed to pass or even to receive a hearing. Labor's many bills—to raise benefits, extend coverage, increase duration, and so forth—also failed of passage. The legislature put together a "package" bill of its own which granted to labor a two-dollar increase in the maximum benefit and to employers a change in the tax system. In his final legislative bulletin to the council members (June 27, 1957) the director of the agency made the pointed observation, "Those 2 bills were clearly treated as a joint 'special order' package—closely approaching the joint package on which the U.C. Advisory Committee might well (or desirably) have reached joint agreement this year *if* the S.U.B. issue hadn't complicated your 1957 negotiations."

It is not strictly correct to say that the council failed to achieve any agreement in 1957. Besides agreeing positively on a bill which the administrator wanted and which made numerous changes in the law to facilitate administration, the council agreed negatively to oppose a number of bills introduced by others than the council. In these agreed-upon actions the council experienced its customary success.

In addition to shaping an agreed bill every two years the council has engaged in multifarious other activities. Limited space requires that these be described more briefly.

The council has always exerted a strong influence on the quasi-legislative process of developing administrative law. Sometimes the initiative has stemmed from council members themselves, usually from someone whose constituents were affected. More often the initiative has come from the administrator, seeking advice or support. Sometimes the process has taken the form of a discussion at a council meeting; sometimes it has been simply a series of telephone conversations. Sometimes it has issued in formal rules; sometimes simply in oral directives. Perhaps the most striking instance of this kind of activity occurred shortly after VJ Day, when the council met with all the local office managers to discuss how the "suitable work" requirement should be interpreted during the expected disturbances of the reconversion period.

The council has often been of help to the administrator in his political relationships. Several instances of such help occurred in 1953, when I happened to be in the state and could observe them for myself. In the first instance, when Congress cut the appropriations for employment security administration to a point which threatened essential efficiency, the advisory council sent a strong protest to members of the key congressional committees and to the Wisconsin delegation. In a second instance, when the majority leader in the Wisconsin Senate publicly announced his disapproval of the director of unemployment compensation,[20] the advisory council let it be known that it was on the side of the administrator. In still a third instance, when the governor proposed to appropriate for general state expenses a three hundred thousand dollar unemployment compensation fund which had been accumulated from penalty and interest payments, the council made suggestions on the extent and method of the transfer which could not have been made with equally good grace by the administrator and which the governor accepted.

The council has also helped the administrator on many occasions in his relations with labor and management groups. It has functioned continuously as a middleman interpreting the agency to labor and management, and labor and management to the agency. Sometimes, too, the council has served as buffer, as in the following instance which occurred in the same year as the others just mentioned: [21] When the canning industry asked to have some (more) of their employees removed from coverage under the unemployment compensation law, the administrator was able to write in reply:

The Advisory Committee members have repeatedly had the present special canning provision thrown at them as justifying rather similar special treatment for other groups. However, I am sending each UC Advisory Committee member a copy of your February 7 letter—and of this letter—and am hereby asking them to send me (promptly) their views on your two suggestions.

[20] *Wisconsin State Journal*, June 10, 1953.
[21] If 1953 is atypical in point of council activity, it is probably in the direction of showing less rather than more activity. The year was a relatively quiet and uneventful one in unemployment compensation.

A literally unique activity of the Wisconsin council consisted of a series of peripatetic public hearings. The advisory council participated in the hearings held by the Legislative Council committee in three cities in 1950 and then obeyed a strong hint of the committee by holding similar meetings of its own in 1952 and again in 1954. The council traveled to half a dozen different cities in Wisconsin and held day-long public hearings in each place in order to give local labor and management people the opportunity to ask questions, voice objections, make suggestions. I traveled with the council in 1954 and observed at firsthand how the council functioned, not only as the voice of labor and management, but also as the voice of the program itself. The council members listened to their constituents at the hearings, but they also lectured to them, telling them what the program could and could not properly do. They were the most impressive when they combined to oppose a witness, whether on labor's or management's side, who proposed something that would have been injurious to the program as a whole. Sometimes in these hearings they explained and defended the actions of the administrator. Yet there were sufficient differences in viewpoint between the labor and management members of the council, and between the council and the administrator, to make these public meetings very lively affairs.

APPRAISAL

Extent of Effectiveness

Council effectiveness is properly appraised by the way council activities affected the three groups chiefly involved—the legislature, the administrative agency, and labor and management.

The Legislature. The preeminent position which the advisory council has occupied in the area of legislation through the procedure of the agreed bill raises the obvious question as to whether Wisconsin legislators have suffered a loss of their prerogatives or have abandoned some of their responsibilities. The favorable conclusions reached by the Legislative Council committee in 1950 when it conducted a formal investigation of council procedures

have been noted.[22] The half-dozen legislators (the more important figures in the field of unemployment compensation) who
were interviewed expressed generally similar views. They welcomed rather than resented the agreed bill procedure. Their
reasons were twofold: It saved them much time and it produced
legislation which was both technically correct and politically
satisfactory. They judged that the common good was adequately
secured because labor and management had naturally adverse
interests in this field and because the agreed bill was subject to
review and final decision by the legislature.

Although all the legislators who were interviewed thought that
the advantages of the agreed bill procedure outweighed the disadvantages, two said they were disturbed by the continuous liberalization which had resulted from it. One said, also, that he and
other legislators disliked what seemed to them the arrogant attitude of the council. The council seemed to think that no one
else adequately understood the complexities of the program, and
grew excited if anyone suggested a change in its agreed bill.[23]

At the public hearing on the 1953 agreed bill an incident occurred which, though small, was a dramatic demonstration of the
fact that final authority is vested in the legislators. The advisory
council members had one by one stepped up before the legislative
committee—the administrator first and then each member—to
state that they were the official representatives of their groups
and that they supported the bill. Then a little, white-haired lady
came up to oppose the massed might of Wisconsin's organized
labor and management and the judgment of unemployment compensation's most experienced administrator. She objected to a
provision of the agreed bill which exempted from the laws of
libel employers who answered the agency's request for information that might lead to the disqualification of a claimant. She
believed that it weakened a fundamental protection of law.
Though the advisory council members insisted that they knew
what they were doing and that there was no danger in this case,

[22] See p. 74.
[23] When the council became aware of this criticism it attempted, with some success,
to allay it. For example, it invited legislators to attend its meetings. Those who attended expressed themselves as pleased with the meetings.

the legislative committee accepted her position and amended the agreed bill—perhaps because they themselves believed her position to be correct, perhaps because they welcomed an opportunity to remind the advisory council where final authority lay.

The Administrative Agency. The administrator and his staff approve of the advisory council without reservation. They admit that the advisory council consumes valuable staff time but consider that it is worth the price. They believe the council has provided aid without meddling. It has been especially useful in: getting provisions enacted that the agency finds necessary for good administration; preventing the passage of amendments unwise either because of their substance or because they would be difficult to administer—the kind of amendments that logrolling easily produces; keeping politics out of the selection of agency personnel; bearing responsibility for controversial decisions and thus freeing the agency for impartial administration; protecting the agency against attacks from labor, management, and political groups; providing technical guidance in the writing of rules and regulations.

Labor and Management. There seems to be general agreement that labor in Wisconsin has gained from the procedure of the agreed bill. The legislative changes listed in Appendix C show a continuous liberalization of the law. Whether the law which has resulted from twenty-five years of amendments stands above or below the medium of all states in point of liberality is difficult to say. Comparison between states is rendered difficult both by the complexity and variety of legal provisions and by the fact that the way in which a provision is administered is often as decisive as the provision itself. In my judgment Wisconsin is at least as liberal as the average state.

But in any case the key question is not whether Wisconsin's law is more liberal or less liberal than that of other states. The key question is whether the law in Wisconsin would be more liberal or less liberal than it is if there had been no agreed bills. None of the persons interviewed—whether they belonged to labor, management, or government—thought that labor had lost by the system; nearly all felt sure that labor had gained significantly by it. True, one employer with a long experience in Wisconsin legislation insisted that no one could be sure that labor would not have got just about as much without the agreed bill as it did with it. He granted, however, that the conservative element in the legislature had been growing in strength steadily and that in 1953 labor certainly could not have got any liberalization without the agreed bill.

With everyone in agreement that labor had profited from the agreed bill procedure, the question naturally arises: Why had management gone along with the procedure? One long-time employer member of the council, who had signed more than ten agreed bills, gave several reasons for his own actions. First, it was the decent thing to do. (This member had an early background of manual labor, which may partly explain the emphasis he put on this reason.) Second, it diminished the danger of federal intervention. (Wisconsin has always been a leader in the opposition to attempts at federalization of the program.) Third, it made for more peaceful labor relations generally. (The leaders on both sides dealt with each other in fields other than unemployment compensation.) Last, it made his work as lobbyist less hectic—he did not have to ride herd day and night over scores of potentially dangerous bills. Employer lobbyists stressed the element of uncertainty attaching to the legislative process. They seemed to look on the agreed bill as "insurance" and to prefer a certain but controlled loss to an uncertain and possibly less acceptable one.

A record of consistently good administration in Wisconsin unemployment compensation has been a real—if minor—reason why employers have been willing to accept successive liberalizations in the program. Both labor and management are interested in good administration in general, but employers have a special interest in two aspects of it. They want a program that permits a minimum of improper payments and yet does not incur high administrative costs. They are under the impression that both objectives, although to some extent incompatible, have been realized fairly well in Wisconsin. The impression has some evidence to support it. Information on improper payments has always been inadequate everywhere; but what evidence is available indicates that Wisconsin's proportion of improper payments is less than the national average.[24] As to administrative costs, there is no doubt that those of Wisconsin have been less than the national average.

The value of the advisory council to labor and management has been discussed here almost entirely in terms of the agreed bill. But while the agreed bill was the chief concern of the council, it was by no means the only one. The labor members were asked whether the council would have a purpose and whether they would continue to serve on it if it ceased to produce agreed bills— either because of irreconcilable differences between labor and management or because both agreed that further substantive changes were undesirable. The member with the longest service on the council said that both possibilities were remote; but that if either did eventuate, the council would still have work to do, although it would not need to meet as often as was its past custom. By "work" he meant chiefly participating in the making of administrative law. He said he would continue to serve on the council because he would want to be in a position to observe and influence the agency as it sat in daily judgment on thousands of individual claimants. The employer members of the council shared this interest, and they, too, declared they would remain on the council. Both labor and management members felt that as council members they had a better window—and, when they needed it, a doorway—into the agency than they would have as private citizens.

Factors of Effectiveness

External Factors. Several characteristics of the Wisconsin unemployment compensation program external to the advisory council itself greatly facilitated the process of arriving at agreed bills. One was that the original Wisconsin unemployment compensation law, enacted three years before the laws of the other states and in the depth of the depression, was unusually limited.[25] There

---

[24] For a survey of the general situation see Joseph M. Becker, *The Problem of Abuse in Unemployment Benefits* (New York: Columbia University Press, 1953).

[25] See p. 70.

was, therefore, unusual room for liberalization in the Wisconsin law. Employers could make concessions year after year and still have a law that was not more liberal than that of other industrial states (although the increase in the maximum benefit to $33 in 1953 made Wisconsin the most liberal of all the states in that respect at that time).

For labor, the continuous liberalization was an obvious help in arriving at agreed bills. It enabled union leaders to return to their constituencies with some new gain each session. If Wisconsin's history had been one of retrenchment instead of liberalization—as has been the case with some states that started with relatively liberal laws—the labor members of the council would have found it very much more difficult, and perhaps impossible, to reach agreed bills. The exigencies of union politics rarely permit union leaders to share the responsibility for taking losses.

A second characteristic which facilitated liberalization was Wisconsin's relatively low rate of unemployment. Both total and covered unemployment rates were lower in Wisconsin than in the nation. This meant lower costs for employers in Wisconsin than for employers in most other states. If the Wisconsin advisory council had been forced to operate in the circumstances of Rhode Island, for example, which since the Second World War has had an unemployment rate double that of Wisconsin, it would have found the task of arriving at agreed bills much more difficult.

A third facilitating characteristic of the Wisconsin program was its strong financial condition, especially after the war. Judged by any of the usual measures, the Wisconsin fund must be considered stronger than that of the median state. The fund's strength was a reflection of the state's low unemployment rate, the chief determinant of cost, but was the result also of adequate tax collections over the years, especially during the war years, when the advisory council foresightedly recommended a special war-risk tax and thus allowed the federal government (through its cost-plus contracts) to build up Wisconsin's fund. The Wisconsin fund could more easily support an increase in benefits in 1953, for example, than could the funds of many other states.

Internal Factors. Other factors which accounted for the effective-

ness of the Wisconsin council were internal to the council itself
and pertained to either its structure or procedures.

The membership of the Wisconsin council was strong.[26] At
least one member of labor and one of management possessed considerable technical competence, and all the others knew the
program fairly well. The membership included the principal lobbyists of labor and management. Most importantly, the members
were fully representative, as John R. Commons understood that
term; that is, they could commit their organizations to agreements
arrived at in the council. This representative quality of its membership explains more of the history of the Wisconsin council
than all its other characteristics combined.

The council's members also possessed that other quality on
which Commons laid so much stress, the quality of "reasonableness." The presence of this quality in the employer members has
already been noted. The quality was present also in the labor
members. It was to be seen to some extent in the Wisconsin CIO,
but was especially marked in the Wisconsin State Federation of
Labor, which was the dominant labor organization in the state.
The WSFL has taken fewer "absolute" positions than have union
leaders in most other states and certainly fewer than its national
leaders. For one thing, the state body has not insisted on the
abolition of experience rating, which has been a fixed goal for
the national, and for most state, labor bodies. For the latter the
issue is not open to discussion, nor is it proper matter for bargaining; experience rating will be abolished as soon as enough legislators can be found to vote against it. The WSFL has not shared
this dogmatic attitude. It saw some important advantages to a
system of experience rating and, so long as the system worked as
it did in Wisconsin, was willing to live with it. Wisconsin employers, encountering agreement in this area, felt their suspicions
and antagonisms allayed and were conditioned to meet labor half-
way in the bargaining sessions.

Neither has Wisconsin labor insisted on the abolition of the
present federal-state unemployment compensation system and its
replacement by a completely federal one, which also is a fixed goal

[26] See Ch. 21, p. 442, for a sketch of the typical Wisconsin council membership.

of the national and of nearly all state labor leaders.[27] On the contrary, Wisconsin labor has joined with Wisconsin employers in actively opposing federalization. In 1943 all three WSFL members of the advisory council (the CIO was not then represented) agreed to an amendment of the law which required Wisconsin to resist federal encroachments on the unemployment compensation program.

Independent action in unemployment compensation has been traditional with the WSFL. During the years when the American Federation of Labor opposed unemployment compensation on principle, the WSFL stubbornly favored it and eventually succeeded in having a program established in the state. When the national body eventually reversed its stand, but favored a single, national system, the WSFL continued to support the plan of independent state programs. Without having changed its original position, the WSFL, formerly to the left of the parent body, found itself to the right.[28]

It is possible that the racial composition of Wisconsin partly explains these characteristics of reasonableness and independence. Wisconsin has a greater than average proportion of Germans, Scandinavians, and Swiss—racial groups which, correctly or incorrectly, have a reputation for quiet orderliness and self-determination. One political analyst at the University of Wisconsin stressed this factor. But I am inclined to regard the race factor as minor, so minor that the influence of a single personality— John R. Commons, for example—would outweigh it.

The bipartite structure of the council was an important factor in the council's effectiveness. It undoubtedly facilitated the process of arriving at agreed bills. It forced the members to concentrate on reaching agreement between themselves in place of fighting each other for the favor and the votes of public members.

[27] In two states union officers (one belonging to the AFL, the other to the CIO) were encountered who said that although officially they were for federalization, privately and off the record they were for retaining the independent state systems. But these were the exceptions.

[28] A professor of labor economics at the University of Wisconsin gave it as his opinion that unions in Wisconsin have always tended to differ from those in other states because in the early days a worker in Wisconsin often was a socialist first and a unionist second.

None of the members of the council wanted to add public members. The relatively small size of the council also fostered a collective bargaining atmosphere. The members studied and discussed problems rather than made speeches about them.

The continuity of the council's membership must be noted in any explanation of its history. It had the lowest turnover rate (4.7 percent) of all the councils in the sample. Continuity facilitated the council's work in two important ways. First, the members came to know each other intimately and developed a tradition of working together. Second, the members developed that degree of competence in the technicalities of the program which enabled them to achieve a significant amount of work in the time available for their meetings. Where there is a rapid turnover among members, much time is spent in explaining and reexplaining elementary notions.

The fact that members are appointed for indefinite terms theoretically protects them from the vagaries of politics, and makes for longer terms. In Wisconsin this provision has probably had little actual influence on the history of the council. A law providing for limited but renewable terms would probably have produced the same results. Members are appointed by the Wisconsin Industrial Commission with the advice of the administrator of the unemployment compensation department. Since the heads of both were unchanged during the entire period covered by this survey, the council would probably have remained untouched under any legal provision regulating terms of office. Furthermore, council members have been appointed on the nomination of their respective groups; so long as that procedure continues as an effective tradition, the legal length of term is relatively unimportant.

The compensation which the Wisconsin council members received did not produce the evil effects anticipated by the theorists. It did not draw to the council people whose main interest was the compensation.[29] A part of the explanation is to be found in the fact that the members were nominated by their organizations.

[29] As happened in other states also, some of the members did not even apply for their expense money; they found the necessary red tape too bothersome.

Since the council wielded real influence, the interested organizations were careful to have effective representatives appointed.[30] The net effect of providing compensation was good. It added a motive for regular attendance at meetings and for doing the kind of preparatory work outside of meetings that makes meetings successful.

Having the administrator of the agency act as chairman of the council worked out satisfactorily in Wisconsin. None of the labor or management members preferred any other arrangement. So much is unique, however, in the Wisconsin situation that it might not be safe to extend the pattern to advisory councils in general. The Wisconsin administrator has long been a national figure in the field of unemployment compensation. He was active in getting the Wisconsin law enacted, and occupied the position of administrator as early as 1934. Typical of John R. Commons's students, he combined the academic and the practical—he was a university professor before he became a government administrator. Again like John R. Commons, he had from the beginning a high esteem for the institution of the advisory council and expended much effort to make it a success. He considered it a greater challenge and triumph of administration to get labor and management to make joint decisions than for himself to make the decisions in their place. Lastly, he was acceptable to both labor and management because he occupied a position between their extremes. His appointment to be administrator was opposed by employer groups twenty years ago because he was a "young radical"; his continuance as administrator has been criticized in recent years by national labor groups because he was too conservative; during the intervening years his position, absolutely speaking, changed very little.

The legal provision authorizing the advisory council to express itself on *all* bills relating to unemployment compensation, while not necessary to advisory council effectiveness, has been useful.

The major procedures of the council have been firmly estab-

[30] There is a circular causality at work here. The kind of person needed to make a council effective is more likely to be appointed if the council is already effective. It is relevant to note that the Wisconsin council was already an influential body before the law was amended to provide compensation.

lished by twenty-five years of experience and have been endowed with a presumption of effectiveness. Among the council's characteristic procedures were the following: irregular meetings, called only when some definite work was to be accomplished, and these meetings fairly long; top staff members present at the meetings; during the preliminary stages of bargaining over the agreed bill, tentative agreements not publicized; a gentlemen's agreement forbidding individual action in support of bills other than the agreed bill and requiring joint action in opposition to other bills; personal appearances of members before legislative committees.

EMPLOYMENT SERVICE

Wisconsin established a state-wide advisory council for the employment service in 1933 to conform with the requirements of the Wagner-Peyser Act. The council was tripartite as the Wagner-Peyser Act required. The size of the council varied, but the number of public members was always larger than the number of either labor or management members. In 1940, for example, the council consisted of five labor, five management, and seven public members; in 1950 it consisted of three labor, three management, and six public members. Members are appointed by the Industrial Commission and serve without compensation.

The council was active and fairly useful during the first few years of its existence, when the program did not yet have its roots down in the state, but accomplished nothing significant thereafter. At a typical council meeting the council listened to reports made by the agency, passed resolutions of approval, and adjourned. According to the man who was director of the employment service during the first twenty years covered by this survey, the accomplishments of the council were not worth the work involved in keeping the council alive. Meetings became progressively fewer after 1936 and almost ceased after 1950.

Wisconsin had local advisory councils long before it had a state council. A public employment office and a local advisory council were established in Superior as early as 1899. These local offices and their advisory councils lost their importance with the growth of the state-wide system under the Wagner-Peyser Act. One local council, however, that of Milwaukee, was still functioning at the time of this survey.

The Milwaukee council, called the "Milwaukee Citizens Committee on Unemployment," has twenty members: five representatives of labor, five of management, and five representatives each of the city and county governments. The committee held its first meeting in 1911 and continued to meet weekly through 1912. Thereafter, until 1950, it met monthly. In the early years the committee functioned like an administrative commission. The minutes show the committee going over all the bills each month and approving expenditures for such items as a telephone "for calling out at $2.50 a month." Gradually, however, the committee found itself with less and less to do, as the national employment service program established itself and became professionalized. Since 1950 the council has met about twice yearly and since at least that time has played no important role in the life of the program.

WORKMEN'S COMPENSATION

Wisconsin's workmen's compensation law, which was the first to go into effect in the United States, dates from 1911. By the early 1920's, if not before, the industrial commissioner had begun the custom of inviting representatives of labor and management and of the insurance industry to attend informal meetings held preceding the legislative session to discuss possible amendments to the law. By the late 1920's the custom had become a formal institution.

The group thus assembled had no standing in law. The industrial commissioner "appointed" its members anew every two years by selecting representatives from nominees supplied by the Wisconsin Manufacturers Association, the Wisconsin State Federation of Labor, and, in later years, by the Wisconsin State Chamber of Commerce and the CIO. He also selected a couple of representatives from the insurance industry. The limited function of the group is indicated by the title under which the nominations are solicited: for the "committee on workmen's compensation legislation." The industrial commissioner or, in his absence, the director of workmen's compensation [31] acts as chairman.

The committee typically begins to meet in the fall preceding a legislative session and holds from six to ten meetings before the session ends. No reliable records exist of the committee's activities, but according to the memories of the participants the committee succeeded in arriving at an agreed bill in every legislative session but one since at least the late 1920's. The only exception they could recall was in 1945, when management refused labor's demands, and labor succeeded in getting the legislature to grant them. The CIO attack on the 1953 agreed bill has already been noted.[32]

This is not the place for a detailed analysis of workmen's compensation; only a few points can be noted that bear on the unemployment compensation program. The Workmen's Compensation Committee achieved its record of agreed bills without the help of one of the circumstances that favored the process in unemployment compensation. The Wisconsin workmen's compensation program did not start behind the other states in point of liberality and catch up. The Wisconsin program has always been at least as liberal as that of the average state and probably more so.[33]

The same leaders of labor and management were on the negotiating committees for both unemployment compensation and workmen's compensation. The relations between labor and management tended to be the same in both committees; moreover, trades were sometimes made of concessions in one program for concessions in the other. In view of this close relationship it is

[31] Workmen's compensation became a distinct department of the Industrial Commission with its own director in 1931.

[32] See p. 75. It was in this session or the preceding one that the CIO proposed an amendment to the workmen's compensation law that would establish a regular advisory council on the model of the one in unemployment compensation. Nothing came of the proposal.

[33] It is very difficult to make accurate comparisons because of the great variety in the provisions of the laws. It is significant, however, that the calculation of a weighted average benefit level shows Wisconsin to be high (first in 1952) in relation to the other states. See H. M. Somers and A. R. Somers, *Workmen's Compensation* (New York: John Wiley & Sons, Inc., 1954), p. 117.

the more significant that the labor and management members did want a formal advisory council in unemployment compensation but saw no need for one in workmen's compensation. The less formal arrangement which had been operative in workmen's compensation for over thirty years was entirely satisfactory to them.

4

THE NEW HAMPSHIRE
ADVISORY COUNCIL

STRUCTURE AND PROCEDURES

THE New Hampshire advisory council began relatively late (1948), but throughout its brief existence it has been unusually effective. In each legislative session through 1957 it managed to achieve agreed bills which were accepted by the legislature. It has been exceptionally influential in the field of administration as well.

The council was established by an amendment to the unemployment compensation law in 1947. The law specifies seven members—three labor, three management, one public—who are appointed by the governor on the recommendation of the director of the agency for three-year terms staggered in such a way that one labor member and one management member come due for reappointment each year.

The scope of the council is limited in the law to unemployment compensation. The limitation reflects the administrative situation when the council was established. At that time the unemployment compensation and the employment service programs were separate divisions. After the two were integrated, in 1950, it was proposed that the council assume responsibility for the employment service too. Since the council as constituted did not fulfill the requirements of the Wagner-Peyser Act, which calls for a woman member, and since the council members were unwilling to change their membership, the commissioner of labor announced that he would appoint a separate council for the employment service, but nothing came of it. In June, 1952, however, after much prodding from the Bureau of Employment Security, the governor did appoint a separate council, which was made up of the existing council and a woman. As of 1957, this special council had not held a meeting.

By law the one public member on the council acts as its chairman. He has refrained from voting, however, because both he and the rest of the council have conceived his function to be that of mediator rather than of arbitrator.

A per diem allowance of $15 was provided for council members by an amendment in 1953. The amount was increased to $20 in 1955.

The council followed no fixed schedule of meetings. Between April, 1948, and April, 1956, it met seventy times, an average of 8.8 meetings per year. Contrary to the experience of most councils, it met with greater frequency as time went on. The first twenty meetings average 6 per year; the next twenty, 8 per year; the last thirty, 11 per year. The meetings occurred at more regular intervals than did those of the Wisconsin council, clustering less around legislative sessions. On only five occasions did more than two months elapse between meetings; the longest interval was only four months. The meetings occupied both the mornings and the afternoons. The lunch custom differed from that of the Wisconsin council in that all the members lunched together, along with several of the agency personnel.

Attendance at meetings was remarkably good. For the period April, 1948, to April, 1956, the council as a whole had an attendance record of 90.2 percent. For the same period the attendance record of employers was 92.4 percent; of employees, 91.4 percent; and of the public, 80.0 percent. In the case of both employers and employees, one individual accounted for most of the few absences. The public member missed so many meetings because he was both owner of and worker in a small business. Emergencies in the shop frequently kept him from attending meetings. He was replaced in 1954, after which the attendance record of the "public" improved.

ORIGIN OF THE ADVISORY COUNCIL

The 1947 amendment establishing the advisory council mentions only its unemployment compensation functions. That fact reflects the origin of the council. It was established primarily as a means of handling unemployment compensation legislation.

Before the advisory council was established, there was no set pattern for the discussion of amendments to the unemployment compensation law prior to their submission to the legislature. If the agency felt the need of support, it usually took its proposals to the Manufacturers Unemployment Compensation Committee and tried to come to an understanding with that group. If labor wanted support it also went to the employers' committee and tried to reach an agreement with them. If employers wanted changes—the less usual situation—they might consult with labor first if they expected opposition from the agency and thought they could strike a bargain with labor; or they might consult with the agency first if they needed the agency's technical advice or if they thought labor would be immovable.

Employers were somewhat better organized than labor and were more influential with the legislature, especially during the earlier years of the program. The Manufacturers Unemployment Compensation Committee had begun in 1939 as an informal gathering of half a dozen employer representatives who found similar problems in the field of industrial relations. After the war the group was organized more formally and focused on unemployment compensation.

Labor had little organization. The state bodies of the AFL and the CIO worked independently of each other, as did also the individual unions within the state bodies. Usually they simply introduced their separate bills and took their chances. An individual labor lobbyist sometimes negotiated with an individual employer lobbyist, but the process was haphazard and depended entirely on personalities.

In the early years of the program these informal discussions between labor and employer lobbyists not infrequently ended with the employer spokesman—the secretary of the manufacturers' association—telling the labor lobbyist: "This is what we are willing to give you this year—if you agree not to fight for more in the legislature. If you fight for more, we will oppose all changes in the law, and you will get nothing. You know that we can lick you in the legislature." In both the New Hampshire State Federation and the state CIO the leadership was divided on the issue of whether or not to enter into such deals. In earlier years the leaders usually refused. But in both unions there were competing factions which favored "dealing." When these factions came to power, informal agreements became more frequent.

It was in the fall of 1946 that the first formal joint meeting between labor and management was held to discuss amendments to the unemployment compensation law. The proposal for the meeting seems to have come from the agency and from the state Federation; the CIO was induced to participate by the state Federation. To induce employers to participate required strong leadership; but even strong leadership might not have sufficed had it not been for two favoring conditions.

In the first place, both labor and management were dissatisfied with the then director of the agency, who was new to the program and understood little about it. Secondly, it seemed inevitable that the 1947 legislature would enact some unemployment compensation legislation favorable to labor. Employers were in the midst of a successful campaign to enact the Willey Bill, the New Hampshire "right to work" bill. Labor indignation was at white heat. Some labor lobbyists refused to speak to the legislators who were responsible for the bill and urged the president of the state Federation to organize a mass protest meeting in one of the ball parks. He refused, arguing that a mass demonstration would only harm labor's cause. Even while he continued to fight the bill, he dealt civilly with the legislators involved. They in turn expressed appreciation of his "civilized attitude" and promised to reciprocate when the matter of amendments to unemployment compensation and workmen's compensation came before them.[1] This attitude of the legislature may have helped persuade employers to meet with labor to discuss unemployment compensation legislation.

---

[1] In the following legislative session, that of 1949, the Willey Act was repealed, with only two dissenting votes in the entire House.

Most of the employers were suspicious of the innovation, and despite the favoring conditions it required strong leadership and some "knocking of heads together" to bring employers to agree to give collective bargaining a trial. At the joint meeting, one employer practically withdrew from the employer ranks and constituted himself an impartial chairman in order to get the two sides started on the discussions.

The joint meeting was successful; out of it came an agreed bill, which was enacted into law by the 1947 legislature. Both labor and management participants evidently were encouraged by their experience, because they provided for its continuance. They included among the amendments of 1947 a provision establishing an advisory council.

Who took the initiative in proposing that a council be established is uncertain. Recent though the event is, the memories of those who were present at the 1946 joint meeting are not clear on this point. Certainly the agency and labor, especially the state Federation, were in the forefront. The agency had for years been under pressure from the Bureau of Employment Security to establish an advisory council. The agency had heard from other administrators how useful a council could be; it had just witnessed in the successful conclusion of the 1946 joint meeting a concrete illustration of how an advisory council might operate. Labor, accustomed to standing outside looking in, was glad to have an official doorway into the decision-making area and naturally favored the idea of an advisory council.

Management may have agreed to a council partly because of outside pressure. But that alone would not have produced the willing and effective acceptance of the council which has characterized New Hampshire employers. Other factors were more important. One was the increased power of organized labor. Both the state Federation and the CIO grew considerably in membership during the 1940's. This growth was especially marked in the CIO (shoes and textiles), which came to equal the Federation in size and perhaps to surpass it in influence.

Although management could usually count on the Senate, the influence of labor in the House was usually sufficient to block management bills in the area of labor legislation. (The chairman of the House labor committee was an official of a CIO union.) A legislative deadlock, therefore, was always a possibility. The existence of such a balance of power favored the operation of an advisory council. Both sides felt that bargaining was necessary, and they preferred to do it around a conference table rather than in the legislature.

Personalities were a considerable factor. There were leaders among the employers who believed in collective bargaining, practiced it in their own plants, and favored its extension to labor legislation through an advisory council. Sherman Adams, later to be chief assistant to President Eisenhower, was highly influential in this direction. He had for years been a member of the Manufacturers Unemployment Compensation Committee. Later, as chairman of the House labor committee, as speaker of the House, and as governor, he consistently urged labor and management to solve their own problems by "getting together." [2]

Parallel developments in workmen's compensation during 1946–1947 probably facilitated the establishment of the advisory council. Over the years, the commissioner of labor had made a number of vain attempts to have some kind of amendment enacted in the workmen's compensation law. Finally in 1945, he got the legislature to authorize a study commission; in 1946 the commission traveled about the state and conducted hearings. In 1947 the commissioner arranged for the legislative representative of labor and three nominees of the manufacturers' association to sit down with him and for the first time work out jointly an agreed bill.[3] Some of those labor and management representatives were the same persons who in 1946 agreed to the establishment of an advisory council in unemployment compensation.

When the advisory council was established by law, the governor accepted the recommendations of the commissioner of labor as to persons to be appointed. The commissioner selected the labor members himself and requested nominees from the manufac-

---

[2] The man who became director of the agency shortly after the advisory council began to function was a former secretary of Sherman Adams and shared his general attitude toward collective bargaining. This helped the council get off to a favorable start.

[3] Joint action leading to an agreed bill has continued to be the pattern in workmen's compensation since 1947.

turers' association.[4] One of the labor members was the president
of the state Federation. The CIO representative was later (1953)
to become president of the CIO; at the time of his appointment,
however, he was a rival of the then CIO president, and for a time
this situation caused friction. The third labor member was from
an independent union. On management's side, one of the representatives was a subordinate of the man who had been chiefly
responsible for the joint meetings of 1946. Another, from one of
the largest firms in New Hampshire, was probably the best unemployment compensation technician among New Hampshire
employers. The third was a personnel director with a long record
of successful labor relations. All three were members of the Manufacturers Unemployment Compensation Committee, and one had
been chairman of it for a number of years. None of the labor
or management representatives was a lobbyist, although one of
the labor representatives had some experience in that capacity.

All but one of the original members were reappointed to second
terms. The unemployment compensation administrator made the
recommendations for reappointment without previously clearing
with labor or management organizations. From the viewpoint of
the agency, most of the original appointees were functioning satisfactorily and the natural course was to keep the same members
on the council. The one exception to this procedure concerned
the CIO representative. To diminish the friction that was set up
because the original appointment was not cleared, the governor
explicitly asked the then president of the state CIO council
whether the reappointment would be acceptable.

ACTIVITIES OF THE COUNCIL

The council exercised practically no influence on the employment service side of the employment security program. In New
Hampshire the employment service antedated unemployment
compensation and operated as a separate agency until 1950. It
had an advisory council of its own before 1940, in the days of the
National Reemployment Service. This council met a few times

---

[4] The reverse of the procedure followed in most states.

and was very useful in the period of emergency. It helped the struggling employment offices obtain quarters, funds, and community acceptance. As the emergency became less pressing, the council became less active. After 1941 it ceased to function entirely.

When in 1950 the employment service was integrated with unemployment compensation under a single director, the existing advisory council assumed nominal responsibilities for the employment service. In practice, however, it concerned itself only with those aspects of the employment service which touched immediately on unemployment compensation, chiefly the conditions under which job offers were made to claimants.

In the field of unemployment compensation, however, the advisory council has operated with signal effectiveness. It has influenced both legislation and administration in the program.

LEGISLATION

In the field of legislation, it achieved agreed bills in five consecutive legislative sessions, and on each occasion the legislature accepted the agreed bill and enacted it into law. The position of the council might be described as one of primacy without complete dominance. Its agreed bills have been accepted, but not always without challenge and not always without modification. In the 1949 session, for example, a legislator who was also a CIO union leader introduced bills that competed with the council's agreed bill. But he acknowledged the influence of the council by appearing at one of its meetings to explain and urge his bills, and in the end it was the advisory council's agreed bill which was enacted. In 1950 the legislature held a special session. When the advisory council asked that no unemployment compensation legislation be handled in this special session but be held over until the regular session in 1951 in order to give the council time to prepare its recommendations, the legislature honored the request.

The council has generally examined the bills sponsored by other groups and has informed the legislature of its judgment on them. In the spring of 1951 the speaker of the House formally requested the opinion of the advisory council on an "outside" bill that had been introduced. During the same session the unemployment compensation agency asked the advisory council to recommend that a "seeking work" requirement be added to the law. When the council could not agree on it, the matter was dropped, and the agency did not proceed on its own authority.

The events of the 1953 legislative session are particularly revealing with regard to both the extent and the limitations of the council's influence. The council began to discuss legislation in its April, 1952, meeting; throughout its fall meetings it formulated, item by item, a list of agreements. Finally in January, 1953, it reached agreement on the two most controversial matters—the scale of benefits and a definition of suitable work—and it wrote finis to the legislative program it would recommend for 1953. This program dominated the 1953 session, but not without being challenged by all three groups concerned—the agency, employers, and employees.

The first challenge came from the agency, which had made a "solvency study" in 1952 and had concluded that an increase in the tax rate was advisable. The employer members on the advisory council refused to accept the conclusion. The labor members favored the agency's recommendation but were unwilling to oppose the employer members. Probably this was part of the price labor had to pay for employer support of the agreed bill. The agency was faced with the decision to drop the matter or proceed independently. It chose the latter and had a bill introduced, but it could not get the legislature to pass it.

The second challenge to council primacy came from the employer side, from one of the largest firms in the state. This firm wanted an amendment to the law which would provide that the unemployment benefits paid to workers retired on pension would be charged not against the firm whose employees were receiving both payments but against the general fund.[5] The firm had previously taken its case to the Manufacturers Unemployment Compensation Committee. After a bitter fight there, it had lost,

[5] This firm had recently been put in the position of having to pay unemployment benefits and pensions to its retired workers.

for the committee had decided to follow the leadership of the employer representatives on the advisory council, who were also members of the Manufacturers Unemployment Compensation Committee and on the council had voted against the proposed amendment. The firm, nevertheless, had a bill introduced in the legislature and was able to generate considerable pressure for the bill. The fight in the legislature was intense, and the agency and the employer members of the council had to carry on the fight against the bill without the aid of the labor members. The labor members did not participate in this fight, partly because they themselves did not particularly dislike the bill but chiefly because by this time there had developed certain complications, described below, which had embittered them. The opposition of the employer members and of the agency was sufficient, however, and the firm's bill was defeated.

The third challenge to council primacy came from labor's side. A bill was introduced to pay benefits to former strikers who were still unemployed after the strike was ended. It was introduced at the request of a CIO local union at a plant where, it was charged, the leaders of a strike in 1953 had been discriminated against in a recall to work. The bill was not, therefore, an official labor bill in the sense that it had been initiated by the state labor bodies. Once introduced, however, it was given official labor support, including that of the labor members on the council. The CIO member of the advisory council made a point of telling the legislature that he had refrained from independent action for a period of five years but that on this issue he felt compelled to give his support despite the opposition of the employer members on the council. Ultimately both House and Senate passed a compromise version of the bill—against not too vigorous opposition.

Some employers considered that labor had violated the spirit of the agreed bill by fighting for this "outside" bill on which the advisory council had been unable to agree. But others thought that labor's action was excused by the merits of the bill, the intense feeling that had been generated among the rank-and-file unionists, and the fact that the bill had not come into the picture until after the advisory council had completed its own agreed bill.

The events of the second and the third challenges offer an opportunity to observe the degree to which the employer members of the council were and were not independent of their constituency, that is, the degree to which they led and the degree to which they followed their fellow employers. In the case of the bill providing nonchargeable benefits for pensioners, one of the employer members of the council told the Manufacturers Unemployment Compensation Committee that he would vote against it in the council no matter how the committee voted.[6] In this position he was opposing his superior in the firm by which he was employed. Under pressure this superior supported the bill before the legislative committee, which joked about the divided representation of the firm. In the case of the bill providing for benefits to former strikers, one employer member who favored it from the start voted against it in the council when he was unable to persuade the majority of the Manufacturers Unemployment Compensation Committee to support it.

Both actions are probably typical of council members. On occasion they find it necessary and possible to act independently of their constituency; more often, however, to be effective they must represent, that is, agree with, the majority of their constituency. Generally speaking, the employer members of the council could not act with as much independence as could the labor members.

The events of the 1955 legislative session seemed to indicate that the primacy of the council was growing to a point where it resembled Wisconsin's. The council had held a score of meetings and agreed on numerous amendments, of which at least fourteen were substantial and half of these controversial. In the course of their negotiations, the council members had considered and rejected the proposal of a local transit union in Manchester. This union had taken over a transit company and wanted to begin operations with a more favorable tax rate than the provisions of the law allowed. It wished, therefore, to amend the law regulating the transfer of experience rates. When the council rejected the proposal, the company, backed by the union, itself had a bill

[6] He believed that the provision violated fundamental principles of a sound unemployment compensation program.

introduced in the legislature. At the legislative hearings the lobbyists of labor and management (none of them council members) appeared in opposition to the bill. The labor lobbyists did so reluctantly (the representative of the state Federation was in the position of opposing one of his own unions) but they recognized and stated publicly that this opposition was part of the price to be paid for an agreed bill.

Various other amendments to the law were proposed by non-council persons, but they were met uniformly by the reiterated argument that "this would violate the agreed bill." The administrator of the agency feared for a time that the legislators would grow annoyed at the repetition of this argument. But his fears were unfounded; both the legislators and the governor welcomed the agreed bill. The governor not only did not resent the agreed bill but praised it publicly, stating that he wished the other agencies of his government could manage their affairs as peacefully and efficiently as had the employment security agency during that session—a statement that may be accounted for partly by the fact that the New Hampshire legislative session of 1955 was unusually turbulent.

By contrast, the 1957 legislative session was relatively quiet and uneventful. The council's agreed bills extended coverage to state employees, made some minor modifications in the disqualification provisions, made the employment security agency a separate department of the state government, and authorized the construction of a new building for the agency. No other legislation was enacted besides the council's agreed bills.

ADMINISTRATION

The advisory council participated not only in the work of legislation but in that of administration—not only negotiating the contract but helping administer it. The council regularly considered proposed changes in rules and regulations before they were promulgated. In 1952 the council held a number of meetings for the specific purpose of arriving at an acceptable definition of "suitable work." A large textile plant had closed permanently, and the agency was referring the dismissed workers to similar but lower-paying jobs in a new plastics factory. A CIO union in the state had become so incensed on this issue that it was agitating for the administrator's removal. Eventually the council agreed on a "suitable work" definition which restored peace.

In 1953 employers on their side were much disturbed and displeased by a change in the agency's disqualification policy whereby benefits formerly denied to women in certain marital situations were allowed by the new policy. The employers resented especially the abruptness with which the change had been made—and without their consultation. The administrator explained that ordinarily he would discuss such a change with the interested parties but that on this matter discussion was pointless. The attorneys of the agency had discovered that the previous policy was in error and that according to the law these cases had to be paid.[7]

The council concerned itself not only with questions of administrative law, as in the above illustrations, but also with administration in the narrower sense. In 1953, for example, the council devoted several meetings to discussions of the crisis forced upon the agency by the cut in its budget. The agency explained that it would either have to resort to biweekly reporting or restrict employment service operations if it maintained weekly reporting. The council reluctantly decided in favor of the second alternative. The agency was inclined to economize further by discontinuing a service by which some companies received weekly instead of monthly reports of benefit charges against their accounts. When the employer members of the council protested the projected discontinuance of the weekly service and the labor members did not insist on it, the agency agreed to retain the service for the time being.[8] The council also determined to bring the agency's finan-

[7] The administrator's judgment was not upheld when the new policy was tested in the state supreme court. The court reversed the agency.

[8] To discontinue the service would save the agency only $200 yearly, and one employer said that the service saved his own firm several thousand dollars a year in improper benefit charges.

cial problems to the attention of the New Hampshire representatives in the United States Congress.

Questions of administration in the narrower sense were usually classified in the council's agenda as being "noncontroversial"—by contrast with more controversial matters like benefits and disqualifications. The contrast was reflected in the important distinction between issues that are bargaining points and those that are to be "settled on their merits." I heard the distinction for the first time when I attended a meeting of the New Hampshire council (I encountered it several times after that in other councils). The agency had presented six technical "noncontroversial" amendments for which it asked council approval. The council approved of five. The employer members asked for more time to consider the implications of the sixth, but they warned the labor members that this amendment was not to be considered a "bargaining point," and the labor members laughingly granted that it should be settled "on its merits." The line dividing these two types of issues probably shifts from time to time; the distinction in each case is always somewhat vague.

APPRAISAL
EXTENT OF EFFECTIVENESS

The director of the employment service division did not feel that her division had suffered because of the council's concentration on unemployment compensation. A director of much experience (she has been with the employment service since 1931), she had concluded that in the employment service there was not enough work to keep a permanent advisory council occupied. When there was a specific need for an advisory council—for example, to discuss the problems of the young, of the handicapped, of displaced persons—she found it more efficient to meet the need by assembling a temporary specialized committee.

The only one of the council members who expressed the wish that the council concern itself more with employment service problems was the representative of the CIO, but he had no clear ideas as to what the council ought to do. The most active em-

ployer representative was insistent that the council restrict itself
to unemployment compensation.[9] The other members were neutral.

In unemployment compensation the council's unbroken history
of agreed bills since 1947 was regarded with general satisfaction.
Everyone concerned—labor, management, the agency, the governor, the legislature—was convinced that the agreed bill produced better results than any alternative.

The labor and management members voiced a sense of achievement that was apart from the immediate specific achievements in
unemployment compensation. They felt that they had helped
establish a sound policy of government by participating actively
in a government program which affected them so directly. The
citizens of New Hampshire were particularly sensitive to this
value. New Hampshire is a state which has many small towns and
no large cities, has the largest English-speaking legislature in the
world—although the entire state numbers only about half a million persons—and makes extensive use of the town-hall meeting
for the exercise of local government. Typical of this spirit in
New Hampshire is its use of tripartite panels (agency, labor, management) at the first-appeal stage rather than the almost universally used single referee, who is an employee of the agency.[10]

Everyone connected with the agreed bill was of the opinion
that the law which had resulted was somewhat more liberal than
it would otherwise have been. Labor, management, the agency,
legislators—all expressed the opinion that labor had gained by
the process. These opinions find some support in the fact that
New Hampshire has a program more liberal than that of the
average state (for example, uniform duration of benefits for twenty-
six weeks)—even though it has more unemployment than the
average.[11]

[9] An attitude traceable in part to his personal interest in unemployment compensation and to the fact that his own firm did not particularly need the employment
service.

[10] A useful by-product of these tripartite appeal panels is a growing body of experienced labor and management people constituting a source from which advisory council members can be drawn.

[11] From 1947, when the council was established, through 1955, duration and maximum amount of benefits increased progressively; duration of benefits was increased

The chairman of the House labor committee, a CIO union official and not a member of the council, remarked that, where previously it had been very difficult to get any unemployment compensation amendments through the legislature, now, with the backing of the advisory council, it was no trouble at all, and he had more time to give to other labor legislation. He was firmly convinced of the superior wisdom of small gains achieved steadily with the support of employers, over the alternative strategy of "shooting for the moon" against solid opposition. He said that on this score he had never encountered any opposition from the national CIO. The CIO representative on the advisory council shared his judgment on the value of the gradualist approach but remarked that he had had to defend it against criticism from the national office.

The members declared that the advisory council was worth while even apart from the merits of the agreed bill. They mentioned chiefly the opportunity it offered them to keep abreast of the program and to keep watch over the agency's decisions on individual cases. One employer member remarked also that he valued the regular contacts it gave him with labor leaders in the state, contacts useful in his other work.

There was general agreement that the best instrument for achieving an agreed bill was the advisory council. The administrator did not think that informal relations with labor and management leaders could adequately take the place of the advisory council. Council membership gave representatives of labor and management more influence and made their activities more effective. Moreover, the advisory council produced better educated leaders of labor and management. The administrator was so impressed with this educational value of the council that he was tempted to rotate the council membership.[12]

The value of the advisory council as an educative force was

---

from 20 weeks to 23 weeks in 1947 and to 26 weeks in 1951; maximum amount of benefits was increased from $20 (1945) to $22 (1947) to $25 (1949) to $28 (1951) to $30 (1953) to $32 (1955).

[12] Actually, he did not yield to the temptation. If he had, he probably would have found that the loss in council effectiveness would have far outweighed the general gain in education.

especially great in a small state like New Hampshire. The state labor bodies were not large enough to have full-time state officials (president, secretary), let alone specialists in unemployment compensation. Similarly, there were few, if any, firms in the state large enough to have full-time unemployment compensation specialists. Alike for labor and management members, the regular, compensated, full-day meetings of the advisory council constituted an important instrument of education.

FACTORS OF EFFECTIVENESS

What were the principal factors which explained the success of the New Hampshire council? A few were mentioned earlier, in the description of the origin of the council. Concerning the remainder, some were external to the council, and some were within the council itself.

Management and labor in the state were well enough organized to be represented effectively, and the organizations left their representatives sufficiently free to negotiate on the council.

In New Hampshire, as in Utah, a little organization went a long way because the state was small and the people were in easy, frequent communication with one another. The manufacturers' association was the principal employers' association, and its unemployment compensation committee was the effective focus of employer opinion. In 1950, when the committee was enlarged from a dozen members to thirty, an attempt was made to get representatives from other than the manufacturing industries. Of those others who were invited, only one, a representative from the retail trades, responded actively.

All the employer members on the advisory council belonged to this committee and were its most active members. Through this committee they kept in touch with the secretary of the manufacturers' association, the chief employer lobbyist. None of the employer members of the council was a lobbyist—a potential weakness in the council. If the secretary of the manufacturers' association (new in 1952) should become very strong and should differ from the council members, the agreed bill would be endangered. The council would be strengthened if its membership were expanded to include a full-time professional representative of employers.

The number of employers in the state who were acquainted with the processes of labor legislation was small; the number who actively concerned themselves with it was smaller still. Attendance at meetings of the Manufacturers Unemployment Compensation Committee was poor. Two of the more active members of that committee had no idea of what was happening in the parallel program of workmen's compensation. They left that area to other people, just as the others left unemployment compensation matters to them. On the advisory council one of the employer members was unaware—until I told him—that he was a charter member. He thought that the council had been in existence long before his membership on it and that other employers had carried the burdens then. The demands of his own business leaves the average employer little time to follow the processes of government, even those that affect his business.

Something of the same sort was true of the labor organizations, and even of the legislature. Only a few labor leaders were aware of what was happening in the program of unemployment compensation or, if aware, concerned themselves with it. The officers of the international unions were busied primarily with the contracts of their own unions and tended to leave general, statewide matters like unemployment compensation to the officers of the state body. In the legislature, too, only a few members—no more than can be counted on one hand—were acquainted with unemployment compensation matters.

The lesson for council membership is clear. Since in the modern complex economy specialization is inevitable, to be effective the council must include the specialists outside government who work or can work with the specialists inside government.

The balance of power between labor and management in the legislature favored the agreed bill. It served as a powerful inducement for both sides to resolve their differences by collective bargaining techniques. Another favorable factor was the history of good labor relations in the state. In the period 1935–1950, New

Hampshire had the lowest strike rate in New England, and the New England rate was only one-third as high as the national rate. Evidently New Hampshire had its share of "reasonableness," one aspect of which was especially important for unemployment compensation—the attitude of labor toward experience rating. As in Wisconsin, the labor representatives on the advisory council were willing to live with experience rating.

One feature of the New Hampshire economy was definitely unfavorable to the agreed bill—the higher-than-average rate of unemployment. Over the period in which the council was reaching its agreed bills, unemployment in New Hampshire averaged 5.8 percent of the labor force, as compared with the national rate of 4.1 percent. As a result, costs of unemployment benefits in New Hampshire over that same period averaged 2.3 percent of taxable wages, as against the national average of 1.4 percent.

The unemployment compensation tax rate in New Hampshire averaged 1.73 percent of taxable payrolls over the same period, as compared with the national average of 1.55 percent. That difference is not great, but it had been kept down only by drawing on the New Hampshire reserve fund, which at the end of 1957 stood at 6.5 percent of taxable wages, as compared with the national average of 7.6 percent. That the advisory council of New Hampshire was able to reach agreed bills despite this obstacle of higher-than-average cost makes it an example more imitable than that of Wisconsin, which did not have to work under this limitation.

The advisory council's unique structure [13] in New Hampshire seems to have been a significant factor in the council's effectiveness. Comprising only seven members, it was compact enough to be a working group. Yet it was large enough to be representative of the major forces in the state. The administrator thought the only lack in that respect was the absence of employer representation from the service and trade industries.

[13] The Delaware law specifies the same structure for its advisory council, but the council does not exist outside the pages of the law. Bills specifying this structure were introduced in Massachusetts (1954) and in New York (1955) but were defeated. California's law was amended in 1955 to specify this structure, and in 1956 such a council was appointed.

No one on the council wanted more public members. Public members were not needed for voting, since matters were not decided on the council by a majority vote, and one public member was sufficient to act as chairman and mediator. Moreover, all the members on the council were well versed in the technical aspects of the program, a situation which would have been difficult to maintain if several public members had to be appointed.

If no one wanted more public members, neither did anyone want to lose the one which the council had. Labor, management, and the agency were agreed that the public chairman was an important factor in the council's success. The effectiveness of the first chairman (1947–1954) was enhanced by both his technical competence (he was a former administrator of the program) and his personality. He thought clearly, spoke fluently, and combined an engaging manner with directness and vigor. His principal limitation was his inability to attend meetings, and it was for this reason that he finally resigned. His successor, a former attorney in the agency, was selected by the labor and management members of the council. His performance in the 1955 and 1957 legislative sessions augured well for the future.

There is nothing in the law describing the chairman's function. He himself had adopted the policy of not voting and acting only as a mediator. At the meetings he listened more often than he spoke. When he spoke, it was usually to sum up, to return the discussion to the point at issue, to remind both parties of the basic principles of unemployment compensation,[14] and to suggest acceptable compromise. He did not prepare the agenda for the meetings; as in nearly all the other states, this was done by the agency, with more or less consultation with the members.

The personalities of the advisory council members contributed greatly to the success of the council. Both sides, labor and management, were predisposed to make collective bargaining work. Despite some very sharp passages between one labor member and one management member, which threatened for a time to de-

---

[14] Such as: "Remember, gentlemen, this is essentially an insurance program," when labor wanted to stretch it to cover too much; or, "Remember, gentlemen, the purpose of this program is to alleviate human misery," when management was straining at legal gnats.

stroy the council's effectiveness, the sessions of the council have been reasonably peaceable.

Compensation for attendance at council meetings was particularly appropriate for a state as small as New Hampshire, where organizations did not have full-time professional representatives. For both the labor members and the public member the compensation was a desirable protection against the financial loss caused by absence from their regular jobs.

The policy of calling the members together only when there was specific work to be done was a wise one. Closely connected with this policy was that of meeting for a full day, morning and afternoon. Both policies helped to establish a tradition of worth-while meetings and resulted in good attendance.

Top agency staff attended the meetings and prepared the minutes. One of the management members expressed the wish to hold council meetings away from the agency quarters and apart from agency personnel and apart even from the administrator; no one else, however, shared his preference.[15] The chairman believed that since the function of the council was to advise the administrator,[16] the administrator should be present at the council meetings the better to understand the mind of the council.

The council usually began work on its recommendations early in order to have them ready by the opening of the legislative session. Thus the council began to prepare for its first session (1949) in June of 1948 and by October had reached agreement on most of its program. It began to prepare for the 1955 session in November of 1953 and by June of 1954 had much of its legislative program—all of the less controversial amendments—completed.

The council usually held a meeting on the day when its main bill was scheduled for hearing, and it adjourned in time for its members to appear before the legislative committee in support of the bill. Top agency staff made the opening, detailed presentation and were followed by the individual council members, who

---

[15] This member knew unemployment compensation well enough and could give enough time to council business to be relatively independent of the agency. But he was exceptional in both respects.

[16] This was another "basic principle" of which he frequently reminded the council members: "Gentlemen, remember, we are not a commission; we are only an advisory council."

recorded their endorsement. These appearances before the legislative committee were regarded by all as an important part of the council's procedure.

Since none of the advisory council members was a lobbyist, the necessary buttonholing of individual legislators was done by the respective legislative representatives of the labor and management organizations. The council would be strengthened if its membership were expanded to include a labor and a management lobbyist.

5

THE UTAH ADVISORY COUNCIL

THE Utah advisory council is a long-lived council which went from strength to weakness and back to strength again. It was really two councils: the old, which operated in the period 1936–1949, and the new, which began in 1949 and was still operating in 1957. Neither the old nor the new council maintained the original structure throughout its life; the old council expanded its membership three times (1938, 1941, 1943), and the new council once (1955). The two councils differed markedly in procedures and relative success.

The original law provided for a tripartite advisory council to be appointed by the industrial commissioner [1] and for a per diem compensation of $10. It did not specify the size of the council or the term of the members.

A council was appointed in 1936, about a year after the enactment of the law (March, 1935).[2] This first council was small, consisting of one public member, two representatives of labor, and two of management. The Utah council was originally structured, therefore, like that of New Hampshire. Although none of the five had been active in drawing up the law, the labor and management members were fully "representative" in the sense that they were the nominees of their respective organizations.[3] One em-

[1] In Utah the employment security program has always been a department of the Industrial Commission, and the state is small enough for the commissioner to be a significant force in the program.

[2] Utah was the first state after Wisconsin to enact an unemployment compensation law. When this law was found to have technical defects, it was repealed and replaced on August 29, 1936, by the present legislation.

[3] A fact to which the administrator of the agency appealed in 1943 when the "representative" character of the council was challenged.

ployer member came from the sugar industry and represented the
Utah Manufacturers Association; the other represented the mine
operators. Both came from high-cost industries, a fact which had
much to do later with the conflict between the advisory council
and other employers in the state. One labor member was the
secretary of the Salt Lake Building Trades Council and represented the Utah State Federation of Labor; the other labor member represented the CIO, which at that time claimed the United
Mine Workers as its largest affiliate. The Utah council was different, therefore, from many others in that the CIO was represented from the very beginning of the council's operations.

From 1938 to 1943, this original council was enlarged three
successive times. In March, 1938, it was enlarged by the addition
of one labor member and one management member. The federal
Bureau of Employment Security had been urging Utah to make
its council more representative by making it larger. When one
of the employer members had to take an extended leave of absence, the agency used the occasion to add another employer member. To balance the employer-labor representation, a labor member from the Railroad Brotherhoods was appointed (presumably
to avoid favoring either the Utah State Federation of Labor or
the CIO) even though the Railroad Brotherhoods have their own
system of unemployment benefits and are not directly concerned
with the state unemployment compensation system.

The Bureau of Employment Security continued to remind Utah
that its council was not in conformity with the Wagner-Peyser
Act if it did not have a woman member. In May, 1941, Utah added
another public member to the council, a woman, who brought the
total to eight members. Two years later, in May, 1943, the old
council was enlarged for the last time. The addition of an employer representative from the distributive trades was the answer
to a complaint from those trades that they had no voice on the
council. Again a balancing labor representative was added, this
time from the United Mine Workers, who had left the CIO and
become an independent union. For some unstated reason another
public member was also added—perhaps to make the number of
council members odd. From that time until its dissolution in 1949,

the council consisted of eleven members: four labor, four management, and three public.

The new council, which began in 1949, retained this structure until 1955, when, as in 1943, in response to a complaint from the distributive trades that they were not represented, the council was expanded to include the two more employer representatives and —by way of balance—two more employee representatives. The council then totaled 15 members: six representatives of employers, six of employees, and three of the public.

The law affecting the advisory council was amended in 1949 to raise the compensation of members to $15 and to limit the term of membership to two years. It also added the very important and unusual provision that appointments to the council be made from a list of nominees to be submitted by the employer and employee organizations.[4]

From its establishment in November, 1936, through November, 1957, the Utah council held a total of 130 meetings. The following table shows the number of meetings held each year.

1936	3	1941	7	1946	9	1949	7	1954	2
1937	3	1942	7	1947	4	1950	9	1955	5
1938	13	1943	8	1948	7	1951	7	1956	4
1939	2	1944	8			1952	5	1957	5
1940	5	1945	6			1953	4		

The old council averaged 6.3 meetings per year; the new council, about 5.3 meetings per year. The lower ratio for the new council reflects the fact that since 1949 the agreed bills have been negotiated outside the council meeting proper. Under the old council the meetings tended to cluster around legislative sessions; under the new council this tendency has almost disappeared—again probably a reflection of the change in the new council's relationship to legislation.

The attendance records of the old and the new councils were about the same. For the entire period, 1936–1957, the attendance record of the council as a whole was 81 percent. The record of the

[4] "The Commission shall appoint a state advisory council composed of not less than four employer representatives chosen from individuals recommended by employers, an equal number of employee representatives chosen from individuals recommended by employee groups. . . ." Utah Employment Security Act, as amended, 1951, p. 27.

public members was 84 percent; of labor, 82 percent; and of management, 77 percent. These records, while not as good as those of Wisconsin and New Hampshire, were above average.

ACTIVITIES OF THE COUNCIL

The Utah unemployment compensation law, enacted in March, 1935, was the fruit of an agreed bill. Gus Backman for the employers and William Knerr for labor selected a joint group to work out a mutually satisfactory bill. Since 1930, Backman has been executive secretary of the Salt Lake City Chamber of Commerce —in Utah a principal channel through which employer opinion flows. He has always been one of the more influential forces on the employer side, and he has also been styled "one of the best-known and best-liked men in Utah." [5] John R. Commons would certainly have categorized him as a "reasonable man." William Knerr, one of the three industrial commissioners and a labor leader of the conservative school, was also a "reasonable man." The leadership of both men tended naturally toward the goal of an agreed bill and helped establish Utah's tradition of labor relations as "thought out, not fought out." When the joint group had agreed on an unemployment compensation bill, Backman appeared before the Senate and asked that the bill be passed without amendments. Knerr did the same in the House of Representatives. Both houses passed the bill in the form agreed upon by the two parties.

The council began to function in the year following the law. During 1936, its meetings were taken up with the formulation of the rules and regulations needed to implement the new law. Early in 1937, the council agreed upon some amendments—technical and minor—and these were enacted into law.

At the meeting of March 30, 1938, the chairman of the Industrial Commission informed the council that its functions included the following: "The Council shall act independently, and if it finds that the Unemployment Compensation division or the Employment Service is administered in such a fashion that it needs correction or changing the council should so inform the Industrial

[5] See the feature article on Backman in *Business Week*, March 7, 1953, p. 78.

Commission." [6] The Utah council never had occasion to exercise this function and hence never traveled, as did the New York council, this exciting but rough path.

The meetings of 1938, held to prepare for the 1939 legislative session, revealed both the early influence of the council and the seeds of its eventual decay. When the council began to discuss possible amendments in the spring of 1938, the question at once arose as to how the work of the council would be related to organizations, especially employer organizations, outside the council. At the meeting of May 25, 1938, the motion was adopted:

. . . that the advisory council act as a master committee in the amending of the Utah unemployment compensation law; that this committee through its representatives urge interested groups to offer suggestions or to propose amendments; that the individual members work with their particular groups, or kindred groups in outlining amendments; that the advisory council take the suggestions of the various groups which should be presented in writing, and collate them into logical and satisfactory amendments; that the completed proposed amendments be transmitted to the industrial commission for their presentation to the legislature; and that the advisory council take whatever steps are necessary to aid in the passage of agreed amendments through the legislature.

The advisory council worked hard to make this ideal a reality. It held thirteen meetings in 1938 and eventually reached an agreed bill which incorporated substantially the agency's program.

But the agency evidently did not consider the advisory council's support sufficient to guarantee passage of the amendments. At the council meetings the administrator repeatedly questioned the members as to whether they were maintaining contact with their organizations and could "deliver" those organizations. He even secured the council's reluctant permission to work directly with labor and management representatives outside the council, especially with the professional representatives of the employers' organizations.

In the end the agency won sufficient support for the council's agreed bill to have the legislature enact it into law. All the

[6] Unless otherwise indicated, quotations in this chapter are from the minutes of the advisory council.

controversial provisions of the bill were of a liberalizing character. The maximum benefit was increased to $16 (from $15), coverage was extended to employers of one or more (from four or more), and the system of experience rating was changed from a charge-back system to a benefit-ratio system. Since labor was opposed to all forms of experience rating but most of all to the charge-back system, the change marked a major victory for labor.

One group of employers had refused to support the experience-rating provision of the otherwise "agreed bill." They wanted to retain the charge-back system, under which the individual employer's tax rate was more proportionate to his own experience with unemployment. They were low-cost employers who had relatively little unemployment, and they resented subsidizing the unemployment of other industries. Moreover, they claimed that the program was full of abuses because employers did not have a financial incentive to police it. This group of employers introduced an experience-rating bill of their own; but with labor and the agency against it and employers divided on it, the bill was defeated. This issue of experience rating was to plague labor-management negotiations until it was finally "settled" in the 1951 legislative session.

The legislative session of 1941 followed the general pattern of 1939. Under the leadership of the administrator, the advisory council arrived at an agreed bill. At the same time that he was working with the advisory council, the administrator was also working with "outside" employers, who in 1941 made a formal protest against being excluded from the deliberations that led up to the agreed bill. In dealing with employers both inside and outside the council, the administrator made much use of the threat of federalization, which was a burning issue in Congress at this time. There is little doubt that this threat was a major factor in winning support for the agency's program. In this session maximum benefits were raised from $16 to $20, maximum duration was increased from 16 to 20 weeks and made uniform for all beneficiaries (a major change), and a special disqualification for married women was added.

The increase in the benefit amount had not been in the advisory council's agreed bill. It was added later, and the way in which it was added revealed the weakened position of the council. The administrator added the provision on his own authority when it looked (to him) as if a federal standard would be enacted to that effect. Although he sought the previous approval of employers outside the council for the amendment, he did not inform the advisory council of the change until after he had already included it in the agreed bill.

In the 1943 legislative session the conflict between the advisory council and outside employers increased, and the outcome, defeat for the council, marked a clear turning point in the council's fortunes.

In its meetings preparatory to the session, the council discussed a number of liberalizing amendments, including dependents' allowances and temporary disability benefits, but gradually came to realize that the general climate of opinion was unfavorable to much liberalization. The Second World War was at its height, manpower was scarce, and unemployment compensation commanded less public sympathy than it had formerly. Moreover, the threat of federalization was no longer as effective as it used to be; the states were winning the struggle for control of their own unemployment compensation agencies. Whereas two years previously the Utah administrator had said he was resigned to the inevitability of federalization of the program and thought other administrators unwise who attempted to block it, in 1943 he joined the others in a unanimous declaration of opposition to federal action.

Gradually the council narrowed its discussions to a single proposal, namely, to extend the duration of unemployment benefits from 20 to 26 weeks and to finance the increased costs by imposing a 1 percent tax on employees. The employee tax was expected to forestall any employer opposition to the extension of duration and also (an unrecorded reason) to make it difficult to introduce experience rating. The advisory council again voted unanimously against any form of experience rating.[7]

---

[7] The council's unanimous vote against experience rating is sufficient evidence that the two employers on the council did not represent employers generally.

The opposition of employers outside the advisory council was more formal in 1943. They appeared at two meetings of the advisory council to state their position. They declared it would not be fair to say to the legislature that because the council's bill was an agreed bill, there was no need for open hearings and a legislative debate. Employers in the distributive trades were especially aroused. They argued that they were already carrying the unemployment costs of other industries and that the proposed amendments would add to the burden. They pointed out that the distributive trades were not represented on the advisory council by either labor or management.[8] Toward the end of the second meeting the secretary of the Salt Lake City Chamber of Commerce proposed a "truce" for 1943—to leave the law as it stood. But he said that if the advisory council pushed for its two amendments, a bill would be introduced to establish the charge-back system of experience rating. The advisory council met this formal challenge to its influence by going ahead with its original agreed bill. The council lost; the bill did not pass the legislature.

There seems to have been a kind of agreed bill outside the advisory council. That is, the labor leaders saw the impossibility of getting the advisory council's recommendations accepted by the legislature as an agreed bill, feared the results of a legislative battle with experience rating as one of the issues, and agreed to the "truce" proposed by the employers outside the advisory council.

After the 1943 trial of strength and the advisory council's defeat, the meetings of the council came to resemble discussion-club sessions. A clear indication of its diminished status was the address which the administrator made at the meeting of May 12, 1943, on the occasion of the induction of three new members. In his description of the functions of an advisory council, he did not even mention the agreed bill. He spoke only of the council's "aiding the agency to trim red tape from procedures" and "acting as a sounding board." He explicitly warned the members

---

[8] The unions in the distributive trades belonged to the AFL, but the AFL representatives on the advisory council came from the building trades in the high-cost construction industry. The management representatives on the council came from mining and seasonal manufacturing, also industries having higher-than-average costs for unemployment compensation.

against thinking of themselves as "representing" groups officially; they were only "reflecting the general feeling" of those groups. This was a far cry from the description of functions that the council itself had adopted only five years before.

From the summer of 1943 through most of 1944 the meetings of the council were taken up with discussions of general postwar problems. In January, 1945, the council unanimously adopted two recommendations which the agency suggested: to extend duration from 20 to 23 weeks, and to link the benefit formula to the cost-of-living index. The (new [9]) administrator had cleared these recommendations with leading employer representatives outside the council, and although there was still some opposition expressed by individual employers, the recommendations were accepted by the legislature as an agreed bill and enacted into law.

In the council meeting of December 18, 1946, the new administrator opened a discussion of the relationship of the council to the legislative session that was about to begin. When he had assumed office, he had continued the former administrator's practice of consulting outside employers. Finding it more difficult in 1946 than in previous years to persuade employers outside the council to support agency policy, he was apparently exploring the possibility of stimulating council activity to an extent that would offset the growing employer hostility outside the council.

He outlined four alternative degrees of council activity descending from the first, in which the council would hold hearings, prepare bills, and see the bills through the legislature, to the fourth, in which the council would "do as it had in the past, just be discreetly active"—that is, quietly make up its own mind, publicly state its recommendations, and let the impact take care of itself. He warned the council that if it chose the first alternative, "it would be necessary for some of the members at least to spend a great deal of their time dealing with the matters of legislation." The council never made an explicit choice, but implicitly, in its operations, chose the fourth alternative.

[9] The agency's former public relations chief became administrator in the fall of 1944, succeeding Ray Adams, the first administrator, who went to Washington to head the new Servicemen's Readjustment Allowances program.

The employer groups outside the advisory council showed their mounting dissatisfaction with council procedure by by-passing the council entirely in the 1947 session and dealing directly with the legislative council of the legislature. They also attempted to by-pass labor entirely, but the administrator of unemployment compensation addressed a letter to the legislative council, urging that it give labor the opportunity to present its views on the amendments proposed by the employers, and warning that not to do so would embitter labor-management relations in general.[10]

The amendments of 1947 were eventually worked out by a group consisting of employers (at that time they were not on the council), representatives of labor (some of them were on the council), and the agency. This was the beginning of the extra-councilar feature of unemployment compensation legislation in Utah. Labor would have been glad to settle for a truce in 1947, but the group of dissatisfied employers was not to be denied. They succeeded in having at least part of their program of "tightening" adopted.[11]

The 1947 session marked a turning point. It was the first time that the program was restricted rather than liberalized or left unchanged. The uniform duration of benefits was changed to variable duration, and although the maximum was increased from 23 to 25 weeks, the increase did not compensate for the loss of uniform duration. The base year was moved closer to the benefit year, and eligibility requirements were raised somewhat—both provisions making it more difficult for irregular workers to draw benefits.

The chief battle raged around experience rating, as usual. The administrator said he would accept (reluctantly) a charge-back system if the logic of the system was carried out completely, to penalty rates. The advisory council declared itself opposed to experience rating under all conditions. Employers outside the council were divided—mainly on the basis of high-cost industry versus low-cost industry [12] but also on the amount of "abuse" in

[10] For a similar situation in New York in 1951, see pp. 196–98.

[11] The agency had reached the conclusion independently that some tightening of the program was in order, and the amendments finally enacted closely reflected the agency's recommendations.

[12] Some of the employer groups that favored a charge-back system: steel, oil, retail

the program. Even some high-cost employers favored a charge-back system because it was the only system, they thought, that would keep the program "clean." In the end, a compromise was adopted by the legislature: a payroll-variation system (the one least objectionable to labor) [13] to go into effect immediately, but a charge-back system to go into effect in 1950. In the meantime a study of the whole problem was to be made in time for the 1949 legislature to take new action if it so desired.

The legislative session of 1949 was a repetition—on a larger scale—of 1947. Without consulting the advisory council, employers went directly to the legislative council with their recommendations. At the November 10, 1948, meeting of the council, the administrator suggested that "the reason for the lack of confidence and interest which had been shown towards the advisory council was due to the fact that it was felt that the business members of the council were too far away from the business groups they represented."

When the administrator spoke before the legislative council, he closed his remarks by pointing out that "in the past labor and management had worked things out across the table pretty well," and he urged Senator McShane, the chairman of the Senate labor committee, to "get labor and management to sit down across the table and discuss the problem."

McShane did so, and soon there were three independent groups working on the 1949 amendments: McShane's group of two labor and two management representatives, only one of whom, the CIO representative, was an advisory council member; the legislative council, that is, its committee on unemployment compensation; and the advisory council. The legislative council held its fire in order to give the McShane group a chance to reach agreement. The council continued to meet into January, 1949, but its activities were, for the most part, ignored. The agency worked

merchandising, auto dealers. Mining, construction, and certain types of seasonal manufacturing were among the opponents of the system.

[13] This system did not induce employers to challenge benefit payments, and it resulted in a smaller spread in tax rates. In 1950–1951 in Utah, after high unemployment, the highest rate was 1.5 percent and the lowest was 0.9 percent, a spread of only 0.6 percent. For the same period the Wisconsin charge-back system produced a spread of 4 percent.

with all groups, of course, and had a substantial influence on the contents of the "package" which eventually emerged and was presented to the legislature as an agreed bill.

The agreed bill of 1949 changed the law in several important ways. The split in the employer ranks enabled labor to win its most desired goal, the retention of the payroll-variation system of experience rating. The provision in the law to introduce the charge-back system in 1950 was deleted. As for the employers, they obtained three of their objectives—in substance, if not in the exact form they desired: the definition of "surplus" (in the reserve fund) was changed to permit an earlier tax reduction; disqualifications for voluntary quit and for fraud were made more severe; and a system of individual (instead of uniform) benefit and base years was introduced. Some changes were also made in the law governing the advisory council, as was indicated earlier.[14]

In 1949 Utah had a new governor (a Republican, the first since 1935), a new industrial commissioner, and a new unemployment compensation administrator. The new industrial commissioner made the new deal complete by appointing a new council.

The labor members of the old advisory council were reappointed.[15] They could speak as authoritatively for their respective unions as anyone else in labor. They were legislative agents, that is, lobbyists. The CIO representative was also an elected representative in the legislature. The public members of the old council had not been unsatisfactory, but neither were they indispensable. Because of their connection with the discredited old council, the commissioner decided to appoint three new public members.

The important changes were made on the employer side. Of the four employer members on the new council, one came from the newly important steel industry; two—one of them the secretary of the Utah Manufacturers Association—had been active in the group which negotiated the 1949 agreed bill outside the council; one, the only employer hold over from the old council,[16] was the

---

[14] See p. 117.

[15] With one unimportant exception: the representative of the Railroad Brotherhoods.

[16] He was a latecomer to the old council and had been at odds with it most of the time.

nominee of the secretary of the Salt Lake City Chamber of Commerce. Thus both major employer organizations were effectively represented on the council.

At the first meeting of the new advisory council, July 1, 1949, the new administrator "explained that it was a misconception that the groups should propose legislation and stated that the group should be the educational center in getting information over to the people." There was a twofold explanation for this surprising announcement. The administrator was anxious to have certain amendments enacted during the next legislative session, and for that he wanted an agreed bill. But he was uncertain about how this new, untried council would work together or how effectively they would be able to speak for their respective sides. Labor and management might select on somewhat different bases nominees for an advisory council and nominees for a negotiating committee. Because he was not sure, the administrator preferred to be free to assemble an additional group, if necessary, that would give the highest promise of effectiveness for the purpose of arriving at an agreed bill. This was the first and primary reason. The second reason was his desire to avoid controversy that might split the council at the very beginning. An *ad hoc* negotiating committee distinct from the council could more easily afford to get into a fight than could a group like the council, that would have to continue meeting over the years. If they started with a controversy, they might never get over it. The administrator wanted the new council to start in an atmosphere of academic discussion, not crucial decision.

When he asked the labor and management organizations for delegates to a negotiating committee, he indicated that the new advisory council members would make very acceptable delegates but left the choice entirely to the organizations. He wanted delegates who would have the power to act and to commit their groups. A committee of twelve was finally appointed. All eight of the labor and management members on the advisory council were included. All four of the added members were legislative representatives—lobbyists. One labor addition was the state Federation president; the other was an assistant to the state CIO president, who was on the advisory council. One management addition was the secretary of the retailers' association, and the other was the working secretary of the employers' Utah State Legislative Conference.[17] It was a strong group.

This negotiating committee began to meet toward the end of October, 1950. The members elected the unemployment compensation administrator as their nonvoting chairman—thus making the structure of the committee identical with that of the Wisconsin advisory council. After a couple of preliminary meetings, the committee began to meet for half a day two or three times a week. Later they met almost daily. Not all of the twelve members attended the meetings with equal regularity, but there was the usual core working group. Eventually the committee agreed on a set of amendments, some of them purely technical, some of them substantive and controversial. Because the amendments were in an agreed bill, the legislature enacted them into law without holding public hearings.[18]

During the period that the negotiating committee was working, the advisory council continued to hold occasional meetings (five between September, 1950, and February, 1951) at which it discussed the progress of the negotiating committee, approved the committee's recommendations, and handled all other advisory-council matters—among them the review of several reports made by a council committee which had been appointed to deal with employment service problems.

The legislative session of 1953, like that of 1943, eventuated in a "truce." Labor wanted certain liberalizations, and an influential group of employers not represented on the advisory council wanted a charge-back experience-rating system and a tightening of disqualifications. The advisory council, the agency, and certain leaders outside the council decided that the only way to avoid a bitter and fruitless controversy was not to open the act to amendment at all. A truce was declared, and the "agreed bill" was an

---

[17] See p. 139.
[18] The agreed bill of 1951 increased the maximum benefit from $20 to $27.50 (the first increase since 1941) and extended maximum duration from 25 to 26 weeks. Two disqualifications affecting married women were lightened. In addition, the tax schedule was modified in order to prevent over-rapid increases in tax rates during periods of heavy unemployment.

agreement not to introduce bills on either side. Each side was able to make this agreement hold.

For the legislative session of 1955, the special negotiating committee of twelve was again established. The members worked even more intensively than before. They began in June of 1954 and met biweekly at first, then weekly, then daily. The agency made a more detailed presentation of unemployment compensation problems than it had ever made to any group in or outside the legislature.[19]

The labor members and the management members of the committee frequently held separate meetings in addition to the joint meetings of the committee, and the administrator of the agency continuously exercised the function of mediator at both the joint and the separate meetings. Twice negotiations seemed to reach an impasse, but each time a way out was found and the committee continued negotiations until it reached final agreement. A copy of the agreement in bill form, accompanied by a letter carrying the signatures of all twelve members of the committee, was sent to both the House and the Senate, and one labor lobbyist and one management lobbyist were deputed to maintain contact with both the House and the Senate during the progress of the bill through the legislature.

The agreed bill of 1955 was enacted into law in February. The new law introduced many changes—in benefits, eligibility requirements, and disqualifications—but the major change was to link the maximum benefit *automatically* to changes in wage levels so that the maximum benefit will always be 50 percent of the average total weekly wage of covered workers in the state.[20] The agreed bill of 1957 contained no substantive changes, partly because the changes in 1955 had been so numerous, partly because in 1957 the maximum benefit increased (from $35 to $37) automatically.

Problems of administration, although minor compared with those of legislation, were important enough to be brought to the

[19] For example, to aid the work of the committee, the agency made a major study—extending over three months—of the characteristics of Utah beneficiaries.

[20] Kansas pioneered, though it no longer has, this provision.

attention of the advisory council from time to time. The relation of the council to such problems is summarized succinctly, as well as illustrated by a detailed example, in the following statement by the administrator of the Utah employment security agency.

The Advisory Council has in an indirect manner been very valuable as a sounding board. You can pretty well tell what public reaction will be by reviewing your program and discussing your problems with the Advisory Council. At least we have found this to be the case. I believe pitfalls have been avoided by discussing "public issues" with the Advisory Council and being guided by their action and reaction. I also believe that adverse public reaction has been eliminated by fully explaining to the Advisory Council why we did what we did or why we purported to do something.

The Advisory Council has not helped in the formulation of rules or regulations after new legislation has been enacted. The Council has not entered into the picture with respect to any operation program. They have not had any influence, nor have we discussed with them problems involved in making decisions with respect to contribution or benefit payment functions.

When our appropriation was cut in 1952, we in the Agency, after considerable thought and analysis, tailored our program to meet available funds, which meant the elimination of some services which we felt essential but were unable to continue because of lack of funds, and which also meant the closing of several of our small offices. An Advisory Council meeting was called, and the facts were presented to the Council together with the curtailed plan of operations. The Council did not accept what, in effect, the Agency had accepted. The members were willing to curtail some of the operations that were necessary but were not willing to close all of the offices which we had recommended closing. The Council realized that the offices were being closed only because funds were not available for their operation, and the Council took upon itself the responsibility of getting sufficient funds for the operation of these offices. A subcommittee was appointed and assigned the responsibility of meeting with our legislative representatives to present to them the position which they had taken. Such a meeting was arranged. Our entire congressional delegation was present and met with the subcommittee of the Advisory Council, myself, Commissioner Wiesley and Gus Backman, whom the subcommittee had requested to join with them in presenting the problem to our congressional representatives. The congressional representatives accepted the position taken that the offices in question should not be closed. Senator Bennett was appointed and requested to take back to Washington the position of the Utah people.[21]

[21] Letter of Curtis P. Harding to the author, December 9, 1954.

EMPLOYMENT SERVICE

Neither the old nor the new council spent much time discussing employment service matters or doing anything about them. In 1941 and 1942 the council spent a number of meetings reviewing reports on manpower problems, but it took no active part in solving them. In 1949 the new council established an employment service committee which held several meetings that year and made plans to publicize the work of the employment service.[22]

During the high unemployment of 1950, the council discussed methods of increasing employment. This, however, was primarily the responsibility of another group, the Committee on Employment and Industrial Planning, and the council did little more than review reports on the situation. In 1951 the council concerned itself briefly with the manpower problems raised by the Korean war, but here too the primary responsibility rested with another group, the Defense Area Labor-Management Committee.

There were other occasions when the council discussed employment service matters, but in general the amount of time it devoted to these matters was small.

WORKMEN'S COMPENSATION

For a better understanding of the legislative history of unemployment compensation in Utah, it is useful to glance at the state's parallel experience in workmen's compensation. The workmen's compensation law in Utah was enacted in 1917; the administration of it was entrusted to the Industrial Commission, which was established at the same time. No important amendments were enacted in the law until 1937, and none again until 1945.[23]

The 1937 legislative session saw the first of a long series of agreements, most of which have been in the nature of "truces," that is, agreements not to attempt to change the law. The many "truces" were the results of labor's fears that if it opened the law

[22] The employment service in Utah accounts for a larger proportion of newly filled jobs than does the employment service nationally. The "penetration ratio" for the major market of Salt Lake County averages about 32 percent, as contrasted with a national figure of about 15 percent.

[23] In 1941, however, an occupational-disability law was enacted, which was in effect an extension of workmen's compensation.

to amendment and secured benefit increases, management would ask for and get offsetting changes in the law in the form of more restrictive eligibility conditions. According to one long-time observer who worked with both labor and management, this fear had no substantial basis; he had not found management particularly anxious to "tighten" the workmen's compensation or occupational disability programs. He thought that management would have accepted "reasonable" improvements in the law.

This same observer thought that labor had for years been making the mistake of bringing into the legislature a multitude of bills on issues that did not concern labor directly and of asking for too much to be effected too quickly in the matter of workmen's compensation. He had urged labor's legislative representatives to concentrate on what concerned labor immediately and in that area to avoid unrealistic demands. He had pointed out to them: "Even in the 1930's, when you had a liberal legislature, you got nothing by that method; your best method is to ask for small improvements each session and to ask for them in conjunction with an agreement worked out with employers."

APPRAISAL

The Utah picture is not so clear as that of Wisconsin or New Hampshire. It is blurred because the advisory council was not the only center of labor-management activity in unemployment compensation and because the effectiveness of the council varied considerably over time. The Utah picture must be represented by a triptych consisting of three unequal panels.

The first panel represents the brief period 1936–1939, when the council was comparatively secure in its position of leadership in unemployment compensation—but only because it had not yet been seriously challenged. The program was new, the New Deal still had momentum, the council was the only officially recognized body representing labor and management, and employers outside the council were not yet fully interested, organized, and technically competent in this new field.

The second panel represents the period 1939–1949, when the

authority of the council was challenged. The challenge came from the side of employers and arose out of the clash between the views of the employer representatives on the council and the views of the real decision makers among employers, who were not on the council. It began as a grumble in 1939, became an open, formal protest in 1943, and accomplished the overthrow of the council in 1949.

Until 1943 there were only two genuine employer representatives on the council (the third was a lawyer whose relationship with the business community was so loose that when in 1943 his membership status was changed to that of a public representative on the council, no one objected). Even after the council was enlarged in 1943, the employer representation did not include the principal employer decision makers, who were to be found among the professional representatives of the employer organizations, the employer lobbyists, and the technical experts. This meant that the "official" and the real spokesmen for employers were not the same. It was a situation which would have produced friction even if the views of the "official" and real spokesmen had been in agreement.

But, as was noted earlier, their views were in serious disagreement, especially on the vital issue of experience rating. Both of the original employer representatives on the old council came from high-cost industries (seasonal manufacturing and mining) and were opposed to experience rating in any form but especially in the form of a charge-back system. In supporting this position, which was also labor's position, they found themselves opposed by the generality of their fellow employers.[24]

There were other differences in addition to this fundamental one. Between 1936, when the original council members were appointed, and 1949, when they were replaced, a number of changes occurred in the economic climate of the state which established a "new regime" and cast on the original employer representatives the vague discredit of belonging to the "old regime."

First among these changes, Utah shared in the general conserva-

---

[24] Although Utah's original law provided a charge-back system of experience rating, the state did not actually get experience rating until 1947, and then not a charge-back, but a payroll-variation, system.

tive swing which began in the 1940's and was epitomized by the metamorphosis of the Wagner Act into the Taft-Hartley Act.[25] The achievements of the New Deal were subjected to a critical scrutiny from which unemployment compensation was not exempt. If anything, the scrutiny was more critical in the case of unemployment compensation. High employment during the war dulled public appreciation for the institution of unemployment compensation, and the unusual wave of abuse which set in during the reconversion aroused suspicion and a demand for reform.

A second change in unemployment compensation came about through the normal shaking-down process that follows the early stages of any new program—the process of finding where the new shoes were pinching. The employers who were being pinched began to demand changes in the law. The demands became more numerous and insistent with the growth of employers' competence in unemployment compensation. In the beginning they had to take the agency's word or join with the agency in guessing. Later the technicians of the large companies could match the agency in expertness (some of them had been drawn from agency staff), and they had the accumulated experience of their own companies as a guide.

A third change took place during the war, when many new industries came into Utah and not only changed the old pattern of employer leadership but also brought with them a more urgent demand for "reform." [26] This twin development further contributed to make the original employer members of the council seem like representatives of an "old regime."

A final development which further isolated the employer members on the council was a change of administrators in 1944. The new administrator was actively Democratic in his politics, markedly prolabor in his convictions about unemployment compensation, and vigorous in all his actions. Employers outside the council developed a strong antagonism to him, and by concomitance they

[25] State labor laws reflected the change. The Utah version of the Taft-Hartley Act was the Klegg-Vest Act, enacted in 1947. In 1955 Utah enacted a "right-to-work" law.

[26] By reform they meant chiefly the getting of an experience-rating provision which would come closer to making each employer pay his own charges and a tightening of disqualification provisions.

extended their antagonism to his advisory council partly because it was his and partly because the employer representatives on the council frequently supported him—in his stand on experience rating, for example.

The third panel represents the period of the council's greatest influence, 1949–1955. The new advisory council as reconstituted in 1949 included for the first time the decision makers on the side of both labor and management and again operated under an administrator sufficiently neutral to command the confidence of both sides. It was chiefly for these two reasons that the new council was influential as the old had never been.

A third reason might be noted. The decision makers on management's side proved less difficult to handle when they were on the council than when they were outside. For one thing, they learned to see the program through the eyes of the agency (and even of labor) as well as through their own. For another, their demands for reform became more realistic as they learned from their experience on the council that their political influence was limited even when the conservatives were in power. It is significant that during the "new regime" no further changes were made in either experience-rating or disqualification provisions, the two most controversial issues.

The Utah experience establishes the reality of two limitations on council effectiveness. An advisory council will not be fully effective if (1) it does not include the decision makers in labor and management and (2) the administrator of the agency is not neutral enough to command the confidence of both sides. The Utah experience demonstrates that the removal of these two limitations, without any other changes, can transform a council from a relatively ineffective to a very effective institution.

AGREED BILLS

The record of Utah in the matter of agreed bills is similar to that of Wisconsin in at least one respect: the original unemployment compensation law and all subsequent major amendments came about through agreed bills. In other respects, of course,

Utah's record is quite different. In Utah not all of the agreed bills were "full and strict" and not all of them came out of the council.

There was no simple and unvarying relationship of the council to the agreed bills. During the period of the old council, some of the agreements were made partly outside the council (1939, 1941, 1945) and some entirely outside (1943, 1947, 1949). Even during the period of the new council, although all the agreed bills were full and strict and were made by all the labor and management members of the council, they were not made exclusively by the council members: none of the public members participated in the negotiations, and some noncouncil labor and management representatives did participate. Nevertheless, the important fact remains: the unemployment compensation law in Utah was the product of an unbroken series of agreed bills.

The Utah legislature welcomed the agreed bills and on occasion even put pressure on the two parties to "get together" with the agency and arrive at an agreement for the legislature to pass.

The legislature worked under the usual—perhaps more than the usual—handicaps. It was in session only every other year, and the session lasted only sixty days. To pass a bill, it was necessary to win a majority of all the elected legislators, not a majority of only those voting. Under such conditions the task of legislating for a complex and controversial program like unemployment compensation was difficult, and the solution offered by an agreed bill was very welcome.

In 1947 Utah improved its legislative mechanism by adding a legislative council. This council is composed of the leaders of both parties in both houses and meets between the regular sessions of the legislature to prepare for the next session.[27] It sifts and groups proposed bills, sometimes persuades the sponsors to make changes in the bills before introducing them, institutes special studies, and engages in other preliminary activities related to legislation. A subcommittee of the legislative council handles unemployment compensation, but because it has to handle many other matters too, it still welcomes the help of an agreed bill in a program like unemployment compensation.

[27] Twenty-seven states have adopted this interim legislative device.

The unemployment compensation agency has always favored the agreed bill and was indeed one of the most active influences both in getting labor and management to agree and in shaping the terms of that agreement. The agency felt it was easier to avoid bad lawmaking, both as to substance and as to administrability of the law, when changes were worked out by labor and management experts under the supervision of the agency than when the law was "made a political football."

Employers were not unanimous on the desirability of agreed bills, but the majority of the decision makers were very definite in their approval. The law which had resulted from eleven agreed bills, while it fell far short of their norms, was about as good, they thought, as any they could have obtained by legislative battles. They also recognized the additional gains in certainty, self-determination, and the preservation of good labor relations that had come along with the agreed bills.

On labor's side the state Federation spoke more favorably of the agreed bills than did the CIO—the usual situation—but both were certain that the way of the agreed bill was the better way. They thought that the program was more liberal than it might otherwise have been (a judgment in which both the agency and employers concurred).[28] In matters of disqualifications and experience rating, two of the most controversial issues, the Utah law has provisions as favorable to labor as those of any state law. Changes in those provisions could only have been unfavorable to labor. The adoption (in 1955) of the provision which automatically links benefits with changes in average wages represents a major gain for labor. In an economy which will in all probability continue to be characterized by inflationary pressures, such a device is clearly to labor's advantage. Instead of having to bargain— that is, give something—for the increase in benefits which inflation calls for, labor will get the increase automatically.

In view of the general ebb of sympathy for favorable labor legislation during the war years and afterward, there is solid ground

[28] For detailed comparisons of the Utah law with those of other states, see four studies published by the Utah Industrial Commission in 1950: *Utah Economy; A Study of Workers Receiving Benefits under the Utah Employment Security Act; Utah Unemployment Insurance; Unemployment Insurance and the Utah Economy.*

for doubting whether labor would have fared better in the legislature than it did at the bargaining table. Additional grounds for that doubt are furnished by the concensus among labor, management, government, and university people that the Church of Jesus Christ of Latter-Day Saints (popularly known as the Mormon Church) has not been sympathetic to unionism.[29] Since the Mormon Church has more influence in the area of public policy —and hence in the legislature—than it has in the private bargaining of employers, labor has had an added reason for preferring the agreed bill. Those who noted this influence of the Mormon Church, however, did not consider it a major factor.

Agreed bills were possible in Utah because the leaders of labor and of management possessed the essential though intangible quality of "reasonableness" to a marked degree. The early leaders, like William Knerr on labor's side and Gus Backman on management's side, typified the "middle leadership" which has thus far been strong enough to bring along the extremists on both sides.

Another reason that agreed bills were possible in Utah was that labor and management were sufficiently organized to be effectively represented. A few individuals on each side could negotiate with authority for their respective groups. Although it was somewhat more difficult for the state Federation than for the state CIO to achieve the necessary centralization of authority, since power in the Federation rested in the hands of the vice presidents, who were heads of various internationals, the leadership was always sufficiently strong to hold the whole Federation to a single legislative policy in unemployment compensation.

Organization among employers in Utah, as elsewhere, was less adequate than among the unions. Employers in Utah did not have even the social security committees that are found in many other states. But in a relatively small state like Utah, whose industries are concentrated in about four centers, a little organization went

[29] Perhaps because, being a major employer in Utah, the Mormon Church has naturally adopted the attitude of an employer. Perhaps because the Utah community was established as a theocratic society and is endangered by the influx of organizations —unions among them—whose headquarters and superiors are outside the Utah community.

a long way. Several of the employer representatives active in legislation emphasized the ease with which they could contact one
another. They were continually meeting in the ordinary course
of business. Moreover, there was much overlapping of positions,
so that the same men were on several committees, and communication and coordination were facilitated. Two of the employer
members on the new advisory council were also members of the
executive board of the Utah Manufacturers Association, which
met weekly, so that coordination of the council's work with that
important body was made very simple. The Employers Legislative Conference, established in 1947, further facilitated organization on the employers' side. The conference, for example, named
the employer representatives to the negotiating committee which
worked out the agreed bill in 1951.

In the early 1940's an experiment was made with a joint labor-
management conference to discuss all labor legislation and try
to work out comprehensive and coordinate agreements. The idea
originated with state Federation and CIO labor leaders, who had
earlier begun to hold joint labor meetings for that same purpose.
The system worked with some effectiveness in the legislative sessions of 1945 and 1947 and then was discontinued, partly because
of CIO disinterest, but more because of the positive opposition
of some employer groups. These latter said they did not like to
see concessions in one program traded for concessions in another
but preferred to see each program handled on its own merits.

The earlier agreed bills had to overcome an obstacle similar
to that in New Hampshire—unemployment benefit costs were
somewhat higher than the national average. Since the war, however, the costs of the program in Utah have been about average—
higher than those of Wisconsin, for example, but lower than those
of New Hampshire.[30]

---

[30] At the end of 1957 Utah compared with the national average as follows:

	United States	Utah
Benefits paid as percentage of taxable wages	1.5	1.1
Reserve fund as percentage of taxable wages	7.6	8.9
Average employer tax rate	1.3	1.3

SPECIAL NEGOTIATING COMMITTEE

The unique feature of the Utah experience was the special committee of labor and management representatives that met outside the advisory council to negotiate agreed bills. In 1947 and 1949 such a committee was understandable as a way around the difficulty posed by the lack of employer decision makers on the council. It was continued in 1951 for the reasons noted earlier. The administrator thought that after the 1951 session the function of working out an agreed bill might return to the advisory council. But the labor and management members on the council preferred the separate negotiating committee and the public members were satisfied with the arrangement, so the special committee continued to negotiate the agreed bill.

The arrangement had a number of advantages. It permitted the inclusion of persons, particularly on management's side, who were expert and influential in unemployment compensation matters but were unwilling or unable to give to unemployment compensation the continuous attention that an advisory council member must give it. The arrangement also guaranteed that all those who engaged in the negotiations would be people with technical competence in both collective bargaining and the unemployment compensation law and that they would be able to meet as frequently and for as long as might be necessary.[31]

The very success of the negotiating committee raises the question: Why have an advisory council at all? In workmen's compensation a similar negotiating committee was called together every two years to discuss possible amendments to the law, and that sufficed. No one of those interviewed thought that an advisory council was necessary in workmen's compensation. Might not the same be true in unemployment compensation?

The same persons—from labor, management, government—who saw no need for an advisory council in workmen's compensation felt sure that there ought to be one in unemployment compensation. They emphasized the education which the advisory

[31] Membership on the negotiating committee would have imposed a financial burden on the public members of the council. The meetings of the committee were long and frequent, and the members received no compensation—not even for their expenses.

council provided. They believed that the education had a perceptible influence on general attitudes and that it lessened the area
of disagreement between labor and management. The agency was
the chief factor in this educational process, but all the council
members were contributory factors.

The experience of one of the employer members furnished a
good example of such gradual education. Before becoming a
member of the advisory council, he was very suspicious of unemployment compensation and voiced his suspicions in public
speeches. Seeing things from the inside during several years on
the council, he grew to esteem the program and the agency highly,
and he became an effective missionary among his fellow employers.[32] He even modified his position on charge-back experience rating. Where before he considered it an indispensable device for keeping the program "clean," he was now satisfied that
the device was not needed for that purpose, at least, but that the
agency could be depended upon.[33]

The public members contributed to the education of the labor
and management members. The question, "Should there be an
advisory council in addition to a negotiating committee?" is in
part the question, "Do public members perform a useful function?" All the labor and management members were in favor of
having public members on the council. The following typical
comments enunciate the basic reasons for their approval. "The
public members introduce a broader point of view than either
labor or management is likely to present." "They keep both sides
from taking extreme positions." "They preserve the atmosphere
of discussion in the council meetings and prevent angry quarrels."
The chairman of the council, though he expressed some doubt
as to how valuable he and the other public members really were,
believed that they had at least an indirect effect on the work of
the labor-management negotiating committee. The reaction of
the public members in the advisory council meetings gave the
labor and management members an idea of what was reasonable

[32] During an interview he remarked to the author on the difficulty of explaining the
program to those who had not had the educational advantage of membership on the
advisory council.

[33] Utah has one of the highest disqualification rates of any state.

and what was extreme in their positions, and they later conducted their bargaining accordingly.

Labor and management members also educated each other. The regular meetings of the advisory council gave each side the opportunity to see problems from the viewpoint of the other side. The advisory council meetings fulfilled this function more effectively than did the meetings of the negotiating committee: the advisory council meetings were more frequent, covered a broader area of topics, and were conducted in the leisured atmosphere of discussion rather than the tense atmosphere of decision.[34]

[34] This was the difference which distinguished the early stages of work of the California study commission, when the participants were merely discussing the problems, from the later stages, when the participants had reached the point of determining the exact terms of the bargain. See pp. 351–52.

6

THE ILLINOIS ADVISORY COUNCIL

ALTHOUGH Illinois was the last state to enact an unemployment compensation law, it was among the earliest to establish an advisory council. The Illinois advisory council [1] held its first meeting on November 1, 1938. It is a tripartite council of nine members: three representatives each of labor, management, and the public. Members are appointed by the governor with the consent of the Senate and serve without compensation. The law fixes the terms of members at two years and provides that all terms expire at the same time. Standing alone, this provision could result in the automatic dissolution of the council whenever the governor delayed to make reappointments. An additional provision safeguards the council from this recurrent danger; the law states that members shall serve until their successors have been appointed. The members themselves, however, have partially nullified this protective provision by a custom of tendering their resignations whenever a new governor is elected.

The duties and powers of the council are spelled out in the law with more than ordinary fullness. The law specifies that the council is to: make recommendations on its own initiative to the agency, the governor, and the legislature; investigate the agency in the performance of its duties; draw up rules of procedure; [2] keep minutes, which are to be public records; and meet at least quarterly.[3] The council elects its own chairman.

[1] The council's official title is Illinois Board of Unemployment Compensation and Free Employment Office Advisors.

[2] The Illinois rules are full and detailed. They were adopted in 1938 and resemble New York's rules adopted in 1935.

[3] For the full text of the law see *Illinois Revised Statutes*, chapter on State Government, State Bar Association edition, Chapter 127, Sections 6, 8, and 10.

Since 1941 the council membership has included a woman, as required by the Wagner-Peyser Act. The Bureau of Employment Security held up a budget request for Illinois in 1941 until the state met the requirement.

In Illinois, as in most states, the council has had no staff of its own, but in 1953 a member of the agency's staff was given special responsibility for the council with the title of council secretary. During legislative sessions he devoted nearly full time to the work of the council; at other periods, much less. His work was more clerical than executive, and he did not occupy the key position held by the council secretary in New York, Ohio, or Pennsylvania.

At the meetings of the council its members did not sit by groups —labor, management, and public—but mingled around the table. (They lunched together also.) Top agency staff members attended the meetings, as did also the director's personal secretary, who took the minutes. Since at least 1943, and probably even prior to that date, the minutes have been taken verbatim.[4]

Council meetings are open to the public,[5] and employers have made much use of this privilege, especially since 1952. A unique feature of the Illinois meetings has been management's "second row," composed of technical advisers to the employer representatives on the council. To understand this "second row" and its importance it is necessary to understand how employers in Illinois are organized.

There are five principal employer organizations in Illinois, known as the "Big Five." They are the Illinois Manufacturers' Association, the Illinois State Chamber of Commerce, the Associated Employers of Illinois, the Illinois Federation of Retail Associations, and the Chicago Association of Commerce and Industry. The first two provide most of the leadership in matters concerning unemployment compensation. Of these two, the Manufacturers' Association is the older and until recently was also much the larger. Since the Second World War, the state Chamber of Commerce has grown greatly.

The executives of the Big Five make up the Joint Executive

---

[4] The verbatim minutes were not regularly transcribed because they were referred to only on the rare occasions when some dispute arose as to exact wording.

[5] Except when the council wishes to go into executive session.

Committee, which is the policy-forming unit for employers in unemployment compensation. In addition there is the Joint Technical Committee composed of a dozen or more persons having technical competence in unemployment compensation. Both of these committees were established in 1937, before the passage of the Illinois unemployment compensation act, in order to pool what technical resources employers had (in the JTC) and to present a united front on policy (through the JEC).[6]

Back of the Joint Technical Committee are the social security committees of the Manufacturers' Association and the state Chamber of Commerce. The former dates from 1936, the latter from 1946. At least three quarters of the active members of the Joint Technical Committee are drawn from the two social security committees. The meetings of the Joint Technical Committee are used primarily to integrate the work of these two committees and to provide for participation by other employer organizations.

The following quotation describes the major steps by which employers in Illinois typically construct a legislative program in unemployment compensation.

The Social Security Committee of the Illinois Manufacturers' Association is now giving consideration to proposed changes in the above act [Unemployment Compensation Act] for submission to the Illinois General Assembly at the next regular session which convenes in January, 1953. A number of recommendations have been prepared by the Committee. These recommendations are reproduced herein.

Member firms are requested to review these tentative recommendations and to submit their comments thereon as well as suggestions for additional changes in the Act. The views so secured will be submitted to our Social Security Committee.

After this legislative program has been approved by the IMA Social Security Committee, the program will be submitted to the Joint Technical Committee which represents the major employer groups who are interested in this subject matter. The Joint Technical Committee will in turn submit its joint recommendations to the Board of Unemployment Compensation and Free Employment Office Advisors, of which Mr. E. F. Mansure, of E. L. Mansure Company and former president of the Illinois Manufacturers' Association, is chairman.[7]

[6] W. J. MacPherson, the vice president of one of the public utilities, was the leader in establishing the Joint Technical Committee and was its chairman until his death in 1947.

[7] *I.M.A. Bulletin,* October 20, 1952, p. 1.

Besides the five steps enumerated in the above announcement there are two others not mentioned. The social security committees take their recommendations to the board of directors of their respective organizations before taking them to the Joint Technical Committee. And the Joint Technical Committee takes its recommendations to the Joint Executive Committee before taking them to the advisory council.

On paper the process looks cumbersome. In practice it was simplified by the fact that the same few key people were active at each step. Thus, the employer representatives who comprised the "second row" at the council meetings were the same ones who started the work in the social security committees, took the resulting recommendations to the Joint Technical Committee meeting, accompanied their principals to the Joint Executive Committee meeting, and were on hand to explain and defend the recommendations when they reached their final destination in the advisory council meeting.

The organization of labor in Illinois is much simpler. Representatives from the Illinois State Federation of Labor, the State Council of the CIO, and the United Mine Workers can effectively speak for organized labor in Illinois. On the advisory council the representative of the Federation has always provided the leadership, partly because the Federation is the largest and most influential of the three organizations, partly because its representatives have been outstanding personages,[8] and partly because the representatives of the other unions have not been willing, for various reasons, to share the burden of detailed work which the council involved.[9]

During the period 1938 through 1957 the council held 96 meetings, distributed by years as follows:

1938	4	1943	4	1948	4	1953	6
1939	9	1944	6	1949	1	1954	6
1940	1	1945	3	1950	0	1955	11
1941	8	1946	3	1951	11	1956	4
1942	2	1947	3	1952	5	1957	5

[8] The state Federation has always been represented on the council by its secretary, Victor Olander being succeeded by Stanley Johnson.

[9] In the entire period 1940–1957 the Federation representative was absent from only two council meetings. The other labor representatives were absent much more often.

For the entire period the council averaged 4.8 meetings a year, but this is an average of two quite dissimilar periods—the period of the "old" council, through 1950, and the period of the "new" council, after 1950. The "old" council averaged only 3.7 meetings a year but the "new" council has averaged 6.8 meetings a year. The meetings of both councils have tended to cluster around legislative sessions. Meetings averaged more than one a month during legislative periods and less than one a year at other times.

The council had a fairly good attendance record. For the entire period 1938–1957 (there was no notable difference between the periods of the old and new councils) the attendance record of the council as a whole was 79 percent; of employers, 91 percent; of the public, 81 percent; and of labor, 66 percent.

The duties of the advisory council have always included the employment service. In Illinois, the employment service was integrated with unemployment compensation as early as 1937, when the Illinois unemployment compensation act was enacted. Before that time the employment service had an advisory council of its own, called the General Advisory Board. The first board was appointed by the governor in 1915.[10] It consisted of five members of whom two represented employers and two organized labor; the fifth was appointed by the governor from a list submitted by these first four. The president of the state Federation of Labor, John H. Walker, and a leading industrialist, Oscar C. Mayer, served as members of the board throughout its life. The purpose of the board was twofold: to correct the deplorable condition into which the employment offices had fallen [11] and to furnish some control over the system of political appointments to the employment offices. This board was very effective in the depression years, but had already lapsed into inactivity at the time the employment service was merged with unemployment compensation in 1937.

[10] A brief historical survey of the General Advisory Board from 1915 to 1930 is given in the *Thirteenth Annual Report*, Illinois Department of Labor, pp. 55–58. Free employment offices in Illinois go back to 1899.

[11] They were inadequately financed, and the impression was general that they existed to provide employment only for unskilled labor and domestic servants and to serve as a sort of charitable institution.

ACTIVITIES OF THE COUNCIL
UNEMPLOYMENT COMPENSATION LEGISLATION

Although the advisory council gave most of its time to unemployment compensation legislation, it did not limit itself entirely to that field. The council also concerned itself with the administration of the unemployment compensation program, and on occasion turned its attention to the employment service program. These other activities of the council are omitted, however, from the following account in order to describe in more detail the council's relationship to legislation, which in the case of Illinois is unusually well documented and unusually instructive.

Until 1951 the main forces determining unemployment compensation legislation in Illinois were outside the advisory council. They had a connection with the council, however, in so far as their results, in the form of agreed bills, were channeled through the council. Moreover, the activity outside the council was such that it could easily have been the activity of an advisory council, and if it had, would have made that council an unusually successful one. For both reasons it is worth reviewing briefly the legislative activity from 1935 through 1949, even though the advisory council had only a nominal share in it.[12]

1935–1936. Illinois employers expected the Social Security Act to be declared unconstitutional and were opposed to any form of unemployment compensation legislation. They rejected even labor's "realistic" bill, which omitted the features most objectionable to employers. In the special session of 1936 they were able to block all legislation dealing with unemployment compensation.

1937. Early in the session Governor Horner appointed a large committee representing employers, labor, and his own office to meet with the appropriate legislative committees. This group agreed on a bill which was introduced in the House. The major

---

[12] For the materials of this review I am much indebted to the excellent study of Gilbert Y. Steiner, *Legislation by Collective Bargaining* (University of Illinois, Institute of Labor and Industrial Relations, 1951). Professor Steiner kindly made available to me the original materials on which that study was based. I reinterviewed for my own purposes all the major figures involved in the events of the period. By a fortunate accident, I had earlier (1946) interviewed the two key figures, Olander and MacPherson, both of whom had died before the Steiner study was begun.

employer organizations, however, denied that the employer representatives on the committee had been empowered to speak for
Illinois employers and repudiated the agreement. In appointing
the representatives of employers the governor probably had not
consulted the employer organizations.[13] Labor then declared itself
free of the agreement and announced its intention of amending
the bill in the House to ask for more than the agreement had
provided.

On May 24, 1937, the Supreme Court of the United States
handed down its decision declaring the federal law constitutional
and making it practically necessary for the Illinois legislature to
pass an unemployment compensation law immediately. This
strengthened labor's position greatly, and the employers agreed
to meet again with labor to work out a bill.

Despite the lateness of the hour, the employers were able to
produce workable proposals on which to bargain. The proposals
came out of what was to become the Joint Technical Committee,
one of whose members was W. J. MacPherson. MacPherson argued that it was wiser to participate with labor and the legislature
in shaping the law then to follow the example of New York employers, who had refused to participate and had got a law which
reflected that fact.[14] Within a short time the labor and management negotiators produced an agreed bill and the legislature
enacted it into law. The bill which employers had to accept eventually was no more favorable to them than the one which they
could have had with labor agreement in 1936.

1939. An agreed bill was reached in this session. It gave employers a change in the tax system which they considered an improvement [15] and gave labor three substantial liberalizations.[16]
The agreement was made outside the advisory council. The negotiators for employers were the same persons who had worked out

[13] This was the first of three repudiations by employers of agreements arrived at
(more or less tentatively) by negotiators. The other two: 1949 and 1951.

[14] The New York unemployment compensation law was one of the earliest to be
enacted (April, 1935); the Illinois law, enacted June 30, 1937, was the last.

[15] From a reserve-ratio to a benefit-wage system.

[16] Coverage was extended from employers of eight to employers of six, the waiting
period was shortened from three to two weeks, and the maximum benefit was raised
from $15 to $16.

the 1937 agreed bill, and who were by this time formally organized in the Joint Technical Committee and the Joint Executive Committee; [17] the principal negotiator for labor was Victor Olander, the secretary of the Illinois State Federation of Labor. The advisory council held twelve meetings in connection with the 1939 legislative session, but it was not in the council's meetings that the effective decisions were made. Olander, it is true, was a member of the council, but he was absent from nine of these twelve council meetings. It is clear from the council's minutes that the council accepted an agreement fashioned outside of itself and merely added an official stamp of approval.

1941. Although both labor and management introduced extreme bills at the beginning of the legislative session, they eventually reached agreement and their bill was enacted. The pattern of agreement was clear by this time, although not publicized. MacPherson and Olander were the indubitable spokesmen for their respective sides. While meeting formally with their respective groups and, in the case of Olander, with the advisory council, they also met informally with one another and worked out an agreed bill which they then persuaded their groups to ratify and support.

The agreed bill of 1941 increased maximum benefits from $16 for sixteen weeks to $18 for twenty weeks, shortened the waiting period from two weeks to one week, and extended coverage from employers of six to employers of one. But it also increased the number of weeks of disqualification imposed for voluntary quits, misconduct, and refusal of suitable work.[18]

In passing the bill the legislature deleted the provision extending coverage, and this led labor to charge employers with betrayal of the agreement. In the light of the general fate of agreements to extend coverage—even in Wisconsin—it seems prob-

[17] Negotiations on the change in the tax system were conducted for Illinois employers by Frank B. Cliffe and Robert W. Leach. The one was from New York, the other from Wisconsin—evidence of the paucity of experts in those early years.

[18] Employers had begun the session with the expectation that under a Republican administration they would obtain more of the reforms they wanted. Their eventual concessions to labor are partly to be explained by their fear of federalization, which seemed imminent at this time. (See Utah, p. 120.)

able that the legislature acted on its own initiative and that the employers were innocent.

The advisory council met nine times in connection with this legislative session. Olander attended these meetings, but he was almost the only labor representative to do so. Of the other labor representatives, one missed five and the other missed seven of the nine meetings. Again the council's minutes give no indication that its deliberations affected the outcome. At most the council gave the agreement its official approval.

1943. Wartime conditions gave both labor and employers grounds for demanding changes in the law. Labor asked for the elimination of the waiting period and for an increase in maximum benefits from $18 to $24 to meet the rise in the cost of living. Employers asked for some stiffening of disqualifications to meet the stringency in the labor market.

This last demand was general throughout the country, and was granted in many states.[19] In Illinois, however, an agreed bill was reached (late in the session after a bitter struggle) which limited itself to a single amendment, an increase in maximum benefits from $18 to $20. As before, Olander and MacPherson negotiated the final decision for their respective sides. The advisory council held six meetings in connection with the 1945 legislative session, but there is no indication that the council's activities had any significant influence on the course of legislation.

1945. When this legislative session began, the end of the war was in sight. There was a widely held expectation that mass unemployment would follow the end of the war. Agreement, following the usual pattern, was reached rather easily that duration should be extended from twenty to twenty-six weeks and minimum benefits raised from $7 to $10.

One incident of this session indicated that the agreed bill pattern had set firmly. A bill had been introduced in the senate which would have qualified claimants for unemployment benefits who became ill or disabled after beginning to draw such benefits.

[19] "Trends in Disqualification from Benefits under State Unemployment Compensation Laws," *Social Security Bulletin,* January, 1944, pp. 12–13.

At the hearings on the bill labor representatives joined employers in opposing it. They stated explicitly that they did so as part of the bargain struck in the agreed bill.

1947. In Illinois as in the rest of the nation at this time public sentiment was not favorable to labor legislation. It was especially hostile to unemployment compensation because of the unusual amount of abuse which plagued the program after the war. In his message to the legislature in 1947, Governor Green cautioned against any hasty action affecting the relations between labor and management in general; but in the area of unemployment compensation he seemed to invite some restrictive action. The governor said in his message: "Unemployment compensation is a splendid program for those who are out of work and want to work. We are determined that it should not be abused by those who remain voluntarily idle."

Employers were unanimous in wanting to tighten the disqualification provisions of the law, but they could not agree on the best strategy. Some wanted a drastic and immediate revision of the law. The leaders of this group were in the state Chamber of Commerce, which was newly come into prominence and was critical of the past policy and strategy of employers.[20] Another group of employers agreed with the program of drastic revision, but thought it wiser strategy to wait until 1949. A third, led by MacPherson, wanted to keep within the limits imposed by the agreed bill procedure and to tighten the program by degrees over time.

The employers composed their differences sufficiently to commence negotiations with labor. But partly because of this disagreement among employers, partly because MacPherson died during the session, and partly because labor preferred no legislation to risking the enactment of severe disqualifications, the negotiators reached no agreement.

The advisory council was urged—by the "severe" school of employers—to make its own recommendations to the legislature, on

[20] The Chamber of Commerce established a social security committee in 1946 of which the chairman was the employer member of the advisory council who had been on the council since 1941 and who eventually became the chief employer spokesman of the "new" council.

a divided vote if necessary.[21] But both the advisory council and the legislature, accustomed to having an agreed bill, waited for one until the end, and the session closed on June 30 without either of them taking action. No substantive amendments were enacted in 1947.

After the event, it is impossible to say who was correct—those who claimed that the reform program could have been put through if all employers had been united on it and had ignored the agreed bill procedure from the start, or those who said the results showed that legislation could be enacted only with labor support. But one thing was certain, the old pattern of reaching agreement was broken. The death of MacPherson would have assured that. But there were other forces working in the same direction. There was the general conservative trend already mentioned, which made some tightening of the program inevitable and to that extent made future agreed bills more difficult. There was also the growth in influence of an employer group (the state Chamber of Commerce) and of a labor group (the CIO [22]), both of whom regarded the agreed bill technique with suspicion.

1949. Both sides approached this legislative session with a chip on the shoulder. The bargaining position of labor was improved over that of 1947. The national elections had shown unexpected support for the Fair Deal nationally, and in Illinois Democrat Stevenson had unseated Republican Green. Moreover, benefits in unemployment compensation had remained unchanged since 1943 while wages and prices had climbed continuously, so that some increase in benefits was inevitable.

Labor began the session by introducing a bill to establish the "ideal" unemployment compensation program. Employers were still determined on "reform" of the law's disqualification provisions, still found considerable public support for such action,[23] but were still divided on the proper strategy. In April the state Chamber of Commerce introduced two bills which embodied

[21] This was one of the few instances of employers seeking to use the advisory council to create propaganda pressure. For another instance see Rhode Island, p. 286.

[22] The CIO secured a place on the advisory council in 1947 and the directorship of the Department of Labor in 1948.

[23] In late 1948, for example, Fulton Lewis, Jr. directed his broadcast every night for a month to the topic of abuses in unemployment compensation.

the "ideal" employer position and it endeavored to unite all the employers in an aggressive drive to get the bills passed. It yielded reluctantly to the proposal of other employers that negotiations with labor be attempted first in the hope of arriving at an acceptable agreed bill.

Olander died in February of this year, thus completing the dissolution of the previous bargaining pattern. In the negotiations of 1949 labor was represented by the general counsels of the state Federation and the state CIO, and employers by two members of the Joint Technical Committee. None of these four was an advisory council member. The director of the agency participated for the state administration.

The negotiators reached an agreement (tentative on the side of employers) which included an increase in benefits to $27 (from $20) and an understanding that both sides would sign a joint letter to the director of the agency urging him to use stricter norms in imposing disqualifications.[24] But when this agreement was presented to the employers' Joint Executive Committee it was repudiated.

While Governor Stevenson called a meeting of all parties and urged them to reach some agreement, a subcommittee of the House Judiciary Committee commenced a series of hearings on the pending bills. These hearings marked the first time an employer member of the advisory council played a leading part in negotiations. He was the employer member who had been on the council since 1941 and who at this time was chairman of the Chamber of Commerce's social security committee. When he testified on the final day of the hearings he said he spoke for "all employers."

When the hearings ended and agreement was no closer, the governor made another and final attempt. On May 25 he called to Springfield representatives of all the labor and employer organizations, and asked them to try again. At this final meeting labor agreed to a "package" which included an increase in benefits to only $25, some tightening of the disqualification and eligibility

---

[24] The second part of the proposal is a reminder that an advisory council can have another important function besides that of influencing legislation. If administrative decisions can change as much as this agreement suggests even without a change in the law, it is important for labor and management to watch over such decisions.

provisions, and some reduction in the employer contribution rate. Employers, however, insisted on more severe disqualifications than labor was willing to grant, and this meeting also broke up without reaching agreement.

After that, there was no alternative. The legislature had to make the decision for the parties at dispute. The subcommittee of the House Judiciary Committee drafted a bill which closely approximated the "package" which labor had accepted at the final conference. The bill was enacted by the legislature without opposition by either labor or employers. But only in that negative sense could it be called an agreed bill.

The advisory council held only four meetings in connection with this legislative session, three of them before the session began. The locus of decision making was so clearly outside the council, especially after the death of Olander, that the council had relatively little reason for meeting. Neither the governor, nor the legislature, nor labor, nor management had looked to the advisory council for leadership in the 1949 controversy. The council held one meeting following the legislative session, in December, 1949, and then did not meet again until 1951, when new personalities on the council and a new task gave the council new importance.

1951. The original chairman of the council having resigned, the governor appointed in his place the owner of a small business (800 employees) who was a former president of the Illinois Manufacturers' Association. He was also an active Republican; evidently Democrat Stevenson was interested more in personal qualifications than in political affiliations. The council proceeded to elect him to the vacated post of chairman. The governor filled Olander's place on the council with Olander's successor in the post of secretary of the Illinois State Federation of Labor.

This "new" council held its first meeting February 13, 1951, and then held seven more meetings in the next two months to discuss proposed amendments to the unemployment compensation law. At the end, the council agreed on a bill which increased maximum benefits to $27 (from $25) and made some minor changes in the disqualification provisions.

This agreement was worked out primarily between the two new

members on the council. It was accepted by the majority of the council, but one employer member protested that it was a poor bargain and refused to vote on it. He was the member who had been on the council since 1941, who had been chairman of the state Chamber of Commerce's social security committee, and who had spoken in the name of "all employers" at the legislative hearings in 1949.

The employers outside the council agreed with the judgment of this protesting employer. They decided not to support the council's agreed bill but to introduce a bill of their own, which, while increasing benefits somewhat, tightened disqualification provisions considerably. The subcommittee of the Judiciary Committee seemed willing to accept the employers' bill in place of the council's bill. Labor then raised the cry of "bad faith" and accused employers of reneging on an agreement made by their official representatives on the council. Matters became so complicated at one point that the subcommittee reported out *both* bills with a favorable recommendation. The full Judiciary Committee finally took over jurisdiction from its subcommittee and held its own hearings.

The chairman of the advisory council had been out of the state but rushed back to testify at the hearings. The chairman of the Judiciary Committee tried in many indirect ways to find out whether or not there had been a genuine agreed bill. The chairman of the advisory council finally said very quietly but directly, "We both know what you are trying to get at, Mr. Chairman. Let me say plainly that this is a bill agreed upon by the employer members of the Advisory Board. There is no doubt about that."

When the hearings had ended, Governor Stevenson again called together the leaders of labor and management and urged them to work out some agreement. Each side appointed two negotiators. Of these only one, the secretary of the state Federation, was an advisory council member. The other labor negotiator was a specialist from the CIO. The two employer negotiators were active in the social security committees of the Illinois Manufacturers' Association and the state Chamber of Commerce respectively and were also members of the Joint Technical Committee. After thirteen hours of continuous negotiation, they reached an agreement which was substantially the same as the council's original agreed bill, except for a couple of minor changes that favored employers.

1953. In the fall of 1951 the administrator laid before the council the problem of long-range solvency. Illinois, like many of the other states, had been given special funds to make a thorough study of its economy and pattern of unemployment with a view to developing an appropriate long-run tax policy. As the study progressed the council reviewed its findings during fourteen meetings held between September, 1951, and April, 1953. It was during this period, when so much of the council's work was of a highly technical nature, that the employers' "second row" came into existence. That is, several representatives from the Joint Technical Committee began to attend the council meetings regularly, sitting not at the table with the council members but in a row behind them. They were there only for consultation and did not take part in the council's discussions unless called upon.

By January, 1953, the council had agreed on a bill whose provisions although described as "noncontroversial," were very important.[25] The bill revised the financial structure of the program, changed a uniform benefit year for an individual one, and made many other technical changes.

In subsequent meetings the council attempted to work out an agreed bill covering the more controversial matters of benefits and disqualifications. It became evident very early that this time there would be no division among employers. The program of the Joint Technical Committee was clearly the determining one. In the council the chief spokesman for employers was not the council's chairman, who in the previous session had held employers to an unpopular agreed bill, but the employer representative who had been on the council since 1941 and who had always been in close touch with the Joint Technical Committee.

Labor proposed a package which would increase benefits and raise the eligibility requirements somewhat. Employers considered this inadequate and decided to take their case to the legislature in an independent bill.

[25] Controversy has degrees. The matter of this final agreement had been hammered out in council meetings marked by many disputes and compromises. But the matter was not as controversial as, say, benefits or disqualifications.

There was a Republican governor (Stratton) in Springfield by this time. Labor had opposed him in his campaign, and the employers expected to find him favorably inclined to their position. But the Republican governor, like the Democratic governor, was primarily interested in an agreed bill. When it became clear that none would be forthcoming from the advisory council, the governor called leaders of labor and management into conference at Springfield. At this negotiating conference the advisory council for the first time had as many as two members present—the secretary of the state Federation and the employer spokesman, mentioned above, who worked closely with the Joint Technical Committee.

No agreement was reached at the conference. Labor then declared that the failure of the advisory council to arrive at an agreed bill obligated both sides to refrain from introducing independent bills. The employer representative denied that this arrangement existed. The governor dismissed them, urging them to meet again and work out their differences. When he called a second conference some weeks later and found that the disputants had not met in the interval, he was much annoyed. He dismissed them curtly and announced that he would take the matter into his own hands.

The employers' bills came closer to being enacted than did labor's, but in the end the legislature rejected the independent bills of both sides and enacted nothing controversial. Oddly enough, both labor and management were relieved that no legislation at all had been enacted and considered that their side had scored a relative victory.

The agreed bill (on the so-called noncontroversial amendments) met a curious fate. It was passed unanimously by both houses, as expected. Then it was vetoed by the governor! The veto message gave no reason for the action, and for months there was only puzzled speculation as to what had happened. The mystery was never entirely cleared, but the probabilities are that the veto represented a combination of confusion and annoyance in the governor's office—confusion over the difference between the agreed and the nonagreed bills and annoyance over the negative results of the governor's conference.

The incident is a striking illustration of the uncertainties attaching to the legislative process. Here was a measure which represented almost two years of intense work—probably the largest single task undertaken by the agency in its history—which was thoroughly understood by the responsible leaders of labor and management and formally approved by them, and which both houses of the legislature had passed unanimously. Yet it all came to nothing because the governor's office did not and probably could not give the necessary time even to examine the history of the measure. It is a telling sermon on the advantages of having an advisory council assist in the legislative process by means of an agreed bill.

1955. Three new faces were at the council table in 1955. The employer member who was council chairman had resigned to accept a post in the Eisenhower administration. As usual, the governor appointed his successor without consulting the employer organizations. The council for the first time elected a public member to the vacant post of chairman, a university professor who had been on the council since 1941.

Two public members had resigned. One of them, an attorney who had been on the council since 1948, was noted for his habit of asking pointed questions about the function of the public members. At a meeting shortly before he resigned he recalled good-humoredly the three legislative sessions through which he had served on the council—1949, 1951, and 1953—and how the final decision in each instance had been made by labor and management representatives meeting separately from the council. He said he could see the reasons for that procedure, but if that was to be the regular procedure he could see no reason for his attending council meetings.

The legislative session of 1955 marked the first time that the *advisory council* produced a strict and full agreed bill. The agreement, which was reached only after many meetings and only at the last moment, included some of the provisions of the ill-fated "noncontroversial" agreed bill of 1953, and in addition raised eligibility requirements, made minor changes in disqualifications, and introduced the principle of "variable maxima" into the benefit formula. This last provision varied maximum benefits in accordance not only with earnings but also with the number of dependents. Although it had been under study for some years by the agency, the explicit proposal to enact it into law came from the employer members of the advisory council. It represented a major break with precedent and was regarded with much suspicion by some employer groups outside the council.

Extremists on both sides disliked the "package" agreed upon. The employer organizations in the state eventually accepted it, but the CIO never did. The CIO declared that it had not been a party to the agreement, and in a sense this was true, because the CIO member of the advisory council had missed many council meetings in 1954 and 1955, including the meeting at which the final agreement was reached. The CIO proceeded to introduce bills in the legislature which were more liberal than the agreed bill. An open struggle ensued on the floor of the House, during which the speaker referred frequently to the fact that an "agreed bill" had been reached by labor and management on the advisory council. The CIO bills were defeated in the House and did not get out of committee in the Senate. The state Federation supported only the agreed bill, explaining to its membership afterwards:

Many bills were introduced by various legislators which were better than the agreement reached. . . . However, when agreement is made, we live up to such agreement and all other bills are sidetracked in order to enact the agreed bill.[26]

1957. An agreed bill which liberalized the benefit formula and softened one of the disqualification provisions was reached by the advisory council in this session and was enacted into law. The advisory council bill dominated the situation without serious challenge.

OTHER LABOR LEGISLATION

In Illinois labor and management have been influenced in their approach to legislation in unemployment compensation by a long experience with agreed bills in two other areas of labor legislation.

The longest experience with agreed bills has been in the regu-

[26] Report of the Executive Board, Illinois State Federation of Labor, October 10, 1955, p. 34.

lation of the mining industry.[27] In 1899 the Illinois State Bureau of Labor Statistics made a thoroughgoing study of the existing regulations, which were in a chaotic condition, and invited a joint conference of operators and miners to review its conclusions. The conferees worked out an agreed bill on the basis of the bureau's study, and the legislature passed the bill without a dissenting vote. For the next few years an informal agreement prevailed that all legislation should be jointly approved.

In 1905 and 1907 the conferees failed to reach agreement, but in 1909 the operators proposed that there be established a Mining Investigation Commission composed of three representatives each of miners, operators, and "experts," with the understanding that all proposed legislation be referred to the commission. The commission was established, and since that time nearly all coal-mining legislation in Illinois has been based on the recommendations of the commission.[28]

The other experience of labor and management with agreed bills was in workmen's compensation. The pattern was begun when Illinois enacted its first workmen's compensation law in 1911. Governor Dineen was faced with a choice between two contrary bills (an employers' liability bill and a workmen's compensation bill), both of which had been passed by the legislature. The governor vetoed the former and signed the latter on the ground that the latter was an "agreed bill" worked out by a commission of six employers and six employees who had been appointed to study the problem of industrial accidents.

Since 1915 almost all legislation in workmen's compensation has been enacted by the method of the agreed bill. Exceptions occurred in the legislative sessions of 1921 and 1923. In 1921 the agreed bill was not quite genuine; it represented only a majority vote and not a unanimous one. Because the representative of the coal operators had not agreed to the bill, the coal operators attacked the bill in the legislature and were able to force some changes in it.

[27] For a full account see Earl R. Beckner, *A History of Illinois Labor Legislation* (Chicago: University of Chicago Press, 1929), and Eugene Staley, *History of the Illinois State Federation of Labor* (Chicago: University of Chicago Press, 1930).

[28] In 1953 the functions of the commission were transferred to the state Mining Board, but the agreed bill procedure remained unchanged.

In the 1923 session labor, probably in reaction to the unpleasantness of the preceding session, abandoned the method of the agreed bill and introduced a bill of its own. Its bill passed the House but was lost in the Senate. In that year labor gained nothing. In 1925 both sides were ready to return to the method of the agreed bill and they have continued to use the method ever since.

The steps leading to an agreed bill in workmen's compensation follow a regular pattern. Labor (always) and management (sometimes) introduce independent bills early in the session. These are extreme bills with no element of compromise in them. They are referred to the proper legislative committee and simply lie there. Later in the session, about March, when both parties are ready, the industrial commissioner arranges a meeting of labor and management leaders,[29] insurance carriers, and members of the legislative subcommittee which handles workmen's compensation bills. The inclusion of the subcommittee members (all are invited to attend and the key ones actually do) seems to have come about through the insistence of the state Federation, according to the statement of R. G. Soderstrom, its president since 1930.

The practice of limiting participation in such conferences to only employers and employees was looked upon by legislators as improper and questionable procedure, and ended 22 years ago when the president of the Illinois State Federation of Labor refused to meet with the representatives of the employers, when the legislature was in session, unless the legislature also was represented in such employer-employee conference.[30]

If an agreed bill is produced by this conference, as it always has been, the earlier bills are allowed to remain buried in committee. Apparently they serve only the purpose of guns in holsters.

APPRAISAL
AGREED BILLS

The Illinois unemployment compensation law as it stood at the end of the 1957 legislative session was largely a product of agreed bills. Legislation had taken the form of an agreed bill in eight of the

[29] On management's side, the Manufacturers' Association and the mine operators provide the leadership.

[30] Illinois State Federation of Labor, *Weekly Newsletter*, December 13, 1952, p. 1.

twelve sessions between 1937 and 1957. Even in 1949, when agreement failed, the bill which the legislature eventually enacted was largely the product of the joint labor-management conferences which had immediately preceded the legislature's decision.

If one may judge from the testimony of the labor, management, and government representatives involved, the net effect of the agreed bills was good. From labor's viewpoint the resulting law was above average in liberality. Would the law have been even more liberal without the agreed bill? The CIO was certain that political methods would have produced greater benefits, at least in the long run. Except for the CIO, however, there was a general concensus—among labor, management, and government people— that the law certainly would not have been more liberal without the agreed bill and probably would have been less so.

It is true that the Illinois law was made somewhat less liberal in the postwar period, but that was part of a nation-wide trend, and the main restrictions were enacted in those years when there was no agreed bill. It is certain that in 1951 labor would have gained nothing without the agreed bill. It is likewise certain that in 1953 the agreed bill proved to be labor's best defense against threatened losses. Labor found the governor and the legislature, conditioned by a tradition of agreed bills, prepared to accept its declaration that there should be no legislation at all if labor and management could not agree.

Employers were divided in their opinion regarding the desirability of the agreed bills. Some stated their position in phrases that might have been used by the CIO: "The agreed bill has been bad for the program; issues should be settled according to principles and not by bargaining compromises." The majority, however, praised the agreed bill technique. They saw in it insurance against disorderly legislation and a contribution to peaceful labor relations. They felt that any increase in costs which the agreed bills may have caused—and they doubted that there had been any large increase— was more than offset by the accompanying benefits.

From the side of government there came the unanimous judgment that the agreed bill had been a good thing for Illinois. The attitude of the governor and the legislature is sufficiently evident in the way they repeatedly exerted pressure on labor and management to come to an agreement. The administrator of unemployment compensation counted among his chief blessings the number of times that amendment of the law was safely carried out by means of an agreed bill.

Of the factors which accounted for the success of the agreed bill in Illinois some were peculiar to labor, some were peculiar to employers, and some were common to both. On labor's side the chief factor was the influence of the Illinois State Federation of Labor. The Illinois Federation is one of the older and more effective of the state federations [31] and has always been the chief spokesman for labor in Illinois.

In the course of its history the ISFL has experimented with all the main methods of achieving labor 's legislative goals: (1) support of an independent labor party; [32] (2) alignment with one of the regular political parties; (3) support of individual candidates on the basis of "reward your friends and punish your enemies"; (4) negotiation with employers.[33] On the basis of its experience the Federation came to the conclusion that the above order represents the order of increasing effectiveness. For several decades the Federation has relied entirely on the last two methods.

The method of supporting friends and defeating enemies in politics has been interpreted by the Federation to require support of an incumbent over a challenger if both are friendly to labor. Thus in 1948 the Federation supported Republican Green, the incumbent, whose labor record had been good, against Democrat Stevenson, the challenger. When Stevenson won, the Federation found itself in the gubernatorial doghouse; it even lost, temporarily, the post of state Director of Labor to the CIO. In 1952,

[31] It was established in 1884. It has been described as "one of the (and quite likely *the*) best managed, and most influential state federations of labor in the land." Staley, *History of the Illinois State Federation of Labor*, p. 563.

[32] The Federation supported the Illinois Union Labor Party (1888), the Populist Party (1894), the Farmer-Labor Party (1920), but all of them failed dismally when put to the test of an election year.

[33] And with administrators. Staley narrates an example. For twenty-five years the Federation had worked without success to regulate the competition of convict labor by means of legislation. In 1909 it finally succeeded by means of direct negotiation. "Though none of these legislative objectives, except that pertaining to road construction, were obtained, and though the law of 1905 remained unchanged, the Federation did succeed in removing practically all just cause of complaint over convict labor competition by direct negotiation with the administrative authorities." Staley, *History of the Illinois State Federation of Labor*, p. 245.

because Stevenson's labor record had been good, the Federation supported him against Republican Stratton. Stratton won, and when he proved friendly to labor (by federation standards) the Federation gave him its support and was returned to favor over the CIO, which refused, as always, to sever its connection with the Democratic Party.

The method of direct negotiation with employers was frequently challenged in the Federation and put to the trial of debate, but it was as frequently upheld.

Edwin R. Wright, president of the Federation from 1906 to 1912, declared:

All the legislation that the State Federation has secured has been a compromise with the employers. Go as far with the employers as you can before you start fighting them. Most employers will go a long way; why start fighting them from scratch? [34]

John H. Walker, president of the Federation from 1913 to 1929, in reporting to the Federation in 1927 on "The Growing Development of Mutual Agreement between Employers and Workers on Legislative Matters," said:

These joint actions are an indication of a better spirit developing in industry . . . . legislation reached by this process is beneficial not only to the workers and the employers, but to the public as well. . . . It is my opinion that this method of solving legislative questions will be adopted more and more as time goes on.[35]

R. G. Soderstrom, president of the Federation from 1930 to the present, defended the agreed bill procedure as it applied to workmen's compensation.

The questions as to whether this method should continue is always open to debate. It is almost certain, however, that any attempt to break away from the long-established practice will, for a considerable time at least, have no other effect than to delay action by the legislature for two years and perhaps more. The procedure has worked out fairly well in the past. Under prevailing conditions State Federation conventions have recommended its continuance.[36]

[34] *Ibid.,* pp. 236–37.   [35] *Ibid.,* p. 426.
[36] Address given at conference sponsored by the Institute of Labor and Industrial Relations at the University of Illinois and printed in the Illinois State Federation of Labor's *Weekly Newsletter,* December 13, 1952.

Although the CIO has generally gone along with the agreed bills —its open opposition in 1955 was an exception—it has not done so with enthusiasm. It has argued that if the agreed bill procedure is necessary at all, it is necessary only because of a defective state constitution which does not give labor the representation in the legislature to which its numbers entitle it.[37] The CIO would like to see Illinois labor concentrate its energies on revising the constitution. The Federation agrees with the CIO that the constitution should be revised, but believes that the situation can be improved only by gradual steps. In 1954 the Federation agreed (despite CIO protests) to a compromise constitutional amendment which required that, beginning in 1956, the lower but not the upper House was to be reapportioned according to population.[38]

The personality of Victor Olander is part of the reason that the ISFL has favored the agreed bill technique. Olander was secretary of the ISFL from 1914 to 1949. His was an intelligent, vigorous, likeable personality, and he became almost a legend in Illinois labor history. His philosophy was thoroughly that of Gompers. In 1920, for example, he opposed the state Federation's alignment with the Farmer-Labor Party. In all the national conventions of the American Federation of Labor he led the opposition against any governmental program of unemployment compensation. When it was finally decided that Illinois should have an unemployment compensation law, he preferred to see its provisions determined as far as possible by negotiation with employers rather than by political pressures.

On the employers' side, also, a single personality contributed greatly to the success of the Illinois agreed bills. The influence of William J. MacPherson was paramount in unemployment compensation in Illinois during the first decade of the program. Mac-Pherson belonged to the "reasonable" school of employers, who thought that industrial relations could be managed without class conflict and without appeal to the state. A background of manual labor in his early years predisposed him to sympathy with the aims of labor, and the fact that he worked for one of the public utili-

[37] True of labor in general, this is especially true of the CIO in Illinois because most of its membership is concentrated in the big unions of Chicago.

[38] The change gave Cook county (Chicago) control of the lower House for the first time.

ties, which typically have low unemployment compensation rates, made it easier for him to follow his sympathies.

After MacPherson's death, in 1947, some change in the pattern of negotiations was to be expected. But even if he had lived, the conditions of the postwar period would have forced some modifications in the pattern, and the agreed bill would have encountered more obstacles than formerly. During the postwar period Illinois shared in the nation-wide trend of employer revolt against former leadership. The reasons for the revolt in Illinois were the common ones [39] and included, in addition, the rise of the Illinois State Chamber of Commerce. The Chamber, which was growing in size and influence, was not averse to criticizing former employer leadership and was supplied with an occasion by the general charges of abuse in the unemployment compensation program during the reconversion period. The Chamber declared that the agreed bills of the past had been made on too-easy terms and demanded sweeping "reforms." For several years the Chamber represented an independent and potentially divisive force in employer ranks.

By the end of the reconversion period, however, the employers had succeeded in establishing a new and satisfactory pattern of negotiations. It was largely built around the Joint Technical Committee and the Joint Executive Committee. Under MacPherson the Joint Technical Committee had been a rather informal organization. MacPherson simply gathered its members together for a few luncheon meetings at the time of legislative sessions—primarily to get their approval for his bargains with Olander. But after the MacPherson era the Joint Technical Committee became an organized work group, and the Joint Executive Committee became the focal point where final and effective decisions were made. Almost equally important to the employers' negotiating pattern were their two social security committees—the one in the Illinois Manufacturers' Association and the other in the state Chamber of Commerce. This hierarchy of employer organizations facilitated the reaching of agreed bills by making it easier to commit all the major employers to a given agreement.

The relatively low cost of unemployment compensation in Illi-

[39] See, for example, the chapters on Utah, Michigan, California.

nois has been an additional factor favorable to agreed bills. In the solvency study which the Illinois agency conducted in 1952 unemployment compensation costs for the decade 1951–1960 were estimated at 1.27 percent of taxable wages under the assumption of a favorable economic pattern and 2.02 percent under the assumption of an unfavorable pattern. These rates represent average or below-average costs for industrial states. This circumstance makes possible a more liberal program at a cost which does not put Illinois employers at a competitive disadvantage with employers in other states and thus facilitates employer acceptance of agreed bills.

Two factors favorable to agreed bills were common to both employees and employers. One was the tradition of agreed bills in other fields. Both employers and employees were predisposed to the use of the agreed bill in unemployment compensation by their long experience with the method in legislation governing mining (since 1909) and workmen's compensation (since 1911). The other was the operation of the "stalemate" theorem, which states that when either labor or management acts alone each finds it relatively easy to block legislation but relatively difficult to get legislation enacted. Labor and management can both recall occasions when they attempted to get legislation enacted in the face of opposition from the other party and failed: in mining (1907), in workmen's compensation (1921, 1923), in occupational disease (1936), and in unemployment compensation (1947, 1949, 1953). Employers could recall other instances in unemployment compensation when they gained little or nothing by refusing the agreed bill offered by labor and taking their case to the legislature (1936, 1949, 1951).

The theorem owes its validity primarily to a sufficiently close balance of political power existing between labor and management and secondarily to the provision of the Illinois constitution which requires that a bill must be approved by a majority of all the members of both houses. In Illinois a nonvoting legislator is as much an obstacle to the passage of a bill as is a legislator voting "nay." When applied to unemployment compensation, the theorem is strengthened by the fact that the legislators regard unemployment compensation as a "hot potato" and are reluctant to antagonize either party by taking positive action in a controversial matter.

Some find it easier to be conveniently absent—for any one of a dozen plausible, safe reasons—when the vote is taken.

The history of the Illinois advisory council is similar in several respects to that of Utah. The history of both is divided into an "old" council and a "new" council, and for both the dividing date was about the same. In the case of both, also, the old council was less effective than the new.

The old council exercised relatively little influence on legislation, including the agreed bills. The fact of the council's existence in law was an official invitation to labor and management in Illinois to strive for agreement, and the council was there to put its official stamp of approval on any agreement that was negotiated. But that was the extent of the council's influence. As long as the Olander-MacPherson team was functioning the actual negotiations were not carried on by the council. After the deaths of MacPherson (1947) and Olander (1949), a wider circle of persons participated in the negotiations, but they were still not council members.

Beginning with the 1951 session the council began to exercise direct influence on legislation, and in each session thereafter its influence increased until by 1955 the council was clearly the locus of decision making in unemployment compensation in Illinois.

The weakness of the old council was caused primarily by its lack of employer decision makers. Because the employer decision makers were not council members, they had to negotiate with labor outside the council. They were not council members because the government was unwilling to appoint them. Whether "government" in this case was primarily the governor or the administrator of the agency is uncertain, but the probability is that major responsibility lay with the governor. This much is certain: Illinois governors have as a rule refused to allow employer organizations, as they have allowed labor organizations, to select their own representatives on the advisory council.

Employer representation was stronger on the new council. In the 1951 session the council's chairman, an employer representative, exercised a decisive influence on the legislation enacted that year, but he had to put forth heroic efforts to defend the council's agreed bill against the attacks of his fellow employers outside the council. By the time of the 1953 session the likelihood of such a division among employers had been minimized; the key members of the Joint Technical Committee had begun to attend council meetings as the employers' "second row." By 1955 the likelihood of division had become still more remote because the employer who had been a council member since 1941 and who was also a member of the Joint Technical Committee clearly had become the employers' chief spokesman on the council.

Employer representation on the Illinois council could still be improved and probably would be if the governor were to adopt the practice of getting nominations from the employer organizations. The ideal panel of employer representatives might consist of one member drawn from the Joint Executive Committee, one drawn from the Joint Technical Committee, and an independent employer. One of the first two might be drawn from the Illinois Manufacturers' Association and the other from the state Chamber of Commerce. The representative of the Joint Executive Committee would have to be a full-time employee of an employer organization; the representative of the Joint Technical Committee might or might not be; the third council member would not be. This description of a balanced employer membership was received favorably by the interviewees among the employers.

Labor's representation on the advisory council has always been adequate. The Illinois State Federation of Labor has been the acknowledged leader of labor in the state, and the Federation's representative on the council has always had the power to commit the Federation to agreements. Labor's representation would be strengthened however, if it included a technician. The addition would give labor some equivalent to the employers' "second row." It would also lighten the load of the Federation's secretary, who has found it increasingly difficult to combine the demands of the growing Federation in a large state like Illinois with the demands of the advisory council, especially in years when meetings were frequent and the agenda heavy, as in 1954 and 1955.

Some of the labor representatives have been lobbyists and have proved useful to the council in that capacity. For example, at a meeting of the council which I attended in 1953, when the council wanted someone to transact a certain bit of business with a legislator (he had introduced an ambiguous bill) it readily found a labor representative who was a lobbyist to whom it could commit the task but it had to go into the "second row" to get a representative from the employers.

It is difficult to assess the importance of the public members on the advisory council. The administrator was sure that at times at least they had been a significant influence. One of the employer representatives remarked that in the 1955 negotiations the stand which the public members took induced employers to modify their position. In that session also when negotiations between labor and management seemed to be bogging down, the public members made two trips to Springfield to discuss the situation with the governor.[40]

On the whole, however, it seems safe to say that the public members rarely, if ever, played a major role in the council's history. If they did, the fact was not reflected in the council's minutes or mentioned by any of the interviewees. The experience of the public members generally has been similar to that of the lawyer member quoted above, who felt left out of important council activities.

The administrator of the agency has been a major favorable factor in the success of the advisory council. He is a strong believer in the value of an advisory council, possesses the qualities of leadership necessary to keep a good council together, has had long experience in the program,[41] and has been acceptable (at least in recent years) to both labor and management. At council meetings he has been active, but has not attempted to dominate; he has tended to talk less rather than more than the average council member.

During its first fifteen years the council always chose its chairman from among its employer members. This is sufficiently different

[40] The governor was a Republican and one of the public members was a Republican committeewoman with a record of thirty years service.

[41] He has been with the unemployment compensation program since its beginning and has been the Illinois administrator since 1942. His official title is Commissioner of the Division of Unemployment Compensation (in the Department of Labor).

from the usual pattern to invite speculation. The men chosen had the qualities which make for a good chairman, but very likely there was an additional reason. Labor probably hoped in this way to enlist more support from employers. This would have been in character for the Illinois State Federation of Labor, which has always regarded the council more as an opportunity for collective bargaining than as an instrument for pressure politics. The chairman of the Illinois council has not been a mere figurehead, as has been the case with many councils; but neither has he been as active as the chairman, for example, in Connecticut, Ohio, or New York. In Illinois, the administrator of the agency has called the meetings, for example, and arranged the agenda.

The fact that members were not compensated for attendance had no clear effect on attendance. The Illinois record was as good as that of many compensated councils, such as those of New York and Ohio. There was no strong sentiment expressed for introducing compensation, and there was some objection against it.

There are four characteristics of the Illinois council which are theoretically debatable and potentially important, but in actual practice none of them has had any perceptible effect, good or bad: (1) Confirmation of appointments to the council by the Senate. (2) Council members' custom of offering their resignations to each incoming governor. That there is danger inherent in this procedure, however, is clear from the experience of the Pennsylvania council. (3) Verbatim minutes. (4) The public nature of the council meetings. This last characteristic has made possible the employers' "second row," but the same effect could have been obtained by the designation of alternates, as is done in the Federal Advisory Council.

Part Three

EXPERIENCE WITH LONG-LIVED

ADVISORY COUNCILS

7

THE NEW YORK ADVISORY COUNCIL

THE New York council was unusually active throughout most of its long life and kept unusually full records of its activities. Participating energetically in every phase of the program, the council held 239 meetings of the full council and even more numerous meetings of council committees during the period covered by this survey (1935–1957). In addition to recording the results of its work in numerous reports to the legislature, governor, and agency, the council kept verbatim minutes of all the meetings of the full council.

The historian of the New York council is thus faced with a problem the opposite of that which faced him in the case of the Wisconsin council. Here the problem is not a paucity of records but a superabundance. As a result the historian must be unusually selective; and the warning voiced in the preface is unusually pertinent. These chapters on individual councils are not complete histories; they are selective descriptions of those traits in each council which are particularly instructive for council theory and which are not equally well illustrated by the experience of other councils.

One such trait in the New York council was its initiative and independence. Another was the prominence of a public member, the council's first chairman, who provided its leadership. In the first trait the New York council was like the Michigan council; in the second, like the Connecticut council. The combination of a very independent council under the leadership of a public member gave rise to some interesting issues of council theory. These issues are stressed in the following account, sometimes, no doubt, at the expense of a more balanced description of the council's entire life.

The council's history falls into two major periods—before and after 1949. The first period (1935–1949) coincides with the term of the council's first chairman and is itself divisible into two minor periods—before and after 1940. Before 1940 the council's activity was very effective; after 1940 its activity was that of a swimmer fighting water too rough for him. In the second major period (1949–1957) the council led a somewhat less energetic, though still active, life.

The New York council consists of nine members: three representatives each of employers, employees, and the public. They are appointed by the governor for six-year terms, which are staggered in such a way that three members come up for appointment every two years. The functions of the council are thus described in the law:

The State Advisory Council shall consider and shall advise the Commissioner upon all matters connected with this article submitted to it by the Commissioner and may recommend upon its own initiative such changes in the administration of this article as it deems necessary. It shall have full investigatory powers, and shall have direct access to all sources of information.[1]

The commissioner referred to is the industrial commissioner, the head of the Department of Labor, of which the employment security agency is a division. In practice the council's principal relationship has been with the director of the employment security division, even though the commissioner has taken a more active interest in the employment security program than the head of a labor department usually does in a large industrial state.

The 239 meetings of the full council were distributed as follows:

1935	8	1940	12	1945	12	1950	9	1955	12
1936	11	1941	11	1946	8	1951	8	1956	13
1937	12	1942	15	1947	9	1952	6	1957	12
1938	15	1943	10	1948	7	1953	9		
1939	13	1944	9	1949	10	1954	8		

There has been some tendency for meetings to cluster around legislative sessions, but not to the same extent as in Wisconsin, for example. In New York the legislature meets every year and the advisory council is always either just completing a legislative session or preparing for the next one.

[1] New York State Unemployment Insurance Law, 1955, Sec. 533.2.

The council averaged 10.4 meetings per year over the entire period. This is the third highest average of all the councils in the sample. There was no significant difference between the first and second major periods. For the period 1935–1949 the council averaged 10.8 meetings per year, and for the period 1950–1957 it averaged 9.6 meetings per year.

The council's attendance record for the entire period was 75 percent. The record of the public members was 84 percent; of the labor members, 72 percent; and of the management members, 69 percent. As usual certain members were absent frequently, while others rarely missed. The first chairman, for example, missed only four meetings in his fourteen years of service (1935–1949).

The council drew up rules of procedure as early as November, 1935. They are given in Appendix B as an example of a very full set of rules. Because they were so early and so full they served as a model for several other states in drawing up their own rules.

The rules of procedure provide for council committees, and several committees functioned effectively. The council was able to act with as much independence as it did partly because it worked through committees, which could meet more often and do more work than could the council operating as a whole. The Committee on Amendments, consisting of the chairman and one labor and one management member,[2] was especially active and important. It was this committee which carried the heavy burden of working out an annual legislative program.

ACTIVITIES OF THE COUNCIL

When New York established its advisory council for unemployment compensation in 1935, an advisory council for the employment service was already in existence. The latter continued to function in its own field, but became less and less active as the depression lightened and ceased to function entirely when the employment service was taken over by the federal government during the war. When the employment service was returned in 1946, it was integrated with unemployment compensation. Its advisory council

[2] Expanded at a later date to include an additional labor and employer member.

was not reestablished, but the functions of the unemployment compensation advisory council were expanded to include the employment service. This council gave more attention than did the average council to the employment service,[3] but like all the other councils it regularly gave by far the greater part of its attention to unemployment compensation.

1935–1939

The council was in operation from the very beginning of the program. It started to work before the telephones were installed and even before the director was appointed. During the first months of the program its work was unusually heavy and unusually influential.[4] It prepared a pamphlet explaining the law, wrote a seasonality provision to be added to the law, struggled with the definition of wages for tax purposes, and made a recommendation on how often employers should be required to report their payrolls.[5]

The council was able to carry on such activities because its membership included some of the few persons who understood the technicalities of the program at that early date. Two of its members had belonged to the group which drafted the original law.[6] One of these was the president of the New York State Federation of Labor, George Meany. The other was a public member, who became the council's first chairman and its most active member until he was replaced in 1949.

Governor Lehman accepted all but one of the council's recommendations for 1936 and all for 1937. Early in 1938 he stated pub-

[3] For example, the council made an early noteworthy contribution by the preparation of its *Manual on the Placement of Minority Groups.*

[4] See the similar experience of other early councils: California, Connecticut, Illinois, Massachusetts, Minnesota, Ohio.

[5] In connection with this recommendation, there occurred a misuse of the council by the agency that is fairly common in advisory council history. The director of the agency told the newspapers that the system selected by the agency for payroll reporting "has been presented to and has the general approval of the Unemployment Insurance State Advisory Council composed of representative employers, employees, and the public." The vote in the council on this matter had been six to three, with all the employer members voting against it. The three employer members wrote a letter to the newspapers protesting this misleading statement.

[6] A group which included no representatives of employer organizations.

licly that he wished to have the council's judgment on any proposed amendment before he presented it to the legislature.

Payment of benefits in New York began in 1938, and the difficulties then encountered furnished the council with an opportunity to establish itself as a major influence. Owing largely to the initiative and energy of its chairman, the council made full use of the opportunity. Early in that year the chairman had spurred the council to begin studying ways of simplifying the tax and benefit procedures.[7] He felt uneasy about the ability of the agency to handle the impact of the first flood of claims. His fears were justified. The administrative machinery proved inadequate from the start, and a multitude of errors and delays occurred.[8] When a wave of public protest arose, the governor issued a statement in June, 1938, assuring the public that his advisory council was looking into the matter. This was the first the council knew of it, but shortly thereafter the governor sent a letter to the chairman, formally requesting the council to conduct an investigation. The letter concluded: "I think no group is better equipped to study the situation." After that public pronouncement the governor could not but support the advisory council's findings.

The legislature appointed an investigating committee of its own. This (Burney) committee soon found itself in difficult technical waters, and since it could not call for assistance on the agency, which was being investigated, it came to rely heavily on the council, especially on the chairman.

In the fall of 1938 Governor Lehman, anticipating the results of the investigations, appointed a new director to the agency. The new director had been selected by the industrial commissioner, who happened also to be new. At the first meeting of the council with these two officials (November, 1938) a pattern of conflict was established which persisted for years. The chairman of the council began the meeting by stating the council's dissatisfaction with the way the new director had been selected. When later in the meeting the industrial commissioner broached the subject of a legislative program

[7] The other members of the council had been willing to wait until there was some experience under the current law.

[8] A not uncommon experience in states which began the payment of benefits early; see, for example, Massachusetts, p. 211.

for 1939, the chairman immediately detailed the steps he had already taken in that direction [9] and made it clear that the council intended to retain the initiative it had been exercising. In view of the disturbed state of the agency, the newness of the commissioner and the director, and the mandate given to the council by the governor, this attitude of the council was eminently sensible at the time.

In the meeting of January, 1939, the chairman quoted a recent editorial in the New York *World-Telegram* to the effect that no legislation should be enacted in unemployment compensation until the advisory council had completed its investigation and made its recommendations. But in March, 1939, the agency, acting independently of the council, introduced some bills into the legislature. The council agreed that its chairman should notify the leaders of the legislature that these were not the council's bills and that the council was preparing its own recommendations. In the upshot the Burney Committee accepted the council's recommendations in their entirety and made them its own. The legislature then enacted them into law by the unanimous vote of both houses. This 1939 legislation marked the high point of the council's influence.

Some of the amendments enacted in 1939 directly affected the advisory council. The Burney Committee was evidently impressed by the role the council had played in policing the previous administration and seemed inclined to cast the council permanently in some such role. The thinking of the committee is clear in the following:

The Advisory Council has disagreed with the Division on certain major questions of policy and of personnel, and has been ignored by it in others.

Various possible remedies for the above situation suggest themselves; better co-operation between the Division and the Council by voluntary action; more explicit provision in the statute for frequent periodical reporting by the Advisory Council directly to the Legislature; giving to the Council by statute effective power in whatever degree may be deemed advisable, from the right to pass on all proposals for major changes in policy or personnel but without veto power thereon to being the executive head of the Division. . . .

[9] At this point a labor member protested against so much individual action on the part of the chairman and reminded him that the Committee on Amendments existed.

It may be well, this year, to go no farther than providing the Council with adequate staff of its own, a reasonable per diem compensation, and more clearly reciting in the act its power to initiate recommendations, and to make investigations, its duty to report periodically to the Legislature, and requiring the Commissioner to consult the Council on all major matters but without giving it veto power thereon.[10]

The recommendations of the last paragraph were carried out by amendments to the law. One amendment provided that the industrial commissioner "shall, in so far as practicable, consult the State advisory council on all matters of major policies and procedures involved in or connected with the administration of this article and he shall inform the council of the action taken in connection with such matters." [11] This amendment had the effect of emphasizing but not necessarily enlarging the council's functions.

Another amendment provided compensation for council members "for each day spent in attendance at meetings or otherwise in the work of the council." [12] The per diem rate was set at a standard rate paid all such state bodies in New York and was raised from time to time as the standard was raised. In 1957 the rate was $40. No ceiling was set on the amount that might be paid to council members in any one year.[13] These three characteristics of the New York provision—a relatively high per diem rate, availability of compensation for committee work, and no annual ceiling—make the New York law the most adequate of the state laws in point of council remuneration.

Still another amendment gave the advisory council the right to have its own staff.

The advisory council may select and nominate an executive secretary and research assistant to aid the council in the performance of its functions, and the commissioner shall appoint the persons so nominated. If the council so recommends, such employees shall be ap-

[10] Legislative Document No. 91 (1939), pp. 38–39.

[11] New York State Unemployment Insurance Law, 1955, Sec. 533.2.

[12] New York State Unemployment Insurance Law, 1955, Sec. 533.1. The broad phrase "or otherwise in the work of the council" was early limited by interpretation of the Bureau of Employment Security to cover only days "on which the member was in attendance at a scheduled meeting of the council itself or a scheduled meeting of a duly appointed committee thereof."

[13] In point of fact, the average council member in the average year received only about $300 during the period covered by this survey.

pointed in the exempt class of the civil service and they shall be removed and replaced by the commissioner at the request of the council. Said employees shall receive such compensation as may be fixed by the council.[14]

This provision the industrial commissioner was reluctant to carry out. At the council meeting of March 9, 1939, she argued against it on the grounds that it indicated distrust of the agency by the council, that the proposed staff of two persons could not do the necessary research work anyway, and that the council would get better service by using the staff already existing in the agency.

The council replied that it did not intend to use its staff to supplant the research work of the agency; the staff would only interpret the agency's work for the council. Without such help, the council said, it could not keep abreast of the agency's plans as they developed; and if it did not keep abreast it would inevitably find itself in the position of having to give a quick vote of approval to complex plans which it did not understand because they were presented to the council only at the end of a long period of work by agency technicians. In brief, the council needed its own staff to avoid becoming a rubber-stamp.

To explain this point one of the employer members, Mr. Marion Folsom, offered the following illustration:

For example, look at the position you put the Council in by this merit rating report. You gave it to us about two days before we had a meeting on it. And we had to take a position on that thing. It put us in an almost impossible position. The way I got out of it, I turned it over to a person who knew as much about it as the person who prepared the report, and he told me the report was unfair and biassed, and I was able to take a position. . . . I am probably a little better situated than the rest of them [the other council members] because I have not only studied the thing for years, but I have two or three economists in my organization who have studied this and can advise me on the subject. I can turn over a report to one of them, and he brings up to me in two or three days quite a few questions, questions on the whole thing; gives me the background, and so forth. That is exactly the kind of functions we contemplate [for the council staff].

This statement contains a clear illustration of the problem which plagues all advisory councils—how to pass judgment on matters that involve technical considerations. It also contains an indication

[14] New York State Unemployment Insurance Law, 1955, Sec. 533.3.

that the problem is usually greater for labor and public members than for employer members.

The council did get its two staff members towards the end of 1939. The executive secretary was a lawyer, who could draft bills and follow legislative developments, and the research assistant was a combination economist and statistician. The council did not keep them long. The war took first one and then the other. After the war various compromises were arranged at different times, but the council never again had two full-time professional people. After the war its usual complement was a typist, a recording secretary, and an executive secretary. Since at least 1949, however, the executive secretary has belonged primarily to the agency and has spent most of his time on regular agency work.

Relations with the New Administrators

Even before the 1939 amendments, the council had been accustomed through its chairman to call its own meetings, arrange its own agenda, initiate proposals for extensive changes in the law, and on occasion to meet in executive sessions from which the director of the agency was barred. The events of the 1939 legislative session all conspired to increase both the inclination and the ability of the council to act with independent initiative. The responsibility placed on the council by the Burney Committee, and even the language used by the committee, would naturally have led the council to see itself as a very active, independent, even controlling body in relation to the agency. The provision of staff (and to a lesser extent the provision of compensation) increased the ability of the council to fill such a role.

The new administrators were unwilling to concede to the council as much initiative and control as the council thought it ought to have, and friction developed from the beginning. The chairman continued the practice of calling executive sessions from which the industrial commissioner and the director of the agency were excluded. The new commissioner protested against this practice to the governor, who remonstrated with the council; the result was that Rule 13 was added to the council's rules of procedure.[15]

The commissioner retaliated on the council in the most effective

[15] See Appendix B.

manner possible. In the spring of 1940 she announced to the council that she was inviting representatives from labor and management to meet with her to develop a legislative program for 1941. To the council's pained question, "Why not us?" she gave a vague answer about there being need for "wider representation." She proceeded to invite twelve labor and twelve management representatives, who selected from among themselves a working group of half that number. Only one council member, a labor representative, was included among the twenty-four invitees.

The commissioner held many meetings with this group in the course of which the group apparently worked out an agreed bill. Then at what was expected to be the last meeting in the fall of 1940, an employer representative unexpectedly announced that the employer organization he represented would not support the agreement unless it included a provision for experience rating. The labor representatives were furious. They said they thought they had been dealing with employer representatives who were able to bind their people to an agreement; the labor representatives had made concessions in the course of the negotiations which could be used against labor in the legislature.

The employer representatives had no adequate answer. Either they had not understood the nature of the negotiations (that is what they said) or they had not brought their organizations along with them as the work of the meetings progressed (this seems more likely). The group broke up in bitterness and did not meet again.

The commissioner salvaged some planks of the "agreement" and had them introduced as administration bills in the legislative session of 1941. The majority of the council opposed these measures and again, as in 1939, apprised legislative leaders of their opposition. Shortly afterward the council presented its own program to the legislature and succeeded in having the legislature adopt a part of it. The council had survived the commissioner's attempt to freeze it out, but only by the narrowest of margins, and the position of dominance it had held in the 1939 session was obviously weakened. The council never regained that dominant position. The main reason, discussed later, was its failure to achieve agreement, but there was also another factor at work. As the program grew beyond the

1939–1940 period of reorganization, the agency became increasingly the center of technical competence and therefore of influence. The council, even with its own staff and even with an unusually active chairman,[16] could not supervise in detail, and still less lead, the planning activities of the agency—not in the state with the largest population, and especially not in a state whose legislature met every year. For example, in March, 1940, while the council was completely engrossed with the legislative session then in progress, the director of the agency announced to the council that the agency's legislative program for the next year, 1941, was already well advanced. Even working at its best, the council could only follow, not lead, such a pace and the council did not always work at its best. In January of 1941 the chairman outlined an ambitious program of work for the coming year and warned that to finish it the council would have to meet at least twice monthly. The council met less than half that often in 1941, and a key labor representative, the secretary of the state Federation, missed nearly all the meetings.

The dispute between the council and the agency was given its most formal expression in the council's annual report for 1942. In the course of analyzing its own functions, the council laid down this principle:

In dealing with problems of administration, the Council should depend largely upon the administrators; in dealing with the broader issues of policy at stake, the administrators should depend largely upon the Council.[17]

In reply the director of the agency wrote:

We cannot agree with the conclusion in their report that "in dealing with the broader issues of policy at stake the administrators should depend largely on the council". . . . It is highly questionable as to whether an advisory group designated as such should ever exercise complete or even partial *control* over the policies to be administered by the Industrial Commissioner.[18]

[16] The governor once offered to compensate him for his great expenditure of time by putting him on a salary; he declined.

[17] See n. 47 of this chapter.

[18] From a report to the industrial commissioner by the director of the Division of Placement and Unemployment Insurance, January 18, 1943.

This dispute of principle was never settled as formally as it was stated. In practice the council continued to attempt, with only partial success, to restrain the director of the agency from acting independently of the council in setting policy.

Inability to Agree

An essential factor in the council's effectiveness in 1939 had been the unanimity of its recommendations. The unanimity had not come easily. It had nearly split on the rock of experience rating. In the original law labor had been able to have the decision on experience rating postponed by relegating it to "further study." This had been the easier because employer organizations had no direct part in drawing up the original law. New York employers, like those of Pennsylvania, had confined their activity to opposing any kind of unemployment insurance law and as a result had no share in determining the provisions of the law that was finally enacted.[19] But with each passing year employers grew more dissatisfied over the lack of an experience-rating provision in the law and more insistent that one be enacted.

George Meany, the chief spokesman for labor on the council, never took the position that experience rating was a matter of principle in the sense that it was not negotiable. He kept the door open to a possible agreement. In the meeting of March 23, 1939, he demanded only that employers should not introduce an experience-rating bill *at that time*. He argued that even if he himself agreed to experience rating on the council, he could not quickly persuade the unions throughout the state to accept it. An educational process would be needed for that. At the meeting of February 20, 1939, he argued:

We have avoided making any divided report to the Legislature and I came in here two or three weeks ago and reported that my people had a number of suggestions to liberalize the law and that I had told them that as long as we work through the council none of those suggestions would go to the Legislature, that we would not put any of those suggestions into the Legislature but in this council; they wouldn't go to the Legislature from this council unless they had the unanimous approval of the council. I told them the reason I had

[19] For the effect of the New York experience on Illinois employers, see p. 149.

done that was that up to the present the council had never submitted two reports or a divided report to the Legislature. Now I also
explained that to assemblyman Burney and Senator Pitcher and Mr.
Penney when I talked to them.

At the council meeting which concluded the 1939 negotiations
and at which the provisions of the agreed bill were settled, Meany
accepted the promise of the employer members that they themselves would not support any experience-rating bill that might be
introduced, even though they could not promise that other employers would not introduce such a bill.

Some employer organizations did, as a matter of fact, introduce
a bill in the 1939 session and succeeded in getting it passed.[20] However, Governor Lehman vetoed the bill at labor's request. This
might be taken as an instance of employers overestimating the
strength of their position. Meany had warned them that they could
not push the bill through against labor's opposition and had coun-
seled compromise.

1939–1942

The period 1939–1942 was a period of transition for the council.
At the end of 1939 the council was clearly an essential part of the
decision-making process. At the end of 1942 it clearly was not. One
minor contributing cause of the decline was continued friction
with the agency, but by far the chief cause was the council's inability to reach agreed bills, and the chief obstacle to reaching
agreement was the issue of experience rating. Had George Meany
remained on the council after 1940 the chance of reaching agreed
bills would have been better. As the quotation above reveals, Meany
had a clear appreciation of the nature and advantages of agreed
bills. On a number of occasions he pleaded with the members not
to go outside the council for the things they wanted and warned
against the danger of making unemployment compensation a "political football." He expressed displeasure that the agency had given
its bills only to Democrats to introduce. The council's custom, he
explained, was to give its bills simultaneously to the leaders of both

[20] The Young-Demo Bill passed the Senate 32 to 14 and the Assembly 93 to 51.

parties. According to some employers (not on the council) Meany
had agreed in the course of private meetings held during the summer and fall of 1939, after Lehman's veto, to work out an acceptable
compromise experience-rating bill in the next legislative session.
The council lost Meany's strong leadership, however, in January,
1940, when he went to Washington to become Secretary of the
American Federation of Labor.[21] In later years other members of
the council would on occasion remind the labor members, especially the newly added CIO representative, of Meany's esteem for
the ideal of the agreed bill.

After Meany's departure the difference on the council over experience rating deepened into a deadlock. The labor members
wanted some liberalization of benefits. The employer members were
willing to support labor in this demand only if labor would support employers in getting an experience-rating provision. When
labor refused, a stalemate ensued which was never resolved by the
council. The labor members were bolstered in their position by
the chairman, who declared that he had to oppose experience rating
on principle and could never consent to any bargain that included
it. If labor seemed even tempted to bargain, he intervened. On one
occasion an employer member expostulated, "Why not let labor
speak for itself?" With both labor and management wanting
changes in the law and with no apparent possibility of getting the
changes through council agreement, the separate representatives
inevitably took themselves elsewhere.

1942–1946

"Elsewhere" was chiefly the Joint Legislative Committee on Industrial and Labor Conditions, commonly known as the Ives Committee. Composed of members from both parties and both houses,
with assemblyman Irving Ives, then majority leader, as its chairman,
it began to operate in 1939. For the first three years of its existence it
tended to leave unemployment compensation legislation in the
hands of those who had previously been active in it—the Burney

[21] At this time the secretary of the state CIO replaced one of the Federation members
on the council. Meany had previously approved of the change, and even advised it, in
order to strengthen the council. For a very different reaction of a state Federation
president, see p. 263.

Committee, the industrial commissioner and her labor-management group, the advisory council. But in 1942 it took the reins into its own hands, and from 1942 to 1946 all major unemployment compensation legislation came out of the Ives Committee.

A striking feature of the Ives Committee was its "rule of unanimity." Ives laid down the rule from the start that no legislation would come out of his committee unless it was approved by all the members. Here labor and management groups had to do perforce what they refused to do voluntarily in the advisory council—accept a compromise bill.

The success of Ives's rule of unanimity was due partly to Ives himself. Ives was an unusual combination of arbitrator and mediator. His political power as majority leader and committee chairman made him a potential arbitrator. His personal inclinations, including his belief that reasonable men could usually come to an agreement, made him by preference a mediator.[22]

But Ives's success was due also to a political situation that favored compromise. The governor and the legislature were Republican, and therefore labor leaders could not expect to get their way entirely; but both governor and legislature were sensitive to labor's demands, and therefore employers also were limited. The governor (Dewey) was especially sensitive because during an entire decade (1940–1950) he was running for office (either the governorship or the presidency) every other year,[23] and in the intervening years he was preparing the "record" on which to campaign.

The situation in the legislature favored compromise because the legislature was divided into three groups: the extreme liberals, mostly big-city Democrats; the extreme conservatives, typically upstate Republicans; and a middle group, composed of some Democrats but consisting mostly of liberal Republicans with important labor constituencies. Neither of the extreme groups was large enough to enact legislation without the support of the middle group. It was this strategic position, in combination with his personal qualities of leadership, which enabled Ives to make his "rule of unanimity" effective.

[22] Ives's convictions on labor-management relations come out clearly in his booklet, *Voluntary Procedures and Process in Labor-Management Relations* (New York: Industry Council Association, Inc., no date).

[23] 1940, 1942, 1944, 1946, 1948, 1950.

The working of the Ives Committee is best illustrated by the legislative sessions of 1942 and 1945. (In the sessions of 1943, 1944, and 1946—after which Ives left New York for Washington—only minor amendments to the law were enacted.) In 1942, with Dewey trying to displace Lehman as governor, there was keen competition for labor's support. Unemployment compensation was certain to be liberalized—because of economic conditions and because the federal government was threatening to take that step itself—and both candidates advocated liberalization. The only question was: How much? The Ives Committee drafted a liberal bill (considerably more liberal that that which the majority of the advisory council had been willing to recommend), which included an extension of duration of benefits from thirteen to sixteen weeks. Then Ives heard that Governor Lehman had prepared a bill which would increase duration to twenty weeks. Ives phoned the printer and had his own bill changed to read twenty weeks.[24]

In 1945 an influential group of employers were insistent that the law be amended to provide for an experience-rating system, and that the system be of the charge-back type. This was the type most objectionable to labor. It was also objectionable to high-cost industries, which regularly drew out of the unemployment compensation fund more than they contributed.[25] The Republican leadership did not think that such an amendment could be enacted but agreed, under heavy pressure, to let the employers make the attempt. The governor, however, would not promise to crack the party whip.[26] The employers' bill was defeated by a close vote, as the leadership had expected it would be. Five minutes later a compromise bill, which provided for a much-watered-down type of experience rating, was introduced by Ives and passed unanimously. This compromise had been devised by the agency in conjunction with the

[24] The chairman of the advisory council publicly criticized this kind of political maneuvering; it was no substitute, he said, for an intelligent development of the unemployment compensation program.

[25] This was the case, for example, with the apparel industry, which was the largest industrial division in the state, accounting for about 10 percent of all covered employment.

[26] According to some employer lobbyists, the governor at first agreed to remain neutral and sign any bill which the legislature passed. But on the day of the final vote the governor yielded to the persuasions of the New York State Federation of Labor and sent word down the line that the bill was to be defeated.

council's chairman and labor members, had been approved by the labor and public members of the council, and had been accepted by Ives as a bill for which he could hope to get the unanimous vote of his committee. The general group of employers had had no share in contriving this compromise, and it left them acutely dissatisfied. They were to continue, throughout the period covered by this survey, to demand a "genuine," that is a charge-back, system of experience rating.

During the years that Ives dominated unemployment insurance he kept in touch with the council, but it is not easy to determine the extent to which he was influenced by it. Some members of the council certainly were influential with the committee in their individual capacities. The executive secretary of the council was at the same time the actuary of the agency and did all the actuarial work for the Ives Committee; he also served as a liaison agent between the committee and the council, keeping each group fully informed of what was being done by the other. The labor members of the council were the authentic spokesmen and chief decision makers for their side. They were certainly listened to by the Department of Labor ("their" department) and by the Ives Committee. But it is likely that they would have been given very nearly the same attention even if they had not been council members. The employer members of the council also had some influence with the committee, although they were not the leaders for their side to the same extent as were the labor members for the labor side. The employer counterparts of the labor spokesmen were outside the council. The chairman of the council continued to be very active during this period. His position on the experience-rating issue was that of labor's, and both morally and technically he probably was a strong support to labor. Since the influence of organized labor was considerable in the Department of Labor, in which employment security was a division, the influence of the council chairman exerted through the labor members may have been very significant.[27]

According to the council's executive secretary, who certainly was

[27] Again it is difficult to say to what extent this type of influence was dependent on his being a council member. After leaving the council he became the official adviser of the CIO in unemployment insurance matters and in all probability continued to exert considerable influence on legislation in this capacity.

in a position to know, "the discussions in the Advisory Council and the thinking of the Ives Committee were closely coordinated" and "the Ives Committee would not consider any legislation that did not have the advance approval of a majority of the Advisory Council." [28] Granted that it is very difficult to trace and evaluate the separate strands of influence that go into the making of a law, this observer can only record as his opinion, based on interviews with all the labor, management, and government persons who were most active during the period, that what influence the council members exerted they exerted not so much as a body but as individuals—in the way and for the reasons just indicated.

During this period the relations between council and agency improved substantially—partly because a new industrial commissioner was appointed—but occasions of friction continued to occur more frequently than in any other council encountered in this sample. The disputes usually involved a question of principle as to the proper amount of dependence or independence each should have in relation to the other. During the 1945 legislative session friction reached a kind of climax which is recorded in the council chairman's report to the council (April 5, 1945) concerning certain bills which the agency had caused to be introduced: "We had considered them in Council and had voted to oppose them. Nevertheless, I found that Mr. Loysen [the director of the agency] was pressing those bills for passage, and I found myself in a very unpleasant and very unwholesome position of having to go to the legislature to lobby in order to defeat those bills." [29]

The chairman also reprimanded the director for accepting invitations in 1945 to speak before employer groups who were interested in securing a charge-back experience-rating system. This 1945 conflict eventuated in an assurance by the industrial commissioner that the director would always present his proposals to the council before acting on them or even before bringing them to the commissioner.

[28] Letter of the executive secretary to the author, March 20, 1958.
[29] Quoted in "Commentary on Bill on Advisory Council" (S. Intro. 2156, Print No. 2296), written by a consultant to the Hughes Committee and dated November 26, 1954.

1946–1949

Ives left New York for the United States Senate in 1946. The departure of Ives did not result in the advisory council's recovering its former influence. During this period, between the departure of Ives and the rise of the Hughes Committee, control was more diffused but was probably exercised chiefly out of the governor's office. The director of the agency was very active during this period and worked closely with the governor's office. He was in touch also with the employer groups outside the advisory council who in 1947 succeeded in again amending the law to give the experience-rating system more of a charge-back quality.[30]

Relations between the advisory council and the agency were on the whole good. The two cooperated on some excellent work in the fields of both unemployment insurance and the employment service. Still, occasions continued to arise when the chairman felt constrained to criticize the agency for acting with undue independence of the council. In 1947 the chairman lodged an especially sharp complaint against the head of the agency's planning unit, who, while serving as adviser to the Joint Legislative Committee on Industrial Conditions and Labor, brought proposals to the committee which the advisory council had rejected or been unable to agree on. In other meetings the chairman voiced complaints against the agency's director, charging that he did not keep the council informed of the agency's planning activities and that he acted with too much independence.

As before, the council was unable to exercise control over legislation because it was unable to reach agreement on the issue of experience rating. The council's ability to reach agreed bills was further weakened during this period by the conservative swing which was making itself felt throughout the country and which was intensified in New York by a vigorous campaign conducted by employers against alleged abuses in the payment of unemployment benefits.[31] The movement for "reform" brought with it demands

[30] It gave a weight of about 50 percent to the factor of benefit wages charged against the accounts of individual employers.

[31] The campaign induced Governor Dewey (1948) to appoint a committee under the chairmanship of Thomas L. Evans to investigate the charges. The Evans report,

for changes in the law which were so unacceptable to the council's chairman and labor members that agreement became impossible.

If labor had rightly interpreted the handwriting on the wall, it might have secured a better bargain for itself. In 1947, for example, when employers won their legislative victory, employers had earlier offered labor a better package in exchange for labor's support than the one which labor ultimately had to accept from the legislature.

During this period the effectiveness of the employer members of the council continued to decline. All three were original members,[32] but with the passage of time they had become less representative of the real decision makers among New York employers. None was the leader of any of the employers' social security committees, none was a lobbyist, and none had any official connection with employer organizations. The one who was potentially the most effective was so busy with assignments in Washington during the war and afterwards that he was able to attend less than half the council meetings held after 1943. The effectiveness of all three members was diminished to some extent by their being identified with the period preceding the conservative swing, when employers had been less successful in achieving their goals.[33] By the end of this period two of the employer representatives were ready to resign and did so.[34]

The first chairman of the council also left the council at the end of this period. When his second term expired, in 1947, he was invited to resign and accept a letter of commendation. He refused, partly because of the way another public member, who had served long and faithfully on the council, had been separated from the council without a letter of commendation. The governor finally replaced him in the spring of 1949, without a letter of commendation. His departure from the council marked the close of an era.

---

completed in 1950, never got further than the governor's office—some say because its strictures were so severe that they would have reflected on the previous five years of the Dewey administration.

[32] One was not an original member in the strictest sense of the term. He came on the council a few months after its inception.

[33] This was a common enough fate. See, for example, the Illinois and Utah councils.

[34] One in 1949 and the other the following year.

1949–1955

A new era was opened by the establishment of the Hughes Committee and by the appointment of a new council chairman, both in 1949. The Hughes Committee was a joint legislative committee [35] deputed to make a "thorough and comprehensive investigation of the administration of the unemployment insurance law, and of all matters and things whatsoever connected with and relating thereto." The committee subsequently became, for good or evil, one of the major landmarks in the history of the New York unemployment compensation law.

In 1950, before the Hughes Committee got into high gear, the new chairman of the advisory council invited a group of three labor and four management people to meet with him and attempt to work out an agreed bill for 1951. The three labor representatives were the labor members on the advisory council; everybody agreed that they were best qualified to speak for New York labor. They were the secretary of the state Federation, the secretary of the state CIO, and the secretary of the I.L.G.W.U. The management representatives consisted of the one employer member left on the advisory council and three others. The three additional members were: the general manager of the Associated Industries and the respective chairmen of the social security committees of the state chamber of commerce and the New York city chamber.[36] The selection of these men indicated where the real influence among employers was in the immediately preceding years.

No one from the agency was an official member of the negotiating group, but top agency personnel participated in most of the group's meetings and wielded considerable influence. The absence of public representatives other than the council chairman made the group similar to the New Hampshire advisory council.

These negotiators held a number of meetings in November and December of 1950. The course followed by the meetings of this 1950 labor-management conference bore a striking resemblance to

[35] Its official title was the Joint Legislative Committee on Unemployment Insurance.
[36] The official titles of these latter two organizations were, respectively, the Empire State Association of Commerce and the Commerce and Industry Association of New York.

that followed by the 1940 conference. The conferees made what seemed to be steady progress and by the end of December had established what seemed to the chairman to be an area of agreement. The chairman arranged for a final meeting to be held in Albany at which he hoped the conferees would "tie up the package" and present it to the governor. The three noncouncil employers arrived late and opened the meeting by declaring that the proposed "package" was unacceptable. They had met the day before with the New York State Conference on Unemployment Insurance [37] and had been told that no agreement would be acceptable that did not include a genuine charge-back system of experience rating. When this demand was refused by the labor representatives, the chairman adjourned the meeting as having no further purpose.

The labor representatives were surprised and chagrined by the sudden turn of events.[38] A part of the explanation was undoubtedly to be found in the Hughes Committee. One of the employers had been working simultaneously as a consultant to the Hughes Committee. When he found the committee willing to accept more of the employers' program than the labor representatives on the conference had accepted, he and his associates simply elected the way of politics over the way of collective bargaining—as labor had done in the days of the Ives Committee.

The chairman of the advisory council entered a protest. He went to the chairman of the legislative committee and told him that his labor-management group had almost completed an agreement. The legislative chairman replied that the norm of his committee was not what labor and management were willing to agree to but what the program required. Labor would never agree, he believed, to the kind of reforms which the committee considered necessary to put the program on a sound basis.

It was for this reason, no doubt, that labor leaders were entirely excluded from the committee's deliberations.[39] The exclusion fur-

[37] See below, n. 53.

[38] One of them, the I.L.G.W.U. representative, had participated in the 1940 debacle, and he particularly resented its repetition.

[39] However, the Hughes Committee did retain as its legal counsel a prominent upstate labor lawyer, who was present at all the committee's deliberations, including executive sessions.

ther deepened the resentment of the labor representatives. What they did not know was that the management representatives were kept almost equally in the dark regarding the committee's intentions. The management representatives were chagrined when the bill finally came out of the Hughes Committee and they saw the modifications which had been made in the employers' original program. As one technician who worked with the Hughes Committee remarked: "Labor, though unseen, was present at all the committee's meetings."

The Hughes Committee eventually reported out the Hughes-Brees Bill, which was passed by substantial majorities in both houses and signed by Governor Dewey early in 1951.[40] The industrial commissioner's report for 1951 described the Hughes-Brees Act as the "complete reorganization of a law basically unchanged since 1936." [41]

Labor reacted violently to the passage of the Hughes-Brees Bill. The I.L.G.W.U. representative on the advisory council, who had been a member for almost a dozen years, sent a strong letter to Governor Dewey resigning and giving as his reason the governor's approval of the Hughes-Brees Bill. Organized labor declared it would defeat the two authors of the act in the next election and worked extremely hard to that end.[42] In its 1951 convention the New York State Federation of Labor denounced the Hughes-Brees Act and, breaking a long-standing relationship of cooperative neu-

[40] Governor Dewey abstained from taking any active part in the legislation, merely stating that he would sign any bill that passed. Labor's strategy to keep Dewey neutral faltered once when the state CIO president issued a press release attacking the governor for the progress of the Hughes-Brees Bill. A few hours later at a press conference Dewey was asked for his opinion of the bill, and for the first time he expressed hearty approval of it.

[41] The fixed-benefit year was replaced by an individual benefit year, and the base year was made the fifty-two weeks immediately preceding the benefit year. In the computation of each employer's experience rating the factor of benefits paid was given more weight. Employers were to receive weekly notices of the charges made against their accounts. The solvency of the fund was better protected. Although the maximum benefit was increased from $26 to $30, the eligibility requirements were also raised (to twenty weeks of employment at a wage of at least $15 per week). The benefit rate was based on average weekly earnings, and request reporting was permitted to most employers. No changes were made in the disqualification provisions, much to the employers' chagrin.

[42] Unsuccessfully, however. Both Hughes and Brees were reelected by larger majorities than previously.

trality with the Republican Party, declared official war on the Dewey administration. Most striking testimony to the feeling aroused— the state Federation and the state CIO campaigned jointly against the Hughes-Brees Bill, thus collaborating on a legislative program for the first time in their history.[43]

The extreme violence of the labor reaction surprised most observers. A part of the explanation was undoubtedly the way in which the changes were made. Angered initially by the abrupt way in which negotiations had been terminated in the labor-management conference, labor representatives grew increasingly resentful as they were systematically excluded from the deliberations of the Hughes Committee. It was the first time since the 1930's that they had been so ignored, and they found it galling. Feeling might not have run so high over the Hughes-Brees Act if some less antagonizing method of enactment could have been found.

The Hughes Committee was continued in existence by successive annual acts of the legislature and continued to be the main legislative channel through which unemployment compensation bills passed. It did not, however, possess the quasi-monopoly of influence which the Ives Committee before it had, nor did it attempt to enforce a "rule of unanimity." The Hughes Committee worked under two disadvantages as compared with the Ives Committee: it had to work without the support of labor, which still resented the Hughes-Brees Act, and, after the election of Democrat Harriman in 1954, without the support of a friendly governor.

These limitations on the Hughes Committee might have given the council an opportunity to recover some of its former influence. But the membership of the council was going from bad to worse. For four years (1951–1954) the council had only one employer member, and for two years (1951–1952) only two labor members—members having resigned and the governor having neglected to fill vacancies.

The lone employer member had further limited the effectiveness of the council by insisting in 1953, after nineteen years on the council, that "it is not within the province of the Advisory Council to propose substantive changes in the law; its advice is limited to

[43] The collaboration did not last beyond the emergency.

matters affecting the administration of the law." [44] The actual wording of the law supports his contention, but the law had never before been interpreted in that sense, and no one else on the council agreed with him. He may have taken this position because employers were a minority on the council, or he may have simply reverted to an original position. He was the employer who had resigned from the chairmanship of an employers' social security committee upon being appointed to the council. At that time he evidently did not consider himself as delegated to help mold policy in the name of employers. But whatever his reason, when he refused to participate in policy discussions on the council it inevitably weakened the council, since he was its only employer representative.

On the last day of the year 1954, in what was almost his last official act, Governor Dewey made eight appointments to the advisory council. He reappointed the three public members and the one employer member, filled the two employer vacancies, and replaced two of the labor representatives with new appointees. The two members who were replaced were the secretaries of the state federation and the state CIO respectively. They had been on the council for many years and were undoubtedly the chief spokesmen for labor in unemployment compensation. They were dropped from the council because they had declared political war on the governor after he signed the Hughes-Brees Act. They were both returned to the council the following year by Dewey's successor, Governor Harriman.

1955–1957

It is tempting to describe this period as the "normal" period, when the council was neither very weak nor very strong, but "average." For the first time since 1949 the council had a full complement of members. The chairman was equally acceptable to both labor and management, and his relations with the agency were tranquil. Like his counterparts on other councils, he allowed the

[44] Annual Report of the New York State Advisory Council on Employment and Unemployment Insurance for 1954, p. 11. This was at the furthest extreme from the position taken by the first chairman of the council in the council's 1942 report (see p. 185).

agency and the executive secretary to make up the agenda and to provide most of the initiative in planning. The council's labor representation was strong; the labor members were the decision makers of their side. The employer members, however, still represented an element of weakness.

The original employer member still refused to take positions on matters of policy, and of the newly appointed members one never attended a meeting. Governor Harriman replaced the latter in the spring of 1957 with a lawyer whose clientele included employers in the garment industry and who, like the employers in that industry, had labor's viewpoint on many crucial issues. That left only the third member to speak for the generality of employers in determining policy. Although he was a competent, widely accepted, effective representative, the employer representation as a whole was not the locus of decision making to nearly the same extent as was the labor representation.

The council's effectiveness continued to be limited by its inability to reach agreement on experience rating, which prevented agreement on some other items, such as the level of benefits, because the exigencies of trading tied all the items into a single package. The government was equally unable to reach agreement. Three times in this period the legislature passed a "package" bill which raised benefits to $45, and three times the governor vetoed it because it contained an experience-rating provision that would increase the taxes on those employers who regularly drew more out of the fund than they put in.

The council was successful, however, in reaching agreement on other, less controversial, matters. For example, it solved the vexing problem of whether and how to pay benefits to workers idled by vacation shutdowns.[45] It also did a thorough job of rationalizing and standardizing the disqualification provisions. The council performed other important tasks of this same kind—as it had done throughout its history. The narration of other events crowded out the account of such successes in previous years, but they were there.

[45] It produced a formula which the agency began to use in 1955 and which the legislature enacted into law in 1957.

In 1957 Ashberry replaced Hughes as chairman of the Joint Legislative Committee on Unemployment Insurance and began an intensive effort to break the impasse over experience rating. More acceptable to labor than Hughes had been, he made much progress toward agreement. In the course of this effort he worked closely with the advisory council. He and his research assistant attended a half-dozen meetings of the advisory council, while the executive secretary of the council attended a number of meetings of the committee. In this respect it was like a return to the days of the Ives Committee.

ADMINISTRATION

Space does not permit as detailed an account of the council's activities in the area of administration as in the area of legislation, but it can be said in general that the New York council was more active by far than the average council. In the council's annual report for the year 1942 there is an impressive enumeration of the council's accomplishments up to that time. The council is credited with such major developments as: a simplified benefit formula, administrative procedures for the prompt payment of benefits, a method for separating the judicial from the administrative functions of the agency,[46] the day-base plan for the payment of partial benefits. The enumeration continues:

In considering technical amendments developed by the Administration . . . in advising the Industrial Commissioner regarding rules and regulations, . . . in calling attention to such subjects as fraudulent benefit claims and employer delinquency in the payment of contributions, and in stimulating the Division's efforts toward improvement of its operations, in reviewing procedures and practices—in all of these varying activities, the Council has been engaged in helping to make unemployment insurance work.[47]

[46] The separation of the judicial from the administrative functions of the agency was almost entirely the work of the council, and especially of the council's chairman. It constitutes one of the best examples encountered in the course of this survey of a council's participation in the administrative function.

[47] Annual Report of the New York State Advisory Council on Employment and Unemployment Insurance for 1942. The excerpt is taken from the section entitled "Role and Function of Advisory Council," which is an excellent treatment of that general topic.

Although the period covered by the report was the council's most influential period, it was not atypical. The council was active in all periods. For example, in 1949 the council participated in preparing a two-volume report on "Organization and Operation of the New York City Offices of the New York State Employment Service," [48] and in 1951 it helped develop a lengthy and detailed "Statement of Policy on the Suitability of Job Offers." These are examples of very formal pieces of work; the council performed much informal work of the same nature.[49]

The council's contribution was especially valuable in the area of administrative law. The director of the agency regularly submitted rules and administrative interpretations for the council's consideration. He said that when administrative law was worked out in this way it stood up better in practice. He also said that a formal council was a better instrument for this purpose than informal contacts. He used informal contacts—he telephoned people, for example, as need arose—but this was no substitute for the council meetings. At a council meeting labor and management were present together; they could criticize each other's arguments and usually they could be brought to some agreement.

APPRAISAL

The New York advisory council was certainly more active and effective than the average council and without impropriety could be included among the councils graded "more effective" in this study. It is on the borderline.

In the course of its long life the council made a number of important contributions to the employment service side of its dual responsibility but like all the other councils devoted most of its attention to unemployment insurance. During its first five years the

[48] This report was a delicate bit of business, for it was made at a time when feeling was running high over the relationship between unemployment compensation and the employment service. The council's nonpartisan character made it ideal for the task.

[49] Further examples of the council's activity in the area of administration can be found under the index heading "advisory council" in David H. Colin's *The Law of Unemployment Insurance in New York* (New York: The New York University Institute of Labor Relations and Social Security, 1950).

council was the principal influence in unemployment insurance. After 1939 it lost this preeminence but continued to exhibit more than average activity until after the war. Its effectiveness was probably lowest in the decade 1946–1955. In 1957 the trend line of council influence seemed to take a definite turn upwards.

The council's preeminence in the early period was due in large part to the quality of its membership, which included, in addition to a very competent public chairman, such employer and employee representatives as Marion Folsom and George Meany. The surrounding environment was also more favorable to the council in the earlier period. At the start of the program there was much to do and there were few who could do it as well as the council members, some of whom had helped put the law through and knew it best. When somewhat later the agency ran into serious difficulties, the situation provided the council with an opportunity to play the role of reformer. The council was equal to the opportunity, thanks in no small measure to the activity and competence of its chairman.

After this initial period of success the council experienced a period of transition during which it was faced with more difficult tasks. Its labor members (and its chairman) could no longer count on sweeping employers along on the full tide of the New Deal but had to learn to bargain with them in a political sea made up of cross currents. Also, instead of reforming a weak agency, it had to learn to get along with a strong one.

The council did not manage the transition very successfully. Its labor and management members were unable to work out mutually acceptable bargains. There were a number of issues on which they disagreed, but the chief one by far was the issue of experience rating. Other difficulties might have been overcome if the obstacle of experience rating had not proved insuperable. In the case of New York this always troublesome issue was magnified because the council's chairman felt he had to oppose experience rating on principle and still more because one of the labor members was from the apparel industry, which would have been seriously disadvantaged by experience rating. If George Meany had remained on the council it is possible—just barely possible—that the council

would eventually have worked out a compromise solution acceptable to both sides. But in fact the council never did, and its effectiveness was correspondingly diminished.

Had labor and management made the compromises required for
agreed bills, each party might have fared no worse than it actually
did under the compromises imposed on it by the Ives and Hughes
committees.[50] The net result in terms of amendments to the law
could easily have been about the same. And there would have been
at least two accompanying advantages. The process of amendment
would have been less open to the vagaries of partisan politics (such
as determined the duration of benefits in 1942) and would have
been less likely to produce embittered industrial relations (such
as accompanied the amendments of 1951.) The agreement on experience rating that was reached after the 1957 negotiations was the
first that promised any stability of peaceful relationships because
it was the first that had any genuine quality of mutual consent.

Had the council been able to achieve agreement, its chances of
exercising influence would have been greatly improved, but after
the first half-dozen years they would not have been assured. This
was because the employer representatives on the council became
progressively less able to speak with authority for the major employer organizations. Beginning at least as early as 1945, and probably before, the major employer organizations did not hope to
work effectively through the advisory council. Their principal leaders were not on the council, and the council's labor members,
strongly supported by the chairman, were determined not to bargain on the issue of experience rating. So the employer organizations
by-passed the council and went directly to politics.

As in the case of some other long-lived councils—for example,
Utah and Massachusetts—the deterioration in the representative
quality of the employer members was gradual. One of the original
appointees had been the general manager of the Associated Industries of New York—an ideal position for a council member. But
he resigned from the council after a few months in early 1936 because he was actively engaged in fighting the constitutionality of

---

[50] In 1941, employers, and in 1947, employees, may actually have lost by taking
their case to the legislature instead of agreeing to a previously offered "package bill."

the New York unemployment compensation law. His successor was chairman of the social security committee of the Associated Industries—also an excellent position for a council member—but he resigned from that position upon being appointed to the council because he considered the position incompatible with the public nature of the council. Evidently he did not consider himself as "representing" employers in the Commons sense of being able to commit an organization. He continued to be an influential figure among his fellow employers, but not as influential as if he had retained his position on the social security committee.[51]

Another original appointee was Marion Folsom, an authority on social security programs and a future member of President Eisenhower's cabinet. At the time of his appointment he was undoubtedly one of the principal voices on the employers' side, but later he became so occupied on the national scene that he gradually dropped out of the circle of major decision makers in New York affairs. The third original appointee was a lawyer, counsel for the Retailers Association, who had persuaded that association to come out for unemployment insurance while the issue was still being debated in the state legislature.[52] He knew the program well and had important political connections, but he was primarily a professional man and was never closely connected with the major employer organizations.[53] All three of these original appointees remained on the council until 1949.

One employer who was critical of the council believed that the only effective way to keep the council membership adjusted to changing power patterns in industry and politics was to make the terms of council members nonrenewable; or at least not renewable

[51] He was the council member who later held that the council had no business discussing matters of policy: see pp. 198–99.

[52] This is one of the few instances in which an employers' organization favored the enactment of an unemployment insurance law.

[53] The three employer organizations most important for unemployment compensation in New York are the Associated Industries of New York, the Empire State Association of Commerce, and the Commerce and Industry Association of New York. These three organizations with about one hundred others are gathered together into one organization called the New York State Conference on Unemployment Insurance, which began in 1937 under the title of Employers Conference on Unemployment Insurance, became moribund with the years, and was resuscitated in 1949 under its present name.

until a member had been definitely separated from the council for a year or more. His reason was that too often neither the governor nor the employer and labor organizations were willing to force a man off the council though they would have welcomed his departure.

The most interesting aspect of the New York council from the viewpoint of advisory council theory is the dispute between the council, especially the council's chairman, and the agency concerning the degree of independent initiative proper to each. As the chairman saw the council, it was to be as active as the agency in planning policy and was even to provide leadership. It was to provide leadership even in very technical matters—such as the "day-base" plan, the experience-rating formula of 1945, and the payment of benefits to claimants involved in vacation shutdowns (to mention three developments which did stem from council initiative). At one time the New York council claimed (as did the Michigan council) that the agency (every official below the industrial commissioner) was to leave all policy determination to the council. The council even objected to a member of the agency's planning unit working with a legislative committee and presenting for the committee's consideration proposals of which the council had not approved.

This conception of an advisory council's function could be defended for a council that had the decision makers of labor and management as members, that had some staff of its own, that was willing to devote a great deal of time (much more than any council other than Massachusetts was willing to give), and that could achieve agreed bills. These are the minimum requirements for such an ambitious function.

The New York council after 1939 did not have these minimum requirements. It did not have the major decision makers of management as members, it did not have adequate staff, it was not willing to give the necessary time, and it was not able to achieve unanimity. This last was the most important lack. The chairman's theoretical position in his 1942 dispute with the director of the agency was weak primarily because the council for which he was claiming preeminence was not a unanimous council. In assigning the privilege of setting policy to a split council he was in effect assigning it to the public members. If a council's labor and management members are unable to agree on policy, then its public members, since they hold the balance of voting power, become the actual arbiters of policy. But this is to allocate power where there is least responsibility. The public members do not have to live with the results [54] of their decisions in the same sense as do the other persons concerned—the governor and the legislature and the labor and management members, all of whom have constituencies to satisfy, and the director of the agency, whose job is at stake. A mere majority vote on any advisory council is normally ineffective precisely because everyone recognizes that it represents nothing more than the view of the public members, who bear the least responsibility.

Did the council's claim to preeminence in initiating and deciding policy increase or decrease its effectiveness? It had both effects, but the positive results almost certainly outweighed the negative ones. The unusual vigor and initiative of the council undoubtedly went far to explain the council's more than average effectiveness. Not many councils (less than half a dozen) could rival the New York council's constant and persuasive influence on almost every phase of the program.[55]

But there were losses also. The vigorous initiative claimed and exercised by the council was to a considerable extent traceable to the chairman, and since he was unalterably opposed to experience rating "on principle," the council's claimed control of policy worked to prevent necessary compromises. One of his reasons for objecting so strenuously to the independent activity of the director was, very likely, that the latter was meeting with pro-experience-rating employer groups outside the council. The chairman wanted to keep control within the council and to keep the council arrayed against experience rating. In this, of course, he had the solid support of the labor members.

It was unrealistic to expect to keep the director of the agency from

[54] For the comment of John R. Commons on this point, see p. 41.

[55] In the matter of initiating technical projects the councils of Michigan, Connecticut, and Ohio were close rivals to the New York council, at least at some periods of their existence.

participating actively in policy formation outside the (divided) council. The director of the agency, as the top government official possessing full-time responsibility for the employment security program, was bound to be a major source of influence in policy formation and to be a working partner of every influential group inside and outside the advisory council.

The term of service for council members was set at six years to overlap the governor's term and thus to guard against the contingency of an entire council being swept in and out of existence every time there was a change of governors. Along with the plan's advantages there is this disadvantage, that one governor can impose advisers, possibly unwelcome, on his successor. An unwelcome adviser is an ineffective adviser. The council's chairman, appointed for the first time in 1935, was reappointed by Democrat Lehman in 1941 and hence had nearly a whole term under Republican Dewey, who was elected in 1942 and on whom he had little influence. Dewey in his turn tried to impose as many appointees as possible on his Democratic successor.

The higher-than-average compensation which the law provides for council members seems to have had no disadvantages and may have had two advantages. It may have improved attendance at meetings, although the council's record was not exceptionally good.[56] Also it may have improved the quality of the meetings. When each meeting costs a sizable sum both the agency and the council members are more likely to take meetings seriously, and the danger of "thin" meetings is lessened.

Two features of the New York experience are unique: it has had some staff of its own, and it has kept verbatim minutes. As to the first, it is certain that having its own staff enabled the council to operate more efficiently. It is also certain that the arrangement did not alienate the council from the agency. If anything, the council's staff members helped link the two together because they remained close and friendly co-workers of the agency staff. It is not equally certain, however, that the added efficiency of the council was worth the added expense; nor that having its own staff will never give a council a false sense of independence from the agency

[56] See Appendix A.

it is supposed to advise, and hence lead to bad relationships. The New York experience was too short—the council had its full complement of staff for less than two years—to be conclusive.

As to the verbatim minutes—they added some importance to the council meetings and they were available to settle disputes. They did not seem to hinder free discussion. The council members stated that they were not inhibited, and a reading of the minutes bears out their statement. An occasional request that something be "off the record" seems to have sufficed for handling the more private business of the council. But the verbatim minutes were expensive. Also, they were rarely read. Shorter minutes of the usual variety were prepared immediately after each meeting —long before the verbatim minutes were transcribed from the secretary's shorthand—and this shorter account was normally the only one which anyone read.

8

THE MASSACHUSETTS
ADVISORY COUNCIL

THE Massachusetts advisory council is notable for its long life, extraordinarily numerous meetings, insistence on its "public" character, and a consequent strong political coloration. The influence of the council was highest in the early period, 1939–1941, after which it declined steadily. By 1949 its influence was minor and so remained until 1955, when an increase was noticeable.

The original Massachusetts unemployment compensation law [1] provided for a nine-member tripartite council to be appointed by the governor for staggered terms of six years. The law stipulated that "not more than five members shall be members of the same political party." The council was to serve without compensation in advising the tripartite commission which at that time administered the employment security program.

The council appointed under this law was short-lived. It functioned about a year and then seems to have disintegrated. The reasons for its disintegration are obscure, but seem to have included the tripartite commission itself, which looked upon the tripartite advisory council as an unnecessary competitor and dominated council meetings to the extent of doing all the talking. Council members like President Lowell of Harvard University could not be expected to remain interested in this passive role.[2]

---

[1] The Massachusetts program became law on August 12, 1935, two days before the Social Security Act was enacted. See Acts of 1935, Ch. 479, Sec. 5.

[2] Nor even in a more active role very long. The governor aimed too high in his appointments.

The Massachusetts agency began to pay benefits in January of 1938 and suffered the experience of some of the other early states such as New York. It failed to handle the first heavy impact of claims satisfactorily and came under such heavy criticism that it had to be reorganized. The reorganization was accomplished by a series of amendments in 1939. Among other changes, the three-man commission was abolished and replaced by a single executive director.

The Massachusetts council was too anemic at this time to do as the New York council and supply the leadership in the work of re-organizing the agency. The Massachusetts council itself had to be reorganized. The changes in the council at this time were made at the insistence, mainly, of one of its employer members. This was the same person who proposed the second reorganization of the council in 1954 (see below). The amendments of 1939 [3] reduced the council from nine members to six (two representatives each of labor, management, and the public) and dropped the limitation on the number of members who might belong to the same political party. (Governor Salstonstall thereupon appointed all Republicans to the new council.) In 1939 amendments provided that members be compensated at the rate of $15 for each meeting and set a maximum of one hundred meetings in a year. (This was amended in 1947 to provide $25 for each meeting for a maximum of sixty meetings in a year.) The amendments also provided that the council should have "suitable quarters and such clerical assistance as the council may deem necessary." This has meant in practice an unusually fine meeting room and a full-time secretary.

Finally the 1939 amendments enlarged the functions of the council in two respects. They provided that the council (1) report quarterly to the governor, annually to the legislature, and (2) "investigate and study all proposals for changes in or additions to the provisions of this chapter pending before the General Court [the Massachusetts legislature] including proposals made by the director, and report to the General Court its recommendations with respect thereto." The 1939 law retained the earlier provision that rules and regulations which affected the property rights of employers or

[3] See Act of 1939, Ch. 20, Secs. 1, 5.

employees were subject to the approval of the advisory council.

These changes strengthening the advisory council were similar to those made in the New York law at this time [4] and reflected a similar situation: the agency had just broken down, and the advisory council was expected to guard against a repetition of the collapse. Like the New York council, the Massachusetts council tended naturally to see itself cast in a semi-administrative role and to become active on a scale not dreamed of by the average council. This partly accounts for the council's unusually frequent meetings.

The Massachusetts advisory council has undoubtedly held more meetings than any other council in the country. From its first meeting, in February, 1939, through fiscal 1957 the council held a total of 1,401 meetings, an average of over 75 meetings a year. The meetings were distributed as follows:

1939	86	1943	99	1947	75	1951	56	1955	59
1940	104	1944	93	1948	55	1952	56	1956	59
1941	107	1945	83	1949	65	1953	54	1957	58
1942	98	1946	84	1950	54	1954	56		

Most of the council's meetings were held in the afternoon and lasted two or three hours. Some, especially in the early years, lasted from morning until midnight; others, especially in the later years, were perfunctory meetings which lasted little more than an hour. The council is required by law to meet at least once a month.[5]

ACTIVITIES OF THE COUNCIL
1939–1941

The council's first year, 1939, was an unusually active one. The new director, faced with the necessity of reorganizing the agency and regaining public esteem for the program, welcomed the cooperation of the council. Of the multitudinous tasks to be performed, the first and most important was to recommend needed

---

[4] The reporting provision was identical with that in the New York law. The provision giving the council responsibility to study *all* proposed changes in the law was similar to the provision introduced into the Wisconsin law at this time.

[5] The most convenient reference for all the legal provisions governing the advisory council is a booklet issued by the Massachusetts Division of Employment Security in January, 1957, entitled *Massachusetts Employment Security Law with Regulations.* Pages 2, 43, and 49 cite Ch. 151A, Secs. 1, 62, and Ch. 23, Sec. 9N, of the General Laws of Massachusetts.

changes in the law. The council, working harmoniously with the director, was able to reach agreement on a number of substantive amendments. It agreed to abolish the tax on employees and to introduce a tax-reduction plan for employers.[6] It also worked out an agreed position with regard to the waiting period, the definition of base and benefit years, the disqualification of voluntary quits, the relation between unemployment benefits and pension payments, and many technical matters of administration. The chairman of the council and the director of the agency brought the council's recommendations to the governor and discussed them with him. Then the entire council appeared in support of the recommendations at the hearing held by the legislative committee. With minor modifications the council's entire program was accepted by both the governor and the legislature and was enacted into law. This was the council working at its best.

The close of the legislative session did not end the council's activity for 1939. At its twice-weekly meetings the council continued to do serious work on significant problems. It helped develop norms for deciding cases of voluntary quitting, prepared a questionnaire to be used by claims-takers in establishing the eligibility of claimants, and proposed a plan whereby the council would participate in the governor's program for full employment. The council also discussed its own functions—deciding at one meeting that its responsibilities included the employment service as well as unemployment compensation, and at another that it did not have the authority to make rules and regulations but only to review those made by the administrator. These are only examples of what occupied the council in its multitudinous meetings during the first year of its existence.

The council continued to be very active in 1940. The administrator brought to the council all his problems, even such matters as the reclassification of agency personnel. Groups with complaints

[6] The council first recommended a flat-rate reduction plan, which was favored by the Associated Industries of Massachusetts in opposition to the National Association of Manufacturers, which favored individual experience rating. The Social Security Board, however, induced Massachusetts employers to drop the flat-rate plan. The board made so many difficulties over the plan that the Associated Industries of Massachusetts abandoned it in favor of the benefit-wage, generally called the Cliffe, plan, which remained in operation in Massachusetts until 1951.

and petitions came before the advisory council to ask for council support. The Board of Review met with the council to discuss legislative amendments that would facilitate the work of the board. Defense manpower problems occupied many meetings at this time. It was in 1940 also that Massachusetts initiated joint meetings with other New England advisory councils to discuss common problems, especially the problem of federal-state relations.

After 1940 controversies between Massachusetts and the federal Bureau of Employment Security were much to the fore. The Massachusetts council was second only to that of Wisconsin in its concern over state independence. It took the lead in calling joint meetings of the New England advisory councils in 1940 and 1941 in order to discuss ways of limiting federal control over the state agencies. One such meeting, held in Boston, was dubbed the "Boston Tea Party."

The controversies touched on many aspects of the program, such as the propriety of federal minimum standards, the obligation to follow employment service directives that came from the Bureau of Employment Security, and the federal proposal for a reinsurance fund. Ironically the council was opposed to a reinsurance fund because it would compel Massachusetts to share with less wealthy states; later the Massachusetts fund was to become one of the weakest in the country.

At one point in this running battle with the federal agency the council went over the head of the Bureau of Employment Security and sent a representative to Washington to present the state's case directly to Congress. Since regular administrative funds, which had to be obtained from the Bureau of Employment Security, were not available for such activity, the council obtained the necessary money from the governor's emergency fund.

The council's influence on legislation was not nearly so great in 1941 as it had been in 1939. Over one hundred bills relating to unemployment compensation were introduced in the legislature in 1941. The council reviewed and expressed itself on nearly all of them, but the opinion of the council was clearly only one, and not the most influential one, of many opinions to which the legislature paid heed. For example, although the council favored retaining the two-week waiting period, the legislature lowered it to one week at the insistence of organized labor outside the council. After 1941 the relation between the recommendations of the council and the actual pattern of legislation progressively weakened.

1942–1948

During this period the administrator continued to bring all the agency's problems to the council at its twice-weekly meetings, and the council continued to express its opinions, analyze all bills submitted to the legislature, write reports, and in general make itself intelligently vocal. The members respected one another and worked together harmoniously—at least until 1945.

In the matter of exerting influence on legislation, however, the council's position progressively deteriorated. After the 1941 session the council abandoned its practice of appearing at hearings and deputed its chairman, one of the public members, to appear in its name. The chairman found that he was accorded only token attention by the legislative committee, which listened to him politely but was obviously anxious to get on to the testimony of the agency and of the labor and management leaders, none of whom were on the council. After a few sessions the chairman, too, abandoned the fruitless practice.

In 1943 the council was weakened by the loss of its most effective employer member. It was further weakened in 1945 by a swing of the political pendulum. Between 1939, when the council was reorganized, and 1945 the governorship had been held by the Republicans and all council appointees had been Republicans.[7] During this period the council had the opportunity to exercise at least the influence which comes from belonging, however remotely, among the political advisers of the governor. In 1945, however, a Democrat became governor, and he felt little interest in an ad-

[7] During the period covered by the second council the governorship was held as follows: 1939–1944 (Republican), 1945–1946 (Democrat), 1947–1948 (Republican), 1949–1952 (Democrat), 1953–1956 (Republican). The Republicans controlled the Senate throughout the entire period 1939–1955 and controlled the House in the periods 1939–1949 and 1953–1955.

visory council which not only could not speak for organized labor and management but did not even belong to his own political party. The six-year staggered terms of the council members and the two-year term of the governor meant that he could not hope to replace many of them during his term of office.

He did have an opportunity, however, to appoint one labor member to the council in 1945. He appointed a Democrat, the first Democratic labor representative in the council's history. The new member (an officer in one of the CIO unions) brought considerable energy to the council and a corresponding amount of conflict. He avowed that in the future the labor members on the council would press labor's demands more vigorously, and he made good his avowal. He remained on the council only until 1949, when a successful and grateful Democratic candidate for governor, for whom he had campaigned, appointed him director of the employment security agency.

1949–1955

By the end of 1949 the council's politics were again in harmony with the governor's—all members were Democrats—but the council's influence did not revive. If anything, it deteriorated further. The new director of the agency, although himself a former council member, held the council in less esteem than his predecessor did and gave it much less time and attention. In 1951 he became greatly displeased with the council for what he termed its weakness in not successfully opposing the employer-engineered amendments of 1951, and thereafter he pointedly ignored the council. He declared that there was no one on the council of sufficient importance to make it worth his while to attend the council meetings. He attended only when the council called him on some specific problem. The council, left without anybody to arrange its agenda, supply it with materials, and guide it through technical problems, worked under a serious handicap. None of its members could spend the necessary time, even if they had the necessary technical ability, to supply fully the agency's missing leadership. The council continued to meet weekly but its influence was greatly limited.

The legislative sessions of 1951 and 1953 provided clear evi-

dence of the council's limitations, but also of the fact that the
council was not entirely without influence. In these sessions major
changes were made in the Massachusetts law similar in character
to those made about this same time in New York and attended by
a similar controversy.[8] The council was definitely not a leading
figure in making the changes. The leading figures were the lobbyists of the state Federation and CIO labor bodies, and the Massachusetts Employers' Council on Employment Security. This last
was an organization which was established in 1950 for the precise
purpose of putting through the 1951 amendments.[9] None of the
decision makers in labor and management and no one in government could recall anything done by the council which influenced
the outcome in a major way. Nevertheless the council continued
to be very active during these sessions. It analyzed all the proposals
being offered and made its views known on each. Very likely the
council exerted some mediating influence by aiding the governor
to choose between the various pressures to which he was being
subjected. For example, in the final stages of the 1951 negotiations,
held in the governor's office, one of the employer members of the
council was active in a personal capacity as a friend of the governor.

In 1954 a bill was introduced to reorganize the advisory council.
Its designer was the employer representative who had been a member of the original (1935) council, had brought about its reorganization in 1939, and had served on the reorganized council until illness caused him to resign in 1943. The bill would have established a council on the model of the New Hampshire council, with
three labor representatives, three management representatives, and
a nonvoting public chairman. The employer members were to be
appointed "by the governor from a list to be provided by the Massachusetts Employers' Council on Employment Security" and the
employee members "from a list to be provided by the Massachusetts
State Federation of Labor and the Massachusetts Congress of Industrial Organizations."

The director of the agency, newly appointed that same year,

[8] In Massachusetts the amendments included the introduction of a reserve-ratio
(in place of a benefit-wage-ratio) system of experience rating, an increase in qualifying wages from $150 to $500, individual (in place of uniform) benefit and base years,
and some changes in disqualifications.

[9] For similar organizations in Michigan and New York, see pp. 326–27 and 205, n. 53.

opposed the bill. He argued that a nonvoting chairman could not break a tie and the council would therefore frequently be without a voice. He also argued that the Massachusetts Employers' Council on Employment Security was too loose an organization and too dominated by large employers to deserve a nominating monopoly. Since neither labor nor management gave the bill strong support, the director's opposition sufficed to kill the bill in the Senate.

The terms of three council members—one public, one labor, and one employer, all Democrats—expired in 1955, and three Republicans were appointed to replace them. (The Republicans had regained the governorship in 1953.) The new labor and employer members resembled their predecessors in that they did not belong to the circle of decision makers. The state labor organizations went out of their way to make it clear that the council did not speak for Massachusetts labor. The new public member, however, who became the council's chairman, was politically influential and technically competent. He was consulted by both the Republican governor who appointed him and the Democratic governor who succeeded to office in 1957, and during the legislative session of 1957 he "spent some seven days at legislative hearings before the Committee on Labor and Industries explaining the effects of the proposed legislation." [10] He worked with the new director in a close relationship reminiscent of the situation on the Connecticut council during that council's early years.

The above account is the shorter because there was no need to include a description of agreed bills reached by labor and management outside the council. There were no agreed bills either in unemployment compensation or in workmen's compensation. In Massachusetts, labor and management have no tradition of working out legislation together. The usual pattern has been for each side to introduce its own bills, and then for the legislative committee (or the governor), having consulted with each side separately, to declare what the final decision is. Neither side has made any serious effort to change the pattern, essentially one of compulsory arbitration, but both have concentrated on attaining the

[10] From a letter of the council chairman to the author, dated April 4, 1958.

political power which would turn the arbitrator's decision in their favor.

APPRAISAL

The council was clearly an influential body during the early period of its operation, 1939–1941. Its influence was felt by the director of the agency, the governor, and the legislature, and was exercised in the areas of both administration and legislation. Thereafter, to the end of the war, the council was important at least to the director, who declared that it was well worth the considerable amount of time he gave it. From the end of the war until 1949, the council steadily declined in effectiveness, and after 1949 seems not to have been a major influence in the program. It may have begun a revival in 1955.

Several circumstances conspired to make the council more influential in its early years. In those years of reorganization there was much to be done and few experienced persons to do it; the council filled a partial vacuum. The director was unusually interested in the council; no other director, probably, in the history of employment security has given as much time to his advisory council as did the director of the Massachusetts agency during the decade 1939–1949. Finally, the council had somewhat more effective members in the early years. One of the two employer members (the same who had been a member of the original council) was the chief technical consultant for employer organizations. Although neither of the two labor members was a labor official at the time of his appointment, both had been. One had been president of the Massachusetts State Federation of Labor and the other had been an officer in his own international union. The chairman of the council was a professor at Harvard University; he was very interested in the program and gave a great deal of time to it.

What the council lacked in ability to speak for organized groups it made up partially in political influence. During the early years the governor, the director of the agency, both houses of the legislature, and all the council members were of the same party. When the director and the council could agree on a program, that program was very likely to be supported by the governor and given careful and sympathetic consideration by the legislature. Governor Salstonstall, who had campaigned in 1938 on a platform of reform in unemployment compensation, knew the council members personally and relied on them. He held the governorship for three successive terms, 1939 through 1944.

The council lost much of its early influence as the result of changes in all these favoring circumstances. As the agency became established, there was less for the council to do (after 1941); the council gradually lost its more effective members (after 1945); the successor of the original director took less interest in the council and eventually ignored it entirely (after 1949); and the governors after Salstonstall relied less on the council, partly because it had become a less effective body, for the reasons just indicated, but also because the political affiliations of its members were often different from the governor's.

The membership of the council normally did not include the official spokesmen for organized labor and management, and the council never exercised its influence by way of agreed bills backed by organized labor and management. What influence the council had was the influence of a member of a political team. This was the lesser influence. A long-time participant in Massachusetts politics (a Republican and an employer lobbyist) was asked by the writer: "In the early years of the council, when the entire government was Republican, who had the greater influence with the legislature—the labor representatives who were on the council and were Republicans but could not speak for organized labor, or the labor leaders who were not on the council and were not Republicans but who could speak authoritively for organized labor?" He replied, "The latter—undoubtedly."

The first director under whom the council functioned (1939–1949) agreed with this judgment but said that it was irrelevant to an evaluation of the council. He held that the council was not intended to exercise influence directly, that is, by making final decisions through bargaining. The council was intended to give the government the advantage of its views and nothing more. He said that "bargaining" had never taken place on the council and no one ever suggested that it should. In his view all the members of the council should be "public" in the sense that they should abandon their partisan interests when they come on the council and should act with the same disinterestedness as the director himself.[11] The labor and employer members of the council expressed themselves in agreement with this view.

Such a view seems necessarily to include a theory of delimiting the decision-making scope of private groups in order to increase that of the political parties. At any rate, as the theory was reduced to practice in Massachusetts, it had the effect of emphasizing the political over the economic factor. Republican governors tended to select Republican labor representatives, and Democratic governors tended to select Democratic employer representatives, and in neither case did the selection bring to the council the respective leaders of these two economic groups. The Massachusetts theory of selection and operation resulted in a council that was relatively ineffective during most of its existence—much less effective, certainly, than the councils of Wisconsin or New Hampshire, which operated on quite a different theory. The Massachusetts experience is the more enlightening in that it constitutes what is probably the most thorough test of this type of council. The Massachusetts council had wide powers in law and was adequately staffed and compensated; it maintained close, harmonious relations with the director, who gave it an unusual amount of time; it was as long-lived as any council and in the course of its life held an extraordinary number of meetings; and it had the experience of being at one time all Republican, at another all Democratic, and at other times a mixture of both. The Massachusetts experience would seem to be an adequate test of the potentialities of this "public" or "political" type of council; the type is not likely to succeed to a greater extent elsewhere than it did in Massachusetts.

If Massachusetts should ever decide to experiment with the type of council which emphasizes the representation of organized, partisan interests, it would find several circumstances in the Massachusetts situation which would favor and several which would hinder the experiment. Among the favoring circumstances is the fairly

[11] The present director, appointed in 1954, holds essentially the same view.

even balance of power that exists between labor and management in the state. Massachusetts differs from most other states in giving its cities, and therefore labor, proportional representation in the legislature. Balanced political power is a favoring condition because it makes the results of political activity uncertain and hence makes joint action in an advisory council more attractive as an alternative.

Another favoring factor is that the chief decision makers among labor and management are not personally antagonistic to one another. They share a mutual respect and would experience no particular personal difficulty in working together.[12]

A final favoring condition is that both labor and management are sufficiently organized so that a few representatives on an advisory council could speak effectively for them. Although the state Federation and the CIO have not been accustomed to work together formally on legislation [13] and have reached their positions on unemployment compensation independently, their positions have usually been in substantial agreement. Employers took a long step toward effective organization when they established the Massachusetts Employers' Council on Employment Security in 1950. Although the Employers' Council is a loose body, it speaks effectively for the majority of employers. The predominant influences in it are the Associated Industries of Massachusetts, which claims to represent over 80 percent of the total industrial payroll in the state,[14] and the Greater Boston Chamber of Commerce.

Among the circumstances in Massachusetts which would hinder the operation of the Wisconsin or the New Hampshire type of council is the above-average rate of unemployment in Massachusetts. This has resulted in the state's having higher-than-average

[12] This was less true before 1947, when one of the state labor organizations had a "wild man"—as they speak of him now—on its staff.

[13] A notable exception to their usual pattern of independent action was their joint action in 1948, when to defeat a right-to-work bill they set up the United Labor Committee of Massachusetts.

[14] In Massachusetts, as in many other states, the chief source of division among employers has been the difference in interest between high-cost (epecially shoes and textiles) and low-cost employers and their consequently different attitudes toward experience rating.

unemployment compensation costs and a reserve fund which has for years been one of the weakest in the country. This situation has made employers less willing to liberalize the program and more insistent on tightening it, which in turn has made labor less willing to deal with employers and more inclined to take its chances in the legislature.

In a situation as difficult as this it may be unreasonable to expect private groups to incur the odium of making unpleasant but necessary changes in the law. Such a situation, it may be argued, must inevitably be handled by the legislature itself. There is a considerable element of truth in the argument, but it is not universally valid.

New Hampshire has had an equally hard problem of unemployment to solve, yet labor and management representatives have themselves managed to agree on the proper solution. Moreover, in Massachusetts the legislature did not do a particularly good job of solving the problem. In repeated sessions the legislature followed the popular path of simultaneously increasing benefits and lowering taxes—the ideal formula for pleasing everybody. Although benefit costs in Massachusetts have always been above the national average, the tax rate imposed on employers was below the national average from 1942 until 1948 and was only slightly above the national average in the two succeeding years. As a result of following this primrose path, the legislature had, by December, 1949, reduced the state's reserve fund to the point where it was the lowest in the country—3.3 percent of taxable wages in contrast to the national average of 8.9 percent. Only then did the legislature find the courage to raise the tax rate and to limit benefits. In 1950 it raised all employers by one-half of 1 percent, and in 1951, besides tightening the benefit side of the program, as already described, it raised all employers to the maximum rate of 2.7 percent. By 1955 the Massachusetts fund was out of danger though still weaker than that of the average state.

An additional though minor hindrance to the operation of a Wisconsin-type council in Massachusetts was the unwillingness of decision makers on labor's side to become members of any type of advisory council. One key figure on labor's side did not want to be hampered in his freedom to attack; another felt obliged to follow a policy of distributing honorific posts widely among the union membership.[15]

The frequency of council meetings might well prove a hindrance to getting the best available council members. Weekly meetings cannot easily be fitted into the busy schedules of decision makers. To induce the decision makers of labor and management to accept council membership, Massachusetts would probably have to reduce the number of council meetings.[16]

The compensation which has been provided for the Massachusetts council has had advantages and disadvantages. Over the life of the council the advantages have probably been outweighed somewhat by the disadvantages.

[15] When the posts have also been remunerative, as in the case of the advisory council, he has felt the obligation even more strongly.

[16] The public member who became chairman in 1955 and who has proved to be one of the most effective council chairmen in the program believes, on the contrary, that even weekly meetings are not frequent enough if the council is to carry out fully the responsibilities imposed on it by law. (See, in this connection, the exhortation of the New York council chairman, p. 185.)

9

THE CONNECTICUT ADVISORY COUNCIL

THERE are two advisory councils in Connecticut, one for the employment service and one for unemployment compensation. The former was never much more than a gesture made to satisfy the Bureau of Employment Security and to fulfill the legal requirements of the Wagner-Peyser Act. It has been inoperative for years. The following account therefore relates only to the advisory council for unemployment compensation.

The Connecticut council has been in existence for more than twenty consecutive years and is therefore one of the older councils in the country. It is a six-man council composed of two representatives of labor, management, and the public. They are appointed by the governor for three-year terms, and they serve without compensation. The council is considered to be advisory to the administrator of the agency, not to the governor or the legislature.

The administrator has called meetings of the council according as he needed the council's advice. He has felt the need only irregularly and infrequently as the following record of the council's meetings shows.

1936 1	1941 1	1946 1	1951 2	1956 0
1937 6	1942 0	1947 3	1952 0	1957 0
1938 2	1943 0	1948 2	1953 3	
1939 1	1944 1	1949 0	1954 2	
1940 1	1945 1	1950 3	1955 1	

In 22 years, the council met only 31 times, an average of 1.4 meetings a year. No regularity marked the meetings. One fifth of all the meetings were held in the first twelve months of the council's existence, whereas during the decade 1940–1950 meetings averaged less than one a year. The administrator of the agency, who was away at war during part of that period, believed that more meetings were held than the records show. There was no way to check his impression; the council minutes were fragmentary and the memories of the council members were vague. The attendance record of the public members was very good (94 percent); of the employer members, good (85 percent); and of the employee members, fair (72 percent). The record of the council as a whole was 84 percent.

ACTIVITIES OF THE COUNCIL

Since the records of the Connecticut advisory council were fragmentary, and a preliminary review of the council's activities indicated that the council had not been a major influence, only such investigation was made as would suffice to bring out the main stages of its development.

1936–1937

The council held its first meeting on the last day of 1936, just one month after the Connecticut unemployment compensation law was enacted. During the next twelve months, the council met on an average of every other month. Because there was much to do and because there were few competent to do it, the council concerned itself with nearly every phase of the program, administrative as well as legislative.

During this period, the leading personage on the council was the chairman, one of the public members, who has held that post throughout the council's history. An actuary by profession, he had the talent necessary to help organize what was essentially a program of insurance. He had been the chairman of the study commission which drafted the original Connecticut unemployment compensation law, and as chairman of the council he continued to give his professional skill and a great deal of his time to the program. During this period and for several subsequent years, he was "Mr. Unemployment Compensation" in Connecticut.

None of the employer and employee representatives had the influence which comes from technical competence and the authority to speak for organizations. The employer representatives were highly respected as individuals by their fellow employers and would have done splendidly on a team that included a technician and a professional representative of the Connecticut Manufacturers Association. The employee representatives, both of them from the Connecticut Federation of Labor, were neither well versed nor particularly interested in the program.

1938–1944

In 1938 the two labor members on the council were replaced by more effective representatives, one of them the secretary of the state Federation. During this period of seven years, the council met only five times—partly because of the war, but principally because another group was doing what could have been the council's work.

Agreed bills were customary in this period, but they were reached through the negotiations of a group outside the council. The group included only two council members: the labor member who was the secretary of the state Federation and the public member who was chairman of the council. The others in the group were the chairman of the Joint Legislative Committee, the director of the agency, and the secretary of the Connecticut Manufacturers Association. The usual procedure for the Joint Legislative Committee was to hold a hearing on all bills relating to unemployment compensation (in a typical session these numbered between 100 and 200) and then for the chairman of the committee to call together the negotiating group and urge them and help them to arrive at what was in effect an agreed bill.

Although negotiated outside the council, the agreed bills were nevertheless real and effective. Because of instructions issued at the annual convention of the Connecticut Federation of Labor, the secretary of the Federation sometimes had to introduce bills which asked for more than the negotiating group had originally included in the agreed bill. But everybody understood that these bills were a formality and that the agreed bill was the real bill. Legislators knew that they could vote for the agreed bill without incurring the displeasure of organized labor or management. While the CIO objected to these agreements—because it was not represented on either the advisory council or the negotiating group, and because on principle it preferred political action to "dealing"—it was not strong enough during this period to interfere effectively.

The agreed bills of this period were facilitated not only because the Federation was in control of the labor representation but also because this was the time of continuous liberalization of the program, before the tightening process had set in. The threat of federalization was one of the factors of this period favoring liberalization; it was particularly effective in producing the liberal agreed bill of 1941.[1]

1945–1947

In this period the pattern for enacting unemployment compensation legislation underwent a change. In 1945 the council member who was secretary of the Connecticut Federation of Labor resigned from both the council and the Federation to accept the appointment of commissioner of labor. As commissioner he had direct control. Since unemployment compensation was a division in the Department of Labor, the new commissioner could and did continue to be active in formulating legislation in unemployment compensation. His activity, however, took a different form. He was no longer merely one of the private negotiators. Whatever bill he favored became the official bill of the administration and as such occupied the first place among the hundred or more bills introduced each session. The Joint Legislative Committee usually started with the administration's bill and related the other bills to it.

The commissioner's bill usually represented a compromise between the extreme labor and management positions. He effected the compromise not as a mediator but as an arbitrator. He did not bring the two groups together and induce them to adopt a common position but listened to each separately and made an independent judgment as to what should be given to each. (The

[1] For a similar situation in Utah, see p. 120.

legislative committee acted similarly when it came to make the final decision.)

This pattern of enacting legislation left the council more than ever out of the main stream of activity, and the council's importance was diminished proportionately. Another change at this time contributed further to that effect. In 1945 the state presidents of the Federation and the CIO were appointed as the labor representatives on the council. Although in theory these ideal appointees should have added to the council's influence, as a matter of fact they further diminished it. They proved to be very poor members. Throughout the three years of their terms they attended only one meeting.

What influence the council had during this period was exercised by two council members: a new employer representative, the counsel of the Connecticut Manufacturers Association, who was appointed to the council in 1946, and the council's chairman, who continued to be consulted by the agency and by the Joint Legislative Committee. An unusual, and somewhat accidental, instance of the chairman's influence occurred during the legislative session of 1945 in connection with the proposal for dependents' allowances in unemployment compensation.

Because employers were strongly opposed to dependents' allowances and only the CIO was strongly in favor of them, there seemed no likelihood that the proposal would be enacted into law. But there came a day toward the end of the legislative session when the Joint Legislative Committee in executive session was tying up the unemployment compensation "package" and the council chairman happened to be in attendance. The committee had reached the conclusion that it ought to do a little something more for labor, and the council chairman was asked for suggestions. When he suggested a modified version of labor's plan for dependents' allowances,[2] the committee snapped it up (it was late in the day) and added the provision to the bill. A very controversial issue was settled that quickly and that easily. The decision makers among

[2] In 1945 the state Federation and the state CIO for the first time had a joint legislative program.

labor and management were surprised when they read about it in the newspapers the next morning.

1948–1957

In 1948 the two labor representatives on the council—the state presidents of the Federation and the CIO—were replaced by the attorneys for the same organizations. These two lawyers were much more active than their predecessors. Together with the counsel of the Connecticut Manufacturers Association, they staged brilliant debates in the council meetings. But the debates led nowhere, and to some observers it seemed that the lawyers were more interested in debating as an end in itself rather than as a means to possible agreement.

In this period, some of the appointments to the council were made for political reasons and the council's influence was thereby further weakened. In 1950 an employer member who had been on the council for thirteen years and who was well versed in the council's problems, competent, and respected by his fellow employers was not reappointed because he was a Republican and the governor was a Democrat. Later that year a public member was replaced for the same reason. She was a former legislator, a former administrator of the National Emergency Relief Administration, and had been on the council since its beginning. She was replaced with a union organizer (AFL). The governor gave as his reason for this unusual action that the other public member (the chairman) was promanagement and that this appointment would balance the council. Three years later a Republican governor decided that if his predecessor could cultivate labor support by such an appointment, he could profitably follow the example. When the term of this labor public member was completed, the governor replaced him with another labor official, the only difference being that this time the appointment went to the CIO.

The period was not marked by agreed bills, in or out of the council. Two changes in circumstances were unfavorable to agreed bills. One was the change from a liberalizing trend to a tightening trend as regards the program of unemployment compensation in the entire country. Although the Connecticut employers seem not to have taken the offensive as vigorously as those in some other states did,[3] their changed attitude made agreement harder to achieve.

The other change was labor's increased reliance on political action to gain its ends. The growing influence of the CIO in the state contributed to this development. The CIO was on principle more inclined to use political methods than was the Federation; furthermore, the CIO had been excluded from the "deals" which the Federation sometimes made with employers. For these reasons the CIO attacked the working arrangement between the Federation and employers and was partly responsible for its abandonment.

But the Connecticut Federation of Labor itself had changed. Between 1935 and 1957 "voluntarism" had lost ground. The man who became secretary of the Federation in 1946 had been a state senator from 1938 through 1943 and even then had been in disagreement with the long-established Federation policy of working out agreements with employers. He believed that this policy resulted in labor's getting only the crumbs from the table. When he himself became Federation secretary he preferred to rely more on political activity and for this end to work closely with the state CIO.

APPRAISAL

The Connecticut council was chiefly characterized by three qualities. It was thin, public, and political. The outstanding characteristic of the Connecticut council was its "thinness." It was thin in numbers—only two representatives of labor and two of management; it was thin in meetings—an average of 1.4 meetings a year over its lifetime; and it was thin in scope—it never aimed at influencing legislative policy directly, by means of agreed bills.

The limitation on the council's scope was self-imposed and reflected the council's emphasis on its "public" character. The council did not attempt to negotiate agreed bills because it held that making "deals" was not the proper function of a public body. The

[3] For example, in Michigan, New York, Ohio, Massachusetts, Illinois, California.

council conceived that it had performed its function when it met on call, considered the matters laid before it, reviewed the relevant data, stated its opinion(s), and adjourned. To some extent this position was forced upon the council. It could not have negotiated effective agreed bills if it had tried; during most of its existence its membership did not include the decision makers of labor and management. It is significant that the council's "best" member—in point of attendance, activity, and influence within the council [4]—has been a public member, the council's chairman.

As between having a "political" or an "economic" coloring, the Connecticut council had rather the former. The council was "political" in the double sense that the members preferred political action to collective bargaining and in the sense that some appointments to the council were made on the basis of the appointee's position in the political rather than the economic hierarchy of the state. The council might have been slightly less political in both senses if the unemployment compensation employment security agency had been a separate administrative unit and not in the Department of Labor directly subject to the commissioner of labor. The commissioner is necessarily more involved in politics than the administrator of the agency; for the higher one goes in the political hierarchy, the more politics, in the narrow sense, matters.

An advisory council in Connecticut would have better prospects of influence if the number of its members were increased, if the membership included the decision makers in labor and management, if the council met more frequently, if it made one of its aims the reaching of agreed bills, and if politics played a lesser role in the appointment of its members.

Such an advisory council would be helped toward agreed bills by two circumstances in the Connecticut situation. First, unlike other New England states, Connecticut's unemployment costs are below the national average and its reserve fund is above the national average. Second, there seems to be fairly equal balance of power between labor and management in Connecticut. Labor

---

[4] His influence was greater earlier than later. His influence rested primarily on his technical competence, which was rarer in the early days of the program before the agency and employers developed technicians of their own.

frequently has more influence in the Senate and management regularly has more influence in the House (the opposite of the situation in Rhode Island.) The balance is sufficiently close to make the results of a test of political power an uncertainty for both parties, and each has a motive therefore for preferring the certainty of an agreed bill.

The director of the agency had a bill introduced in 1957 that would have reorganized the council. Among other changes, it would have increased the membership from six to eight by increasing the number of the public members from two to four. This change would have deepened the "public" coloration of the council and probably would have lessened the likelihood of agreed bills. The bill, however, did not pass.

10

THE OHIO ADVISORY COUNCIL

THE advisory council of the Ohio Bureau of Unemployment Compensation [1] was established by law in December, 1936, held its first meeting in October, 1937, and has been active ever since. The provisions under which this council began to operate were revised in 1939, but have remained essentially unchanged since then.

The law as revised [2] provides for a council of seven members to be appointed by the governor with the advice and consent of the Senate. The council is tripartite: two labor, two management, and three public representatives.[3] They are appointed for seven-year terms [4] staggered in such a way that one member's term expires each year. The members receive compensation of $20 a day "while attending meetings of the council or while engaged in the necessary business of the council," up to a maximum of $2,000 in any one year.

The law gives the council a wide field of activity: "The advisory council may conduct research of its own, make and publish reports, and recommend to the administrator, the board of review, the

[1] Although the Ohio State Employment Service was integrated with the Bureau of Unemployment Compensation in 1938, the name of the agency was not changed. In 1941 the advisory council recommended unanimously that the name be changed to the Department of Employment Security, but the recommendation was ignored.

[2] All the following citations are taken from *The Ohio Unemployment Compensation Law (Annotated) 1955–56*, pp. 12 and 14 (sections 4141.05 and 4141.08).

[3] The law does not actually specify "public" representatives, but "persons whose training and experience qualify them to deal with the difficult problems of unemployment compensation, particularly with respect to the legal, accounting, actuarial, economic, and social aspects."

[4] This gives the Ohio council the longest fixed term of any of the councils.

governor, or the legislature, needed changes in the act or in the rules and regulations of the bureau."

The law also endows the council with two bits of administrative power: the administrator must have the approval of the advisory council before he can draw money out of the special administrative fund, and the council decides when the amount of this special fund is excessive; further, the council acts as arbitrator between the administrator and the board of review and promulgates rules regulating the payment of claims when these two authorities cannot agree.

The law further provides that "the chief of the division of research shall act as secretary of the advisory council" and "may not be removed without the consent of the advisory council, nor may the duties of his office be altered, suspended or abolished without the consent of the advisory council." This unique provision was devised to safeguard the council's channel of information. The division of research is normally the nerve center of an employment security agency. Having the chief of the division as its secretary, the council is provided with the best possible channel of information; and having a veto on his removal, the council is provided with the means to defend him against possible retaliation by an irritated administrator.

The only member of the agency who regularly attends the council meetings is this secretary. Other members of the agency, including the administrator, attend only as they receive a specific invitation. When they are called in to present some material, they usually leave the meeting after they have done so. The council members feel that they can discuss their affairs more freely if they are by themselves.[5] The council's secretary apprises the agency administrator of the council's actions only as directed to do so by the council.

The council's secretary is much more than a recording secretary —although he does take the minutes of the council meetings. As the council's main link with the agency, he has played an active role in arranging the council's agenda, supplying it with materials, and

[5] For experience with a similar procedure, see Michigan (pp. 317, 328–29) and New York (p. 183). See also New Hampshire (p. 113). In Ohio the procedure gave rise to none of the unpleasantness which marked the New York experience.

guiding the work of analysis. But since he is only a subordinate official in the agency, he has not attempted to lead the council as the administrator of the agency might. His relation to the council has been more like that of the executive secretary of the New York council than like that of the chairman of the Wisconsin council.

Because the council's link with the agency is through someone other than the administrator himself, the Ohio council has been more independent of the agency than are most councils (though not so independent in either structure or operation as the Michigan council, for example) and has had to supply its own leadership to a greater extent than is required of the average council. The Ohio council has been able to do this with some success largely because of the competence of its chairman.

Its chairman since 1945 has been a university professor who has been a member of the council since 1939. During the early years the council rotated the chairmanship among its labor, management, and public members, but found the professor chairman so satisfactory that it insisted on his keeping the job. His attendance record at council meetings for the period 1939–1957 was 95 percent. A number of circumstances combined to make him unusually effective in the post: his field of teaching included unemployment compensation, he lived in Columbus, he had an engaging personality, and his work outside council meetings was compensated.

Another reason why the council has been able to maintain a fairly high level of independent activity has been that it made extensive use of committees. All its more difficult tasks were accomplished through committees, which changed as needs changed. Most of the committees operated efficiently and produced reports. Their work was facilitated by the availability of compensation for work on a committee, even a committee of one.

The frequency of its meetings was still another reason why the council was able to keep functioning actively and efficiently even though it was less closely associated with the administrator of the agency than is the average council. The Ohio law requires the council to meet at least monthly, and in most of the years of its existence the council fulfilled this requirement. From its first meeting, in October, 1937, through December, 1957, the full council held a total of 326 meetings. In addition there were even more numerous meetings of council committees. The meetings of the full council were distributed by years as follows:

1937	13	1942	17	1947	13	1952	4	1957	11
1938	55	1943	15	1948	9	1953	16		
1939	40	1944	18	1949	9	1954	12		
1940	21	1945	19	1950	4	1955	7		
1941	14	1946	12	1951	7	1956	10		

In total number of meetings Ohio is second only to Massachusetts. During the first twenty-four months of its existence, October, 1937, through September, 1939, the council held 113 meetings, an average of more than a meeting a week. After 1940 the number of meetings declined sharply, partly because the work of founding and reorganizing the agency was completed, and partly because the council became less ambitious as the result of some rebuffs suffered in 1940 and 1941.

The attendance at meetings was fair. The record of the council as a whole was 76 percent; of labor, 79 percent; of the public, 77 percent; and of employers, 71 percent. As is the case with most councils, the missed meetings were not distributed evenly within the membership. In each of the three groups, there were some individuals who missed more than half of the meetings and others who missed scarcely any. In recent years employers have had the best, instead of the worst, attendance record.

ACTIVITIES OF THE COUNCIL

The council has always been active in matters of administration, including administrative law, but was especially active in its early years. Like other councils which have begun with the agency, the Ohio council was caught up in the rush of things that needed to be done to get the program started. For example, the council helped choose the first executive director of the agency, and a little later supplied the struggling agency with an actuary and a systems expert to help it set up the original benefit payment procedures.[6] There

---

[6] The services of the actuary and systems expert were offered by one of the public members, who was connected with a large insurance company.

was so much to be done in 1937 and 1938 that the council sometimes met twice a week.

The agency had been functioning for little more than a year
when it was reorganized early in 1939. The reorganization was
brought about by several factors. There was a general trend at this
time to bring unemployment compensation and the employment
service under one head and to replace commissions by single directors. The Ohio reorganization included both of these changes.
But the chief factor was political. By 1939 the New Deal had lost
some of its momentum in Ohio, and Democrat Davey was replaced
by Republican Bricker. The new governor and legislature of that
year wished to lessen the influence of the previous administration
and also of organized labor in the agency. The reorganization enabled the governor to replace the former three-man commission,
whose chairman had been a labor man (United Mine Workers),
by a single administrator who was later to become the executive
vice president of the Ohio Chamber of Commerce.

The reorganization extended to the advisory council: it was
dissolved and a new one formed. Three members from the old
council were reappointed to the new one (one each from the labor,
management, and public groups); the four additional appointees
were new. With the reorganization came many new administrative
problems and with the beginning of benefit payments (January,
1939) came more. The new council was as busy as the old had
been and it continued to meet twice weekly. On one occasion when
some regulations were proving unworkable, the council was called
into emergency session by the governor to approve a new set of
regulations. In 1939 the council was clearly an important institution.

The council's activity was not confined to administration but
extended to legislation as well. The minutes of the council for the
years 1940 and 1941 indicate that the council ambitioned a more
direct relationship to legislation in those early years than it did
later. The council even manifested interest in the possibility of
working out agreed bills. The council's later position—that agreed
bills were not part of its function—seems to have been a change
from its position in those early years. At its meeting of May 9, 1940,

the chairman "instructed the secretary to write to the Chairman
of the Illinois Advisory Board to determine the procedures followed by that Board in obtaining an agreed bill and putting it
through the Illinois Legislature without dissent." The minutes
do not record whether the council learned the true situation—
that the Illinois council merely approved agreed bills which were
reached outside the council—or what conclusions the Ohio council reached regarding its own "powers and duties under the law
and frequency of meetings necessary to fulfill its duties." [7]

Evidently the council expected to play an important role in the
1941 legislative session and made intensive preparations for it.
In July and August of 1940 the council sent letters to employer,
labor, and public organizations, inviting them to submit proposals
for amendment of the Ohio law. It sent similar letters to a selective
list of small employers, and through the newspapers extended the
same invitation to the general public. At its two-day meeting in
September the council discussed "future procedures of the council
in giving detailed consideration to proposed amendments and in
holding public hearings" and in November the council decided
to divide its membership and hold simultaneous hearings in the
northern and in the southern parts of the state.[8]

Also in November the council requested a meeting with the
governor "to ask whether he desires that they [the council] draft
amendments which he would present to the legislature." The governor met with the council but did not commit himself further
than to say that he "thought it desirable for the council to continue its work on such amendments as were absolutely necessary
to the satisfactory operation of the law."

In December the council invited the Ohio League of Women
Voters to submit suggestions for improvement in the unemployment compensation law. The league probably surprised the council by concentrating on the council itself and insisting that the
council should have no rule-making powers (as a matter of fact,
it had none) and that the council members should serve without
compensation.

[7] Minutes of the Ohio advisory council, meeting of June, 1940. Subsequent quotations are from the council's minutes unless another source is indicated.
[8] It seems that this decision was not carried into effect.

In March, in the midst of the 1941 legislative session, a public member of the council visited the New York advisory council and brought back a glowing account of that council's wide powers and great influence, an account possibly obtained from the New York council's public chairman. At that time it was not yet clear that the New York council had passed the peak of its influence and had begun to decline.

The extent of the council's influence on the 1941 legislation is uncertain. Had the council been able to arrive at an agreed bill its influence would probably have been considerable. Its two labor members could speak for the Ohio State Federation of Labor (at that time the effective spokesman for Ohio labor), its two employer members were influential with their fellow employers, and the administrator believed in lobbying energetically for the legislative program he wanted. But since the council could not reach agreement, the probabilities are that the direct influence of the council as a body on legislation was small.[9] Perhaps one item on the agenda of the council's meeting in November, 1941, is an implicit admission that the council's influence had been minor. At this meeting the council again "discussed various ways of making the Council more influential."

Certainly in succeeding legislative sessions the council never again came as close to being a direct major influence on legislation. In 1942, for example, when the council held public hearings in preparation for the 1943 session, only the representatives of the Ohio State Federation of Labor put in an appearance. The CIO and the leaders of the employer organizations sent word that they were otherwise occupied on that day.

At many of its meetings during 1943 and 1944 the council discussed the coming problems of reconversion, and in February, 1945, it secured a meeting with the governor (Lausche) to discuss its conclusions with him. But the meeting did little to strengthen the council's position. There would seem to be a rebuff implied in the governor's statement that "he would prefer the Council to furnish data relative to proposed amendments, rather than specific

[9] This statement does not deny that the council may have exercised significant influence indirectly, or through its individual members, or on administration.

recommendations." Perhaps it was this experience which decided the public members to abstain "on principle" from the kind of bargaining activity that is involved in reaching agreed bills.[10]

The events of the 1949 and 1951 legislative sessions made it very clear that the council was not an important direct influence on legislation. In both sessions major changes were made in the unemployment compensation law—in 1949 in the direction of liberalizing the law and in 1951 in the direction of tightening it [11]—but in neither session did the advisory council play an important part. In both sessions the battlefield was wide and the fighting was fierce, but the council was certainly not at the center of it. It is significant that these action-filled years were years of less frequent, not more frequent, council meetings.

The event which dominated the years 1954 and 1955—the CIO's initiative petition—was entirely independent of the advisory council, but that very fact sheds light on the council's position among other forces influencing the unemployment compensation program in Ohio. The CIO had abandoned hope of ever persuading the Ohio legislature to enact what the CIO considered an adequate unemployment compensation program, and in 1954 it decided that the time had come to use a new method.[12] It had recourse to the device of the initiative petition by which it could force the legislature to vote on the CIO proposals and if the legislature rejected them could take them directly to the electorate.[13] The CIO suc-

[10] Or perhaps it merely confirmed them in a position which they had held from the beginning but which they had modified to accommodate the labor members of the council (all of them state Federation representatives), who did wish to reach agreed bills.

[11] The changes in 1949 are traceable to the high unemployment of that year, to the appointment of a new, more liberal administrator, and to the Democratic majority in the state Senate. The changes in 1951 were on the pattern of changes made in the New York and the Massachusetts laws at this time and were part of the long-bottled-up drive of employers to tighten the program. The Ohio changes included more amendments to the disqualification provisions than did the changes in the other states.

[12] The CIO had grown rapidly since the beginning of the war. Growth in steel, autos, and rubber had doubled the membership of the CIO in Ohio. By 1954 it was at least as large as the state Federation. (It had been given its first post on the advisory council in 1946.)

[13] In Ohio the initiative petition requires the signatures of 3 percent of those who voted in the last gubernatorial election, including 1.5 percent in each of at least 44 of Ohio's 88 counties. In 1954 this meant about 80,000 signatures. Such a petition is

ceeded in getting its proposals put on the ballot, but at a special election held in November, 1955, the proposals were rejected by 63 percent of those voting.

Though the CIO initiative petition was an unusually dramatic move, in one sense it fitted the general pattern of unemployment compensation legislation in Ohio. Labor and management have always followed independent courses in introducing legislation. There have been no agreed bills in or out of the advisory council. Leaders of the state Federation have several times suggested the use of the agreed bill technique, but the CIO and employers have been cold to the idea, and neither the governor nor the legislature has tried to pressure the two parties to reach agreement. In this respect Ohio's history resembles the history of Massachusetts rather than of Utah or Illinois.

In another respect, however, Ohio resembles Utah and Illinois rather than Massachusetts. Workmen's compensation in Ohio has had a long tradition of agreed bills. If the memories of labor and management negotiators are correct, in the entire period 1922–1951 there were only three failures to reach an agreed bill.[14] In 1953, 1955, and 1957, however, the negotiators were unable to reach agreement—possibly an indication that the old tradition is broken and that in the future workmen's compensation will resemble unemployment compensation as regards legislative procedure.[15]

The legislative session of 1957 was literally a unique one for unemployment compensation: no amendments of any sort were enacted.

APPRAISAL

The public character of the Ohio council has been prominent in both its structure and its procedures. It has had three repre-

sufficient to initiate action on the part of the Ohio General Assembly. If the action of the Assembly fails to satisfy the petitioners (as happened in this case), the petitioners can put their proposal on the ballot by getting the signatures of another 3 percent of the qualified electors, similarly distributed by county.

[14] In all these negotiations the Ohio State Federation of Labor and the Ohio Manufacturers Association supplied the leadership.

[15] Since 1955 workmen's compensation has resembled unemployment compensation in still another way—it has had an advisory council closely modeled on the advisory council in unemployment compensation.

sentatives of the public to only two each for employers and employees. One public representative has been the council's chairman since 1945 and so active as to earn the title "the working member of the council." Another public representative is the only member to have been on the council throughout its entire existence. The provision of compensation for work done outside the council meetings has made it easier for public members to give time to council business. The council has operated with more than average independence because it has met at its own call and apart from the administrator of the agency and his staff. Although the secretary of the council has been an agency staff member and has been very influential in council affairs, he has not attempted to subordinate the council to the agency. Finally, the council has refrained on principle from lobbying and from the bargaining that might lead to agreed bills because these activities involve representing partisan interests, and the council has held that it should represent only the "public" interest.

The Ohio council is the leading example of the "public" type of council. The Connecticut council was equally "public" but it was not nearly so active as the Ohio council and hence its potentialities were less. The Ohio council has probably been about as effective as a public-type council can be. If its influence could be appraised accurately, there would be available a fair measure of the possibilities of this type of council. Unfortunately, the appraisal of the Ohio council's influence cannot be very accurate. What influence it exercised was of the indirect rather than the direct sort, and therefore by its nature difficult to measure. It is certainly significant that the two administrators with the longest and most successful terms of office declared emphatically that they would not have liked to be without an advisory council. But they were unable to indicate the exact form the council's influence took.

With respect to the employment service it is likely that the Ohio council exercised more influence than the average council. The council's chairman and its executive secretary and at least one administrator of the agency (1947–1951) were intensely interested in the employment service and regularly brought its problems to the attention of the council. Nevertheless, the influence of even the

Ohio council was probably minor in the employment service program. This was the opinion of all those interviewed.

The influence of the council was more marked in the unemployment compensation program, especially in the field of administration and administrative law. The council's frequent meetings and the long experience of some of its members with the program both helped to that end. Some of the council's activities in the field of administration have been exemplified above. The emphatic appreciation of the two administrators just cited probably rested on the council's role in the solution of administrative problems. One of the administrators related the following incident as typical of that role. A week after his appointment to office (in 1947) a batch of new regulations was put on his desk for his signature. His staff expected him to sign the regulations immediately, but he declined to do anything about them until after he had laid them before the advisory council. As a result of the council's consideration, a number of improvements were made in the regulations before they were put into effect.

Although this administrator valued and used the council, he did not find it entirely adequate. Its representation of labor and management was too thin, and he had to go outside the council for necessary contacts. He built up what he called his unofficial advisory council composed of persons in key positions in labor and management organizations. By his "unofficial advisory council" he meant, not another group which functioned as a group, but persons on whom he called individually to handle anything that affected the organization with which the person was associated. He made explicit agreements with these persons that he would not handle these matters through anyone else, and in return secured their support and cooperation.

Looking back over his years in the agency, he judged that making this arrangement was one of the wisest things he had done. Asked whether the arrangement would not have worked even better if these key members had been members of the official advisory council, he said he believed it would have. But when he was asked whether this unofficial advisory council did not make an official council unnecessary, his answer was decidedly in the negative. His informal contacts with individuals could not, he thought, replace his relations with a council—which acted as a body, met regularly, and had official status.

The council's influence has been least manifest in the most important area, legislation. During the last decade it has refrained on principle from the most direct kind of influence—through agreed bills and lobbying—and except for a rare memorandum sent to the governor has contented itself with exercising the undocumented influence of personal contacts and the indirect influence of education. It is very probable that some of the council members exerted considerable influence, at least occasionally, through their personal contacts with key people in politics and with leaders in the organizations of labor and management. The reports of the council, competent in their analysis and well written, had genuine educational value and were given wide circulation. The council sent copies not only to the governor and the legislature but also to newspapers, to leaders in labor and management, and to some civic organizations.

Its biennial report to the governor and legislature has labored under the serious disadvantage of always appearing late. In Ohio the legislature convenes early in January of the odd-numbered years, and the governor's message to the legislature opens the session. But the council's report has never appeared before February, and at least twice it appeared as late as May. This, despite many resolutions taken by the council to get out its report in time for the governor to use it in his message. The delay has usually been connected with some difficulty in satisfying the council's employer members.

One highly placed state official said that he never read the council's reports. He did, however, readdress them to a friend who taught in the state university and the act of readdressing indicates that he attached some importance to the reports. One technician who worked for an employers' organization declared that while the council certainly had no direct influence on legislation, it did make "valuable contributions." He did not specify what contributions he had in mind, but he must have included at the very least the council's reports.

Why did not the council exercise more direct and important influence on legislation? Certainly a major part of the explanation is to be found in the council membership. As noted above, the public members have been emphasized in the composition of the Ohio council. These public members have been of the highest caliber, but they are still only public members; and unless public members happen to be active politicians they rarely influence legislation directly. Moreover, in the case of Ohio the public members were opposed "on principle" not only to the bargaining involved in reaching agreed bills but also to such direct procedures as putting the council's recommendations into bill form and appearing at legislative hearings in support of those recommendations.

The labor and management membership on the council has been too small and has not included enough of the technicans, lobbyists, and decision makers of the respective sides. Until very recently the labor membership never included a technician. Labor representation was stronger in the earlier period of the council. In the later period, especially after 1944, the labor members on the council were not able to speak authoritatively for organized labor in Ohio. The governor appointed some members not because their organizations nominated them or because they were experts in unemployment compensation matters but because they supported him politically in his campaign.

The employer representation on the council has been reasonably strong—although here, as with labor, the limitation to two representatives has made it impossible to secure simultaneously decision makers and technicians and adequate representation of the various organizations.[16] One of the employer representatives has been on the council since its second beginning (1939) and is influential in the rubber industry, which is influential in the Ohio Chamber of Commerce, which is very influential in unemployment compensation matters. That chain of connections plus his long experience have made him as adequate a spokesman for employers as one person could be. The other employer position has been occupied successively by three persons. The present (1957) occupant is head of the compensation department of a large firm and is there-

[16] Organizations of employers in Ohio are unusually numerous, perhaps because industry in Ohio is unusually diversified both qualitatively and geographically.

fore in constant contact with the program on a technical level. Both employer representatives are members of the social security committees of the Ohio Chamber of Commerce and of the Ohio Manufacturers Association and make a combination about as strong as can be obtained with only two representatives.

Employer representation on the council would have been strengthened further if it had included the professional spokesmen of employer organizations. The principal organizations in unemployment compensation matters have been the Ohio Chamber of Commerce, the Ohio Manufacturers Association, and the Ohio State Council of Retail Merchants. The Ohio Chamber of Commerce is one of the largest and best organized chambers in the country. As in Illinois and several other states, the state Chamber of Commerce since the war has led a "reform" movement in unemployment compensation.

The Council of Retail Merchants has been active since the original law was enacted. The man who is the present chairman of the council was once employed by this group to help draft the original bill.[17] The retailers have generally tended to be somewhat more liberal than the other employer organizations—at least as regards benefits, if not as regards disqualifications—perhaps because they see retailers as deriving a more immediate gain from the spending of unemployment compensation benefits.

The employer organizations are unusually well staffed with former members of the Ohio Bureau of Unemployment Compensation. The executive vice president of the Ohio Chamber of Commerce was the first administrator of the bureau; the secretary-treasurer of the Ohio Manufacturers Association was formerly a member of the bureau's board of review; the men in charge of unemployment compensation for both the Council of Retail Merchants and the Ohio Chamber of Commerce were formerly technicians in the bureau. The presence of so many bureau "alumni" in employers' organizations is an advantage to both employers and the bureau; at the very least it diminishes conflict arising out of misunderstanding.

There was a chorus of agreement that a technician working for

[17] For a similar situation, see New York, p. 205.

an employers' organization would not make the best advisory council member. The technicians themselves agreed with this judgment. They believed that because they were identified with a specific employer organization they might not be acceptable to all employers. They also mentioned the disability of not having enough authority to form policy.[18] One executive—as influential in Ohio unemployment compensation as any one person might be—offered the added objection that such technicians would be inclined to liberalize the program too much since they were not "genuine employers" and the costs of liberalization would not come out of their pockets.[19]

The practice of having the chief of the division of research and statistics act as the secretary of the advisory council, and of giving the council some control over his status, seems to have worked well in Ohio. The gains have thus far been large enough to hazard the danger of division within the agency. The danger was at its maximum in 1952, when a new administrator tried to dismiss the division chief and the council prevented it. After a brief period of acute conflict, during which the council won the support of the governor, the administrator accepted the situation, and the agency continued to operate with unimpaired efficiency. The danger remains, however, that a serious conflict between an administrator and an advisory council so entrenched might disrupt the agency.

Despite the recommendation of the Ohio League of Women Voters, the council members have continued to be compensated for their services. The arrangement seems to have had no undesirable effects as yet, and has probably resulted in the council doing more work. The provision by which members are compensated for work done outside council meetings has been particularly helpful. Without such a provision it is unlikely that the committee work would have been as effective as it was; certainly the chairman could not have given so much time to the affairs of the council.

Although the requirement in the law that the council meet at

[18] The force of this objection would be much weakened if more than two places on the council were open to employers. It would then be possible to have a combination of technicians and those holding posts of authority.

[19] This was the reverse of the usual argument according to which others than "genuine employers" should be kept off the council because they are too intent on making a record for themselves by saving money for their bosses. See p. 443.

least once monthly has not been rigidly adhered to, it has had the effect of increasing the number of meetings held, and the frequency of meetings has undoubtedly contributed to the effectiveness of the council. The type of council which emphasizes its public element depends more than others on frequent meetings to exert influence.

The long, seven-year term of the members and the provision that the Senate confirm the appointment of members seem not to have been significant factors, for good or evil, in the council's history.

11

THE NEBRASKA ADVISORY COUNCIL

AS enacted in 1937 the Nebraska unemployment compensation law provided for an advisory council composed of two representatives of employers, two of employees, and three of the public. Amendments enacted in 1941 reduced the number of public representatives to two, set the term of council membership at four years, and provided compensation of $10 for each day of active service.[1] The amendments of 1941 also integrated the employment service with unemployment compensation and extended the duties of the advisory council to include both programs.[2]

In Nebraska employment security is a division of the Department of Labor, and the commissioner of labor, who has fewer duties than his counterparts in other states—his department does not include workmen's compensation, for example—exercises active control over the employment security program. The law specifies that the function of the council is to advise the commissioner and that it is to meet at his call. By the terms of the law the commissioner has the power to appoint the council members, but in practice this power has been exercised by the governor—on the theory that the governor may do whatever his subordinates have the power to do. The governor has sometimes made council appointments without consulting either the commissioner of labor or the director of the division of employment security.

The Nebraska council ranks among the longest-lived councils. It met for the first time in December, 1937, and has held meetings

---

[1] This was increased to $15 in 1947 and to $20 in 1955.

[2] The 1941 amendments changed the name of the division from "Unemployment Compensation" to "Placement and Unemployment Insurance." A 1949 amendment gave the division its present name, "Employment Security."

every year since that time except in 1940. By the end of 1957, the council had met 42 times, an average of two meetings a year. The following is a complete list of its meetings by years.

1937	1	1941	1	1945	2	1949	1	1953	2	1957	1
1938	3	1942	3	1946	3	1950	3	1954	2		
1939	3	1943	1	1947	1	1951	1	1955	1		
1940	0	1944	3	1948	4	1952	3	1956	3		

Employer members attended 98 percent of these meetings; employee members, 95 percent; and public members, 95 percent. The attendance record of the council as a whole was 95.5 percent, the best of all the states in the sample.

A public member served as council chairman until 1945. In that year a newly appointed employer member, the executive secretary of the Associated Industries of Nebraska, was elected chairman. The council retained him in the post until 1956, when, at his request, a public member was again elected chairman.

ACTIVITIES OF THE COUNCIL

During its first few meetings, the Nebraska council, like all the early councils, found itself faced with the administrative problems attendant on the establishing of a new program. But thereafter the council concerned itself entirely with unemployment compensation legislation, beginning with the 1939 legislative session.

In 1939 a group of employers outside the council were very active in the legislature and had a bill introduced which was designed to tighten the disqualification provisions drastically.[3] At its meeting of February 27, 1939, the council discussed what action it ought to take with regard to the bill. This council discussion provided examples of two major viewpoints on how a council should function —according to unanimous or majority vote. The labor representatives favored the rule of unanimity. They held that unless they and the employer representatives could reach agreement, the council should recommend to the legislature that no action at all be taken. The rule of unanimity would have worked to labor's advantage in this instance, since no legislation would represent a labor vic-

[3] One of these provisions postponed benefits for two months in the case of a claimant whose salary was more than $50 per week.

tory, and the labor representatives may have proposed it less as a permanent principle than as a temporary expedient. The second viewpoint was voiced by the regional representative of the Bureau of Employment Security, who was present at the meeting and insisted that the vote of the majority always determined the position of the council. In this case the viewpoint probably represented a statement of permanent principle. "Advisory councils," he added, "usually publicize the position they take by issuing a statement to the newspapers."

In the end the council managed to agree unanimously on a recommendation that the offending bill "be not enacted at this time." But because the council membership did not include decision makers among employers at that time, the council's recommendation was ignored, and many of the bill's provisions were enacted into law. After this setback in 1939, the council members lost interest. When two attempts to assemble a quorum in 1940 failed, the council ceased to function.

In 1941 the programs of unemployment compensation and employment service were integrated in a single division, and this reorganization provided the opportunity to appoint a new council. This council seems to have become the effective locus of decision making. It agreed to legislative "truces" in 1943 and 1947, and in all the other sessions—1945, 1949, 1951, 1953, 1955, 1957—the council formulated the amendments which were enacted into law.

The most important agreed bill was that of 1949, which made major changes in the law. Some of the changes were similar to those made earlier in the Michigan law (copied later in the laws of Ohio and New York) and included request reporting and the sending of a copy of each benefit check to the employer concerned.

In reaching the 1949 agreement the council had to reverse itself at one point and thereby provided an apt illustration of the forces at work in Nebraska decision making. The executive secretary of Associated Industries was in Europe during the latter part of 1948, and his place on the council was filled by an alternate. The alternate, an official in a public utilities company, agreed with the rest of the council on an agency-sponsored increase in benefits to $22 (from $18). The alternate was either unaware that the executive secretary had previously settled with other employers on a maximum increase to $20, or he was unconcerned.

When the executive secretary returned, a special meeting of the council was called—on New Year's Eve—to hear the protest of certain employers, mainly the retailers of Omaha. At this meeting the council voted unanimously to change the benefit amount in the agreed bill from $22 to $20. The labor members, knowing that they could not win a legislative battle against employer opposition, agreed to the change in order to save the employer members of the council from embarrassment and to build up some employer good will for future negotiations.

In the 1955 session the employer members made a partial return of the favor. In the previous session, 1953, the council had agreed to an increase in eligibility requirements which excluded some seasonal workers. The labor members of the council had voted for the increase after they had cleared—they thought—with the unions affected by the change. Later they found themselves bitterly criticized.[4] In the 1955 session the employer members joined with the rest of the council to recommend some easing of the requirements.

The CIO, which has been represented on the council for only three legislative sessions,[5] endorsed the agreed bill of 1951, but not those of 1953 or 1955. The refusal of the CIO representative to endorse the last two agreed bills had the approval of the employer members of the council. They recognized that he would only injure himself with his fellow unionists if he approved the agreements, and they knew that his refusal to approve would make no difference in the legislative results.

The commissioner of labor has not used the council to any significant extent in the formulation of administrative law. He has not called the council into meeting frequently enough for that. Instead he has consulted informally with the leaders of manage-

[4] The criticism was twofold: that too many workers had been excluded by the change and that the labor bargainers had got too little in exchange for their concession.

[5] The CIO was given one of the two labor places on the council in late 1949 by the governor, who was looking for support in a forthcoming political campaign. At the time both the state Federation and employers were displeased, but they have since become reconciled to the appointment.

ment and labor, usually the secretary of Associated Industries and the president of the state Federation, both of whom were easily reached in Lincoln.

The commissioner has used the council in the performance of another task, however, which is almost unique. The Nebraska law gives the commissioner of labor the unusual power to prescribe by general rule the contribution rate applicable to each covered employer for each calendar year. Understandably, the commissioner has hesitated to exercise this remarkable power entirely on his own responsibility. He has, therefore, always asked the council to approve the schedule of rates which he proposes each year. For the employers on the council this opportunity to participate directly in the determination of their own tax rates has been an important value of the council. For the labor members the opportunity to withhold support of a proposed tax schedule (even though the support is merely moral, and not legal) has represented one of their few solid bargaining points when the council comes to work out an agreed bill.

The Nebraska council has twice discussed proposals to establish a local advisory council in Omaha. The first proposal was made in 1944 by the agency. The director of the agency thought that a local advisory council might be a means to improve labor-management relations in Omaha, which at that time were very strained. The advisory council approved the proposal, but only on condition that compensation be provided for the members of the local council. When the federal Bureau of Employment Security refused to grant funds for such a purpose, and the agency shortly thereafter became immersed in the turbulent reconversion period, the whole idea was forgotten.

The second proposal, made in 1950, had a different origin. Some employers of Omaha, chiefly members of the Nebraska Small Businessmen's Association and the Omaha Retailers Association, feeling that their interests were not properly represented on the state council, hoped to redress the balance by a local council, which would be under their control. The state council unanimously disapproved of this proposal, the identical one they had unanimously sanctioned six years earlier. The employer members on the council did not want their authority challenged, and the labor members recognized that the challenging group of employers were more conservative than the employers on the state council. This drive for a local advisory council weakened the following year, 1951, when the president of the Nebraska Small Businessmen's Association was appointed to the state council.

APPRAISAL

After 1943, when the council was reorganized, amendment of the unemployment compensation law was regulated by the council's agreed bills. To that extent the Nebraska advisory council was an influential institution. The agreed bills were made possible by the fact that the labor and management representatives on the council could speak authoritatively for their respective sides. On management's side, the Associated Industries of Nebraska was the only state-wide employer organization and was usually regarded by both employers and the legislature as the chief spokesman of employers in unemployment compensation matters. The executive secretary of the association, a council member since 1945, was always able to give assurance that Nebraska employers would support any bill he agreed to on the council. Before giving this assurance, he always secured the approval of his board of directors and he usually had discussions with other employer organizations, especially the Nebraska Small Businessmen's Association and the Omaha Retailers Association. The Nebraska Small Businessmen's Association came into being in 1947 as a vehicle for putting a right-to-work provision into the state constitution. After this was accomplished (by a popular vote of 212,443 to 142,702), the organization was continued by some of its members and became a rival of Associated Industries. It failed to attract adequate support, however, and was eventually disbanded in 1956.

On labor's side, the Nebraska State Federation of Labor was always the recognized spokesman in unemployment compensation matters. The Federation was much larger than the CIO and had more influence—little though it was—in the legislature.[6] The

[6] Both legislators and employer lobbyists have tended to freeze out the CIO by dealing almost exclusively with the state Federation.

Federation's position was not normally determined by the Federation's representative on the council. This individual was not a decision maker in his own right but took his directions from the Federation's president, who normally made the final decision to accept or reject the employers' offer. The president's lobbying activities brought him into frequent contact with employer spokesmen and he sometimes struck bargains with them. Undoubtedly, however, he was influenced by the views of the Federation's council representative, and the Federation's position was always expressed officially by its representative on the council and at the council meeting.

The agreed bills represented a judgment by both sides that they had more to gain by agreement than by conflict. Employers found the agreed bill both simpler (one or two council meetings substituted for many days of lobbying activity) and safer (the agreed bill forestalled the possibility of other, less desirable, legislation).[7] Employers also valued the opportunity to determine their own tax rates.

On their side, labor leaders judged that they had more bargaining strength in dealing with employers than in dealing with the legislature. The Nebraska legislature was dominated by agricultural interests, whose position was the stronger because legislative reapportionment was overdue and the city population (and therefore organized labor) was underrepresented. Also, because the salary of legislators was so low that only persons of independent means could afford to serve, the legislature included a disproportionate number of retired businessmen, lawyers, ranchers, and small-town editors. This legislature was suspicious of labor legislation in general and of unemployment compensation in particular.[8] Generally labor could rely on no more than a third of the total votes in the legislature on bills directly affecting labor.

In dealing with employers labor was dealing with those who at

[7] One employer lobbyist recalled how a legislator introduced an unemployment compensation bill which he intended as a help to employers but which would have caused them considerable trouble. They caught it at the last minute and only by much work were able to have it sent back to committee.

[8] One of the labor leaders cited his own relatives, small-farm holders, as examples of the attitude of farm dwellers. They were so hostile to organized labor that they thought his own profession a disgrace to the family.

least understood labor's problems and the machinery of unemployment compensation. Labor found that employers were willing to
pay something for the cooperation which labor could give or withhold in the matter of an agreed bill and that employers could not
afford to antagonize labor unduly in the area of unemployment
compensation because they were under the necessity of getting
along with labor leaders outside the legislature—in the regular
industrial relationships where labor had more power. For these
reasons labor preferred bargaining with employers to fighting with
the legislature and saw the agreed bill as the lesser of two evils.

Two additional factors help to explain why the labor leaders
accepted the agreed bills and made less of a legislative fight than
might have been expected. First, by temperament they were more
inclined to reasonableness than to militancy. Some observers
thought that by harder bargaining labor could have got more
than it did on certain occasions (for example, in 1949 and 1953),
when labor agreed to amendments which employers wanted very
much. Second, labor leaders placed unemployment compensation
low in their scale of relative values. Given the choice of a gain in
unemployment compensation or in workmen's compensation, for
example, they would always choose the latter. On at least two occasions they actually made such a choice.

The program which has resulted from the agreed bills, while
not so liberal as the programs in industrial states, is about as liberal
as those in the other agricultural states outside the South. This is
the norm, as a matter of fact, which was generally used by employers
in their negotiations with labor.

The agreed bills of labor and management were entirely acceptable to the legislature, which because of its structure and size
found them more than ordinarily helpful. The Nebraska legislature consists of only one House,[9] and this one House has only
forty-three members, who meet only every other year for a legislative session which lasts only four to six months. In this short
period these few legislators must transact all of the state's business.
Each legislator is busier and has more responsibility than even the

[9] Nebraska adopted the unicameral form in 1937 under the influence of George W.
Norris. This single House, although elected on a nonpartisan ballot, has always been
composed of a majority of Republicans.

average state legislator. Certainly in Nebraska the agreed bill has represented a greater than usual contribution to expeditious legislation.

The director of the employment security division was a major factor in the success of the council's operation. He was one of the more experienced directors in the country, having held the post of director since the beginning of the program. He placed a high value on an advisory council and worked to keep it functioning effectively. He declared that a matter as complicated as unemployment insurance did not lend itself too well to the pulling and hauling of the legislative process and recalled compromises made hastily on the floor of the legislature which resulted in nonworkable and even contradictory provisions. Being under the merit system the director was not closely linked with politics; [10] he was also acceptable to both labor and management. Such a director could easily function as the council's chairman—on the pattern of Wisconsin.

The public members of the council seem not to have exerted any important influence. The experience of one of them is typical. A personal friend of two governors, he had served on several other state boards. In his work on these boards, he had several times gone directly to the governor to urge his views. He had never done so in the case of unemployment compensation. He had no reason to believe that the governor would welcome his intervention— there was nothing he could tell the governor which the director of the agency could not tell him as well or better.

Nebraska's advisory council, like its legislature, is smaller than average. However, it has probably been large enough. There is little reason to think that making it larger would have made it more influential. No important group was excluded from representation nor have technicians been allowed to go to waste. Indeed the paucity of technicians among both employers and the unions —but especially among the latter—is a characteristic of the state.

The practice of compensating council members seems to have had more advantages than disadvantages. It has been particularly helpful to the labor members. Since labor in Nebraska does not have many full-time state officers, service on the advisory council

[10] The commissioner of labor generally assumed responsibility for political decisions.

may mean the sacrifice of a day's pay. For the sake of the labor members, the council has held its meetings whenever possible on Saturday or on some other nonwork day.

The council's meetings have not been frequent. They have sufficed, perhaps, for the limited functions of approving a rate schedule each year and determining the essentials of an agreed bill every other year. But the labor members would like the council to perform more functions, and therefore to meet more frequently. They would like the council to participate more in the development of administrative law. They would also like the council to operate more like a study group—raising fundamental questions and considering the data relevant to the answers. Labor's chief objection to council meetings as they have been conducted is that the employer members have come not to discuss but to dictate and have proffered terms for an agreed bill as an ultimatum resting on political power rather than as a reasoned conclusion that is subject to challenge. Negotiations of that nature require very few meetings, but labor would like to see a change in the nature of the negotiations. A change is not likely to occur, however, until labor either acquires more technical competence or wields more political influence.

12

THE MINNESOTA ADVISORY COUNCIL

THE Minnesota advisory council has undergone more changes, probably, than any other council. Some of the changes were minor legal modifications which left the council essentially the same,[1] but some were substantial changes made in the structure of the council without any change in the law. The law has always provided for "an equal number of employer and employee representatives" and "such members representing the public as the appointing authority may designate." This flexible provision has enabled Minnesota to experiment with six different council structures, as listed in Table 1.[2]

During the period 1938–1957 these various councils held a total of 112 meetings. In addition, an executive committee of the council, which functioned almost exactly like the full council, held fifty-two meetings. The distribution of meetings by years was as follows (the figures in parentheses refer to the meetings of the executive committee):

1938	66	1943	4	1948	1 (2)	1953	1 (1)
1939	9	1944	3 (14)	1949	1 (1)	1954	1 (2)
1940	0	1945	3 (10)	1950	3 (5)	1955	3
1941	2	1946	1 (10)	1951	1 (3)	1956	3
1942	0	1947	3	1952	2 (4)	1957	5

Nearly three quarters of the meetings of the full council were held in the first year and a half of the council's existence. Between 1940 and 1957 the full council met only thirty-seven times, an average of 1.8 meetings per year. The executive committee met

---

[1] For example, the amendments of 1939, 1941, 1945, 1947, and 1953.

[2] In 1958 a seventh structure was tried: two additional nongovernmental public members were appointed, making the total number of council members thirteen.

more than twice that often during the years that it operated. Between 1944 and 1954 the committee met fifty-two times, an average of 4.7 meetings per year.

TABLE 1

STRUCTURE OF THE MINNESOTA EMPLOYMENT SECURITY
ADVISORY COUNCIL 1938–1957

Period	Representatives of Employers	Representatives of Employees	REPRESENTATIVES OF THE PUBLIC			Total
			Not from Government	From Senate	From House	
March, 1938–June, 1939	1	1	1			3
June, 1939–June, 1941						*
June, 1941–June, 1943	2	2	2			6
June, 1943–Sept., 1945	2	2	2	3	3	12
Sept., 1945–Feb., 1947	4	4	2	3	4	17
Feb., 1947–Dec., 1955	2	2	3	2	2	11
Dec., 1955–Dec., 1957	3	3	1	2	2	11

* The council was not operative during this period.

The many changes in the structure of the council make a single, composite attendance record almost meaningless. However, there were nine years of the period under survey when the structure of the council remained unchanged—1947 through 1955. During this period the attendance record of the whole council was 78 percent; of the labor representatives, 88 percent; and of the employer and public representatives, 76 percent each.

The original law provided no compensation for the council, but successive legislatures amended the law to provide for per diem stipends of $10 (1941), $15 (1947), and $25 (1953).

The members of the first council were appointed according to an interesting procedure. The Industrial Commission secured a single nominee from the Minnesota Employers' Association and one from the Minnesota State Federation of Labor. These were the state's leading employer and employee organizations; there has never been a state chamber of commerce in Minnesota, and in 1938 the CIO in Minnesota was unimportant. The two nominees were allowed to nominate a third person to represent the public, and these three were then appointed to the council. Although this method of appointing members was certainly one reason that the first council was so effective, the procedure was not followed in the appointment of any subsequent council.

The first council, which began in March, 1938, was immediately given the task of setting up a merit system to govern the selection of personnel for the new unemployment compensation program. This initial task forced the council to operate more like an administrative than an advisory body. It had several employees and its own budget, and it concerned itself with such minor administrative details as having a telephone installed. It called its own meetings, of which there were seventy-five in the first twelve months of its existence beginning in March of 1938. The council members were not compensated for their work and until September of 1938 were not even reimbursed for their expenses.

The council completed its task of setting up the merit system by June of 1939, when it ceased to function. In that year the agency was reorganized,[3] and the director was so preoccupied with the task of reorganization that he felt he could not give the time necessary to reassemble the council and start it off on a new task.

A new council was not appointed until two years later, in June of 1941. Its revival came about as the result of two pressures—one stemming from Governor Stassen, who had instructed the Minnesota agency to set up an advisory committee on defense manpower, and one from the federal Bureau of Employment Security, which at that time was reminding all the states of the Wagner-Peyser Act requirement that an advisory council must be established in connection with the employment service.[4] Since the new council came into existence after the employment service and unemployment

[3] The employment service was integrated with unemployment compensation, and the three-man commission was replaced by a single director. Later, in 1953, the division of employment security was elevated to the rank of a separate department.

[4] Public employment offices in Minnesota go back to 1905, and at various times there were advisory councils connected with them. The most recent one, which consisted of fourteen members, ceased to function in 1936, when it became impossible any longer to assemble a quorum.

compensation had been integrated in Minnesota (1939), it was given responsibility for both programs.

The new council was double the size of the original one. Representation was expanded to include three additional members: a woman, a representative of the CIO, and—to keep the balance— another representative of employers. The addition of the CIO resulted in the loss of the council's most influential member, the state Federation president, who refused to serve with the CIO and whose place was taken by another state Federation representative. This council never got off the ground. Only two members appeared at the first meeting, and only four at the second. No more meetings were called until June of 1943.

There were two principal causes of the 1941–1943 lapse. One was the war and its accompanying disturbances, especially the federalization of the employment service in 1942. The other and more important cause was the activity of the two chief decision makers of employers and employees, the research director of the state Federation and the general manager of the Minnesota Employers' Association. These two individuals were not council members but were very active outside the council. They assumed the responsibility for representing their groups and insisted on working directly with the agency rather than through the council. In the hope of obtaining an agreed bill in the 1943 legislative session, the director spent all his available time with these two decision makers rather than with the council.

His hope was not realized, and the 1943 session proved a turbulent one. Some amendments were enacted (they included a considerable tightening of the program along with an increase in maximum benefits from $16 to $20), but only after a bitter labor-management struggle which the governor and the legislature were anxious not to see repeated. The governor [5] suggested, in general, that the advisory council be revived and strengthened and, specifically, that legislators be included in the council membership.

In June of 1943 the council was revised along the lines of the governor's suggestion, and the membership was again doubled. The six original members were reappointed, and six legislators were

[5] Stassen was governor from 1939 to 1943, when he resigned to accept navy duty.

added. Three of the new members were from the Senate and three from the House. They were drawn from among those who were especially active in unemployment compensation and included the two chairmen of the committees that handled unemployment compensation bills in the Senate and in the House, respectively. One of the six new members, a senator, was considered a representative of employers; another, a member of the House and a union official in private life, was considered a representative of employees; the other four were considered to represent "the public." The four "public" legislators were as a matter of fact equally divided as to proemployer and prolabor leanings.

The actual selection of council members was made by the director of the agency, who submitted the names to the governor for approval and appointment. The Minnesota Employers' Association declared itself dissatisfied with this method of appointment, insisting that the association should have had the privilege of nominating the representatives of employers. The director replied that the two employer representatives originally on the council had proved satisfactory and deserved to be reappointed, and he gave the following explanation of the norms which had guided his choice of the six legislators:

We did not clear with any employer organization on the appointment of the employer representative from the Senate nor with any employee organization on the appointment of the employee representative from the House. . . . It was my feeling that inasmuch as these two men were members of the Legislature, that while they were selected on the basis of vocation, they could better function on the Advisory Council if they were under no obligation to any group or organization in connection with the appointment to the Council.[6]

The director offered to allow the general manager of the Minnesota Employers' Association to name one additional representative to the council, but the offer was declined.

This large council of twelve proved unwieldy, and the agency suggested that an executive committee be established. Such a committee was appointed, composed of the employer representative of the original three-member council, the "labor" legislator, and one of the "public" legislators. Thereafter the agency made more use

[6] Internal memorandum of the agency, dated June 28, 1943.

of the executive committee than of the full council. Indeed, a reliance on this committee was one of the characteristic features of the Minnesota council.[7]

Between June of 1943 and September of 1945 [8] the executive committee met twenty times and the full council six times. Most of the work of the full council consisted of reviewing and approving the work done by the committee. Many of these meetings were devoted to preparing an acceptable policy with regard to suitable work in the war and reconversion periods; the rest of the meetings were taken up with preparing a set of acceptable legislative amendments for 1945.

The 1945 legislative session saw the council achieve its only strict and full agreed bill. The bill relaxed some of the disqualifications which had been tightened in 1943 and increased the benefit duration from sixteen to twenty weeks. The agreed bill had been made possible by the vigorous leadership of the director of the agency and by the threat of federal action, which seemed imminent in 1944 and 1945. Besides, in the previous session some legislators had promised labor leaders that if they would "go along" in 1943, changes in the most offending provisions would be worked out in 1945.

The validity of the agreed bill was assured by the participation of the general manager of the Minnesota Employers' Association and the legislative representative of the state Federation. Although these two decision makers were still not members of the advisory council, they met frequently with the council's executive committee, where most of the work was done, and participated fully in the negotiations which led to the agreed bill.

Employers were dissatisfied with the 1945 results. They complained that the agreement had been of the shotgun variety and objected that the advisory council did not properly represent employers. In an attempt to satisfy this objection the governor appointed (September, 1945) two more employers to the council, one of them a representative of small business. To balance the council, as required by law, the governor appointed two more employee

[7] For a somewhat similar situation, see New York, p. 177.
[8] At the end of this period the council was again reorganized.

representatives, making a total of seventeen members.[9] A new chairman, dean of the state university law school, was appointed to replace the original chairman, whom illness had kept inactive for almost three years.

Between the fall of 1945 and the fall of 1947 [10] the executive committee, which had been reconstituted, held fourteen meetings and the full council five. The meetings were concerned with various problems of "administrative law," employer proposals to change the experience-rating system, and labor proposals to liberalize benefits. At the full council meeting in January of 1947 agreement was reached on a number of employer-sponsored amendments to the experience-rating system. At the next meeting, in February, the labor members asked that the agreement be voided unless or until agreement was reached on some labor proposals also. The chief labor spokesman at this meeting was a noncouncil member, the legislative representative of the state Federation, who attended as the proxy of one of the regular labor members of the council. He had not attended the meeting at which the agreement had been made. His chief opponent was another noncouncil member, the general manager of the Minnesota Employers' Association, who also attended as a proxy member. When these two decision makers could reach no agreement, the previous council agreement became meaningless. The two carried their fight to the legislature but could achieve no clear victory there. The legislature decided to enact no amendments at all in 1947.

After the 1947 session the advisory council was reconstituted once more, but this time by the simple expedient of dropping members. Two employer and two employee representatives were dropped along with two of the legislators, thus reducing the size of the council from seventeen to eleven. The director had come to the conclusion that a smaller council would be more efficient and simply took advantage of circumstances in 1947 to achieve that end. The members who were dropped had either not been attending meetings, or were unable to continue to serve, or, in the case of the legislators, were not reelected.

[9] See Table 1. The additional member from the House represented an accidental and temporary situation.

[10] At the end of this period the council was again reconstituted.

This council met less frequently than previous councils. In 1948 and 1949 the executive committee met three times and the full council twice. The legislative representative of the state Federation and the general manager of the Minnesota Employers' Association attended both of the full council meetings. The issues of 1947 were again at stake in 1949, and the result was the same, a deadlock.

In the 1949 session the council was able to reach only two agreements. One was that the chairman would present to the legislative committee the arguments of both labor and management on the council. He did so, but found it to be a waste of time. The legislative committee listened to him politely but neither asked questions nor offered comments and was obviously only too anxious to get on to those witnesses who could speak with some authority— the director of the agency and the leaders of labor and management.

It was also agreed, or at least understood, by the council that the agency would introduce a bill which would reflect the director's understanding of the positions which labor and management had taken on the council and his judgment as to what was a reasonable compromise between them. The bill which the agency introduced became the starting point for legislative consideration and was substantially the same as the bill which eventually was passed.

The final compromises which determined the amendments of 1949 were arrived at in a conference in a legislative corridor. Conferees were a few key legislators, who included two of those on the advisory council, and the two chief spokesmen for labor and management, neither of whom was on the council. By the final agreement labor got an increase in benefits from $20 for twenty weeks to $25 for twenty-five weeks, and employers got a revision in the tax system which gave more weight to the individual employer's own experience with unemployment and lowered the minimum tax rate to 0.1 percent. In substance this was the agency's bill with one modification. The agency, as well as the employer representatives on the council, had wanted to keep the minimum rate at least as high as 0.5 percent; but the greater influence of employers outside the council, especially those represented by the general manager of the Minnesota Employers' Association, forced the modification in the agency's bill.

In reviewing the events of this period, the director later wrote: "While the Advisory Council was not in complete accord in its thinking on needed legislation, it performed an important function in clarifying the issue through open discussions, thus assisting the legislative committees in arriving at their conclusions." [11]

In the period between the legislative sessions of 1949 and 1951 the committee met seven times and the full council three times. Most of the meetings dealt with problems of defense manpower and with the solvency study which Minnesota began in 1951. An attempt to arrive at an agreed bill failed. Employers were willing to let benefits go to $30 for twenty-six weeks but insisted on raising the minimum qualifying amount from $300 to $500. Labor was unwilling to raise the qualifying amount higher than $350, and there negotiations stalled. The legislature declined to break the deadlock and did not enact any substantive legislation in unemployment compensation in 1951.

Between the 1951 and the 1953 sessions the committee met five times and the full council three times. The solvency study continued to occupy the council—it was published in 1952—and a beginning was made at the meeting of December, 1952, to work out an agreed bill for 1953. One part of the solvency study was an examination of the characteristics of low-earnings claimants. The findings of the study had the effect, as both labor and management remarked, of narrowing the area of dispute over the minimum qualifying amount. The dispute could not be entirely resolved, however, and when the director saw that the council was heading toward a deadlock like that in 1951, he did not call any further meetings but prepared an agency compromise bill which he pushed vigorously in the legislature.

The committee in the House found itself divided on the bill. The committee chairman thereupon instructed the spokesmen for the state Federation and the Minnesota Employers' Association

[11] From the *Twelfth Annual Report to the Governor on the Administration of the Minnesota Employment Security Law*, p. 28.

to "go off by yourselves and talk this thing out; come back when you have agreed on something." Under this pressure they reached agreement on a bill which raised the qualifying requirements to $500 (from $300). The legislature approved the bill unanimously. Neither the state Federation nor the CIO were happy about the bill but agreed to it lest the increase in benefits be again delayed as it had been in 1951. They followed the customary procedure of letting legislators know that labor would not hold it against them if they voted for the bill. The CIO did not list the bill at all in its "box score"—published at the end of every session to show how each legislator voted on bills of interest to labor—and thus avoided the dilemma of either praising what it had officially opposed or condemning what it had unofficially accepted.

Between the 1953 and the 1955 sessions the committee met twice and the full council four times. The negotiations and final results in 1955 were similar to those in 1953. With the agency acting as mediator and the legislative committee as arbitrator, labor and management were steered to an unhappy agreement on a bill which raised maximum benefits to $33 but also raised the minimum qualifying requirement to $520. The advisory council as such took no part in this final agreement.

In 1955 a new director of the agency, a former labor official, was appointed, who decided to reorganize the advisory council. He persuaded the governor to retain the same four legislator members, but to reduce the number of public members to one and to appoint three labor and three management members who were the genuine decision makers for their respective sides. These eleven members constituted a strong council.

The new council began to meet toward the end of 1956 and attempted to work out an agreed bill for the 1957 legislative session. The council reached agreement rather quickly on eight administrative amendments desired by the agency and on a recommendation for universal coverage. It also reached agreement in general terms that both benefits and taxes would have to be increased. Twice during the legislative session the director of the agency urged the labor and management members to meet privately between council meetings and work out a final, concrete agreement in these two areas. No agreed bill, however, came out of the council on either benefits or taxes.

The director, disappointed with the performance of the council in these two crucial areas, decided in 1957 to have the governor appoint two additional public members, thus bringing the total number of council members to thirteen. If labor and management reached an agreement, he reasoned, the public members would go along with the agreement; if labor and management failed to agree, the public members would themselves establish a council position to which the agency could appeal.

Toward the end of 1957 the council embarked on a comprehensive study of the employment security program and the Minnesota economy similar to the solvency study of 1951–1952. In deciding to undertake such a study, the council, which included the chairmen of the legislative committees responsible for unemployment compensation, agreed that it was unrealistic to expect the legislature to conduct the study and that it would be impossible "to hold the interest of legislators during a busy season [even] to thoroughly explain the legislation being considered." [12]

Workmen's Compensation. Although in the history of Minnesota full and strict agreed bills were rare in unemployment compensation, they were common in workmen's compensation. Labor and management leaders said that agreed bills in workmen's compensation have been customary in Minnesota since the beginning of the program, and they expected that pattern to continue.

APPRAISAL

Like most state councils, the Minnesota council devoted very little of its time to the problems of the employment service,[13] but concentrated on unemployment compensation. In this program it exercised some influence on both legislation and administration, the degree of influence varying with circumstances. Its influence on

[12] Minutes of the advisory council for November 26, 1957.

[13] In 1952 the employment problems of agriculture were made the responsibility of a separate advisory council, which seems to have functioned effectively. For a similar situation, see pp. 337 and 359.

legislation seems to have been negligible in the first three legislative sessions of its existence, 1939, 1941, and 1943. In 1945, however, the council achieved a strict and full agreed bill which was accepted by the legislature without change.

In the sessions following 1945, the council's influence on legislation was less direct and measurable but was probably significant. The council influenced legislation indirectly by influencing the legislators on the council, the decision makers of labor and management, and the director of the agency. Key legislators who were council members were present at most of the council discussions (their attendance record through 1952 was over 50 percent) and very likely their judgments were formed partly by what they heard at the meetings. Frequently also the two chief spokesmen for labor and management, the legislative representative (later the secretary) of the state Federation and the general manager of the Minnesota Employers' Association, attended meetings of the council and of the committee. What narrowing of differences they achieved by study and discussion they achieved in the council. They found the council the best place for getting together, reviewing the relevant data, and testing their tentative positions.

If the advisory council influenced the director—and it probably did—that was its most significant influence. The director of the Minnesota agency was unusually influential for several reasons— because he had been director since almost the beginning of the program,[14] because he was unusually competent and personable, and because in Minnesota the executive officers of departments are accorded large freedom of action in attempting to shape legislation.[15] An eloquent testimony to his influence was the fact that the leaders of both labor and management considered him a more formidable adversary than they did each other. The advisory council helped determine not only the quality of this influence but also its quantity—by increasing the number of influential persons he might win to his point of view in the favorable environment of study and discussion which the council provided. On this point

[14] He became director in 1938 and resigned in 1954 to become head of the Bureau of Old Age and Survivors Insurance.

[15] One indication of that freedom is their privilege to come onto the floor of the legislature while it is in session.

one legislator remarked: "It is easier for him to sell his ideas to the advisory council than to the whole legislature."

The most important limitations on the legislative effectiveness of the council were two: the inability of labor and management leaders to agree and (until 1956) the absence of these decision makers from the council membership. Even though they could not reach agreement, if they had been council members the council would have been an important body with at least potential effectiveness. They were not council members primarily because of the director of the agency. The director's unhappy experience with the professional representatives of labor and management in 1943 had led him to fear that their presence on the council would reduce the council to "a cat and dog fight." On the other hand, even though they were not council members, if they could have reached agreement they would have found in the council an effective vehicle for transmitting that agreement to the legislature. But agreement on substantive matters was practically never reached.

By contrast, the labor and employer members of the council's executive committee got along well with each other and could frequently agree personally on what the solution of a problem should be. However, they were not in a position to give effect to their agreement because they could not speak officially for organized labor and management. Thus their agreement was far from being decisive, especially in the area of legislation. Their influence was greater in the area of administration—in such matters, for example, as determining the policy for suitable work and supporting the agency's request for new quarters.

The new council of 1956 held more promise than previous councils because it had the decision makers of labor and management as members, because it was workably small, because it did not rely overmuch on an executive committee, and because the limitation of public members to one emphasized the function of the council to work out a bargained agreement rather than to "settle" issues by a vote. This council was given very little time to prove itself, and the addition of more public members in 1957 may have been premature.

Two features of the Minnesota political scene have had special relevance for the advisory council. First of all, the legislature meets for only ninety working days every other year. The brevity of the session makes the legislators more than ordinarily dependent on the full-time professional representatives of organizations or, alternatively, on an official advisory council. Second, because the state legislature is elected on a nonpartisan basis, the political machine is not as important an institution in Minnesota as it is in other state legislatures. A smaller proportion of the legislators are young men with a political future to build, and a greater proportion consists of retired editors, farmers, businessmen, who having sufficient personal means to indulge in politics, and having sufficient personal standing in their local communities to be elected, tend to be independent agents once they are elected.

This second characteristic of the Minnesota legislature has both favorable and unfavorable relevance for an advisory council. Its relevance is favorable in so far as it makes the work of the professional lobbyist more difficult. Since the legislators are not members of a political party, they must be contacted and persuaded individually. On three separate bills a lobbyist typically must line up three different sets of supporting legislators. The uncertainty and difficulty of this procedure serve as an added inducement (thus far insufficient) to the professional representatives of labor and management to use the simpler and more certain procedure of an agreed bill in the advisory council. This same characteristic of the legislature has unfavorable relevance for an advisory council in so far as it diminishes the certainty that an agreed bill will be accepted by the legislature. In such a legislature it is easier for a few independents who dislike unemployment compensation—perhaps because of some unpleasant personal experiences with the program—to force changes in even an agreed bill.

In Minnesota the two political parties [16] are the Republican Party, which controlled the governorship from 1939 to 1953, and the Democratic Farmer-Labor Party. The latter, established in 1944, comes close to being a labor party. Since Minnesota labor, especially the CIO, is thus committed to one political party, labor leaders may show an increasing inclination to use politics rather

[16] They function only in elections for national and all-state offices.

than collective bargaining as the vehicle for attaining their objectives. As yet this inclination is not pronounced, perhaps because of the drag of tradition. Minnesota, like many another state, has had a long tradition of AFL leadership and one of those long-term, influential state Federation secretaries. The secretary of the Minnesota State Federation of Labor was in office for over twenty years and established what has become a deeply ingrained pattern for the settling of problems by negotiation whenever possible.

In Minnesota, as in most other states, the cities and therefore labor are underrepresented in the legislature. This is one reason that labor has been favorably inclined toward negotiation. It knew it would be fighting at a disadvantage in the legislature. The same reason makes employers less anxious to settle problems outside the legislature. Although they too may see advantages in a private settlement—because the legislature is never a certain factor—they will not pay so high a price for a settlement, in terms of concessions to labor, as they otherwise would.

COUNCIL STRUCTURE AND PROCEDURE

The original three-member council conducted itself so much like an administrative body that its experience is not especially instructive for advisory councils. The method by which its members were appointed, however, may have some applicability to advisory councils: the leading organizations of labor and management nominated their representatives and these nominated a mutually acceptable public member.

Minnesota experimented with several different council structures. The largest, with seventeen members, was clearly too large; everyone connected with its operation agreed that it was unwieldly. And yet in one important sense it was not large enough. Labor and management were allotted only two places each; this was not enough to give adequate representation to both officials and technicians.

Legislators have been members of the Minnesota council since 1943. There is no doubt that they have made the council more influential, and there is no evidence that they disadvantaged the council in any way. It is questionable, however, whether the council needed three members from each House; two, possibly one, might have sufficed.

It is likely that Minnesota used the device of the executive committee too intensively. The employer and employee members of the full council who were not on the committee tended to lose interest in the council because at its infrequent meetings they were asked to do little more than review and give routine approval to the work of the committee.[17] If the committee had consisted of the chief decision makers of labor and management, the use of the device would have been more justifiable—though it is debatable whether even such a committee should be used continuously.[18]

ADVISORY COUNCIL IN TEMPORARY DISABILITY INSURANCE

In 1953 Minnesota decided to investigate the desirability of a temporary disability insurance program. The governor entrusted the task to the employment security agency and appointed a "Special Advisory Council on Sickness and Disability Insurance" to work with the agency. The regular unemployment compensation council might have imitated profitably this special council, which was on the whole more effective than the regular council.

The special council consisted of eleven members, four representing employers, four employees, and three the public. From these a working committee of seven was chosen, which was structured like the New Hampshire advisory council—three representatives each of employers and employees, and one public member, who acted as chairman. Of the three employer representatives, one was the general manager of the Minnesota Employers' Association and the other two were members of the Senate and the House, respectively. Of the three employee representatives, one was the secretary of the state Federation and the other two were members of the Senate and House. These six employer and employee repre-

---

[17] Two of these members served on other state advisory councils in 1954—one on a council of industrial relations and the other on a council of public welfare. Although their work on these councils was harder and carried no compensation, they said they enjoyed the work much more because they were exercising real influence.

[18] Utah made only occasional use of its negotiating committee.

sentatives, together with the director of the agency, were undoubtedly the decision makers in the state. The chairmen of this working committee was a university professor who had the three requi-
sites for a successful mediator: he was entirely acceptable to both
parties, was technically competent, and could give to the task as
much time as could the principal negotiators themselves.

The members of the working committee were few enough and
competent enough and influential enough to find meeting with
each other worth while. They held many meetings and produced a
thorough analysis of the problem. While they did not arrive at
complete agreement, they did decrease the differences that had
separated them at the beginning.

Their final report listed eight areas of agreement, the last of
which constituted a statement of principle. That statement could
well stand as the theme of this book: "Whatever we do, one of
our concerns should be to encourage rather than discourage the
working out of their own problems by employers and employees."

Part Four

EXPERIENCE WITH OTHER
ADVISORY COUNCILS

13

THE RHODE ISLAND ADVISORY COUNCIL

IN Rhode Island, as in many states, an advisory council functioned in connection with the employment service before the enactment of the Social Security Act and was very active during the early years of the depression, especially in 1933 and 1934, when it helped establish the emergency employment offices. As the employment program lost its emergency aspect, however, and became more of a routine operation, the interest of the council members began to slacken. When unemployment compensation came into the picture, in 1936, it had the effect of further lessening the status and hence the activity of the employment service council. The employment service was reestablished as part of the unemployment compensation agency, which was administered by a tripartite board. The board, because it was tripartite, tended to think of itself as displacing the similarly constituted advisory council and left the council with few functions to perform. The council was kept alive, however, by the persistence of the employment service director and continued to function until 1942.

In 1942 the employment service in Rhode Island, as in all the states, was federalized and the War Manpower Commission was established. The War Manpower Commission made an advisory council superfluous and the council ceased to function until 1946. But almost all the former members of the employment service council served on the War Manpower Commission, which operated under the director of the employment service. When the employment service was returned to Rhode Island, in 1946, its director persuaded some of the former WMC members to remain with the employment service in the capacity of an unofficial advisory council.[1]

In 1948 this same director became chairman of the tripartite board which then was administering the combined programs of cash sickness benefits, unemployment compensation, and the employment service. The director brought with him his unofficial advisory council. After extended consideration, the board was unanimous in its opinion that there was a need for an advisory council to act for the agency as a whole and to advise with respect to all phases of its program, rather than be restricted to the placement functions only. Subsequently, in this same year the board, through its chairman, effected a reorganization of the council, which still remained unofficial, for the Rhode Island law did not as yet provide for a council.

While the original plans called for reorganization along the lines of a tripartite council, deference was made to the wishes of the employer and employee members, who saw no advantage to the inclusion of public representatives. Hence, when reorganized, the council consisted of sixteen members—eight representing employers and eight representing employees. The new council also was larger than had been planned originally. Six employer members representing major industrial employer organizations[2] had been selected. Also, six employee representatives (two from the Rhode Island State Federation of Labor, two from the CIO, and two from the Industrial Trades Union of America[3]) were selected. However, the building trades and the machinists, both branches of the AFL, claimed sufficient independence to insist upon separate representation. Their wishes were respected, and thus the number of employee representatives was brought to eight. To balance the

---

[1] This unofficial council proved very helpful in 1946, when a flood of "abuse" charges was overrunning the employment security program nationally and was especially high in Rhode Island. See Joseph M. Becker, *The Problem of Abuse in Unemployment Benefits* (New York: Columbia University Press, 1953), pp. 41, 43.

[2] Associated Industries, the Industrial Cabinet of the Providence Chamber of Commerce, the Retail Cabinet of the Providence Chamber of Commerce, and the trade organizations in textiles, jewelry, and metal trades. In Rhode Island at this time textiles and jewelry accounted for over half of all manufacturing employment, which accounted for over half of total employment.

[3] An independent textile union in the north of the state, formerly affiliated with the AFL.

council membership, two more employer representatives were appointed, one from the insurance business and the other from among the cost accountants.

This council, which held its first meeting in September, 1948, retained its bipartite character for less than a year. Rhode Island had established a cash sickness program in 1942 [4] and this was administered by the Unemployment Compensation Board. However, in the cash sickness law, provision was made for the establishment of an advisory council with respect to the cash sickness program alone. This council consisted of seven members—the two chairmen of the respective labor committees in the Senate and in the House, three representatives of organized labor, and two representatives of the public, one of whom was a doctor, representing the medical profession. The labor members on this cash sickness council in 1948 were also representatives of labor on the unofficial council mentioned above, and in 1949 the labor members suggested that the two councils be merged. This was done by an amendment to both laws in the 1949 session of the legislature. The provision for an advisory council in the unemployment compensation law was part of a bill which reorganized the agency by abolishing the tripartite board and establishing a Department of Employment Security, to be administered by a single administrator. At the same time, the cash sickness section of the law was amended to abolish the then existing advisory council for the cash sickness program. As a result, the new law provided for a council consisting of nineteen members—eight representing labor, eight representing management, two legislators, and a doctor—and responsible for the three programs of unemployment compensation, employment service, and cash sickness.

These 1949 amendments gave the employment security council its first legal status. The law provided that the advisory council serve at the pleasure of the governor and without compensation. Its function was to advise the administrator—no mention was made of advising the governor or the legislature.

This council functioned during the five legislative sessions be-

---

[4] It was the first such program to be established in the country; in 1952 its name was changed to Temporary Disability Insurance.

tween 1949 and 1953 and held a total of forty-five meetings, an average of nine meetings a year. If the meetings are grouped according as they cluster around legislative sessions, they can be represented as a steadily declining line: 1949 (16), 1950 (14), 1951 (8), 1952 (5), 1953 (2). This same line describes equally well the general course of the council's waning effectiveness, and after its meeting in January, 1953, the council became totally inactive.

A new council was appointed in 1954, organized on conventional lines: three representatives each of employers, employees, and the public. Between its first meeting, in June of 1954, and the end of 1955 it held ten meetings, an average of 6.7 meetings a year.

Neither of these councils had a particularly good attendance record. On the first council the attendance record of the employers was 75 percent and of the labor members 72 percent. The doctor and one of the two legislators were absent from practically all the meetings. On the new council the attendance records of all three groups were identical and all were poor—only 60 percent.

The Rhode Island council has followed the unique custom of holding its meetings in the evening. The members receive no compensation for meetings and many of them were unable to take time from their regular jobs during the day. Since the state is small (no part is more than an hour's drive from Providence), the council members arrange to meet for a buffet supper at five o'clock and begin their meeting at about six. In recent years the typical meeting has been short, lasting an hour or an hour and a half. These evening meetings may be one reason why the attendance record was not higher: members must have found it difficult to attend meetings after a day's work.

ACTIVITIES OF THE COUNCIL

The council's best years were its first two, the legislative sessions of 1949 and 1950. In the 1949 session the council played a crucial role. Beginning with monthly meetings in the late fall of 1948 and continuing with weekly meetings in early 1949, the council analyzed and unanimously recommended such legislative changes as the adoption of the flexible week, the allowance of vacation pay, the allowance of pension payments, and the liberalization of benefits in the temporary disability insurance program. All these recommendations were enacted into law.

The council also reached agreement on extending coverage to one or more, but its recommendation was not accepted by the legislature. The council discussed the revision of the benefit structure and the establishment of a system of dependents' allowances, but was unable to reach agreement on these issues. It gave considerable attention to the crucial problems of the tax structure and experience rating. It approved of the agency's proposal to make a solvency study and appointed a committee of the council to discuss with the governor the possible harm to the economy if the impending tax on payrolls were to be put into effect; subsequently the impending tax was postponed by the legislature. Later in the year the council met with the Board of Review to discuss the application of the new provision which permitted vacation pay. At another meeting the council discussed and agreed upon a definition of suitable work. The council's schedule was a full one in 1949.

In the 1950 legislative session the council was almost but not quite as active and effective as in the previous session. The agency presented for the council's consideration a series of proposed amendments, some of them restrictive in nature. They were based on an elaborate solvency study just completed, which showed that the unemployment compensation program was in danger of bankruptcy. When it reviewed the findings of this study, the council gave its unanimous approval to most of the agency's proposed amendments, and a bill incorporating these amendments was introduced in the legislature.[5]

The two *ex officio* council members, the respective chairmen of the Senate and House labor committees, adopted opposite positions with respect to the council's agreed bill when it got into the legisla-

[5] The proposed amendments in unemployment compensation included: changing to an individual base and benefit year; increasing eligibility requirements; making duration of benefits a function of weeks worked; liberalizing the provisions governing the waiting period and partial benefits; extending coverage. The council also approved of the elimination of dual payments in temporary disability insurance and workmen's compensation. The labor members of the council, lacking adequate technical advice of their own, asked for a special meeting with the agency's staff to learn the implications of some of the proposed changes.

ture. The chairman of the Senate committee, who had attended all the council meetings, saw the bill successfully through the Senate. The chairman of the House committee, who had attended none of the meetings, opposed the bill when it got to the House on the ground that it was antilabor. He was a member of a building trades union, and the unions in that industry were opposed to the bill. He and the labor faction supporting him attacked the increase in qualifying requirements [6] so violently that the labor members on the council withdrew their support of that part of the bill, saying that they had not fully understood it when they approved of it. The House eventually passed the bill but only after amending it in such a way as to make it meaningless. The agency and council recommended, therefore, that the governor veto it, and the governor did so. The other parts of the council's program, however, were enacted into law, including the individual benefit and base years and the liberalized waiting period and partial benefit provisions.

The labor members were not the only ones to retract a vote of approval in 1950. At one of its meetings the council approved the program of federal assistance for states which (like Rhode Island) were in financial difficulty. One of the employer members, who represented the Associated Industries, unaware that his organization opposed the plan, voted for it and later had to ask to be allowed to retract.[7]

In June of 1950 the council lost its chairman, an employer member who was influential among employers, widely accepted by labor, and one of the council members who understood the program very well. It was a serious loss, though it is doubtful that his continuance on the council would have made any substantial difference in the council's subsequent history. The environmental forces were too strong for that.

During its first years the council operated in a more favorable environment than was to be its lot thereafter. In 1949 and 1950 the

---

[6] In 1950 Rhode Island had the unrealistic low requirement of $100 earned in the base year, but the opposing factions insisted on retaining the requirement unchanged.

[7] Associated Industries of Rhode Island, like the National Association of Manufacturers, favored federal "reinsurance," which required repayment, but not federal "assistance," which did not.

council was acting under the spur of a nation-wide recession but with the support of a reserve fund that had been built up during the war and the immediate postwar years. Rhode Island, with its textile industry, had prospered more than the average state in the immediate postwar period, but it lagged behind the rest of the country in recovering from the recession. After 1950, while other states were enjoying prosperity, Rhode Island continued to have much higher-than-average unemployment. While other states were liberalizing their unemployment compensation programs, Rhode Island saw its reserve fund shrinking at an alarming rate and had to call on its employers to submit to higher taxes and its labor leaders to accept benefit retrenchments. It was the worst possible situation for negotiating agreed bills or even for planning with calmness. Tempers wore thin as the council continued to work under an ever-increasing strain.

The council began work for the legislative session of 1951 with a meeting in December, 1950, at which a committee of six was appointed to study the new list of legislative recommendations submitted by the administrator. In the course of its 1951 meetings the council agreed on recommendations to extend coverage and liberalize partial benefits (in both the unemployment compensation and temporary disability insurance programs) and to limit pregnancy benefits and eliminate dual payments (in the temporary disability insurance program). But on the issue of raising the qualifying requirements in unemployment compensation, the council still could reach no agreement. The labor members were unwilling to accept the agency's recommendation, insisting that it called for more discussion.

The labor members also insisted that council discussions be kept strictly private. The council had been operating on an unwritten law of unanimous voting and the only council actions which were given publicity were those which had the support of the entire council. But the reluctance of the council to accept certain proposals induced the employer members to demand the right to issue minority reports to the press and thus bring their case to the public. The labor members demurred, insisting that unless council action was unanimous it was not publishable.

The press was excluded from the council meetings, but information leaked out on the dispute over qualifying requirements and on other issues dividing the council. Council members would no sooner reach home after a council meeting than reporters would be telephoning to learn what had happened at the meeting. These "leaks" aggravated the situation within the council and increased the difficulty of arriving at constructive recommendations.

While the council was engrossed in this internal strife, the governor had a bill introduced (March, 1951) embodying most of the administrator's recommendations. When the council protested at being thus by-passed, the governor explained in a letter that since new legislation had to be introduced before the forty-second day of the session he could not wait longer for the council's recommendations.

By the fall of 1951 the council showed definite signs of breaking up. One of the employer members, who represented the most depressed industry of the state, released a statement to the newspapers in which he dubbed the council a "do-nothing council" and explained that although the program was faced with threatened bankruptcy, the labor members could not bring themselves to recommend the necessary restrictive measures and by a "rule of unanimity" were preventing the employer members from taking action. To emphasize his protest, he resigned from the council.[8] The chairman of the council, a labor member, in an answering letter to the papers, twitted him with adopting "cry baby tactics."

A committee of the council had been revising the rules of procedure, and in October, 1951, the council approved the revised rules. The council reiterated its rule, which had been violated in the past, that no publicity be released unless authorized by the council and that all such publicity be released through the chairman. The revised rules also provided for majority and minority reports in place of the former practice of requiring unanimous decisions. The employers still found room for complaint, however. They protested to the press that the majority vote was always and would always be in favor of labor because the two "public"

---

[8] For the opposite and more usual picture (labor resigning in protest), see the chapter on the Pennsylvania council, p. 301.

members, who were the chairmen of the labor committees in the legislature, were really labor representatives.

The 1952 legislative session was for the most part a repetition of that of 1951. The administrator again presented a number of recommendations for the council's consideration, some of which would not only have raised taxes but have tightened the program on the benefit side. These recommendations were based upon a report of a special study commission appointed by the administrator and seemed a necessity in the face of the continued drain on the reserve fund. Again the council was unable to agree, and again the governor, in order to meet the deadline for the introduction of new legislation, introduced these amendments as an administration measure. In a letter to the council he pointed out the reason for his action and requested the council to consider the proposals and advise him with respect thereto. After this bill had been amended to satisfy some labor objections, it was passed by the House but was defeated in the Republican Senate in a move of partisan politics (the governor was a Democrat).

The end of the 1952 session also marked the end of the advisory council as a potentially significant influence. After a last desultory meeting in January, 1953, the council became completely inoperative. In the 1953 legislative session the governor took the reins into his own hands from the beginning. He called meetings with labor and management groups separately and brought them to accept a bill substantially the same as the one which had failed of passage the year before; in 1953 it passed both houses without difficulty. The bill raised the qualifying requirements to thirty times the weekly benefit amount (the same formula which had been accepted and then repudiated by the advisory council in 1950) and made the disqualifications for voluntary quit, refusal of suitable work, and fraud more severe. It also abolished the old advisory council and set up a new one organized on different lines.

The new law specified a council of the conventional sort, tripartite, with three representatives each of employers, employees, and the public. The change was not based on either special study or expert knowledge. The study commission which the governor had established to prepare the legislative recommendations for 1953 had decided, almost incidentally to its other work, that (1) the advisory council needed a fresh start and a change of personnel, (2) a change in the council's structure would be the easiest way of accomplishing a change in its personnel, (3) the previous council had been too large. The nine-member tripartite council was different, it was smaller, and its structure was that used by most states; so it was adopted without further discussion.

The members of the new council were appointed in December of 1953 and held their first meeting in July, 1954. They constituted a fairly strong council. All of the three employer representatives were officers (two presidents and a treasurer) in large firms. One was the leader of the left wing of employers and the other a leader of the right wing (he himself was not on the extreme right). One of them accepted his appointment only after he got an iron-clad guarantee from his "wing" that he could commit them to positions that might involve compromise. None of the three was a technician or a lobbyist, which was a weakness in their representation. Two of the three labor representatives had been on the former council; none of the three was either a technician or a lobbyist. They were, however, on the executive boards of their respective state organizations. Of the three public members, one was a university professor, one was a doctor (for the temporary disability insurance program), and one was a woman (to comply with the Wagner-Peyser Act).

This council led a less turbulent and a less eventful life. It went along holding its hour-and-a-half meetings each month, listening to reports presented by the agency, passing an occasional resolution, having few fights but exerting relatively little influence. What influence it exerted was chiefly in the field of administration—for example, it approved the agency's new policy on tax refunds and supported the agency in its request for more administrative funds in the temporary disability insurance program. In the field of legislation it exerted no perceptible influence. The governor's program of amendments in unemployment compensation for 1955, for example, was based more on the work of his study commission than on the recommendations of the advisory council—a situation which the council resented but could not change.

Although the Personnel Committee on the Employment Service had no formal connection with the advisory council, it deserves at least mention here because it performed some of the work that an advisory council usually does. This committee consisted of employer technicians who as part of their work dealt regularly with the agency and who, therefore, could help both the agency and themselves by learning more about the agency's operations. They comprised an informal group without official standing of any sort. The group was formed in 1950, when the director of the agency invited a number of technicians to meet with some of his staff to learn how the agency operated and to have their questions answered. For the first couple of years the discussions of the group were confined to the employment service but were extended later to include unemployment compensation. The group had some similarity to employers' social security committees in other states; but this one maintained the kind of regular relations with the agency and had the kind of window into the agency which usually only an advisory council has. The group was particularly useful to the agency when new regulations had to be devised and installed.

APPRAISAL

The first council was a very effective institution for about two years, and even in the later, less effective years it was probably an important agent in bringing Rhode Island citizens to recognize the dangers facing the program and, when some groups seemed inclined to "gut" the program, in counseling moderation and in showing how to tighten the program without undermining it.

During 1949 and 1950 the council, acting in conjunction with the director, was easily the predominant influence in employment security. Its effectiveness had several sources. First of all, during this early period the council was operating in an environment which both called for and made possible some liberalization of the program without an increase in taxes—the most favorable environment for the reaching of agreed bills. Second, the council members came as close to being representative of their groups as was possible in a situation marked by factionalism. The absence of public members in the ordinary sense was not felt as a lack, and the presence of two legislators seems to have been a net gain. The legislator from the Senate was a considerable help to the council at the stages both of deciding on recommendations and of getting the recommendations enacted into law. The council was effective also because it enjoyed excellent leadership in the persons of its first chairman and the director of the agency. The latter combined competence and personality with an unusually strong conviction of the value of a good advisory council. In his twenty years with the program he had never grown discouraged over the greater-than-average difficulties of building a good council in Rhode Island.

Six principal factors limited the council's success and eventually killed it. Two of the factors were in the council's environment and four were in the council itself. The first was an unusually high rate of unemployment and the consequent need to tighten the program. After the immediate postwar years, Rhode Island had to live with an insured unemployment rate almost double the national average. In addition to the usual causes of unemployment, the state had the sick textile industry and the highly seasonal jewelry industry. Combined with a fairly liberal program,[9] this high unemployment resulted in a ratio of benefits to taxable wages which was significantly above the national average ever since Rhode Island first began to pay benefits in 1938. Even though the Rhode Island tax rate was also above the national average,[10] it was not sufficient to keep the reserve fund safely beyond the threat of bankruptcy. The council always had to work in the shadow of that threat. After 1949 the employer members became insistent, almost clamorous, for "reform," while the labor members were reluctant to assume responsibility for changes that would be very unpopular with their constituents. It was the worst possible environment for successful collective bargaining. The

[9] Not the most liberal, and less liberal now than formerly, in relation to other states.
[10] Except for the period 1947–1949 all Rhode Island employers always paid the maximum rate of 2.7 percent.

fact that labor was strong in the state government made the situation more difficult. The necessary but unpleasant changes in the law could not so easily be attributed to "the opposition." In highly industrialized and highly unionized Rhode Island organized labor is probably stronger than in any other state.

Factionalism was a second factor that contributed to the council's difficulties. Both the labor and the management groups were badly split and hence found that they could not achieve unified action even on their own side of the table. It was more difficult in Rhode Island than even in most large states to secure unity among either employers or employees. Here again this was traceable to the nature of the basic economic problems confronting the state.

Among employers there was a sharp clash of interests, especially over the issue of experience rating, between industries with high unemployment and those with low unemployment. This chasm seemed unbridgeable. The employers' most ambitious attempt to compromise their differences and find common ground was the Trade Association Joint Council. Established in 1951, it was composed of six employer groups: Associated Industries, the Providence Chamber of Commerce, and the trade associations for textiles, jewelry, contracting, and metal trades. The Trade Association Joint Council initiated joint meetings with labor in 1952 in an attempt to work out agreed bills covering unemployment compensation and workmen's compensation. The meetings were unsuccessful and were not repeated.

Among labor groups there were similar, though not-so-deep divisions caused by industrial differences. Industrial differences, for example, were the reason why some labor leaders welcomed an increase in eligibility requirements in exchange for higher benefits while others bitterly opposed the increase under any conditions. Other divisions within labor were caused by political rivalry, including rivalry for political jobs. This was a more important cause of division within labor ranks in Rhode Island than in the average state, because labor in Rhode Island has a greater-than-average share in political power.

Within both groups—labor and management—there were significant divisions which were attributable primarily to differences in personality. One employer, for example, who was very active in unemployment compensation and who was more liberal than most of his fellow employers, frankly attributed the difference to his personal experience with unemployment during the depression years. On the new council, in 1957, one employer representative from the textile industry went along with the other employers in favoring a charge-back experience-rating system even though it would hurt the textile industry because he believed in experience rating as a matter of principle. On the issue of whether employee contributions should be restored in unemployment compensation,[11] there were in the same industry and in the same union leaders who advocated and leaders who opposed the idea.[12]

The operation of all factions was facilitated in Rhode Island because in this family-sized state, government tended to be more direct than in larger states. Each splinter group, and even individuals, could take their problems directly into the governor's office or directly to their representatives in the legislature and did not necessarily depend on the official lobbyists of large organizations. Moreover, business within the legislature was to a considerable extent conducted by means of informal caucuses. The representatives from the smaller districts, who might be no good at all in floor debate, could be very potent in a caucus, especially if a proposed bill—a bill to increase eligibility requirements, for example—threatened hardship to their district. The entire situation made it very difficult for the council to be the center of effective decision making.

Incompatible personalities on the council were a third factor in its decline. If the same groups represented on the council had been represented by different persons, the council could have functioned with less friction.

A fourth factor was the lack of "professionals" on the council. There were no technicians among the members and, except for

[11] Rhode Island taxed employees for unemployment compensation until 1942, when the cash sickness program was begun and the accumulated employee taxes were transferred to the new program.

[12] The idea was effectively killed by the opposition of the governor, who feared that another widespread tax would be politically unpopular.

the president of the CIO,[13] none of the full-time managers of either labor or employer state-wide organizations. As for lobbyists, the council had a couple of labor members who spent at least some time at the legislature during sessions, but it had none of the employer lobbyists. One of the most important of these latter said that he worked exactly the same during as before the council's existence—which is another indication of either the council's ineffectiveness or the operation of factionalism.

A fifth factor may have been the large number of persons at the council meetings. Its nineteen members made the Rhode Island council the largest in the country, and the council meetings were usually augmented by members of the Board of Review, several of the agency staff, and a university consultant. Such large meetings invited speechmaking rather than discussion and solid work, and speeches were made. The large membership did, however, make possible more adequate representation of the various factors —a consideration of some importance in Rhode Island.

A sixth factor was the poor attendance at meetings, and probably also the brevity of the meetings. Little serious work can be accomplished in meetings lasting only an hour, or an hour and a half, and poorly attended. Better meetings might have resulted if the council members had been compensated for attendance.

The above appraisal applies almost solely to the first council. The experience of the second council during the period covered by this survey was too brief to justify a final judgment.

[13] He left the council in the spring of 1949 to take a position on the Board of Review, but he continued to attend the council meetings (members of the Board of Review have a standing invitation) and to caucus with the labor members of the council (some of whom resented it).

14

THE PENNSYLVANIA ADVISORY COUNCIL

IN Pennsylvania there were two short-lived advisory councils before a third achieved something like stability. But even the third council lasted less than five years.

The first council was appointed by the governor in 1938.[1] It had nine members (three representatives each of labor, management, and the public) who served without compensation and without fixed terms in advising the secretary of the Department of Labor with respect to both unemployment compensation and the employment service.[2] This council held its first meeting on June 27, 1938, and like other early councils was very busy for a time helping to solve the administrative problems of a new program. Its reports and recommendations were directed to such matters as simplifying the law, simplifying agency procedures, and securing adequate working space for the agency.

This first council came to an end six months after it began, when a new governor was elected. The law made no provision for the council to continue beyond the term of the governor by whom it was appointed, and since the new governor did not reappoint the council members, the council simply ceased to function.

[1] Much earlier, in 1915, Pennsylvania had a "Bureau of Employment" to which were attached a number of local advisory councils. Each council consisted of six members: three representatives of labor, one of whom was not to be a member of any employee organization, and three representatives of management, one of whom was not to be a member of any employer organization. The members were expected to meet monthly and to serve without compensation. If the history of these councils could be told it would probably be very instructive; but the necessary documents are lacking, and in any case it lies outside the scope of the present study.

[2] Pennsylvania had already integrated the two programs in one division; it was among the earliest states to do so.

It was two years before the new governor got around to appointing another council. This second council held its first meeting on March 26, 1941, and functioned sporadically for a year and a half, until the end of 1942, when it too became a fatality of the change of governors.[3]

The new governor, Governor Martin (1943–1946), never appointed a council, and his successor, Governor Duff (1947–1950), did not do so until almost at the end of his term, so that the council's second period of hibernation lasted more than seven years. During this period the agency was reporting at intervals to the federal Bureau of Employment Security: "We shall soon appoint an advisory council."

Labor, especially the state Federation, kept urging the reactivation of the council, and in 1949 the governor gave his approval to the idea. At the same time the legislature amended the law to guarantee the continuity of the council's existence and to safeguard it from the automatic dissolution which previously had occurred whenever there was a change of governors. The new provision stated that council members "shall serve until their successors have been appointed and qualified."[4] Another, and very unusual, provision stipulated that "the members of such council shall be appointed by the Governor within 30 days of the passage of these amendments."[5] Later, in 1951, the council itself recommended that the law be amended to provide fixed terms of six years, staggered so that there would not be a complete turnover in council membership each time a new governor was elected. The legislature, however, did not see fit to act on the recommendation.

Another 1949 amendment provided that the secretary of labor, in whose department the division of employment security was located, be an *ex officio* member of the advisory council and that he "appoint an executive secretary and such other personnel as he shall deem necessary to aid the council in the performance of its functions." This provision may have been inserted at the sug-

[3] In Pennsylvania the governor's term is four years, and he may not succeed himself.
[4] Section 204 of the Pennsylvania unemployment compensation law, edition of 1957. Subsequent citations of the law are to this section and edition.
[5] The attorney-general later ruled that this provision was advisory, not mandatory.

gestion of the secretary of labor himself. The secretary seems not to have favored the reactivation of the council, but by this amendment he was assured of a certain amount of control over whatever council might be appointed.

The third advisory council came into existence early in 1950. Its employer and employee members were appointed by the governor from a panel of names submitted by the major employer and employee organizations. On the employers' side these were the Pennsylvania Manufacturers' Association, the Anthracite Institute, and three chambers of commerce—the state Chamber and those of Philadelphia and Pittsburgh. A brief description of these organizations may be useful by way of background.

The Pennsylvania Manufacturers' Association was differentiated from other such state groups by the extent of its political and insurance activities. In politics it had aligned itself openly with the Republican Party and the Grundy machine; its president was the Republican national committeeman in 1953. Insurance was for the Pennsylvania Manufacturers' Association (as for its New Jersey counterpart) a major activity which dictated many of the policies and determined some of the membership of the association.[6] The Anthracite Institute is the somewhat misleading name of the principal association of mineowners in the coal industry. The voice of the Institute carried great influence in Pennsylvania because coal mining not only was a major industry in the state but also had long been a "sick" industry. The industry's workers made more than average demands upon the unemployment compensation fund and its employers bore more than the average tax burden. For both reasons the needs and wishes of the coal industry were given more consideration than those of the average industry when Pennsylvania made decisions affecting its employment security program.

All three chambers of commerce had social security committees and each committee had a number of excellent technicians. Among the employer organizations the chambers of commerce were probably in the best position to make contributions on the

[6] Thus Wanamaker's, a department store, bought Pennsylvania Manufacturers' Association insurance and was an association member; Philco, on the other hand, a manufacturing company, did not buy insurance and was not a member.

technical side. The Philadelphia and Pittsburgh chambers did not always agree, for they reflected the political rivalry that split Pennsylvania into an eastern and a western faction.

The three employer members appointed to the council in 1950 represented respectively these three major employer groups: the manufacturers, the mineowners, and the chambers of commerce. None of the appointees, however, was a professional representative of any of the employer organizations; they were all executives in individual firms which belonged to one or another of these organizations.

On the employees' side there were likewise three major organizations: the Pennsylvania State Federation of Labor, the Congress of Industrial Organizations, and the United Mine Workers. The state Federation was by far the largest of the three.[7] The UMW, which left the AFL in 1937 and the CIO in 1942, exercised considerable influence on the employment security program in Pennsylvania because the coal industry in that state was, as remarked above, both large and "sick." These three organizations were not required to submit a panel of nominees to the governor but were allowed to designate their representatives on the council. The CIO designated its president (he was also at that time a member of the Federal Advisory Council), and each of the other two organizations designated its secretary. The governor then appointed these three as council members.

Three public members, one of them a woman, completed the council membership. The public members have always supplied the council with its chairman, and one of their number, a university professor, was probably the council's most active member.

This third council held its first meeting on May 18, 1950, and until its dissolution in 1954 held a total of eighteen meetings (most of them full day) which were distributed by years as follows:

| 1950 | 9 | 1952 | 2 | 1954 | 1 |
| 1951 | 2 | 1953 | 5 | | |

The attendance record of the council members at these meetings was good and was almost identical for the three groups. The em-

---

[7] The Pennsylvania Federation is unusually well organized and has the largest staff (twelve members) of all the state federations in the country.

ployee members had an attendance record of 85 percent; the employer and public members both had a record of 83 percent.

ACTIVITIES OF THE COUNCIL

The third council was the only one to remain in existence for more than a brief period and is the only one under consideration in the remainder of this chapter. The activities of the council were centered around the legislative sessions of 1951 and 1953. At its first meeting, on May 18, 1950, the council decided to "give particular emphasis to the development of a legislative program and endeavor to obtain agreement upon necessary amendments to the Pennsylvania unemployment compensation law." [8] At its second meeting it selected three areas for immediate consideration —partial unemployment benefits, experience rating, and the appeals procedure—and appointed three committees to study them.[9] The committees were active. In addition to their own meetings, they held joint meetings with other interested groups. One committee, for example, met with the agency's Board of Review; another met with the Pittsburgh Chamber of Commerce. At the July meeting of the full council each committee met separately in the morning so that it would be able to present its report to the entire advisory council in the afternoon. At the December meeting each committee met the day before the full council meeting.

On the basis of the committees' work the council was able to reach agreement on extensive revisions of the appeals procedure [10] and on a recommendation to leave the experience-rating formula unchanged for the time being. With regard to partial benefits, difficulties and differences were so profound that the council decided to make no recommendation at all. This was the substance of the council's first report to the governor in January of 1951 and

[8] From the minutes of the council. Subsequent quotations in this chapter not otherwise identified are from the same source.

[9] An "executive committee," set up at the suggestion of the agency, existed for a time. Intended as a work group to prepare the agenda, it did little more than rubber-stamp what the agency proposed. It was abandoned within the year as a needless additional procedural step.

[10] The entire council had visited New York to examine the appeal procedures of that state.

at that time it was looked upon as the council's complete legislative program for the year.

The council's report constituted an agreed bill, but not in the full sense. That is, both labor and management had other changes they wanted to see enacted, and they continued to work separately outside the council to that end. The employers worked mainly through the Employers' Conference, a loose federation of all the employer organizations, which was established in 1943 to put an experience-rating provision into the law.[11] After the conference achieved its immediate goal in 1943 it became relatively inactive until 1949, when it was revived. In early 1951 the leaders of the conference prepared a number of amendments which they asked the agency to support.

This employer move fitted in with the plans of the agency, which expected to take a more active part than formerly in preparing legislation. The former secretary of labor had been accustomed to maintain a direct and detailed supervision over the affairs of the employment security division (located in the Department of Labor) and to insist during legislative sessions on working out proposed amendments in his own office. Some of this unusual interest was traceable to the secretary's assistant, who was a former unemployment compensation technician. But a new secretary was appointed (at about the same time as the new advisory council) who was inclined to allow the director of the division more autonomy. The director saw in this circumstance, coupled with the existence of the new advisory council, an opportunity to provide really effective leadership in the 1951 legislative session. If the council could be brought to agree on a substantive bill prepared under the leadership of the agency, there was every reason to expect that the legislature would accept and enact such a bill.

The director decided, therefore, to continue the meetings of the council in the hope of broadening the council's agreement to include some of the more substantive, and controversial, issues.

[11] The original law did not permit experience rating, reflecting in this respect, as in some others, the fact that employers had had no share in its drafting. The Pennsylvania employers had gambled on the election of a Republican president in 1936 and the repeal of all the social security laws. Like New York employers they had spent their energies working to repeal the laws rather than helping to shape them.

Before calling the next meeting he prepared a legislative package consisting of a modified version of the employer proposals (employers were expected to be willing to compromise their demands in exchange for agency support), two liberalizations in benefits for labor (an increase in maximum benefits from $25 to $28 and the introduction of the New York "day-base" plan for partial benefits), and some technical amendments which the agency felt it needed for the sake of more efficient administration. The agency then called a meeting of the advisory council (April 29, 1951) to discuss and—the agency hoped—to approve this package or something like it.

Labor's first reaction was a violent one. It objected to several of these proposed amendments, charged that the agency had been working separately with the employer representatives, and said that in any case it disliked being presented with a ready-made package. One of the labor representatives asked:

Has it been the practice of the advisory council in the past to receive from the agency a bundle like this that actually comes as a recommendation from the Bureau for the advisory council to approve? If it isn't, maybe we are departing on a dangerous practice. The best position of the Bureau is an impartial kind of position.

Not all of the employer members were satisfied either. Some segments of management, particularly in the coal industry, were strongly opposed to the day-base plan for partial benefits. After some discussion it was agreed that since the council members had not received the seven-days notice stipulated by the rules of procedure, the council should not take action on the proposed bill at this meeting but should meet again the following week.

At the meeting of May 2, 1951, the employer members moved that the "noncontroversial" sections of the package bill be approved first [12] and that then the controversial sections be voted upon section by section; wherever agreement was impossible majority and minority reports should be prepared for the governor and the legislature. The vote on this first motion was six to three in favor, labor dissenting.

[12] Among these were some experience-rating amendments which employers had asked for.

The labor members, who had apparently decided in the week's interval that the agency's package represented the best bargain they could hope for, countered with a motion "that the council approve the proposed amendments contained in the document *in toto*." The vote on this second motion was six to three against, labor favoring.

Then the employers moved that the package be accepted with the exception of the day-base plan. To compensate labor for the loss of this plan employers offered a greater increase in benefits than was provided in the original package bill. They offered an increase both in benefit rates ($30 instead of $28) and in duration of benefits (26 weeks instead of 24 weeks). The vote on this third and final motion was six to three in favor, labor dissenting. To the UMW representative the day-base plan was the most important part of the package, for much coal mining was characterized by part-week employment. For the same reason the employer representative from the mining industry preferred to make any concession rather than this one. Both labor and management from the other industries viewed the matter differently, but deferred to the overriding necessity felt by their mining confreres.

The labor members caucused at this point. After only a short conference they announced they were resigning from the council and walked out of the meeting. On the same day they sent a joint letter to the governor tendering their resignations. It was the council's first anniversary.

The legislature then took over and eventually (September, 1951) passed a series of amendments that were very close to the provisions of the compromise proposed by employers in their third and final motion. The legislature gave employers a tax reduction and gave labor an increase of maximum benefits (to $30, which in 1951 was the highest basic maximum paid by any state) and an increase in duration (to 26 weeks).

As far as final results were concerned the legislation of 1951 might as well have been handled by way of an agreed bill. The labor members argued that their resignations had influenced the governor and the legislature to give them more than they otherwise would have received from that source; which is probably true. But it was not more than they could have gotten from employers in an agreed bill.

The council did not meet again until nearly a year later, July 29, 1952. By that time the labor members had reconsidered their resignations and at the request of the governor had reassumed council membership. At this meeting the council compiled a list of eight problem areas and assigned them to a "Committee of Research" consisting of one representative each from labor and management and the public. This committee remained in existence during the next two years and became the working committee of the council—although not quite to the same extent as did the "Executive Committee" of the Minnesota council.

Guided by the Committee of Research the council proceeded to hold a series of meetings during 1952–1953 in the course of which it worked out its recommendations for the 1953 legislature.[13] The completed recommendations were presented to the governor in the "Report of the State Advisory Council on Unemployment Compensation for the Year 1953." This report was a substantial document which set out each recommendation very clearly in nonlegal language, explained the issues involved, presented the main arguments for and against each recommendation, and indicated the way each council member had voted. It was admirably adapted to fulfilling one of the council's chief functions, that of helping the legislature make its decisions in the light of full knowledge.

The report indicated that the council had reached unanimous agreement on a number of recommendations labeled "noncontroversial" [14] and on a recommendation to increase eligibility requirements. When the labor members later encountered criticism for agreeing to the eligibility recommendation they said that they had not fully understood it when they voted for it.[15] Although they did not ask to have their vote changed, it is possible that they worked privately against the recommendation; the legislature did not enact it despite this "unanimous" vote of the council.

[13] During these meetings the labor members repeatedly warned the rest of the council that they would have nothing to do with a "package bill."

[14] Which included, however, a stiffening of the disqualification for pregnancy and a softening of the voluntary-quit disqualification.

[15] See pp. 253, 284, 347–48.

On four other recommendations the report indicated a divided vote, with labor getting the support of the public members on only one of the four, namely, the recommendation to increase maximum benefits from $30 to $35. The other three recommendations were: requiring pensioners to requalify for benefits after retiring; rescinding the noncharging provisions of the law (on the score that they weakened employer interest in the program); disqualifying all employees during a vacation shutdown.

During one of the meetings which had preceded the report an employer representative had suggested a package bill which would include all four of the disputed issues. But another employer had flatly refused to agree to any increase in benefits on any terms, and the leader of the employee representatives had responded by saying that he would not agree to a benefit increase on conditions which would make it impossible for anyone to get it.

In any event, none of the council's recommendations which were based on a divided vote were enacted into law. Of four other amendments that were enacted in controversial areas, two favored employers (a tightening of two disqualifications) and two favored labor (a small increase in partial benefits and an easing of one disqualification). The crucial decision not to raise the maximum benefit was made outside the council and in a sense outside the unemployment compensation program. The governor was insistent that something would have to be given to labor to balance a reduction in corporation taxes which had been given to employers,[16] and employers said that they would prefer to see an increase of benefits in workmen's compensation rather than in unemployment compensation. The legislature accordingly increased the maximum benefit in workmen's compensation while leaving unemployment compensation unchanged, with the result that for the first time in the history of the two programs the maximum benefit was not the same for both. A bill which also increased benefits in unemployment compensation had been passed by the House but had been killed in the Senate. Labor was told by the

[16] On another occasion in another legislative session employers were given to understand that if they wanted to get a certain unemployment compensation amendment they would have to drop their opposition to a beer tax which the governor wanted. Such bargains, which cross the borders of distinct programs, are less common than those which are contained within the limits of a single program.

Senate that if it fought for the unemployment compensation increase it would lose the workmen's compensation increase as well. Labor accepted this as a fact and subsided.

After the legislative session was ended in 1953, the council members busied themselves with three important problem areas: temporary disability insurance, delinquent taxes, and the long-term solvency of the unemployment compensation fund.

In the matter of temporary disability insurance the council made a report to the governor which was notable for its entire lack of recommendations. The labor members had insisted from the beginning that no recommendation be made. They had reason to think that the secretary of labor and the governor were more favorable to labor's proposals in this matter than was the advisory council. Besides, the CIO showed little interest in having any legislation enacted, but seemed willing to leave the matter to be settled by collective bargaining in each industry.

The council's investigation into delinquent taxes was begun at the insistence of one of the employer members. He had become suspicious of the situation in the coal industry where hard-pressed mineowners who had fallen behind in their taxes were warning the agency not to insist on payment because that would be merely to close more mines and cause more unemployment. The council began its investigation by requiring the agency to make a full report to the council on the facts of the situation.

In the matter of fund solvency the council encountered its most difficult and its most urgent task. The task was difficult because it involved a study of the entire Pennsylvania economy and was urgent because the state's reserves were dangerously low. It followed upon an earlier study (1951) called the Adams Report after Professor John F. Adams (he was later to be a member of the advisory council and still later director of the agency) which had warned that the fund was in danger. The agency of course did the actual research work, but the council's Research Committee followed each step of this solvency study and wrote a part of the final report. The council reviewed and approved this report, certifying that it was an impartial and accurate statement of the facts—thus performing the function upon which John R. Commons laid so much stress.[17] With regard to this report and a later supplement, one of the council members wrote:

It would never have been released had it not been for the Council. Unfortunately it was not brought to the attention of those who could do anything about it and were disposed to do so. The Governor didn't learn about it until the depletion of the Pennsylvania fund had become a political issue about September 1, 1954.[18]

In 1954 the council came to an abrupt and unexpected end. It began the year with a meeting, in January, that seemed to hold great promise, but then never met again. In the January meeting, at which all the members were in attendance, the council laid out an ambitious program of work for itself—that is, the executive secretary of the council and the chairman of the Research Committee laid out the program and the council adopted it. This program committed the council to continue its work in the areas of temporary disability insurance, delinquent taxes, and fund solvency and to begin work in the following new areas: (1) the relation of unemployment compensation to the guaranteed annual wage; (2) the relation of unemployment compensation to labor disputes, especially lockouts; [19] (3) the agency's need for more administrative funds (recently curtailed); (4) employment service practices and procedures—an area the council had hitherto neglected entirely; (5) the characteristics of Pennsylvania beneficiaries—an area suggested by the Federal Advisory Council. A separate council committee was established for each area of study.[20]

Why did the council abandon this program of work? Why did the council never meet again? The answers are not entirely clear but certainly include the circumstance that two of the proposed studies were unpopular with influential groups. One was the study of the financial structure of unemployment compensation, which threatened to make too clear that certain industries were a drain

[17] See p. 45.

[18] From a letter to the author, January 14, 1955.

[19] Had the council studied this area its findings would have had particular pertinence in 1955, when in the course of the Westinghouse strike the agency decided that the strike had become a lockout and that the workers were entitled to benefits. Employers successfully appealed this decision to the Pennsylvania Supreme Court.

[20] None of these committees produced a report.

on the fund and also that the program as a whole needed higher taxes. The other was the study of characteristics of beneficiaries. The agency and some, though not all, of the labor representatives feared that the results of such a study would prove embarrassing, and embarrassing or not, would do more harm than good.[21]

Another reason that the council abandoned its program was the political changes of 1954. In the fall of the year, a new governor (a Democrat) was elected and a little later a new director of the employment security program was appointed. Four members of the council (two of the public and two of the labor members) resigned because, they said, they wished to give the new governor the opportunity of choosing his own advisory council. Their action had the exact effect which the 1949 amendment ("the members shall serve until their successors have been appointed") was designed to prevent. The new governor delayed to appoint new council members and the council ceased to exist.

In the case of the labor members who resigned, this result may have been intentional. Labor may well have reached the conclusion that in the changed circumstances of 1955 an advisory council would be more of a hindrance than a help. The governor who had just taken office owed much to labor's support and to the heavy unemployment which Pennsylvania experienced in 1954–1955; in the area of unemployment benefits labor may have expected to get more from the government than from the advisory council. If this was labor's expectation, it was not a mistaken one. Labor obtained, among other liberalizations, the literally unique provision of thirty weeks' duration of benefits uniform for all beneficiaries.

The atmosphere of the 1955 legislative session was such that an advisory council probably would have accomplished little even if one had been in existence. During this session the government— the governor's office and the new director of the agency—took over decision making in the program to a degree that left little room for the bargaining of an advisory council. The changed situation is here described clearly:

[21] This attitude has been characteristic of the Pennsylvania agency. See Joseph M. Becker, *The Problem of Abuse in Unemployment Benefits* (New York: Columbia University Press, 1953), p. 91.

Commencing in 1955, full responsibility for proposing, formulating, and explaining amendatory legislation in this field was accepted by the administration for the first time in more than a decade. Essential information for legislative planning was furnished directly by the administration to committees of the General Assembly and was also made available to all interested parties. Representatives of the Bureau of Employment Security, together with spokesmen for other groups, appeared before the legislative committees with the result that the merits of proposed amendments were debated and acted upon in the open and on the basis of informed opinions on all sides. In the light of these developments it may have been felt that there were no practical purposes which the Advisory Council could serve for the present.[22]

The "present" extended for at least several years. At the end of 1957 the council was still inoperative.

APPRAISAL
INFLUENCE OF THE COUNCIL

There is no doubt that the council was very influential when it was able to reach unanimous agreement and had (as it always did) the support of the administrator. When those who were most interested and most expert agreed, there was no one in the legislature, or in the office of the secretary of labor, or in the office of the governor who had either the incentive or the technical competence to object. Most of the council's agreements were limited to administrative matters and to some of the less controversial legislative issues.

When the council was divided—as it usually was on the more controversial legislative issues—it had relatively little influence. As the council's executive secretary expressed it at the council's last meeting:

I think it was generally recognized by the time we wound up at the end of the 1953 session that where there is a split on issues the way the vote goes doesn't mean a hoot in a boot. The Council is not a court or executive body and no court or legislative body or anyone else is going to be impressed by a 5–4 or 6–3 vote of the Council.[23]

[22] Letter to the author from the director of the Pennsylvania Bureau of Employment Security, April 27, 1956.
[23] From the council minutes for January 28, 1954.

Even when the council was divided it exercised some influence through its reports. Its 1953 report was such a clear and convenient exposition of the main issues and of the main arguments for and against each issue that it was used by the legislators in their debates and probably influenced them.[24] It was also used by the labor and management people most interested in the program, especially the members of the social security committees of the employer organizations. The joint council-bureau report on the solvency of the unemployment compensation fund contributed significantly to an understanding of that problem and, certified as it was by the council as being an impartial, accurate study, inevitably exerted influence. Speaking of the council's reports, the secretary of the council said:

They are the media for explaining problems in as simple terms as possible to those who do take action that counts. I can think of no better comparison to what such a report can be than an "educating brief" presented to a court which lacks sufficient familiarity with the issues to make an intelligent, practical precedent decision without good counseling.[25]

The members said that they found work on the council a valuable educational experience. It automatically kept them abreast of developments and gave them the right to ask for whatever special information they might need. This "window" value of the council is higher in Pennsylvania than it might be in some other states because Pennsylvania makes less use of public hearings. The important legislation of 1951 and 1953, for example, was enacted without the holding of hearings. The council members also valued the education received from each other. In this they agreed with the council's secretary:

The council is a chance to hear one another's view points on the adequacy and soundness of the benefit program and proposed amendments to the law. Perhaps more is accomplished by this alone than some of us have realized even when there are few immediate tangible evidences of such consequences. I think the employment security program in general can profit from more conversations between those whose primary concern is on the contribution side and those who look

[24] The report came out in January—early enough to be of use. The equally good reports of the Ohio council were less influential because they lacked this timeliness.
[25] From the council minutes for January 28, 1954.

primarily to the benefit aspects of the system. After all there is not much chance for mutual understanding and cooperation unless people meet and sit down and talk things out.[26]

The advisory council exerted no influence on the employment service; it did not concern itself with that side of the program. This situation was entirely satisfactory to the director of the employment service, who could see no significant function for the council to perform. The program, he said, no longer had to be sold to the public as in the early years; [27] since the program was part of the United States Employment Service, its major policies were set nationally; and the director and his staff had a more effective listening post in their multitudinous regular contacts with employers and employees than the few advisory council members could provide.[28]

MEMBERSHIP OF THE COUNCIL

The council was always able to boast of a fairly strong membership. The three labor representatives have been as good as could be appointed in point of both authority and competence. They were the ones most worth educating through the advisory council because they were the ones most capable of committing their groups to an agreement. The representative of the United Mine Workers was especially valuable to the labor group because he had more ready access to the governor, who came from a mining district in the state and was sympathetic to miners.

The employer representation is, as usual, less easy to appraise. If not quite as strong as labor's representation, it was not weak. Although all three representatives were "genuine employers," and their number therefore did not include either a professional lobbyist or a representative of an employer organization, one employer came very close to combining both these functions and another was quite active in the Employers' Conference. Between

[26] *Ibid.*

[27] For example, all the schools in Pennsylvania now accept its services for the vocational testing of graduates.

[28] When this person later (1955) became director of the entire bureau, including unemployment compensation, he retained this opinion of the council; see above, p. 307.

them they maintained adequate contact with the full-time professionals in the major employer organizations, who in turn were in close contact with each other through the Employers' Conference and through what might be called interlocking directorates —that is, they belonged to two or more organizations and were on the social security committee of each organization.

The public representation on the council was better than average. One of the public members was something of an expert in unemployment compensation and was also one of the council's hardest workers. Standing on these two bases of authority, he was able to exert a perceptible influence in the council. The influence of the other two public members was less measurable, but was sufficient to cause labor and management to contend for their support. In the opinion of several observers the public members had been helpful on a number of occasions in preventing abuse arising from collusion between employer and employees.[29]

AGREED BILLS AND THE COUNCIL

The mining industry made the task of the advisory council difficult in Pennsylvania, much as the textile industry did in Massachusetts and Rhode Island. Mining was a sick industry in Pennsylvania, and the liberalization of the program could proceed no faster than the mining industry could bear. Since mining accounted for far more than its share of unemployment benefit claimants, it constituted a heavy drain on the unemployment reserve fund and resulted in a high tax rate for mineowners. Further, the objectives of the council members who came from the mining industry—both labor and management representatives —were often different from those of their fellow labor and management members. For both reasons the mining industry was an obstacle in the path of agreed bills, which are reached most easily when liberalization of the program is economically bearable

[29] For example, arrangements to secure both vacation pay and unemployment benefits, or both pension payments and unemployment benefits. Such arrangements were sometimes encountered where the employer was already paying the maximum unemployment tax rate and was not averse to aiding his own employees at the expense of other employers. On such issues divisions in the council were more likely to follow industrial lines rather than labor-management lines.

and when labor and management is each united on its own side of the table.

With regard to the possibility of agreed bills in the future, the legislative representatives of the heavy industries, where decision making in unemployment compensation used to be centered and where unemployment difficulties are still prominent, were pessimistic. Among their reasons for pessimism was the belief that employers generally would not be willing to hand over to a few representatives—of whom most might be from industries not plagued by unemployment—the power to commit all of them to some bargain struck with representatives of labor. On the other hand, the representatives of the chambers of commerce and in general those who were most active in promoting the Employers' Conference were optimistic. They pointed out that employers had, as a matter of fact, achieved a united position in 1951 and again in 1953. They also pointed out that in 1951 the legislation actually enacted could very well have been the result of an agreed bill.

The labor representatives on the council expressed themselves somewhat inconsistently on the subject of the agreed bill. They said, "The success of the council depends on the public members," by which they meant that the success of labor depended on winning the vote of the public members. Yet, they also declared emphatically, "The council is no good," by which they meant that even when they managed to win a majority vote on the council it did them no good in the legislature. Although they understood, and would admit when pressed, that a mere majority vote on the council was of little value and that a unanimous vote could be achieved only by collective bargaining, in their conversation they automatically reverted to the vote-taking procedures of the council and pinned their hopes on winning the votes of the public members. The inconsistency may have been simply the reflection of a fundamental preference for collective bargaining overlaid by a belief that employers were neither interested in it nor capable of it.[30] It is significant that the labor representatives did not have a very clear notion as to where decision making was

---

[30] The CIO representative on the council favored the idea of collective bargaining, provided only that the employer representatives on the council could commit all the major employer organizations—which he doubted.

centered on the employers' side. Apparently labor and management in Pennsylvania have not been accustomed to getting together regularly and working out compromises at any stage in the legislative process.[31]

Except in the 1955 legislative session, labor would have done about as well by accepting an agreed bill as by taking its case to the legislature. In 1955, however, labor clearly gained by choosing political action over collective bargaining. In fact, the results of the 1955 Pennsylvania legislative session provide what is probably the clearest example of how it may be to labor's advantage, at least in the short run, to work through government rather than with employers.

STRUCTURE AND PROCEDURES OF THE COUNCIL

The council's activity was terminated three separate times (in 1939, 1943, and 1955) by the combination of indefinite terms for council members and the members' custom of resigning whenever a new governor took office. In theory, this automatic, recurrent dissolution is prevented by the present form of the law, which was amended in 1949 to provide that the council members serve until their successors have been appointed. In fact, however, the council is still vulnerable—as witness its dissolution in 1955. The law as it stands requires too much of both governor and council. It requires the governor to take the positive step of pushing still-functioning members off the council and thus to incur the danger of hurting feelings and making new political enemies. It requires the council members to remain on the council even when they are not sure the governor wants them to remain.

The experience of Illinois with a similar system shows that the system can be made to work; but the experience of Pennsylvania shows that the system has an inherent weakness. Although no law is proof against the unwillingness of either governor or agency director to have a council, the Pennsylvania law would be strengthened if it were amended in accordance with the council's recom-

[31] In this respect Pennsylvania resembled Massachusetts.

mendation to the legislature in 1951 that members be appointed to the council for staggered terms of six years.

The council adopted rules of procedure as early as its second meeting (June, 1950). They were a full set of rules, modeled on those of New York and adopted only after a council committee had examined the rules of other state councils. The minutes reveal, however, that on very few occasions did the rules make a difference in council action.

One rule was added later, in February, 1953. In the meeting of that date the council debated and decided against the practice of voting by proxy. The council feared that the practice might lead to excessive absenteeism on the part of council members and to blind voting on the part of the proxy holder. The council argued that "a member has to live with the program" to know how to vote on some issues, and that it is impossible to foresee accurately what turns the discussion might take and what bargaining compromises might be presented during the meeting itself.

The Pennsylvania council resembled the councils of New York and Ohio in having an executive secretary but differed from them in so far as its secretary depended not on the council, or even on the agency, but on a unit of government outside both, the Department of Labor. Its secretary took directions from three separate superiors: the council, the agency, and the secretary of labor. This arrangement could easily have produced friction. That it did not was owing principally to the fact that the secretary of labor after 1949 did not attempt to maintain any detailed control over the council and its secretary.

Since the work of the council did not engage the whole of its secretary's time, the director of the agency began to use him for special tasks until the secretary's time was about equally divided between council and agency. Some council members and on one occasion the secretary of labor raised a question as to the propriety of his working for two masters. Experience seems to have proved, however, that the arrangement was advantageous to the council. The secretary's dual capacity enabled him to establish between the agency and the council the close liaison which is essential to a council's effectiveness. Because he served both council and agency he could more easily keep the council informed of what was happening in the agency, steer the council away from action that would be opposed by the agency, and secure from the agency the statistical and clerical assistance which the council needed.

To some extent he served as a substitute for the director of the agency in the task of interpreting the agency to the council. To that extent the arrangement may have disadvantaged the council, for there is no adequate substitute for the director himself.

At the last meeting of the council the most active members were two college professors, the council's secretary and the council's chairman. These were the two who did most of the talking at the meeting, who developed the council's work program, and who assigned the committees to do the work. The preeminence of these two may have been a sign of the council's declining vigor, for they were the two members with the least economic and political stake in the council's actions. It can be laid down as a fairly reliable rule that the most effective councils are those on which the labor and management members and the director of the agency are the most active members.

15

THE MICHIGAN ADVISORY COUNCIL

DURING the first decade of its operation, the Michigan employment security law did not have a provision for an advisory council. Perhaps the fact that a commission administered the program made an advisory council seem unnecessary. But in 1947 the law was amended to provide for a council, and in 1948 one began to function.[1]

In 1947 Governor Sigler came into office on a platform which included reform of the unemployment compensation agency. The governor appointed an acting administrator, who recommended, among other changes, that the four-man commission be replaced by a single director and that an advisory council be established to give labor and management an alternative form of participation for the one which they would lose through the abolition of the commission. The legislature saw fit to disregard the first part of the recommendation and to follow the second: it kept the commission but provided for an advisory council.

Why the legislature established the advisory council is obscure. It is certain that neither labor nor management had asked for a council. The labor and management representatives who were most active in the 1947 hubbub of amendments were barely aware of the advisory-council provision among the other proposed amendments. The Bureau of Employment Security had been reminding Michigan for years that it was out of conformity with the Wagner-Peyser Act in not having a council, but the Bureau's

[1] An earlier advisory council for the employment service had the usual history of such councils: active and effective during the depression, becoming less active as conditions of employment improved, giving way to manpower committees during the war, and never reviving.

pressure had been growing less rather than greater over the years. Besides, the council established by the legislature in 1947 was still not in conformity with the Wagner-Peyser Act.[2] Some observers of the Michigan scene were of the opinion that the council was established as a watchdog to prevent a repetition of the financial irregularities alleged to have occurred under the previous administration.

Another explanation was suggested by some of the Michigan labor leaders. The 1947 amendments to the law were unfavorable to labor, and as a partial recompense labor was to be given a greater voice in the administration of the law. This was to be done in two ways. First, labor was to have two of the four places on the commission, and to this end the 1947 amendments specified that two of the four commission members must be representatives of employees.[3] Second, an advisory council was to be established on which labor would have half the members. The weakness of this explanation is that since labor's influence was increased effectively by the change in the commission, there was no real need to create a council for this purpose. This explanation makes the advisory council almost an afterthought.

The most likely explanation is that Senator Bonine, chairman of the Senate labor committee, wanted an advisory council. The senator was the most influential single figure in the events of 1947, and he liked the idea of an advisory council. He liked it primarily because he thought that labor and management on an advisory council might learn to work together—even achieve agreed bills— and thus lessen the bitter tension which marked their relationships at that time. He was probably influenced by the success of the Wisconsin council in that respect, for the advisory council he proposed was modeled on that of Wisconsin, which limited council membership to representatives of labor and management.

[2] The Michigan Employment Security Commission occasionally reminds the advisory council that the Wagner-Peyser Act requires that council membership include public members and at least one woman.

[3] Previously the law had merely required that no more than two of the commission members were to be of the same political party, and the way this provision was administered resulted in labor's never having more than one representative on the commission—and he was not from the CIO, the dominant labor organization in Michigan. Since 1947 one of these two has always been from the CIO.

The Michigan law specifies a council of eight members, four to represent employers and four to represent employees. The members are appointed by the governor for staggered terms of six years, and serve without compensation. The responsibility of the council is stated simply but comprehensively: "It shall be the responsibility of the advisory council to make recommendations, (1) to the commission, on policy, and (2) to the governor, the legislature, and the commission, on proposed amendments to this act." [4]

The council proposed that the director of the agency act as council chairman—following again, perhaps, the example of Wisconsin. The director was the secretary of the commission, however, and the commission at that time was suspicious of the council as a possible rival and would not consent to his serving both bodies. The council, therefore, elected a chairman from among its own members. The chairman was always chosen from among the labor members, and the secretary from among the employer members.

The Michigan council lived an unusually independent existence. It always called its own meetings and prepared its own agenda. Between council and agency there was less official liaison than even in the case of Ohio. No official of the agency met regularly with the council. Agency personnel attended the council's meetings only by invitation, usually to supply information, and left when their business was completed. The agency did not receive a copy of the council's minutes and had no other direct source of knowledge of its activities.[5]

The records of the council are fragmentary. Although the minutes for the years after 1952 are nearly complete, those for the years prior to that time were lost when the council changed secretaries. Hence it is difficult to follow in detail the earlier activities of the council.

The council held meetings with at least average frequency. As nearly as members could estimate, the council met about fifty times between its first meeting, in August of 1948, and the end of

[4] Sec. 421.3a of the Michigan Employment Security Act, 1955.
[5] The agency's assistant director was not even certain whether the council kept minutes.

1955—an average of about seven meetings a year. The council's most active period was the three years from 1949 through 1951, when it averaged nearly twelve meetings a year.

ACTIVITIES OF THE COUNCIL

The environment in which the Michigan council began to function was not favorable to its success. The amendments of 1947 had been in the nature of a "reform," and the bitter struggle which accompanied their enactment had left labor-management relations in unemployment compensation at their lowest ebb. The reform had been started in Michigan, as in some other states,[6] by a group of disaffected employers revolting against their accustomed leadership. In Michigan there was this difference, that the revolt was not directed against employers who were council members; in Michigan at this time there was no council.

The revolt came from within the Michigan Manufacturers' Association.[7] For a year prior to 1947 a group of employers had been meeting independently of the association and planning far-reaching changes in the unemployment compensation program.[8] In the meantime, the general manager of the Michigan Manufacturers' Association, John Lovett, had agreed with some labor leaders, probably the AFL, to an increase of two dollars in maximum benefits and did not have in mind any other substantive changes. At a final meeting of employers, however, the insurgent group prevailed on the meeting to override Lovett, and as a result the employers' recommendations for 1947 became a proposal for a major revision of the act.[9]

Many of the employers' recommendations were enacted into

[6] For example, in Illinois, Utah, New York, California.

[7] Not, as in Illinois, from a rival organization like the state Chamber of Commerce; in Michigan there is no state chamber.

[8] These changes, which included request reporting, sending employers copies of benefit checks, and tightening of eligibility and disqualification provisions, became the model for changes in other states, such as Ohio, New York, Massachusetts, Nebraska.

[9] The provision increasing benefits by two dollars was incorporated in the employers' bill because Lovett had already committed himself; but a young legislator, who later became chairman of the Senate labor committee, noticed the provision as the bill was about to pass and insisted that it be deleted.

law, but only over bitter labor opposition. The advisory council thus began its existence at a time when labor-management relations in unemployment compensation were most strained and an agreed bill least likely. Management was determined to hold on to everything it had gained, and labor stated emphatically that it was merely biding its time until the turn of the political wheel would enable it to undo all the 1947 changes.

The council's first meetings, in late 1948 and early 1949, were taken up with the administrative changes necessitated by the legislative amendments of the previous session and with proposed amendments for 1949. The council was unable to agree on the amendments. Employers were unwilling to concede what labor wanted and was sure it could get from the legislature. Labor knew it could count on the new governor,[10] in whose election the CIO had played a vital part, and on the new director, who clearly favored labor. Labor was probably correct in this judgment. By the amendments enacted in 1949, labor gained not only some easing of eligibility requirements but also an increase in maximum benefits from $20 ($28) to $24 ($32).[11]

The meetings of the council in late 1949 and through 1950 continued to be taken up with both administrative and substantive problems. Some of the administrative problems could be solved by rules and regulations, which the agency could enact; others required technical amendments to the law, which only the legislature could enact. As far as one can judge from the fragmentary

[10] Governor Mennen Williams was elected in 1949 and was reelected in 1951, 1953, 1955, and 1957. Between 1935 and 1957 the Republicans held the governorship for five terms and the Democrats for seven. Both Senate and House have been under Republican control in all sessions except those of 1937–1938 and 1941–1942. The long dominance of the Republican Party in the legislature has been due in large part to the system of districting the state. In the early 1950's districts were reapportioned according to population, but through careful gerrymandering the Republican control was not disturbed.

[11] The higher figures, in parentheses, apply to beneficiaries with dependents. Dependents' allowances were added to the Michigan law in 1945. The manner of their enactment was reminiscent of the way they were added to the Connecticut law (p. 229). In Michigan a bill was under discussion which liberalized unemployment benefits, when a rural legislator rose to say that he was against the bill because it increased benefits for single men but that he would not mind increasing the benefits of men with dependents. The bill was amended accordingly and passed forthwith, without the lobbyists for either labor or management having anything to do with it.

minutes, the council did solid work in helping to solve both these kinds of administrative problems.

In the area of substantive legislation the council worked during this period with a study committee of the legislature. The study committee hoped that the meetings would lead to an agreed bill. The labor members of the council hoped that the meetings would lead to the undoing of the amendments of 1947. The employer members looked on the meetings as an opportunity to educate the committee in the fundamental principles which underlay those amendments.

To attain their objective the employer members prepared a six-part statement on "Fundamental Public Policy," which the labor members signed. The employers then proceeded to build their case on this "unanimous statement of the advisory council." The statement was correct enough, but all six parts were employer oriented in their emphasis and were intended to provide the basis for a second statement, "Giving Effect to the Public Policy of the Michigan Unemployment Compensation Act." This second statement contained such conclusions as: "No further upward revision of benefit levels is needed or desirable. . . . It would be economically unsound to extend benefit duration beyond the present 20-week period. . . . The members of the Advisory Council believe that the experience rating provisions of the Michigan law should be approved and strengthened." On the last page were blank spaces for the signatures of the labor members.

Appended to the statement was a note: "This statement was prepared in the hope that it might be agreed to unanimously by both employer and employee representatives. The employee representatives have decided that they will submit a separate statement of their position." The employer members could not possibly have expected labor to sign such a statement. It was clear that they were using the council meetings primarily to get a hearing for their ideas rather than to negotiate an agreement. When this became evident the joint meetings ended and the legislative committee acted on its own; in two all-night sessions, with the director of the agency as adviser, the committee worked out a compromise bill. Labor was favored by an increase in maximum benefits from $24 ($32) to $27 ($35). Employers were favored by a change in the director of the agency.

The director appointed by Governor Williams had aroused the same kind of employer opposition as had the director of the Massachusetts agency at about the same time—and for the same reason: he seemed very partial to labor and hostile to employers. The final result was also the same, but in Michigan the reaction was quicker and took a different route. First, the legislature transferred from the governor to the Unemployment Compensation Commission the power to appoint a director.[12] The commission then removed the director. His successor would have to be acceptable to both sides—since labor and management had equal voice on the commission—and nearly two years elapsed before labor and management could agree and a new director was appointed. This agreed-upon director introduced a measure of stability into the office. Before his appointment Michigan had changed directors ten times in thirteen years; since his appointment there has been no change.[13] He has managed to remain in office because he has been the sort of impartial, nonpolitical administrator envisaged by John R. Commons.[14]

An unofficial arrangement made about this time increased the potential influence of the advisory council. The commission members and the director were given to understand that their task was simply to administer the law, not to interpret it or recommend changes in it; these latter functions were reserved to the advisory council. The employer members of the commission accepted this limited view of the function of an administrative body. The labor members of the commission did not. Without the cooperation of the employer members they could not, of course, function in the forbidden area as a commission, but they could and did continue to work in it as individuals. The director had to accept the limitation—and in the explosive situation that then existed was glad

[12] The governor retained his power to appoint the members of the commission, but since these appointments required the consent of the Senate, the legislature still had a measure of control.

[13] Appointed acting director in 1950, he became director in 1952 and remained in office through the period covered by this survey.

[14] And see Leiserson's remark, p. 34, n. 6.

to do so—but he continued nevertheless to exercise considerable influence. Any full-time, expert administrator is always a prime influence in determining the policy of the program he administers, the more so as the parties affected by the program—in this case labor and management—cannot agree on what they want. A legislative leader, for example, declared that the constant disagreement on the council left him no choice but to seek his advice from the director of the agency.

Beginning in late 1951, when Michigan completed its solvency study, and continuing into 1952 and 1953, employers concentrated on trying to change the tax system while holding the level of benefits unchanged.[15] Their aim was to change the Michigan benefit-ratio system into a reserve-ratio system resembling Wisconsin's, a change that would relate the cost of unemployment more exactly to each employer's own experience and would cause the tax rate to move more counter-cyclically. They formulated their proposals in a bill and had it introduced in the legislature.

The legislature took the employers' bill and after, as usual, adding something for labor (an extension of duration from twenty to twenty-six weeks) passed the bill in both the 1952 and the 1953 sessions.[16] In both sessions Governor Williams vetoed the bill at the request of the CIO, which wanted an increase in benefits and some changes in disqualifications and was resolved to block the tax changes desired by employers until employers agreed to better terms. The state Federation doubted the wisdom of this strategy, especially in 1953, when there was an acute manpower shortage in Michigan and unemployment benefits were not a strong talking point. Typical AFL strategy would have been to accept the bill in 1952 and work for something better in the succeeding sessions.

The advisory council met only a few times during 1952 and 1953. Most of the joint study and discussions during this period took place between two technicians, one representing the employer members of the council and the other the labor members, although

---

[15] "Employers" rarely refers to a monolithic group. There were many employers who fought the proposed tax changes, especially employers with a record of over-average unemployment. In 1951 and in 1952 an employers' technical team traveled the state, trying to win their fellow employers to the proposed system.

[16] The Michigan legislature began to hold annual sessions in 1952.

neither of the two was a member of the council. The council reviewed the completed work of these technicians but was unable to reach an agreed bill on the basis of it.

The council did not as a body exercise any positive influence in either 1952 or 1953, but in 1953 it did exercise an unfortunate negative influence. The agency, prohibited from recommending amendments, had given the council a long list of technical changes in the law which the agency needed for more efficient administration and had asked the council to approve them. The council neglected this list while it continued to fight over substantive issues. Eventually the labor members became disinterested in what was from their viewpoint fruitless negotiation and would not attend further meetings. The last council meeting in 1953 was held on January 7. The deadline for introducing new bills passed without the council's having taken any action on the needed administrative amendments, and the agency was compelled to manage as best it could for another year. This obstructing of the passage of the technical amendments, the council's only contribution in 1953, did not enhance its reputation.

The council did not meet again until a year later, on February 19, 1954. Even at this initial meeting of the new session it became clear that the council was still split on the issues which had divided it during the two previous sessions and that it could not expect to reach agreement in the 1954 session. During the rest of this session, therefore, labor and management carried on their maneuverings outside the advisory council.

The legislative deadlock was nevertheless broken in 1954. Employers introduced their former bill (vetoed in 1952 and in 1953) with two additional provisions: some minor tightening of disqualifications and a small increase in benefits. But labor, by great effort and the expenditure of one hundred thousand dollars on publicity, was able to get several amendments into the bill, including an amendment for a larger increase in benefits.[17] Labor's cause was helped by the high unemployment in 1954 and was

[17] Out of these negotiations came Michigan's pioneering system, now spreading to other states, of the "variable maximum." It seems to have been devised by employer technicians in Michigan.

given strong support by a group of young Republicans in the House. The amended bill was passed in the legislature by a nearly unanimous vote and was signed by the governor.

For the next two years the council began to meet more frequently (though not so frequently as during its first three years) and to take on more of the appearance of a peaceful work group. In 1955 the council produced an agreed bill which was both extensive and complex, including a long list of administrative and semisubstantive matters which the agency had submitted for council consideration. After the council had worked through the list in detail and reached agreement, the legislature enacted all but two of the recommendations into law. A fly in the 1955 ointment is indicated by the following comment made by a labor member of the council: "The council did agree upon certain recommendations made by the Commission this year for amendments to the law, but since it was introduced in the Legislature [as House Bill No. 190] the Republicans have attached some amendments to it which we are in disagreement with, and from now on the labor members at least will approach any such recommendations by the Commission with a great deal of suspicion." [18]

Something similar seems to have occurred in the 1956 session. The advisory council agreed on a number of administrative changes, which were introduced as House Bill No. 295. Then some legislators attempted to amend the agreed bill in ways which were highly objectionable to labor. Labor used this experience as the occasion for issuing a statement on the council in early 1957. In this statement, which was sent to the governor and the legislature, labor expressed dissatisfaction with the council because it "had made no recommendations in recent years for substantive improvements in the Act" and proposed "the expansion of the Advisory Council from eight to twelve members with the additional four members representing the public in order to revitalize the Advisory Council, place it in conformity with the requirements of Federal law and permit it to function effectively in its stated legislative purpose." Nothing came of this proposal, and thereafter council activity almost ceased.

[18] From a letter to the author, May 11, 1955.

APPRAISAL

Like most advisory councils, the Michigan council exerted practically no influence on the employment service side of the program. On the unemployment compensation side, in the eight legislative sessions covered by the period of this survey (1949–1957) it achieved an agreed bill only once, in 1955, and this bill, although it was extensive and important, was confined to technical and semisubstantive amendments. The council has never managed to reach agreement on the more controversial, substantive issues of the program.

The council has done little in the way of issuing reports of its own or authenticating studies made by the agency. Its technical committee did some solid work in revising the tax structure, but two of that committee's three members were not members of the council. For labor and management the council constituted a window into the agency, but this advantage was minimized by the unusual degree to which the council operated independently of the agency. On the whole the council has not been an institution of major importance in the development of the Michigan employment security program.

The council's lack of influence cannot be explained by the calibre of its membership. Thus far the Michigan governors have allowed labor and management to nominate candidates for the council. The labor members urged this procedure on Governor Williams when he balked at appointing certain employer nominees who were active opponents of the governor. Labor said it preferred to deal with employers who could speak authoritatively for their organizations. The council membership has always included the principal decision makers of both labor and management. With one exception, these have not been drawn from the top echelons of either group.[19] Michigan is characterized by giant unions and giant companies. This fact makes it less likely that council members will be top officials, but also makes it less necessary. The division of labor that of necessity accompanies great size

[19] The exception: the secretary of the Michigan Federation of Labor, which is the smaller of the two state labor bodies.

gives to lower officials considerable decision-making power. The labor and management representatives on the council have been adequate for their job and have made the council a potentially powerful body.

In Michigan the representatives of employers can the more easily speak authoritatively for their constituents because there exists an organization, the Michigan Employers' Unemployment Compensation Bureau, which represents and services the employers of the state in all matters pertaining to unemployment compensation. This organization, established in 1947 with the name Michigan Manufacturers' Unemployment Compensation Bureau, Inc., took over the functions previously performed by the Social Security Committee of the Michigan Manufacturers' Association. It was established primarily to achieve coordinated employer action; but there was an additional reason. The "reform" groups among the employers wanted to separate employers' unemployment compensation activity from the Michigan Manufacturers' Association, whose unemployment compensation policy was not to their liking. John Lovett, general manager of the association, had long been accustomed to set policy in unemployment compensation by making deals with labor, usually with the AFL. The "reform" employers considered his unemployment compensation policy too easygoing and believed that they would have a better chance to change it by working through a new organization set up outside the old pattern of control.

Another reason for the establishment of the bureau was to unite all employers, and not merely manufacturers, in a single organization. To emphasize this aim, in 1952 the word "Manufacturers' " in the title was replaced by "Employers'." Since 1952 the membership of the bureau has grown greatly, and while it is far from including all employers, it does include practically all the large employers and enough of the others to make it clearly the chief spokesman for Michigan employers in the area of unemployment compensation. The lobbyists of other employer organizations or of particular companies are expected to coordinate their activity with the bureau's in everything pertaining to unemployment compensation.

The bureau is both a service organization—it answers questions, responds to calls for help, and publishes a monthly bulletin—and the chief locus for employers' policy formation. It holds an annual meeting, at which it elects directors, who appoint the bureau's manager and secretary. The board of directors, numbering twenty-one, meets quarterly or oftener. There is also a five-man executive committee which meets irregularly to handle business on a more continuous basis. The executive committee has generally included two of the employer members of the advisory council.[20]

The existence of very large companies and unions has guaranteed the presence of capable technicians. A marked feature of the Michigan council has been its use of technicians, even of those who were not members of the council.[21] Two noncouncil technicians, one from labor and one from management, worked with the council so closely and so constantly that at least twice the secretary of the council listed them in his minutes as council members. The availability of technicians has been one reason that the Michigan council has been able to function as actively as it has while keeping the agency at a distance. Most councils would find it too difficult to conduct their own meetings on their own initiative to the extent that the Michigan council did.

As remarked before, the structure of the Michigan council was probably modeled on that of Wisconsin with the hope that it would prove as successful as the Wisconsin council. But the history of the Michigan council has been as unlike Wisconsin's as its structure has been similar. Some of the reasons for the difference have been in the council's environment, others in the council itself. Labor relations have always tended to be more acrimonious in Michigan than in Wisconsin, and they had become especially bitter in unemployment compensation just at the time the council began to function. In Michigan the dominant labor organization has been

[20] In addition to the Michigan Employers' Unemployment Compensation Bureau there is in Detroit an organization called the Employers Unemployment Compensation Forum, which comprises technicians from various companies in Detroit and meets monthly. It grew out of a custom of meeting informally at a dinner. The forum is primarily a clearinghouse of ideas and does not attempt to set policy. It is entirely separate from the bureau, which it antedates, but the manager or secretary of the bureau usually attends the monthly meetings of the forum.

[21] See the Illinois and the federal councils for a similar use of technicians.

the younger, more militant CIO, and the turbulent history of the UAW-CIO has set the tone; in Wisconsin the dominant labor organization has been the older, more conservative AFL. Also, because Michigan's CIO has tended to identify itself with a political party more closely than has Wisconsin's AFL, labor-management differences in Michigan have shown more of a tendency to become political differences. Further, Michigan's unemployment rate has been consistently higher than Wisconsin's, and a high unemployment rate is an added obstacle for an advisory council to surmount.[22] Finally, the early Michigan law contained many more provisions that employers wanted to change than did the early Wisconsin law; during the very years that Wisconsin employers were agreeing to successive liberalizations in their law, Michigan employers were demanding that their law be tightened. The latter situation is much less conducive to agreed bills than the former.

The Michigan council has been very independent of the agency, and this has been one of its chief weaknesses. The weakness has been manifested partly in diminished activity but much more in lessened unity. The council is composed of only labor and management members, and one of the two groups is certain to supply—or attempt to supply—leadership. Somebody has to "organize" the council, just as the majority party has to "organize" the legislature. Somebody has to decide when meetings will be called and what the agenda of the meetings will be. Somebody has to be prepared to make proposals and to present supporting material for the proposals. In Michigan the employer members have generally attempted to fill the role, and the situation inevitably has led to employers trying to make use of the council to further the projects which were of most interest to employers. The development of the "Fundamental Public Policy" (1949–1950) and the prolonged and difficult work on the revision of the tax structure (1951–1953) are examples of the way the council was set to work by employers for employers.

Understandably the labor members of the council were suspicious of this employer leadership. As one of them expressed it: "It is generally the opinion of the labor members that the em-

[22] See the chapter on Wisconsin, p. 84.

ployers only want to use the Council or to meet when it may suit their purpose." [23] Organized as it is in giant unions and having technicians of its own, labor in Michigan was better able than labor in most states to compete with management; but even in Michigan the contest was not an equal one. Employers could put more and better-trained men on a given project for a longer time than could labor. As a result labor was not always an enthusiastic partner in the work of the council but came along to the meetings (which usually have been suggested by employers) somewhat reluctantly and suspiciously.[24]

The council would have profited by some neutral leadership —by the agency alone, as in Wisconsin, or by the agency and a mutually acceptable public chairman, as in New Hampshire. If the structure and procedures of the council were recast on the model of Wisconsin or New Hampshire, labor, including the CIO, *might* experience a renewal of interest in the council as a mechanism for collective bargaining. And it might not; although the CIO originally approved of having only labor and management representatives on the council, experience with the arrangement brought a change of mind, and the CIO has twice attempted to amend the law to include public members. That may be a sign that the CIO has ceased to regard the council primarily as an opportunity for collective bargaining and is prepared to use it for propaganda purposes, which is the way that employers seemed to have used it in the early years.

There has been one feature of the Michigan scene which was favorable, in a way, to agreed bills. That has been the ease with which deadlocks could develop. In Michigan the stage has always been set for a deadlock on three successive levels: on the level of the council, where there were four labor and four management members and no way to break a tie; on the commission level, where there were two labor and two management members and no way to break a tie; and on the legislative level, where both houses were Republican but the governor was a five-time Democratic winner

[23] From a letter to the author, May 11, 1955.

[24] Except on those occasions when the agency was working actively with the council, as it was, for example, while the council was preparing its agreed bill on the technical amendments of 1955.

who could and did veto successfully the legislature's unemployment compensation bills. During the period covered by this survey, however, the threat of a deadlock has not been sufficient to induce an agreed bill at the council level.

One of the more interesting aspects of the Michigan scene is the coexistence of the advisory council with the commission. Since both are similarly structured in that each restricts its membership to representatives of labor and management, the question naturally arises as to whether both are necessary.

Despite the similarity in structure between the two bodies, there have been significant differences in personnel, especially among the employers. Two factors principally account for the differences. First, the council can more easily draw members from the higher echelons of labor and management because it demands of its members less time and routine effort than does the commission, which meets at least weekly and must bear the day-to-day burden of administration. Second, Governor Williams would not have been willing to appoint to the commission, which he considers an official extension of his own person, some of the employer representatives whom he appointed to the advisory council, which he considers to be a forum for the expression of private opinion and an opportunity for collective bargaining.

The function of the advisory council is clear. It can carry through difficult analyses (with the aid of the technicians it has attached to itself), can commit the major employer and employee organizations to an agreement, and can lobby an agreement through the legislature.

The function of the commission, given an effective council, is not equally clear. The two bodies usually reach identical decisions on important matters because the major battle lines are drawn between labor and management and hence are the same for both council and commission. The commission's chief functions could be performed, and as a matter of fact are often performed, by the executive-director working with the advisory council. In 1954, for example, the director took his list of proposed amendments to the advisory council and to the commission, but it was from the advisory council that he obtained the more thorough analysis and the final decision. Certainly one reason why the commission has been retained is that employers see it as a check on the power of the governor over the agency. Given a prolabor governor, which Michigan has had since 1949, employers would fare less well if the agency was administered by a single director appointed by the governor than they would if the agency was administered by a commission on which employers constituted half the membership.

The commission was valuable to the director as a shield. Placed as he was between two powerful and antagonistic groups and without the protection of civil service, the director needed the bipartisan support assured by the commission. The commission also had the effect of making labor and management less dependent on the advisory council than they would otherwise have been. The commission gave them a window and door into the agency very similar to that supplied by the advisory council.

The future of the council may be more of a success story than the past has been. Labor and management are sufficiently organized to make a strong council possible. Labor relations in Michigan in general have become less warlike in recent years, and the unemployment compensation program in particular has settled into something like a groove so far as its major structural features are concerned. If the advisory council could be reconstituted on the model of either the Wisconsin or New Hampshire councils, its members might very well succeed in working together with sufficient effectiveness to justify the existence of the institution.

16

THE COLORADO ADVISORY COUNCIL

THE Colorado law, enacted in 1936, provides for an advisory council of eleven members: four representatives of employers, four of employees, and three of the public. They are to be appointed by the governor for staggered terms of four years and are to serve without compensation.

A partial council was appointed in May of 1940, under pressure from the Bureau of Employment Security, but it was never completed and it never met. Under continued pressure another and complete council was appointed in April of 1941. This council held some meetings (probably very few) during the war years, but there is no record of its activity before May 26, 1944, when minutes began to be kept. From that date through 1957 the council held thirty meetings, an average of 2.3 meetings yearly. As the following table shows, the frequency of meetings decreased in later years and averaged less than one per year after 1950.[1]

1944	4	1948	4	1952	1	1956	0
1945	5	1949	0	1953	0	1957	0
1946	4	1950	8	1954	1		
1947	2	1951	0	1955	1		

The attendance record of the council as a whole was 59 percent. The record of employers was 73 percent; of labor, 57 percent; and of the public, 47 percent. The Colorado council is near the bottom of the list both in frequency of meetings and in attendance at meetings.

[1] Most meetings were held immediately prior to or during legislative sessions, which before 1952 held only in the odd-numbered years. Starting in 1952, the Colorado legislature began to hold a short session in the intervening years to handle budget measures.

One of the public members served as chairman until he left the council in 1947. The council then voted, on the motion of the employer members, to have the director of the agency serve as temporary chairman. In 1950 the council unanimously elected him permanent chairman, and he continued to serve in that capacity throughout the period covered by this survey.

ACTIVITIES OF THE COUNCIL

The council concerned itself entirely with unemployment compensation matters and almost entirely with legislation. The first legislative session for which its activities are recorded is that of 1945. In that session the council unanimously approved an increase in the duration of benefits from sixteen weeks to twenty weeks, keeping the benefit amount unchanged at $15. This represented an agreed bill only in a modified sense, for although the labor members voted for the council bill, they announced at the same time that their groups would introduce other bills asking for much more.[2]

Labor might have saved itself the trouble. Even the council's agreed bill, with its mild provisions, failed to pass. At the meeting of March 29, 1945, the council was warned that this might happen. One of its employer representatives, a lobbyist and the council's one direct contact with the legislature, reported that the legislature simply was not interested in unemployment compensation, that the council's bill was considered technical and difficult, and that the bill probably would not move unless the council secured a definite legislator to sponsor it. The council's chairman, a public member, demurred, saying that it was a mistaken idea of the nature of the council to think of it as a lobby. As it turned out, the council did not lobby for its bill, the labor members continued to demand more than the council bill provided, and whether for these or other reasons the bill did not pass and no substantive unemployment compensation legislation was enacted in the 1945 session.[3]

[2] All of the council's "agreed bills" were of this qualified sort, except in 1953, when there was a firm understanding that both sides would work for the council bill alone.

[3] In 1945 the legislature established an occupational disability program and may have felt that this was enough labor legislation for one year.

In 1947 the council unanimously agreed on increasing benefits to $18 for twenty weeks (from $15 for sixteen weeks). In this session the council attempted to meet with the legislative committee handling unemployment compensation but did not succeed. The committee was too busy and was not interested. However, the legislature eventually passed a bill which embodied the council's recommendations.

In 1949 the council unanimously approved an increase in benefits to $21 for twenty-six weeks along with a tightening of the disqualification for voluntary quit.[4] Labor leaders outside the council vigorously attacked the council's bill and repudiated any approval given it by the labor representatives on the council. The legislature finally passed a bill which raised the maximum benefit amount to $22.75 but left the benefit duration unchanged and tightened the voluntary-quit disqualification as recommended by the council. The net result for labor was about the same as it would have been if labor had supported the council's agreed bill.

The 1949 developments brought to a head the issue of organized labor's relationship to its representatives on the council. This issue influenced the outcome of elections held by the Colorado State Federation of Labor at this time. The incumbent officers (president and secretary) had recommended to the convention that the Federation withdraw from the advisory council because labor always played a purely passive role and had to accept whatever employers cared to offer. The candidates opposing the incumbents maintained that labor ought to remain on the council because the council was at the very least a listening post and could become more than that if labor put more effective representatives on it. The opposing candidates were victorious in the election, and one result of their victory was the appointment of the Federation secretary to the council later that same year, 1949. This was the first time that an official of either state labor organization had been a member of the council. (The secretary of the state CIO was appointed to the council in 1953, after which the labor representation on the council was as strong as could reasonably be desired.)

---

[4] "Good cause" for quitting was to be limited to causes "attributable to the employer."

The council made an auspicious start in 1950 in preparation for the 1951 legislative session. It held more frequent meetings in 1950 than in any other year, and it arranged a series of luncheon conferences with the legislative committees.[5] At this time the employer members of the council seemed to be more interested in the council than were the labor members. The idea of meeting with the legislative committee had come from one of the employer members, and the attendance record of the employer members in 1950, while not good, was much better than that of the labor members.

The council could not agree on any legislation for 1951, and none was enacted except for the deletion of the clause "attributable to the employer" which had been added to the voluntary-quit disqualification in the previous session. This change was made largely at the insistence of the director of the agency in support of the labor members.

In 1953 the council came closest to achieving an agreed bill in the full sense. With the director of the agency playing an active mediating role, the council reached agreement on a number of amendments, including an increase in maximum benefits from $22.50 to $28. Labor's joint legislative board, comprising the leaders of the state Federation, the CIO, and the Railroad Brotherhoods, formally approved this agreement and voted not to support competing bills. The secretary of the state Federation did, however, introduce a conflicting bill—raising benefits to $35—because the Federation's annual convention, held before the council agreement was made, had passed a resolution directing him to do so. But everyone understood that he would not fight for his bill, so it did not in any way impair the validity of the council's agreed bill.[6]

The subsequent developments of the 1953 legislative session were most unexpected and convinced labor's negotiators that they had been wise to work through the procedure of the agreed bill.

[5] Two such conferences were held but were so poorly attended by the legislators that the whole idea was dropped.

[6] At the next convention the state Federation granted its secretary the freedom to make the best bargains he could with employers on the council and to introduce or withhold bills. For a similar action of the California State Federation of Labor, see p. 355.

The House committee unexpectedly amended the bill and deleted the increase in benefits. Labor appealed to the governor, citing the fact that this was an agreed bill and threatening to resign from the council. The governor announced that he would veto the bill unless it was passed in its original form. The House, annoyed by what it called executive interference, promptly passed the bill in its amended form. The Senate seemed ready to concur. At this point the director of the agency and the employer members of the council went into action. It was only through their vigorous efforts that the legislature was finally persuaded to reverse itself and to pass the bill in its original form. Labor leaders concluded that if it was so difficult to pass a liberalizing bill even with the support of the employers, it would be impossible to do so against employer opposition.

In the 1955 legislative session there was little chance for an agreed bill. At the one council meeting held in preparation for that session, employers demanded that benefits received under the Old Age and Survivors Insurance (OASI) program be considered as disqualifying income under the unemployment compensation program and they refused to approve of any increase in benefits, arguing that in Colorado the average benefit was already more than 50 percent of the average wage of beneficiaries. Labor, therefore, introduced its own bills which provided as usual for changes so extensive in the law that they had no chance of passage.[7]

The Senate committee, on which labor had one strong friend,[8] prepared a compromise bill of its own, granting employers the OASI disqualification and granting labor part of one of its numerous demands, namely, a reduction in the waiting period.[9] The council played no part in preparing this compromise—as its labor representatives made very clear when they were later attacked by some unions on the ground that they had agreed to the OASI disqualification.

[7] Even at that the bills of Colorado labor did not go so far as those drawn in the national labor offices. For example, instead of the $45 proposed by the national CIO bill, the Colorado bill was content to ask for $35.

[8] He was partially lost to labor in 1955, when he was elected mayor of Denver.

[9] From two weeks to one week. The labor bills had demanded the elimination of the waiting period entirely.

Partly because of a disagreement between the director of the agency and the secretary of the state Federation, no meeting of the council was held in 1956 or 1957 in preparation for the 1957 session. In this session, for the first time in a generation, labor found itself in a position of control. The results were evident in the unemployment compensation amendments: the maximum benefit was increased from $28 to $35 and the maximum duration from 20 to 26 weeks. Some disqualifications were softened, while OASI benefits and SUB payments were declared nondisqualifying.

ADVISORY COUNCIL ON FARM LABOR

As mentioned before, the regular advisory council concerned itself almost exclusively with unemployment compensation and generally ignored the employment service side of the program. The employment problems of farm labor, however, received the attention of a special advisory council, which began to function in 1949. It consisted of employer representatives only, six in all, of whom two were the executive secretaries of farm organizations and four represented the largest firms in the sugar and canning industries. Like similar councils in other states, its chief concern was the recruitment of farm labor for the seasonal crops. Recruitment included providing transportation expenses, arranging housing, getting clearance from the Mexican and United States governments, and many other tasks. At first the council met only annually. As its competence and success increased, the number of its meetings also increased to three or four a year. The director of the agency found this council very useful and was enthusiastic over its accomplishments.

ADVISORY COUNCIL ON WORKMEN'S COMPENSATION

In most states agreed bills are more common in workmen's compensation than in unemployment compensation, but in Colorado the opposite has been true. Agreed bills, even in the diluted form which characterized most of those reached in unemployment compensation, have been practically unknown in the workmen's compensation program, which was inaugurated in Colorado in 1915. Since at least the early 1930's labor has customarily introduced "ideal" bills, which the legislature has regularly ignored. For a dozen years beginning with the early 1930's labor was unable to gain any increase in the low maximum benefit of $14, not even in 1937, when twenty-seven members of the legislature were Democrats and only thirty-three votes were needed to pass a bill. The spokesman for employers once (1941) proposed to the then president of the state Federation that they try to arrive at agreed bills, but nothing came of the proposal. The president was unable to convince his constituents that they would gain more by accepting the limited but certain gains of agreed bills than by fighting alone for their own bills, which the legislature never enacted. Labor continued to work independently until 1955.

In 1953 a formal advisory council for the workmen's compensation program was established at the instigation of one of the state senators, a mineowner. The council consisted of seven members: two representatives of the legislature, three of employers, and two of employees. By law the membership was restricted to insurers in the state department, but the labor representatives (the state Federation and the state CIO secretaries) were included at the governor's insistence. They were included under the formality that they had employees (about a dozen each) insured in the state department. The industrial commissioner, in whose department workmen's compensation is located, acts as the council's chairman. In the 1955 legislative session, which was the council's first opportunity to function, the council reached an agreed bill without difficulty, and the bill was enacted into law without opposition.

APPRAISAL

During the twelve years of its recorded history the Colorado council was influential only in the area of unemployment compensation legislation and only moderately so there. It exerted no influence on the employment service, and almost none on administration and administrative law. Its influence on unemployment compensation legislation was confined to four agreed bills, none of which involved more than a minimum amount of study and a minimum number of meetings. Three were not agreed bills in the full sense; though the labor members of the council grudgingly accepted the agreement as the best they could obtain from employers, they made serious efforts to obtain something better from the legislature—stopping short only of such efforts as might antagonize legislators and jeopardize the agreed bill. Of the three agreed bills, one, in 1949, was violently repudiated by labor outside the council. Only the last, in 1953, was an agreed bill in the full sense, both labor and employers working actively for it and for it alone.

The agreed bills profited labor and satisfied management. Labor, because it never, until recently, had much strength in the Colorado legislature,[10] almost certainly gained more through the agreed bills than it could have gained from the legislature directly. Except for the sessions of 1955 and 1957, labor was never able to induce the legislature to grant more than the employers offered; in the 1953 session it needed the positive and vigorous support of the employers to obtain even that.

Labor might have made even better use of the council to offset its weakness in the legislature if it had been represented on the council by more effective spokesmen. But it was not until 1949 that labor put itself in a position to make the most of the council's potentialities by getting its strongest representatives appointed to council membership. The 1953 agreed bill would have been impossible without this strong representation and is the best example of what it can accomplish.

The employer members of the council have generally regarded the device of the agreed bill with favor. It appealed to them as an alternative to the uncertainty of the legislative battle. Before 1951 that uncertainty was aggravated in Colorado by a legislative provision which required all bills to be introduced within the first fifteen days of the session but allowed them to be introduced by

[10] Charles C. Killingsworth notes that Colorado "includes in its law almost every restriction on unionism ever advocated." He adds, however, that the laws are not applied so strictly in Colorado as in some other states which have less severe laws. *State Labor Relations Acts* (Chicago: University of Chicago Press, 1948), p. 42.

title only. A legislator might introduce a score of bills consisting only of titles on the possibility that he might want to attach a body to one of them later on. The total number of bills introduced would run as high as two thousand. A lobbyist was never sure when an apparently dead bill consisting only of a title would come to life, take on a body, and be enacted into law before the lobbyist knew what was happening. In 1951 Colorado forbade the introduction of bills by title only, and the total number of bills diminished thereafter. But there still remained the practice of introducing many bills with a body merely on the possibility that the introducer might want to urge passage of the bill, possibly in an amended form, later on. In this situation employer lobbyists valued the convenience of an agreed bill.

Although the employers found the agreed bill a convenience for which they were willing to pay a price, their strong position in the legislature made them unwilling to offer a high price or to bargain over the price. They were accustomed to make a single offer to labor on a take-it-or-leave-it basis. Agreements were reached, if at all, by this simple procedure rather than by way of long discussions carried on over many meetings, as was done, for example, by the council in Utah, where the position of labor was about the same as in Colorado.

The employer representatives on the council always included the decision makers. That generally meant a representative of the utilities, the executive secretary of the Denver Retailers Association, a representative of Colorado Fuel and Iron (by far Colorado's largest firm), and the insurance manager of Colorado's largest sugar-producing firm. The last-named was the employers' chief spokesman in unemployment compensation matters. Besides being connected with one of Colorado's more important firms, he was active in Colorado politics. For over a quarter of a century he functioned both as a Republican party worker and as an employer lobbyist, helping to elect several generations of legislators and working with them in the legislature. Also he had a high degree of technical competence in unemployment compensation. His successor in the sugar firm—he retired in 1956—will not necessarily succeed him in this large sphere of influence because some of the qualities upon which his preeminence rested were personal.

The Manufacturers Association of Colorado has generally provided the leadership for employers in unemployment compensation. The Colorado State Chamber of Commerce and the Denver Retailers Association have been less active in recent years than they were earlier. A relatively new employer group is the Colorado Trade Executives' Institute. Set up after the war, it consists of the executive secretaries of the various employer associations in the state. It meets about twice monthly—more frequently while the legislature is in session—and discusses all matters of importance to employers. It was fostered by the Colorado Public Expenditure Council, another relatively new employer organization and one that has become a major center for employer research and legislative planning. Neither of these last two was an important influence in unemployment compensation, but either could easily become so through changes in personnel and consequent changes in patterns of representation.

To have been more influential, the advisory council would have had to meet oftener and become more of a work group. That its meetings were so few, especially in recent years, was owing to some extent to a lack of interest on the part of the agency director. The director was interested primarily in the employment service, to which he devoted perhaps three quarters of his time and attention. But in the employment service program he found, as did administrators in other states, that an advisory council was not effective —with the exception, again as in other states, of the advisory council for agricultural employment. Another reason that the director was not more interested in the council was the unequal strength of labor and employers. Employers were so much stronger in terms of both political power and technical competence that they could limit their bargaining on the council to a take-it-or-leave-it offer. In such a situation frequent council meetings were hardly necessary. Indeed, the council itself was hardly necessary. The director could have achieved the same results by a few informal contacts—especially since he and the decision makers among labor and management resided in the same city, and that city the seat of government.[11]

If the council had met more frequently, and if management and labor had become accustomed to working with each other and with the administrator, the take-it-or-leave-it procedure of reaching an agreed bill would probably have changed for the better. Whether or not that effect followed, the council would certainly have become more active in the area of administration and of administrative law. An example of the possible usefulness of such activity was provided by the events of 1954. Labor's chief spokesman, a member of the council, attacked the director of the agency for falling behind in the prompt payment of benefits. The attack was bitter and was public (it was featured by the newspapers), and an investigation later established that it was without much foundation. It is just such unfortunate and unnecessary conflicts that advisory councils can prevent. This particular attack might never have occurred if the council had been more active. Had the council met several times in 1954—instead of once—so that labor leaders were kept apprised of developments as the recession of that year deepened, the problem which occasioned the attack might have been worked out peacefully in a council meeting instead of being fought out bitterly in the public forum.

[11] Colorado is one of the few states whose chief city is also its capital.

17

THE CALIFORNIA ADVISORY COUNCIL

IN the course of its relatively long life the California advisory council has undergone a half-dozen changes in both structure and function, as outlined in the following calendar.

1934–1939: A seventeen-member council, for the employment service only
1940–1942: A twelve-member council, for the employment service only
(1943–1946: Dormant)
1947–1949: A new twelve-member council, for the employment service only
1950–1953: The same council, for the employment service and, unofficially, unemployment compensation
1954: A new twelve-member council, for the employment service and unemployment compensation
1955–1957: A new seven-member council, for the employment service and unemployment compensation

The history of the California council is more closely connected with the employment service than is that of any other council; indeed, as the calendar indicates, until 1954 the council was limited by law to the employment service program only.

Early records are fragmentary. A council was appointed some time in 1934, apparently to bring the California employment service—established in 1915—into conformity with the 1933 Wagner-Peyser Act. Originally a tripartite council of seventeen members located in the Department of Industrial Relations, it was of considerable help to the struggling employment offices during the period which preceded their integration with unemployment compensation. In July of 1936, one year after the passage of the California Unemployment Reserves Act, the employment service and its advisory council were integrated with the new unemployment compensation program to constitute the Department of Employment.[1]

A question immediately arose as to the status of the advisory council in the new department. The attorney general ruled that its status was unchanged and that its authority extended, as before, only to the employment service. In the fall of 1937 the council offered to extend its activities to unemployment compensation, but the five-man commission [2] which administered the Department of Employment politely declined the offer on the ground that the commission was already performing all the functions that a council might perform. Had the commission been established before the council, it is possible that there would have been no council.

As employment improved in 1938 and 1939, the California council shared the experience of all other employment service councils—its meetings became less frequent and less well attended. The reorganization of the agency in 1939 was used as an opportunity to dissolve the old council and appoint a new one. In September of 1940 a smaller, twelve-member council was appointed which consisted of four representatives each of employers, employees, and the public.

The new council revived the discussion as to whether the council's duties should include unemployment compensation, but the answer of the commission was still in the negative. The available minutes of this council cover the period March, 1941—September, 1942, and show that the council occupied itself with recruitment for the aircraft industry, agricultural placement, housing, racial discrimination, and similar employment service problems.

The council ceased to function after 1942. It is more than a coincidence that the council's last meeting occurred in the same month, September of 1942, that saw the establishment of the Area War Manpower committees. There were two such committees in California, one for the northern part of the state and one for the southern, each committee consisting of five representatives of employers and five representatives of employees. These com-

---

[1] California was probably the first state to use this title for the combined programs; in recent years the title has been adopted by a number of other states.

[2] Two representatives each of labor and management and one of the public.

mittees were very influential, for their membership comprised the real leaders among labor and management in their respective areas, they had the state manpower director as their chairman, they met at least every other week, and they had quasi-legislative authority. Performing all the major tasks relating to employment, they left the advisory council nothing to do which could justify its continued operation.

In 1944 and again in 1945 the California agency considered reconstituting the council but decided to wait until the employment service was returned to state control. This was done in November of 1946, and in 1947 the governor appointed a new council. It consisted, like the previous council, of twelve members who were to serve without compensation and at the pleasure of the governor as an advisory body to the agency in all matters pertaining to the employment service. This was the beginning of what might be called the "modern" council.

The membership of this council met precisely the standards of the Wagner-Peyser Act, satisfied most of the requirements customarily laid down by academic writers on the subject, and must have pleased the Bureau of Employment Security. The employer members were entirely free from the taint of professionalism: one was the president of his company, another was the owner of a small business, still another was a farmer. All the labor members, on the other hand, were full-time professionals.[3] The public members included a representative of minority groups (a Negro), a representative of veterans' interests, and a woman active in women's organizations. The woman public member was elected chairman.[4] But this apparently ideal council accomplished very little.

The council met for the first time in October of 1947 and for the last time just six years later, in October of 1953. During this period the council met forty-two times, an average of seven meetings a year. The council's attendance record was fair, 69 percent. The record of the public members was 77 percent; of the employer

---

[3] Two were representatives of international unions, one of a city central, and one of a state council. Two were from the California State Federation of Labor and two from the CIO.

[4] As in most states, the public member was only the nominal chairman. It was the agency which called the meetings, prepared the agenda, and supplied the materials.

members, 69 percent; and of the employee members, 62 percent. The meetings were held in various parts of the state and usually lasted from mid-morning into the late afternoon.

At its third meeting the council, having first discussed and reluctantly admitted the fact that it was limited by law to employment service matters, drew up a precise statement of its functions:

It was agreed that the purposes of the council might be summarized under three headings: 1. Investigation of specific employment service problems and the development of recommendations on them for the guidance of the Department. 2. Development of legislative recommendations relating to the employment service operations. 3. Assisting the Department in every way possible in developing good public relations in all communities of the state and among all groups. It was agreed that this latter function would probably be fundamental to the other two.[5]

Early in 1948 the council set up five committees: for veterans, agriculture, union-labor relations, special placement problems, and public relations. Only the public relations committee showed evidence of much activity, and that activity consisted only of sending letters to employer organizations urging them to use the employment service. During the 1949 recession the council discussed the problems of full employment and during the Korean War the problems of mobilization. The council's contribution to the solution of these and other employment service problems was generally confined to listening to, and sometimes discussing, reports made by the agency.

Like its predecessor, this council (especially two of the employer members) wanted its scope extended to include unemployment compensation. It had made this request as early as the meeting of December 27, 1947, and had continued to press the issue at subsequent meetings. Thus at a joint meeting with the commission in April of 1949 the council argued: "So far the council has little to show in the way of positive accomplishment; and hence needs to have its functions enlarged." The commission continued

---

[5] From the minutes of the advisory council for December 5, 1947. The first and second seem to be phrased from the viewpoint of the governed and the third from the viewpoint of the government.

obdurate, but finally in May of 1949 the council went directly
to the governor and secured his oral approval to extend its scope
to include unemployment compensation.[6]

In the following year, 1950, the council made its main bid for
recognition and significance. It requested that the names of the
council members be added to the agency letterhead. It recommended to the governor that he appoint two members of the
council to a five-man steering committee on employment stabilization. It secured the unpaid services of technicians from several
private firms to review the procedures of the agency and suggest
improvements. It passed a resolution that the agency double the
time allotted to the fraud program. Finally, it asked that "three
members of the council (one each from labor, management, and
the public) be designated to confer with other persons who are
interested in legislation affecting unemployment compensation
with a view to making recommendations to the 1951 legislature." [7]
Nearly all these stirrings of activity emanated from one member
of the council, an employer representative. Nearly all of them,
also, were without effect.

The proposal that the council make recommendations to the
legislature encountered opposition from an unexpected quarter.
The council's labor members opposed it, and apparently for
several reasons. First, they expected that the public members
would usually vote with the employer members; this seems to
have been their chief reason. But, further, they recognized that
they were not the decision makers in labor, and they feared (or were
forbidden by their principals) to take independent action on the
council lest they interfere with the plans and strategy of labor's
real leaders—who were outside the council and who, often enough,
dealt privately with management's decision makers, also outside the
council. And a still further reason for their hesitancy to make
recommendations in unemployment compensation may have been
two "blunders" which they committed in 1950. They had voted
with the rest of the council to approve the Knowland amendment
and to oppose federalization of the employment service, and both

---

[6] The law, however, was not amended to recognize this extended scope until 1955,
when the council was reorganized.

[7] From the minutes of the advisory council for July 14, 1950.

recommendations were directly contrary to the official position of the national labor bodies.

It is true that when certain bills favoring labor were introduced in the 1951 legislature the labor members of the council moved that the council go on record as approving them. But when the employer members protested that the council should take a position on all bills or no bills, the labor members after a long discussion reverted to their original position and offered the following resolution, which the council adopted unanimously:

In the future, this Council shall not act as a body on any state legislation which is controversial, or which would affect the substantive provisions of the California Unemployment Insurance Act, but will confine its recommendations to technical and noncontroversial proposals designed to facilitate the administration of the act.[8]

The council's resolution to avoid all controversial issues was an assurance, if any assurance was necessary, that its influence would be nominal. In the legislative sessions of 1951 and 1953—the council's first opportunity to use the authority granted in 1950 to extend its scope to unemployment compensation—the council's entire activity consisted of discussing in desultory fashion some of the nearly two hundred bills on unemployment compensation introduced in each session and of listening, months later, to the agency's review of the legislation enacted.

The real influence in California's unemployment compensation program was outside the advisory council, and until 1953 the pattern of decision making was fairly stable. The chief spokesman for labor was the California State Federation of Labor, which was the largest labor organization in the state and had a well-staffed central office. In unemployment compensation matters it operated chiefly through two officials: its executive secretary and its attorney, the latter of whom was a former employee of the California unemployment compensation agency and knew the program thoroughly. Other labor groups were active, but usually they had to channel their activities through the state Federation, and therefore through these two men, or run the risk of having

[8] From the minutes of the advisory council for February 16, 1951.

their bills lost in the legislative maelstrom of one to two hundred other bills on unemployment compensation.

Management also was represented by two chief spokesmen. One came from the retailers' association (its general manager) and the other was an attorney, representing, among others, the movie industry. The trade and service industries have been relatively more important in California than in most states,[9] and the retailers have given more attention to unemployment compensation than is usual among these groups. In 1935, when the unemployment compensation law was under debate, the president and managing director of the California Retailers Association played leading parts in drawing up the law. The latter has continued to be the chief agent used by employers in the construction of their program for unemployment compensation and in the presentation of the program to the legislature. He has usually worked with an attorney supplied by the movie industry. The latter is the counterpart of the state Federation attorney and equally well versed in the technicalities of the program.

None of these four were members of the advisory council, but during most of the program's existence they were the chief decision makers for their respective sides. They were not entirely free agents, of course, the employer representatives even less so than the labor representatives, but they were the focal points at which decisions took shape, and they exerted a preponderant influence on those decisions and on the legislative strategy and tactics to be employed.

The legislative session of 1953 and the events that led up to it provide the best stage on which to see the real decision makers at work. The agency had embarked on a "solvency study" in late 1951 and on the completion of the study in 1952 had asked the governor (actually the agency had the advisory council ask the governor) to appoint a seven-man commission to review the find-

[9] In 1951, 48.4 percent of all employment in California covered by unemployment compensation was in the trade, finance, and service industries; the comparable national figure was 37.2 percent. In manufacturing the proportions were reversed: California had only 32.3 percent of its covered employment in manufacturing, as against the national figure of 45.7 percent.

ings of the study and recommend necessary changes in the law.

In making his appointments to the study commission, the governor followed the recommendations of the agency. For labor he appointed the two state Federation officials mentioned above and the educational director of the state CIO. This CIO representative was the lone council member appointed to the study commission, and he had only recently joined the council. For management the governor appointed, besides the attorney from the movie industry, two employer representatives who were leading figures in the California postwar drive to interest employers more in unemployment compensation and to organize them for unified action. The chairman of the commission was the dean of a school of business administration. He had much prestige in his own field but perhaps lacked some of the technical knowledge needed to function with full effectiveness as the mediator of such a group of unemployment compensation "professionals." The commission had the services of a full-time secretary who was a former director of research in the unemployment compensation agency. By any standards this was a strong group.

The commission proceeded to make the most exhaustive study of unemployment compensation that had been made in California. It held numerous meetings throughout 1952, meetings which sometimes ran three days consecutively and occasionally lasted from nine in the morning until midnight. Gradually it established tentative areas of agreement and by October was in a position to ask the governor to make the forthcoming report of the commission the object of a special message to the legislature. The governor agreed to do so in view of the importance of the matter and the amount of work which the report represented.

At this point the commission suspended meetings until after the November elections should be completed in order to keep its work free of political implications. It expected to have its report and an agreed bill ready to present to the governor at its first meeting after the elections.

The commission met again, as planned, in late November and then suddenly fell apart. In the course of this last meeting the commission reached the unexpected decision that it could not agree on anything. With that decision it brought its work to an abrupt end without so much as making a report.[10] The program's most ambitious and promising attempt at labor-management participation sank beneath the waves, leaving no trace but some roiled waters.

What had happened? The answer cannot be given in detail because the commission members had agreed at the very beginning, and were quite faithful to their agreement, to keep the meetings confidential. It is possible, however, to piece together the general course of events. It seems that the commission members came to the early meetings with the responsibility to represent particular interests strong upon them. Cautious sparring and some emotional oratory marked the first stages of their work. Then they began to grow into something like an academic research team, interested primarily in problems as problems, in questions of fact and factual answers. They had at their disposal the research resources of the agency and some graduate students, and they themselves were competent, strong personalities. They found the meetings intellectually stimulating and enjoyable, and as they worked they grew insensibly closer together with a feeling of common purpose. Their rule not to reveal to outsiders—not even to their own groups —what was being done in the meetings abetted their transformation from representatives of particular interests to academic analysts.

But eventually the day arrived when they had to make concrete recommendations on the basis of their analysis. Immediately and necessarily their representative role reasserted itself. They became hard bargainers, knowing that they would have to take back to their constituents any agreement they made and stand judgment on it. Cautiously they began to put together a tentative "package" to be fashioned later into an agreed bill. The exact contents of this package were never made public, but almost certainly the package contained at least two unpalatable items, an increase in taxes and a tightening of eligibility requirements.

At this point it became necessary for the commission members

[10] In order to salvage part of the valuable work done by and for the commission, the agency itself later published a 400-page volume entitled *A Source Book on Unemployment Insurance in California*. But this was in no sense a report of the commission.

to abandon their rule not to share their deliberations with other groups; they had to inform their respective groups of the proposed agreed bill and to enlist their support for it. The labor representatives seem to have been successful. The employer representatives, however, seem to have found that they could not get sufficient support for their side of the agreement. An influential group of employers, sufficiently organized since about 1951 to be independent of the traditional pattern of employer leadership in unemployment compensation, laid down an ultimatum that they would not support any agreement that increased unemployment compensation costs by so much as a penny.

It seems to have been this ultimatum which brought the work of the commission to an end. The commission members felt that there was no point to their serving merely as a channel for decisions made outside the commission by persons who had not shared the experience of the commission and to whom it was impossible to convey briefly the fruits of that experience. They decided that the usefulness of the commission was ended. The day on which this decision was reached was called by the labor representatives "Black Sunday." [11]

The study commission having broken up without making any recommendations for legislative action, the agency itself prepared five bills for introduction in the 1953 legislature. This was an innovation: the agency did not usually present a substantive legislative program of its own. But the director hoped in this way to salvage something from the work that had been done. The agency bills provided for a new tax schedule which would delete the zero rates and an increase in eligibility requirements which would eliminate over 100,000 marginal workers. The agency's package was probably not a great deal different from that on which the study commission had almost reached agreement.

Somewhat later the employers introduced a so-called omnibus bill modeled closely on the agency's proposals. It had been worked out by employer and labor lobbyists under pressure from the legislature to "get together" on necessary amendments and was intro-

---

[11] This failure of collective bargaining in California bears a resemblance to the experiences of New York in 1940 and 1950.

duced with the unofficial and reluctant approval of the labor leaders. On the employer side the decision to support the bill had been made by the customary leaders and in the customary way, that is, without much consultation with other employers.

The omnibus bill was immediately challenged by a group of employers who were affected adversely by its provisions. This group, probably the same which had upset the near-agreed bill of the study commission, was composed of several elements. One element consisted of the low-cost employers; they would have been the ones with relatively little unemployment, especially in the utilities.[12] They did not altogether trust the established employer leadership, which was rooted in the higher-cost industries of retail trade and motion pictures. A second element consisted of employers of a conservative cast of mind who were concerned over the "abuses" in the program. This group had earlier (1950) organized the Inter-Association Unemployment Insurance Committee, which was originally intended to represent employer interests at appeal hearings but had rapidly evolved into an investigation force. In January of 1953 the committee had made dramatic disclosures of abuses, which the Hearst papers, political foes of the governor, publicized widely. This group of employers felt that the established employer leadership was not active enough in pressing for reforms.[13] The third element consisted of employers engaged in manufacturing. During the war and postwar periods manufacturing had grown from an insignificant part of the California economy to a very important part, a change which the established leadership pattern did not fully reflect. The newcomers were not disposed to accept the traditional leadership without some questioning.[14]

Such employer conflict was unprecedented in unemployment

[12] The utilities are more important in California than in most states. Until 1953 the firm with the largest California payroll was a telephone company. (In 1953 the Douglas Aircraft Company took over the number-one position.)

[13] Later, in November of 1953, this group succeeded in having its candidate, the manager of the Inter-Association Unemployment Insurance Committee, appointed director of the agency.

[14] The second and third elements were roughly identified with the southern part of California, while the established leadership was located in the northern part, so that the division between employers took on a geographical dimension as well.

compensation, and there was no established machinery to resolve it. A hurried meeting of employers was called at Sacramento. The insurgent group was successful in getting employer approval for an amended version of the original bill and in getting the legislative committee to report out the bill favorably. But when the bill reached the floor of the legislature the judgment of the old-time employer leaders was vindicated. The insurgent group was proved to have misread the political map and to have overestimated the strength of the employer position. Labor was able to have the bill remanded to committee by an overwhelming vote. The omnibus bill died, as did all other major unemployment compensation legislation.[15] The net result of all the preparatory work that had been done for the 1953 session was a stalemate.

In looking back on the session both the labor and the management members of the study commission expressed some relief that they had not made recommendations. In their tentative package agreement both sides had made concessions which, although helpful to the program, would have been hard to sell to their respective groups. The chairman of the Senate committee that was charged with unemployment compensation matters recognized that the situation was difficult for both sides, especially for labor. When he was interviewed in 1953, shortly after the events just narrated, he declared that it was unrealistic to expect private individuals to incur the odium that necessarily attaches to such difficult decisions. The burden, he said, must be borne by the legislators, and he himself was prepared to bear it even if it meant, as he expected it would, his defeat in the next election.

Employers, especially the insurgent group, were surprised and disappointed at the results of the 1953 session. Perhaps they had been made overconfident by the Republican sweep in the California elections of 1952 and—in that same year—by the dramatic disclosures of improper payments in unemployment compensation. Labor, which was on the defensive in the sessions of 1951 and 1953,

[15] Two minor bills unfavorable to labor were passed by the legislature, but at the insistence of labor the governor vetoed them. The only substantive amendment enacted was one which tightened the disqualification relating to quitting work for marital or domestic reasons.

considered that it had won a victory in 1953 by preventing the enactment of any legislation.[16]

In 1953 the state Federation made an important change in its legislative procedure which facilitated the reaching of agreed bills. The Federation's legislative representatives were given greater freedom to choose from among the numerous resolutions of the annual state convention those that had more chance of passage in the state legislature and, while concentrating on these, to neglect the rest.[17] This change increased the ability of the labor lobbyists to maneuver and to engage in collective bargaining with the employer representatives.

The 1953 legislative session had been crowded with major events in unemployment compensation, but, since all of them occurred outside the advisory council, they served only to emphasize what had been growing painfully clearer each year, that the council was a figurehead and incapable of exerting any real influence in the program. If anything further was needed to make that clear, it was the new policy adopted at this time by the state Federation. The Federation's representative on the council began to remind the other members that by law the council was established only for the employment service program and hence had no right even to discuss unemployment compensation. The other members protested that in 1950 the governor had approved orally of a wider scope for the council, but the Federation representative insisted on the written law.[18] By the fall of 1953 the morale of the council was so low that several members were talking of resigning. Three of them in separate interviews made the same bitter statement, that the council was nothing but a convenient front for the

[16] It was the more certain of this by 1954, when the new governor, Goodwin Knight, redeemed an election promise by putting through the legislature a bill which increased unemployment compensation benefits by five dollars. The governor did not consult employers at all but had the director of the agency draft a bill which he then forced through the legislature by swift and direct action. This was a "free gift" to labor in the sense that labor did not have to make any concessions to employers in order to obtain it.

[17] This change was accomplished only after a major struggle in the 1953 state Federation convention, and the vote on the final motion was very close.

[18] During a meeting which the writer attended, whenever the council got onto unemployment compensation the Federation representative with elaborate obviousness unfolded a newspaper and buried himself in it.

director. The end was clearly in sight, and it came the following year.

A change of governors in 1954 (Knight for Warren) resulted in the appointment not only of a new agency director but also of a new advisory council. The new council was potentially stronger than any that had preceded it; it was the first to include the major decision makers of labor and management. When the secretary of the state Federation could not be accommodated on the council as a labor representative—because labor politics made it impracticable not to reappoint the labor representatives of the former council—he was appointed as a public member.[19]

This council functioned for about a year, holding a half-dozen meetings in that time, and without debating the matter concerned itself with unemployment compensation as well as with the employment service. This council was vigorous but probably too officious and too independent. On one occasion two of the employer members expostulated with the administrator over the length of time consumed by agency employees in coffee breaks. On another occasion the council called a meeting on its own authority and excluded the administrator of the agency from it. When the administrator protested, he was told by the council's chairman that the council worked for the governor and not for the administrator. This pattern of activity may have been one of the reasons that the council was allowed to "rest" after its first few meetings.

In 1955 the agency underwent the most thorough reorganization in its history. Among other changes, the commission was replaced by a single director and the law governing the advisory council was completely rewritten. The new law provided for a council of seven members (three representatives each of employers and employees and one of the public) to be appointed by the governor and to serve at his pleasure without compensation in advising the director. Further: "The council may select and nominate an executive secretary and the director shall appoint the person so nominated who shall be exempt from civil service, removable by

[19] There is only a surface similarity between this California and the Connecticut (see p. 230) appointments. The Connecticut appointment of a labor official as a public member was made for political purposes and weakened the council; the California appointment was intended to strengthen the council, and it did.

the council and shall receive compensation as determined by the council." [20] An echo of the difficulty experienced under the immediately preceding council may be heard in the unusual phrases, "A State Advisory Council . . . to act *only* in an advisory capacity for the purpose of discussing problems relating to the *administration* of this division" and "No action taken by the Advisory Council shall limit or control the discretion vested by law in the director." [21]

Acting under this law, the governor proceeded to appoint a strong council which included all four of the decision makers mentioned earlier.[22] This council began to function in March, 1956. One of its more interesting features is its limitation to matters of administration only. Everybody concerned—the legislative and executive branches of government and the advisory council members themselves—interpreted the word "administration" in the law to exclude policy matters and everybody seemed satisfied with the interpretation. The period of council experience which falls within the scope of this survey is too brief to be very instructive, but eventually it should shed some light on the debate over the proper interpretation of the term "administration" in the New York law.[23] The California council is attempting to operate as the New York employer claims the New York council should be operating.

OTHER ADVISORY BODIES

Shortly after the Second World War the director of the California Department of Employment assembled a group distinct from the advisory council but intended for a task ordinarily performed by an advisory council. The group was called simply the "Labor-Management Committee" and consisted of about eighteen (the number was variable) representatives of labor and management. The director of the agency acted as chairman. The function of this committee was to advise the director in the formulation of administrative law, that is, in the task of making rules, regula-

---

[20] *California Unemployment Insurance Code,* 1955, Sec. 355.
[21] *Ibid.* Italics supplied.   [22] See pp. 348–49.   [23] See pp. 198–99.

tions, and precedent decisions. The employer members attended meetings much more regularly than did the labor members; often the only labor representative present was the state Federation attorney mentioned earlier. The new director who was appointed in 1954 increased the number of committee members to sixty. His laudable intention was to make more people more active in the program, but he found that scarcely half of the members attended meetings and that of these only the same handful continued to be articulate. The remainder quickly found themselves beyond their depth in the economic and legal technicalities of the program. The new director who was appointed in 1955 did not see any need to continue the committee in addition to the new, and (it was hoped) newly effective, advisory council. During 1957 the council, concentrating on administration, performed all the functions the committee could have performed.

Since 1946 the California Department of Employment has administered not only the unemployment compensation and employment service programs but also a program of disability compensation. There is no official advisory council for this program, but representatives of labor and of the insurance companies have customarily held meetings to work out agreements. In 1951, for example, when labor and management were unable to reach any agreement in unemployment compensation, this group reached an agreement to increase the maximum benefit rate in disability compensation.[24] A similar situation exists in the workmen's compensation program. There is no official advisory council, but labor and management representatives have long been accustomed to meet with the director of the program and to work out agreed bills. Although labor, management, and government representatives expressed general satisfaction with this procedure for the programs of disability compensation and workmen's compensation, and saw no need for an advisory council, the same persons were definite in their opinion that a formal advisory council was desirable for the program of employment security.

[24] Much to the displeasure of some employers, who feared that this increase of the rate in disability compensation would pull up the unemployment compensation rate. Until this time the maximum benefit rate in the two programs had been kept at the same level.

In 1948 the director of the Department of Employment assembled an unofficial advisory council for farm-labor placement problems. Originally he selected its members from among the professional secretaries of farm organizations, but when these proved difficult to handle, he replaced them with farmowners. Like other directors with similar agricultural advisory councils, the California director said that he had found this council to be of real value.

APPRAISAL

The council which began in 1934 seems to have been of some assistance to the struggling employment service program during the first couple of years, but its contribution was negligible during the next decade. The council which began to function in 1947 likewise never made more than minor contributions to either the employment service or the unemployment compensation programs. The council which began to function in 1954 lasted less than a year. It must be concluded that during most of the period covered by this survey the California council was never a major influence. The council which began in 1956 had yet to prove itself at the time of this survey, but it showed much greater promise.

The council's lack of influence during most of its life could be laid in large part to two limitations. First of all, until 1954 the council was limited by law to the employment service, and the experience of all the states indicates that it is very difficult to maintain an effective or even an active advisory council in the employment service. The difficulty is so great that thus far no state has had any notable success in overcoming it.

This limitation alone, if it had been strictly enforced, would probably have sufficed to guarantee a relatively inactive council. It was not strictly enforced, however, and the council kept going beyond it into unemployment compensation territory—at first unofficially, then (1950) with the oral approval of the governor, and finally (1955) with legal authorization. In this respect the California council is one of the best examples of the difficulty of having a good council in the employment service. Even in California, where the council was directed by law to concentrate its attention on the employment service, we find the council spending more and more of its time on unemployment compensation matters. The explanation is expressed succinctly in the council's 1949 complaint: "So far the council has little to show in the way of positive accomplishment; and hence needs to have its functions enlarged."

The extension of the council's scope to include unemployment compensation did not, however, make the council an influential body. The council labored under still another and much more serious limitation—it did not include the decision makers of labor and management. Until the council was reorganized in 1954 and again in 1955, its membership almost never included those who were able to speak effectively for the major labor and management organizations. The single exception was the representative of the CIO, but the CIO itself was not labor's principal voice in California.

The agency shared in the responsibility for this limitation. The agency had participated in the selection of the council members and had deliberately avoided certain decision makers, especially on management's side. The agency gave the council more than its share of time and attention, but nothing the agency could have done would have made an effective force out of the council that was appointed.

When it became evident that this council was an ineffective, unimportant body, the agency encountered an additional obstacle in getting the decision makers on the council—they were not interested in becoming members.[25] Council membership always entails a cost of time, and the decision makers, especially on labor's side, did not consider the returns worth the cost. Labor's recognition of the council's ineffectiveness is strikingly exemplified by its insistence that the council should not even discuss unemployment compensation matters.

The most effective labor-management groups that worked in the field of employment security in California were the Area War

[25] They became interested in 1954 and 1955, however, when the council was reorganized, and each side knew that the other side was putting up its best men for council membership.

Manpower committees of the war years and the study commission of 1952. There is some significance to the fact that both were structured like the Wisconsin advisory council—their membership was limited to the decision makers of labor and management and one neutral member who acted as chairman and mediator.

The 1952 study commission probably comes close to being a picture of what the ideal advisory council in California would have looked like. Its members were the decision makers of labor and management, and they functioned like a study group under the guidance of the agency, digging deeply into real problems and looking for real answers. Even though the commission did not achieve an agreed bill, the participants in the work of the commission received an education which could not but bear fruit in the leadership they later provided for their groups. If the commission members had been members of a permanent advisory council and had continued to meet regularly with one another, they might have reached agreed bills in later legislative sessions [26] and certainly would have been an active and effective group in the development of administrative law.

The most recent council, which began to function in 1956, is structured much like the study commission and promises to make the future history of the California council more of a success story than it has been in the past. The fairly equal balance of power between labor and management in California politics and some tradition of labor-management cooperation in state-wide programs—for example, in the manpower committees during the war and in workmen's compensation and in temporary disability insurance in recent years—are two California conditions favorable to the growth of an effective council. For the social scientist the most interesting aspect of this strong council is the unusual provision limiting it to matters of administration; the experience of such a council should prove very instructive.

[26] By the end of the 1955 session most labor and management leaders realized that the unemployment compensation program was just about what it would have been if the tentative agreed bill of the study commission had been accepted in 1953.

18

THE FEDERAL ADVISORY COUNCIL

THE Wagner-Peyser Act of June 6, 1933, establishing the United States Employment Service, included a provision for a Federal Advisory Council:

The Secretary shall establish a Federal Advisory Council composed of men and women representing employers and employees in equal numbers and of the public for the purpose of formulating policies and discussing problems relating to employment and insuring impartiality, neutrality, and freedom from political influence in the solution of such problems. Members of such councils shall be selected from time to time in such manner as the Secretary of Labor shall prescribe and shall serve without compensation.[1]

Two months after the passage of the act Madame Perkins, then secretary of labor, appointed a council, which held its first meeting on August 14, 1933. It was a large council (employers and employees were each represented by fourteen members and the public by twenty-two) and it had a distinguished membership. For example, it included among the employer representatives Marion B. Folsom, a future member of a President's cabinet; among the labor representatives William Green, then president of the American Federation of Labor; and among the public members Robert Maynard Hutchins, who was chairman of the first meeting.

From 1933 to 1939 the council was concerned solely with the employment service. In this area its history paralleled the early employment service advisory councils in the states: first a period of influential activity; then a period of slow decline—as the em-

[1] 48 Stat. 113, U.S.C. Tit. 29, Sec. 49 j (a).

ployment service program became established and its mode of operation routinized, as the depression lightened and work relief projects dwindled, and as interest swung to the new unemployment compensation program and its pressing problems.[2] Meetings and attendance at meetings declined until by 1939 the council was in need of rejuvenation.

Beginning in 1939, the council experienced a series of organizational changes. Most of them were connected with the checkered fate of the employment service, which began its wanderings in this year. On July 1, 1939, the employment service was moved from the Department of Labor to the Social Security Board (in the Federal Security Agency) because much of its work and all of its funds were coming from its relationship with unemployment compensation, and unemployment compensation was administered by the Social Security Board. The board decided to reactivate the council and enlarge its scope to include the unemployment compensation program. This council was made up of most of the members of the old council and a few new appointees who were especially familiar with unemployment compensation.

At the first meeting, June 21, 1940, one of the members of the old council[3] argued for two separate advisory councils, one for each program, declaring prophetically that in a single council the employment service would be submerged by its more colorful twin, unemployment compensation. After some discussion the council members voted to leave the decision to the Social Security Board, and the board decided on a single council, to be called the Federal Advisory Council for Employment Security. In closing the council meeting, Arthur Altmeyer, chairman of the Social Security Board, stated a principle which was applied with typical thoroughness in his own state of Wisconsin and which has been one of the guiding lines of this study: "It is only through representative advisory committees that bureaucracies can be kept on tap instead of on top."

The council met only three times. Its first meeting, held just after the fall of France, was taken up largely with problems of

[2] Unemployment compensation began to pay benefits nationally in 1938–1939 in the midst of the sharpest increase of unemployment in its history.

[3] Mr. Millard W. Rice, representing the Veterans of Foreign Wars.

the defense program. The second meeting, held January 9–10, 1942, shortly after Pearl Harbor, was concerned almost entirely with mobilization for war. The third meeting, held October 29–30, was conducted under the joint auspices of the Social Security Board and the War Manpower Commission, for in September, 1942, the employment service had been transferred to the WMC for the duration of the war. The WMC set up a Labor-Management Policy Committee, which performed most of the work that an advisory council for an employment service would do, and the Federal Advisory Council held no more meetings until after the war.

When toward the end of 1945 the WMC went out of existence, the employment service was not returned to the Social Security Board but was transferred back to its old home, in the Department of Labor.[4] During 1946 and 1947 the director of the employment service in the Department of Labor and the director of unemployment compensation in the Social Security Board were separately considering the reactivation of an advisory council. Arthur Altmeyer suggested a joint council for the two programs, but the director of the employment service did not favor the idea. At the latter's request the secretary of labor reestablished a "Federal Advisory Council of the United States Employment Service" on January 5, 1948.[5]

This council consisted of thirty-one members, of whom six represented employers, six represented employees (divided equally between the AFL and the CIO), five represented veterans (one for each of the five principal veteran organizations), and fourteen represented the public. Very few of the thirty-one had been members of the original (1933–1939) council; this was largely a new group. The representatives of labor and of the veterans had been appointed after consultation with their respective organizations; the representatives of employers had not. The USES said that it

[4] The transfer followed a political struggle between organized labor and organized employers, the latter preferring the employment service to be in a "neutral" agency like the Social Security Board.

[5] General Order No. 38. This document, revised several times, constitutes the main statement of the council's authority, functions, and procedures. The document which the council later drafted for its own use, "Functions and Procedures of the Federal Advisory Council," is based on General Order No. 38.

wanted employers who were representative of but not dependent on employer organizations, "whose official views are readily available in any case." [6]

This council held only one meeting, on January 30, 1948. Only fourteen of the thirty-one members were present and nothing much was accomplished. The meeting was taken up chiefly with introductions, welcomes, and the election of officers. In March labor made a near-successful effort to have unemployment compensation transferred to the Department of Labor in order to integrate it with the employment service. But at this time the political pendulum was swinging away from labor. On July 1, 1948, instead of unemployment compensation joining the employment service in the Department of Labor, the employment service rejoined unemployment compensation in the Social Security Administration.

The council followed the employment service to its new home and was reorganized. Its functions and membership were extended, for the second time, to include both the employment service and the unemployment compensation programs, and its name became again the "Federal Advisory Council for Employment Security."

This council held its first meeting September 17–18, 1948, when it organized itself into five work committees, one of which was a committee on "Aspects of Unemployment Insurance." The membership of this committee exemplified the weakness which was to plague the council for many years. Of its four members only the labor representative was in direct contact with unemployment compensation problems, and he was far from expert in them. The two public members were both from the field of welfare, and the employer representative, a vice president of a department store, had her experience chiefly in the employment service program.[7]

This first meeting was also the last under the auspices of the

[6] Letter of the director of the USES to the secretary of labor, January 7, 1946.

[7] One of this committee's unanimous recommendations was "that wide publicity be given to the fact that fraudulent claims constitute only one-half of one per cent of total benefit payments." No informed employer would have concurred in that recommendation at that time.

Social Security Administration. The odyssey of the Federal Advisory Council was not yet ended. The unexpected election of President Truman reversed the political pendulum and in August, 1949, the entire Bureau of Employment Security—the employment service *and* unemployment compensation—was transferred from the Social Security Administration to the Department of Labor.[8] Employers argued against the transfer on the ground that the Department of Labor would be biased in its administration of the program. In answering this argument Secretary Tobin pointed out that the Federal Advisory Council would accompany the Bureau of Employment Security, and he promised: "I will consider very carefully the advice of these men and women in the administration of this bureau, if Congress sees fit to transfer the bureau to the Department of Labor." [9]

The council made the move to the Department of Labor without change of name or membership and held its first meeting in its new home September 14–15, 1949.[10] The "modern" Federal Advisory Council may be said to have begun with this meeting and is the only one under consideration in the remainder of this chapter.

The "modern" council held twenty-one meetings during the period 1949 through 1957. This represents an average of only 2.3 meetings per year, just slightly above the minimum of two meetings per year stipulated by the secretary of labor.[11] In addition to these meetings of the full council, however, there were numerous meetings held by the council's committees, and it was in these committee meetings that the council did the greater part of its work. The meetings of the full council were distributed by years as follows:

[8] There it has remained.

[9] From the hearings held by the Committee on Expenditures in the Executive Department, U.S. Senate, 81st Congress, 1st Session, July 21–29, 1949.

[10] The legal basis for the Federal Advisory Council as presently constituted is provided by Section 3 of Reorganization Plan No. 2, 1949: "The Federal Advisory Council, established pursuant to Section 11 (a) of the Act of June 6, 1933 . . . is hereby transferred to the Department of Labor and shall, in addition to its duties under the aforesaid Act, advise the Secretary of Labor and the Director of the Bureau of Employment Security with respect to the administration and coordination of the function transferred by the revisions of this reorganization plan."

[11] General Order No. 38.

1949	2	1952	3	1955	1
1950	2	1953	3	1956	3
1951	1	1954	4	1957	2

The listing reflects the resignation of labor from all federal advisory bodies in 1951 and a shortage of funds in the first half of 1955.

Attendance at the meetings of the full council was fairly good. Because the Federal Advisory Council draws its members from all parts of the country, it cannot be expected to show as good an attendance record as the state councils, whose members do not have as far to travel. Through 1955 the record for the council as a whole was 71 percent; for the public members, 64 percent; for employers, 73 percent; for employees, 80 percent.[12]

The law does not specify the number of council members and the number has fluctuated from time to time. During most of this period council membership totaled thirty-five: fifteen representatives of the public, including four representatives of veterans, and ten representatives each of employers and employees. Beginning with the fall of 1955, council membership was reduced to twenty-seven—eleven representatives of the public and eight representatives each of employers and employees. The reduction was aimed at making the council more of a working group, one in which all of its members could participate more actively.

The term of council membership was indefinite until 1952, when it was fixed at two years. The change was probably made to give the secretary of labor more control over the membership. It is easier to replace a member whose term has expired than one whose term is indefinite. The turnover in the "modern" council has been moderate. For the period 1949–1955 the turnover rate for the council as a whole was 17 percent.[13] For the council's three groups the rates were: public, 21 percent; employers, 16 percent; employees, 10 percent.

[12] Representatives of the AFL had an attendance record of 74 percent; those of the CIO, 86 percent. This difference can be attributed in part to the greater distances which the AFL representatives had to travel and in part to the fact that more of the CIO representatives were technicians, who were less burdened with administrative responsibilities.

[13] Turnover rate: actual changes in membership as a percentage of total possible changes per year.

The secretary of labor appoints the council's chairman and its secretary. The latter is an employee of the Bureau of Employment Security and is occupied nearly full time in council business. A verbatim transcript of each council meeting was made until 1954, when the secretary of labor ordered the discontinuance of the practice throughout his department. He believed that the practice encouraged "talking for the record" rather than working for solutions.

The president of the Interstate Conference of Employment Security Agencies is privileged to attend all of the council meetings. Committee chairmen of the Interstate Conference are sometimes invited to attend the meetings of those council committees that relate to their own committees. These Interstate Conference guests (they have no voting rights) are invited because the individual states have most of the legislative and operating responsibilities in the employment security program.

ACTIVITIES OF THE COUNCIL

Like all the state councils, the Federal Advisory Council gave unemployment compensation the greater share of its attention, but, unlike many state councils, it did not neglect the employment service entirely. It discussed at length, for example, such employment service operations as counseling and testing and entered thoroughly into such problems as defense mobilization and migrant farm labor and "wetbacks." It brought in reports with constructive recommendations on: selective placement (1952), minority groups (1953), older workers (1954), handicapped workers (1955), veterans (1955). In all these areas the committees of the council developed reports on the basis of which the full council discussed the problems intelligently and fruitfully. But although the employment service was not neglected, unemployment compensation occupied most of the council's time and occupies most of this chapter.

The chapter does not attempt to tell the full story of the council's activities, but as usual emphasizes the aspects that have particular relevance for this study. Two such aspects are the council's discussions of its own functions and the problem of getting the "right" employer representatives. Since both of these aspects were highly controversial, to emphasize them is inevitably to convey an impression of more controversy and less agreement than actually existed. To counterbalance that impression it may be well to state at the very beginning that an analysis of all the resolutions and reports of the "modern" council shows a much greater area of agreement than of disagreement. About three quarters of all recommendations on unemployment insurance and all those on the employment service were unanimous, or virtually so.[14]

The council's discussions of its own functions turned chiefly on the question of how important it was for the council to reach agreement. At the council's very first meeting, September 14, 1949, the chief CIO spokesman raised this question and gave the CIO's answer:

I think there is a problem as to what extent we should try in this council to reconcile our diverse points of view. It seems to me that those points of view need to be expressed and made clear to the Bureau, and the Bureau has to make its own decisions.

During its first year of activity the council was required to consider repeatedly this central question of whether and to what extent it ought to try to reach agreement. Because the question is central, because the federal council discussed the question more adequately than any of the state councils, and because on the federal council national leaders were speaking, this early discussion seems worth reporting in detail and, where possible, in the exact words of the participants.[15]

President Truman had asked Congress in July of 1949 to enact

[14] Examples are: recommendations for extension to coverage of employers of one or more, to federal civilian employees, and to ex-servicemen; shortening the period before a new employer can get experience rating from three years to one year; a proposal for beneficiaries' surveys; employment service improvement; special services to youth, the handicapped, and veterans; policies on minority groups; the occupational analysis program; the study of state administrative costs in 1952; legislative activities of the Interstate Conference; and frequent resolutions on appropriations.

[15] The participants have kindly granted permission to be thus quoted. The American Federation of Labor representatives who are quoted wish it to be clearly understood that these quotations do not represent a blanket approval of the agreed bill technique and still less of specific agreed bills that have been negotiated by state advisory councils.

federal standards in unemployment compensation which would require the states to liberalize their laws in respect to coverage, benefits, and the conditions of eligibility and disqualification. He also asked Congress to act promptly, in view of the high unemployment then existing. Secretary of Labor Tobin brought the President's proposals to the council at its December meeting and asked for the council's opinion.

After some general discussion the employer members caucused and then came back to the meeting with a proposal that a study committee be appointed to explore the matter more thoroughly than the full council could do at this one meeting. It was evident, they said, that the President's proposals could not, without modification, command unanimous council agreement, but they thought that a committee might be able to work out some acceptable compromise. John Lovett, general manager of the Michigan Manufacturers' Association and the chief spokesman for employers on the council, said, in making the motion:

I suggest that we have an opportunity to study and to bring back to this group some constructive suggestion on the part of the employer representatives. If we cannot be constructive, if we cannot approach these problems and find some areas of agreement, then I think the purpose of the Council is pretty futile. . . . I don't know how much influence our action would have on Congress. But if we don't go to Congress with some kind of a constructive agreement, then I think the Congress will readily assume that the Council isn't a very effective body. And I would much rather go to Congress within those areas that we can agree on saying that we can reach agreement on those, than to go to the Congress and say that the Council was unable to agree on anything.

The chief spokesman for the AFL representatives replied to Lovett's suggestion:

I think that what Mr. Lovett has suggested has some definite possibilities in it. The real question he has raised is one that confronts all these Advisory Councils and groups. . . . They sit around in a vacuum and make suggestions, and then the administrators go off and do what they were going to anyhow. . . . now what we are up against is all of us trying to find the technique by which an Advisory Council can advise in a way that has meaning. . . . now, how do we consult effectively? There is a possibility of taking a vote on these issues. Well, suppose there was a vote and out of the thirty members there was a 17–13 division. Have we discharged our responsibility? I don't know.

Another AFL representative remarked: "A report that has a majority of labor and public representatives voting against employers, or a majority of only employers and the public voting against labor, is not a very effective report."

The CIO representatives argued against Lovett's motion. They declared that the CIO was opposed in principle to accepting any set of standards less liberal than those of the President, which were already less liberal than those advocated by official CIO policy. Furthermore, they believed that the employers' motion was mainly a device to delay council action. The President was ready to push for legislative action when Congress reconvened in January, and the CIO did not want to see action delayed until a committee of the council could study the matter. One CIO representative said: "Why a postponement? If you disagree now you will probably disagree sixty or ninety days from now. Why not push the whole thing and have all the votes if you are going to do it at all?" The CIO representatives probably expected the public members to vote with labor in support of the President's recommendations and they hoped that the President, riding the wave of his recent victory, could get his recommendations enacted by Congress.

The suggestion was made that since the employers had caucused to prepare their motion (for a study committee), the labor members should hold a brief meeting to decide on their answer. They did so, and came back with a substitute motion: that the Council proceed with its discussion of the President's proposals at this meeting and that a committee be appointed to review the minutes of the meeting, select the areas of agreement, and put these together in a report to the secretary of labor. If the secretary wanted anything more, he could consult the full minutes for the differing opinions of the various groups. The labor representatives were unanimous in making this motion; the AFL representatives had been converted to the CIO strategy either because they were convinced of its wisdom or because they saw the need of presenting a solid front.

One of the public members thought the labor proposal the only sensible one and explained why he thought so.

Is it necessary to have any kind of agreement here? This is an open discussion. A record is being made and it is going to the Secretary of Labor. The Secretary of Labor is a member of the Truman administration. The Truman administration has policies which we hope it will recommend to Congress. The Secretary of Labor will go up there and express the administration's viewpoint. Labor will go up and express its viewpoint and management will be well represented with all its lobbies. So why unanimity? Why any kind of recommendation? Everybody expresses their viewpoint and then they go up on the hill and brawl it out. That is the usual procedure.

Professor Edwin E. Witte of Wisconsin, one of the founding fathers of social security, was a member of the Federal Advisory Council at this time and entered the discussion at a crucial point to say:

I think that in this general field of labor-management relations—and I include Social Security in that field—we have made the soundest progress by what might be called collective bargaining, the conference method. Consequently, I am not sure that we can arrive at any significant areas of agreement, but I would certainly like to find out whether there is any possibility of that. . . . I think that we will never make any substantial progress merely by the method of having either labor or employers, when they can control Congress, put through some legislation which the other side violently objects to.

In making his point Witte cited the example of the Senate Advisory Council on Social Security in 1948:

It was an Advisory Council that didn't do all the things that I would like to have seen done, and it made some recommendations that I perhaps wouldn't want to endorse. But despite the fact that some members still dissent from some of the recommendations [a reference to some of the labor members] I think we now have a bill before Congress, that has passed the House, which will make considerable improvement, by reason of the fact that we had a Social Security Advisory Council.

The CIO's reply to Witte's plea was a motion to reject Lovett's suggestion of a study committee and to make the record of the council's discussion the total contribution of the council. The director of the Bureau of Employment Security entered the discussion at this point to say that in his opinion the secretary of labor would not find this the most helpful contribution of the council. He said that despite the need for action in the coming session there was enough time for a study committee to explore the possibility of some agreement. The CIO's motion was defeated 17–5, one labor representative voting with the majority. Then Lovett's original motion was acted on and adopted by a vote of 17–3, none of the CIO representatives voting.

A study committee of five members was then appointed—the chairman of the council and the leading spokesmen for the AFL, the CIO, and employers. The committee met six times in 1950—January 18 and 19, February 21, March 20 and 29, May 8.

During these committee meetings there occurred occasional instances of the same AFL-CIO difference in attitude toward reaching agreement that had marked the meeting of the full council. The Federation's approach was typified by the statement: "I can agree on an area that is short of ultimate objectives, and I think that it is probably worth doing." The CIO's approach was typified by its often repeated motion to end discussion and have a vote. One reason that the CIO was unenthusiastic about trying to reach agreement is indicated in the following statement:

This tendency towards harsher disqualifications is one of the respects in which the unemployment insurance system has moved backward in the last ten years; and in many cases the improvements that were made in maximum benefits to keep up with the cost of living and rising wages were made on condition that the labor groups would agree to stricter disqualification provisions. They were faced with a very unpleasant compromise.

The study committee set itself to write a report consisting of four sections: (1) the history of unemployment compensation, (2) the objectives of unemployment compensation, (3) failures to reach the objectives, (4) recommendations for approaching the objectives more closely. At the first committee meeting the chairman suggested that they draft the first three sections of the report in such a way as to leave two avenues open when they came to the last section and the recommendations: "First, that we say nothing about areas in which there is no agreement, and second, that we indicate the areas on which we agree and those on which we disagree." As the committee continued to work, it found itself adopting the first alternative, but in an unusual and unforeseen form. The committee eventually agreed upon and released a set of recommendations, but it never agreed upon and never published the first three sections of its intended report, which presumably were to constitute the basis for the recommendations.

The committee met on January 18 and 19 and completed a rough draft of the first three sections. The full council met on January 26 and 27 and, after suggesting changes in the draft, authorized the committee to rewrite it and send it to the secretary of labor as the official report of the full council—if the committee could agree unanimously on the final version.

At this point two objections were raised which demonstrated that not all the council members understood what was involved in the agreed-recommendation technique. One of the employer members not on the committee stated that he wanted an opportunity to register dissent, if necessary, from parts of the committee's report. The AFL spokesman replied:

Mr. Chairman, I do not believe in doing anything to deprive any member of any right of dissenting or of expressing his own point of view, but this question goes further than it looks because there has been a lot of give and take here. I think the employers have relaxed on some of the positions they have taken at times, and we have given in on a number of things. . . . if we start writing dissents from specific things on which we do not have one hundred percent agreement, all we will do is just fly apart into as many directions as there are members of the Council, because there are things we have agreed to here as a whole, as a part of a give-and-take proposition, that I would dissent from as not being one hundred percent representative of my point of view.

Then one of the public members, a representative of a veterans' organization, announced that even if he signed the report he might want to dissent from it later in testifying at the congressional hearings. He argued:

It is my understanding that the Federal Advisory Council is a legal entity created by law. And it has an entity separate and apart from the organizations that may be represented. And even if we adopt something unanimously, it is not binding upon the organizations we represent or binding upon us as individuals, but merely on the Council as a separate legal entity.

The chairman merely replied: "An individual who voted to indorse this report would be in a paradoxical position if at a later time before a congressional committee he disowned it one hundred percent." In the end the council reaffirmed its authorization that if the committee could achieve unanimity its report would stand for the unanimous report of the full council.

The committee met again on February 21 and March 20 and managed to agree on the fourth section of the report, which was entitled simply "Conclusions." The "Conclusions" were recommendations for state, not federal, legislation. They were couched in general terms for the most part, but did include such specific recommendations as coverage of one or more, benefit maximums that would allow most benefit payments to equal 50 percent of wages, and "a duration of benefits of at least twenty-six weeks in a benefit year." The "Conclusions" also contained the statement: "Disqualification provisions now in existence in many states which deny benefits to workers who are genuinely unemployed should be corrected." These recommendations constituted a more liberal position than the employers' national leadership had ever before adopted, and to that extent the negotiations yielded a gain for labor.

In its subsequent meetings, on March 29 and May 8, the committee attempted to complete the first three sections of the report. But differences between labor and management widened instead of narrowing. At the second of these meetings Lovett brought in a new draft which was so different from the one on which the committee had been working that the chairman announced there was no longer any hope of reaching agreement. It is likely that Lovett had been criticized by his fellow employers in Michigan [16] for his concessions to labor in the "Conclusions," and he was trying to recover some of the ground he had given up. It is likely, also, that his technicians back in Michigan had showed him how

[16] See the chapter on the Michigan advisory council, p. 318, for a somewhat similar, though earlier, experience of Lovett.

many interpretations could be given to such phrases as "50 percent of wages" or "twenty-six weeks' duration." When his proposed new draft was rejected he asked to be allowed to append a statement to the "Conclusions," which had already been transmitted to the secretary. The labor people immediately pointed out that in that case they would have to append a statement of their own, and all previous agreement would be canceled out.

At its final meeting, on May 8, the committee agreed to let the "Conclusions" stand but to abandon the effort to complete the first three parts of the report. The secretary of labor thereupon made the "Conclusions" public, transmitting them to the President, the state governors, and the members of Congress. The chairman of the committee later reported to the full council that "the responses from members of Congress and the state governors were in general quite favorable."

Subsequent meetings of the council continued to exhibit the same differences of opinion regarding the function of the council that had marked the debates of 1950. One example must suffice. In 1951 the council discussed the extension of unemployment compensation to employees in agriculture. The Bureau of Employment Security suggested that the council recommend extension to the larger employers, those employing eight or more. The agency thought that the proposal thus limited might have a chance of getting through Congress. The CIO spokesman objected, saying:

Most of you probably know the CIO is on record for covering all workers under Unemployment Insurance; and as we understand it, there is no reason for us to compromise on that in this Advisory Council. On a Congressional Committee you may compromise in order to get action, because you are at the point where compromises are made. We do not feel that this Advisory Council is the appropriate point for such compromises.

The CIO spokesman went on to say that the advisory council should not be concerned with what was politically feasible.

Professor Witte of Wisconsin again took the opposite viewpoint:

I think that is a very wrong conception of what this Council is concerned with. . . . What I call the purely theoretical approach to problems in past experience in this country and particularly in the Social Security field, has been completely fruitless. We can make resolutions to our heart's content without producing any effect if we do not take into account the possibility of something like agreement between labor and industry and the other groups here represented; because if you do not you are just perhaps pleasing some people whom you represent but it doesn't mean any accomplishment whatsoever.

The council held only one meeting in 1951 because in that year labor withdrew temporarily from all federal boards and councils. Meetings were more frequent in 1952, but attendance at them was poor. The meetings in the spring of 1952 marked the low point of the council. At the March meeting only two AFL representatives were present and at the May meeting there were none. Lovett had died in March, and shortly thereafter Folsom announced his intention of resigning. Soon there was only one employer remaining on the council who was expert in unemployment compensation, and he was not influential with the employers' organizations.

In the fall of 1952 the council took on new life with the appointment of new members, including two very proficient public members and two employer members who were nominees in a sense (they had been cleared with the employer organizations beforehand) of the National Association of Manufacturers and of the Chamber of Commerce of the United States. Both new employer members were officials in large companies, one in General Motors and the other in General Electric, and both introduced the innovation of bringing technicians with them to the council meetings, establishing a "second row" very much like that of the Illinois advisory council.[17]

The council and its committees entered upon a period of intensive activity, most of which must be passed over here [18] in order to give a fuller account of the council's continued discussion of its own function and structure. The two new employer members began to propound an interpretation of the council's function very similar to that hitherto held only by the CIO. They said that

[17] These technicians were allowed to serve as alternates for their principals in discussion and committee work, but they could not vote.

[18] Some brief examples of committee activity are given below.

the council was not so much an opportunity for labor and management to reach agreement as it was a forum in which labor and management could state officially their differing and uncompromised positions.

It is likely that the employers were influenced by the results of the presidential election of 1952. They may have expected to find more favor with the new administration than they had with the old and as a consequence to be free of the obligation to work out compromises with labor. These expectations were the obverse of the CIO's in 1950 [19] and were due for the same disappointment. Labor proved to have as effective a veto on employer proposals under the new administration as employers had had on labor's proposals under the former administration.

As regards the council's structure and procedures, employers had long been dissatisfied with certain features of them and during this period made serious efforts to change them. One source of dissatisfaction was the method of appointing employer representatives. Employer organizations were not allowed, as were labor organizations, to nominate their own representatives to the council. Employer dissatisfaction on this score began to win recognition in 1954 and occasioned some changes in council procedures. In January the council's Committee on Functions and Procedures approved the employers' proposal that the major employer organizations be allowed to nominate some representatives to the council. The committee agreed with its labor member, however, that the proposal should not be made a part of the official document on functions and procedures. The committee first decided to include it in the letter transmitting the document to the secretary but later decided to have the chairman of the council communicate it to the secretary orally.

In the spring of 1954 the respective presidents of the National Association of Manufacturers and of the Chamber of Commerce of the United States submitted the names of four nominees to the secretary of labor, pursuant to a previous understanding with the secretary. At the time, the employers expressed satisfaction

[19] See p. 371. At one point during the 1950 discussions John Lovett had said to the CIO representatives: "Would you take the same attitude if you had another President and another Secretary of Labor?"

with the new arrangement, but their satisfaction proved to be short-lived. In June of that year the terms of the two most effective employer representatives—the two whose appointment had been antecedently cleared with the National Association of Manufacturers and the Chamber of Commerce of the United States—expired. The two organizations asked [20] that their original nominees be reappointed, but the secretary declined, saying that he wished to rotate appointments "in order to better acquaint responsible persons in the business community with the particulars of Employment Security," [21] and replaced both of the former representatives. He did, however, make the replacements from a list of nominees supplied earlier by the employer organizations.

The employer organizations did not hold with the rotation principle. They thought the council too important to be used primarily as an educational device. Further, they suspected that the secretary's chief reason for the change was to get rid of two members whom the Bureau of Employment Security found troublesome. The principle of rotation had not been applied to the labor or the public members, and there were two other employer representatives who were retained as members of the council although they had been on the council longer than the two who were released.

Further negotiations took place in the fall of the year between the secretary and the respective presidents of the two employer organizations. The negotiations seem to have resulted in a more satisfactory understanding, which is mirrored in the secretary's general assurance that the Department of Labor "would certainly welcome your nominations and suggestions for persons qualified to serve on the kind of group contemplated." [22]

Another source of employer dissatisfaction was the role played by the public members on the council. Employers believed that the Department of Labor systematically used the public members to put employers at a disadvantage. They charged that the department first selected the public members so as to assure a ma-

[20] In letters to the secretary dated respectively May 21 and July 6, 1954.

[21] From a letter of the Secretary of Labor to representatives of the National Association of Manufacturers and the Chamber of Commerce of the United States.

[22] From a letter of Arthur Larson, acting secretary of labor, to the president of the Chamber of Commerce of the United States, September 17, 1954.

jority vote in favor of labor and then used this majority vote for propaganda purposes. In referring to council action the department did not always mention that the vote was a divided one, with labor and the public on one side and all the employers on the other, but merely announced that "the Council" had recommended so and so. This happened, for example, in 1953 with regard to the Mills-Mason Bill, and in 1954 with regard to the President's recommendation for raising benefit maximums.

The employers made several proposals aimed at "reform" of this aspect of the council. One proposal was to appoint the public members from a panel of nominees supplied equally by the labor and management members. Some public members made a counterproposal, that "council action" require the support of three fourths of the council's members. Either proposal would have sufficed to prevent the department from misusing a majority vote, but neither was acted upon.

A more radical proposal made by employers was to establish separate advisory councils for labor and management in the Department of Labor so that each group could advise the secretary separately. Employers argued that in this way their advice would not be lost to the secretary by being buried in the majority advice of the council. A bill, H.R. 4018, was introduced on February 14, 1955, to give effect to this proposal, but it did not get out of committee.

The most drastic proposal of all was that the employers withdraw entirely from the council in the Department of Labor and become a separate advisory council for employment security in the Department of Commerce. The secretary of commerce could then speak for employers in matters touching employment security in the same way that the secretary of labor speaks for organized labor. This proposal did not get beyond the talking stage.

Matters reached a climax in 1955, when the employer members of the council proposed that the council abandon the whole procedure of voting and confine itself to the making of reports—as many reports as there were different opinions. When this proposal was rejected, the employers ceased to participate in any vote that was taken.

The secretary of labor seems to have reached the conclusion in

the course of 1955 that there was some justice in the employers'
complaint that the council was being used for propaganda purposes. He could see that the Department of Labor was in danger
of losing the cooperation of the employer organizations entirely
if they were not satisfied on this point. In a letter to the chairman
of the council, November 28, 1955, he warned against overempha-
sis on the matter of voting, which "has frequently resulted in
mere maneuvering for position." The secretary wrote:

It is my belief that the maximum help the Council can give us will
not be through formal votes on the issues discussed, but rather through
the preparation of carefully reasoned statements which summarize the
positions taken during the Council discussions. In such statements, the
Council could indicate how it divided if there was disagreement, but I
would be more particularly interested in the reasoning which led to
each of the positions taken. Such a memorandum on each policy issue
considered by the Council would be of great value to me and to the
Department.

At its first meeting in 1956 the council revised its procedures
on a trial basis to take cognizance of the secretary's observations.
Under the revised procedures, the purpose of council discussions
on a specific proposal was the production of a single report for
the use of the secretary. The report would first identify the areas
of agreement, with the reasoning supporting such agreement.
Where divergence existed, the report would identify the areas of
major disagreement and the groups who held the different positions. On the request of any four members, any vote indicating
disagreement on any section of the report was to be made a part
of the record going to the secretary.

Under the revised procedures the former bitter controversy over
the council's proper functions ceased. An excellent example of the
council at work under the new procedures is furnished by the
council's discussion in 1956 of the relations between the Bureau
of Employment Security and the Interstate Conference of Employment Security Agencies. A committee was established to study
the problem, and as the council chairman tells the story:

The Committee reviewed the problem, looked at the evidence, studied
the record, and wrote a report. The reaction was explosive. One would
have thought that the Committee had just proposed the abolition of
unemployment insurance altogether. The committee met again and

conferred with a group representing the State Administrators and the Interstate Conference. We went over the report line by line, item by item. Some suggestions were highly acceptable, some were dubious, some of the things we said could have been put perhaps in a bit clearer manner, and at last the committee met by itself and revised the report. I am pleased to tell you that in spite of the tension and excitement generated by our first report, when our Committee met to revise it, there was little disagreement. And when it was submitted to the Advisory Council it was accepted unanimously. This example shows how much can be accomplished if you're willing to sit down with an open mind and discuss the issues with the courtesy and understanding that this democratic process requires.[23]

In order to give a connected account of the council's struggle with the problems of its own functions and structure, it was necessary to pass over the many other matters with which the council was occupied in its meetings during this same period. It will be worth while to glance briefly at some of this activity, especially as manifested in the work of the committees.

The Federal Advisory Council made more use of committees than did any of the state councils. All of the following committees functioned at some time during the period of the "modern" council (1949–1957): Benefit Adequacy, Benefit Financing, Disqualifications, Farm Placement, Administrative Costs, Fraud and Overpayment, Annual Report, Functions and Procedures, Intergovernmental Relations, Improvement in Employment Security, Occupational Analysis, Minority Policy, Counseling and Placement, Handicapped Workers, Veterans' Problems, and Older Workers. Of these, the first four held an average of six meetings each, and the rest an average of two each. It is not feasible to describe the work of all of them, but one project carried out by one committee is worth touching on briefly because it exemplifies the thorough work of all the committees and also because it illustrates a perennial problem of all advisory councils.

The Committee on Benefit Adequacy had the difficult task of deciding what was the norm of "adequacy" and whether existing benefit provisions met the norm. In a number of long meetings

[23] William Haber, "Functions of the Federal Advisory Council," *Proceedings of the Twentieth Annual Meeting of the Interstate Conference of Employment Security Agencies* (Washington, D.C.: U.S. Department of Labor, 1956), p. 21.

the committee determined the exact form of the key questions that needed to be asked, and examined the evidence available for answering each question. The committee could reach no agreement on substantive recommendations but did agree on the need for more evidence and recommended to the Bureau that it make a pilot study of the adequacy of existing benefits for current claimants.[24]

The committee concerned itself actively with this pilot study. In the course of its work it got into problems so technical that the Bureau established a Technical Committee on Benefit Adequacy to help the council committee. To this technical committee the Bureau appointed technicians drawn solely from the Bureau and from the states. The employers thereupon demanded that they be allowed to put a technical watchdog of their own on the technical committee. They argued that the groups represented on the council ought to examine and approve the methods by which the Bureau proposed to conduct its investigation before the actual investigation began.

The labor and public representatives objected, saying that this was a technical problem beyond the council's competence and that the council would have to trust the agency in such matters. They had other reasons for objecting which may have weighed even more in their judgment. They suspected that the employers' proposal was a device for delaying the inquiry; also, they realized that where choices had to be made between different methods of gathering data the cause of labor was likely to be served better if the Department of Labor could make those choices without employers' supervision.

The employers continued to insist that there was little hope of the council's agreeing on the results of the investigation if there was a dispute at the very beginning over the method of the investigation. One of the most moderate of the employers urged that even if the council was not given the right of veto over the agency's methods, the agency technicians should at least be required to consult with the council so that this preliminary diffi-

[24] This recommendation represented a compromise reached only after a prolonged debate in which employers argued for extending the investigation in various directions and labor insisted on limiting it.

culty would so far as possible be out of the way when the council came to interpret the results of the investigation.

The council's final decision on this issue took the form of an amendment to the "Functions and Procedures of the Federal Advisory Council": "Meetings of such a [technical] committee may be attended by a [council] committee member or a person designated by him." [25] The last phrase, "or a person designated by him," gave employers the right—which they used—to put a technician of their own on the technical committee. (They recruited their representative from one of the professional polling organizations.)

The issue of the council's relation to technical work was raised in another connection when the Committee on Financing made its report.[26] The committee chairman, a public member, reported the many hours the committee had spent on purely technical problems and raised the question as to whether such work represented a proper use of an advisory council. A labor and a management representative both maintained that there was no way of avoiding such technical work; the program had reached a point of development where many crucial decisions turned on technical considerations. The council seemed to agree that this was so. The council recognized, however, that public members were at a disadvantage in this kind of work because they could less well afford to give the time required and recommended to the Bureau that it compensate public members in some way that would not violate the Wagner-Peyser Act—perhaps by hiring them as technical consultants. The Bureau was in sympathy with the recommendation but decided that the law would not permit it.

APPRAISAL
EXTENT OF COUNCIL INFLUENCE

The employment service program was accorded more attention by the Federal Advisory Council [27] than by any of the state coun-

---

[25] Sec. B, No. 1 (d). This amendment was adopted by the council in January, 1954.
[26] Council meeting of October 26, 1953.
[27] As indicated earlier, only the "modern" council is under discussion here.

cils. The federal council's greater-than-average interest in the employment service stemmed from several circumstances: the history of the council has been very closely interwoven with the history of the United States Employment Service; some of the council's members have always been appointed precisely because their predominant interest was the employment service; the director of the Bureau of Employment Security was formerly the director of the United States Employment Service; the Bureau of Employment Security, and therefore its advisory council, has a wider opportunity to exercise influence in the employment service program than in the program of unemployment compensation.[28] For all these reasons the Federal Advisory Council has devoted a significant amount of time and attention to the employment service.

The council was very active in some projects, as previously noted. There were other projects to which the council gave a passive sort of attention—merely listening to reports and giving unanimous approval to whatever the employment service was doing or was planning to do. But since the policies formed in Washington for the employment service were applied nationally, and since the national leaders of nearly all the affected groups (labor, management, veterans, minority groups, educators) were on the council, even this passive attention probably had its influence. The Bureau was very likely influenced at the planning stage by the knowledge that the council would later review its program, and when the council's review turned up nothing objectionable, it must have been a valuable confirmation that the program could be put into practice safely.

Although the Federal Advisory Council did not, like many of the state councils, entirely neglect the employment service, it did, like all the state councils, give much more of its time to unemployment compensation. In appraising the council's influence on the unemployment compensation program it is convenient to consider, first, Congress and then other groups whom the council might have influenced.

---

[28] The reverse is true for the state employment security agencies and their advisory councils; they find greater opportunity for exercising influence in the unemployment compensation program.

The council's potential influence on Congress was normally limited to the areas of coverage and taxes because it was only for those areas that Congress was accustomed to legislate; Congress normally left the other areas to the individual state legislatures. Since even in the areas of coverage and taxes Congress had acted only infrequently, there have not been many opportunities for the council to influence legislation directly. But there have been some opportunities. One, for example, occurred in 1954, when Congress amended both the coverage and the financing provisions of the law. The amendments enacted were substantially in accord with the recommendations of the council. Of course, the influence of the federal council on Congress can probably never be as decisive as the influence of a state council on a state legislature; Congress is much harder to "deliver" than any state legislature.

Outside Congress the council's influence extended to the following groups (here enumerated in an order roughly approximating increasing influence): officials of the state governments, the state advisory councils, the secretary of labor, the director of the Bureau of Employment Security, and the council members themselves.

The council was least influential in its relations to the officials of the state governments—legislators, governors, administrators—but even here it may have exercised some influence. It has been quoted on occasion in support of some amendment which a governor or administrator wanted.

Its influence on the state advisory councils was probably somewhat greater. The national leaders of labor and management are on the Federal Advisory Council; the positions they take and the arguments they employ are always likely to be picked up and used by the state leaders. From time to time the Bureau of Employment Security sends selected materials of the Federal Advisory Council to the state administrators with a recommendation that they communicate the materials to their own state councils. At one time the federal council discussed the advisability of the Bureau's sending such materials directly to the state councils, but decided against it. The decision was probably a wise one. Most state administrators would have resented any direct federal influence on their advisory councils, which they regard as strictly their own.[29]

As was to be expected, the influence of the council was greater within the Department of Labor than on groups outside. In recent years relations between the council and the secretary of labor have been closer and more vital than formerly. Secretary Mitchell generally consulted the council's recommendations before discussing issues on which he had to take a personal stand, and he felt that he spoke with more authority at meetings with the President's cabinet and the Council of Economic Advisers because he could quote the arguments and describe the attitudes of the council members, who were the leaders of their respective groups. Within the department, the council's relations have been closest, of course, with the Bureau of Employment Security, and council reactions have definitely influenced Bureau thinking.

The most important influence of the council has been exerted on its own members, who have been educated by their participation in its activities.[30] They have had access to the best source of data in the country, the Bureau of Employment Security, and to the sharpest minds in the program, the Bureau technicians and fellow council members. Representatives of all three groups admitted to having their opinions on substantive matters changed by their work on the council. Since the council is composed of the national leaders in the field of employment security, what these council members think can have a significant long-range influence on the development of the program. From the viewpoint of the Bureau these were persons well worth instructing and trying to persuade.

FACTORS OF COUNCIL INFLUENCE

Structure

The potential influence of an advisory council is chiefly determined by the quality of its membership. In this regard the Federal Advisory Council has been fortunate. The council has

[29] A few states have even refused the federal request for copies of minutes of meetings held by their state councils.

[30] A former member of the council, with one of the best-known names in social

always possessed a number of first-class members—members who besides being knowledgeable in the field of employment security exercised considerable influence outside the council. There have usually been three or four in each of the three groups represented who met that standard.

The labor representatives have always been named by the national offices of the AFL and the CIO, which have consistently refused to submit a panel of nominees from which the secretary of labor might choose. As a result the labor representation on the council has been strong. It has included the authentic experts and decision makers on labor's side. As between the AFL and the CIO, the CIO representatives *as a group* have attended council meetings more regularly, have shown more technical competence, and have taken a more continuously active part in the discussions. The chief reason for the difference seems to be that more of the CIO representatives have been staff people, technical specialists in the field, while more of the AFL representatives have been state Federation officials chosen partly to get a wide geographical and policy representation. The AFL seems to have felt the need to strengthen its representation, for in 1953 it decided "that AFL technicians should accompany official representatives at meetings of the Federal Advisory Council in the future." [31]

Employers have been the group with the weakest representation on the council. Although there have always been a couple of employer council members who were very competent and who commanded the confidence of the employer organizations, the employer members as a group have not been the equal of the labor group in their technical grasp of the program, nor have they been to the same extent the decision makers for their side. This weakness has limited the council's influence in every direction— on federal and state governments, on the labor and public members inside the council, and especially on management leaders outside the council. The chief cause of this condition has been the refusal of the Department of Labor to let the major employer

security, remarked in a letter to the author that he had resigned from the council "with some regrets, as I learned a good deal about employment security in the meetings and through the correspondence I had on its activities."

[31] Social Security Committee of the American Federation of Labor, minutes of meeting, November 12, 1953.

organizations name their own representatives to the council. It was not until 1952 or 1954—depending on how "nominee" is defined—and then only for two of the ten employer places, that the department began to accord to the major employer organizations the same formal privilege of making nominees that it had always accorded to the labor organizations. However, it must be recognized that, for reasons discussed in Chapter 20, it is intrinsically more difficult to determine who properly represents employers.

The various proposals which employers made to change the structure of the council amounted to attempts to eliminate the public members. The case for the inclusion of public members on advisory councils is stronger for the federal council than for the state councils. In the first place, there is more likelihood of getting expert and influential public members for a council that can draw on the whole country.[32] For example, some of the federal council's public members have been writers whose work has influenced long-range trends in the whole program of employment security. In the second place, public members can participate in the function of "investigation" more effectively than in the function of bargaining, and among the federal council's functions "investigation" is more important than bargaining. Some of the federal council's public members have made valuable contributions to the work of "investigation," especially those who were university professors specializing in this field. However, it must be observed that it has been as difficult on the federal as on the state level to find public members who commanded the confidence of both sides and were not looked upon as belonging to either.

The participation of public members in the work of the council would be facilitated if some way could be found to compensate them, at least for their work on the committees. The possibility of compensating them as technical consultants might be reexamined.

The public members have remarked on occasion that they ought to take a more independently active part in council matters, and even supply leadership. They could do this by working out programs and proposals of their own and inducing labor and

[32] The state councils have always found it more difficult to fill the public places satisfactorily than the labor and management places.

management to accept them. Though theoretically sound, this approach runs the danger of irritating labor or management or both. And if that should happen and a struggle ensue, the public members would probably be the losers. Normally public members can command neither votes nor contributions to political campaigns and hence can exert little direct influence on a governmental program. It is perhaps for this reason that the public members have urged that a press conference be held after each council meeting—the press being almost the only major channel of influence open to public members. The secretary, however, has not seen fit to permit such conferences. All releases to the press must be made by the secretary himself. This would seem to be the wiser arrangement, for otherwise the council would almost certainly become an instrument primarily for propaganda rather than for investigation.

The secretary of labor has always appointed one of the public members to be the council's chairman. The chairman [33] of the Federal Advisory Council has not been a figurehead (as is the chairman of many a state council) but has been a real force— appointing committees, steering and summing up discussions, making crucial decisions on the when and how of voting, rearranging agenda, suggesting labor or management caucuses, and personally discussing council problems with the secretary of labor and the director of the Bureau. Although on occasion he has felt obliged to remind the Bureau not to take important steps without consulting the council, he has himself not forgotten the essentially dependent position that an advisory council must maintain in relation to the agency it is advising. While avoiding the danger of becoming a rubber stamp, he has likewise avoided the danger of becoming an unwisely independent chairman.

Functions and Procedures

The council debated whether it was an important part of its function to reach agreed recommendations. Typically the CIO saw less value in this function than the AFL, whose attitude is

[33] The "modern" council has had two chairmen: William Haber (1948–1954) and Fedele F. Fauri. The evaluation given here applies equally well to both.

reflected clearly in the following paragraph taken from the meeting of the AFL Social Security Committee on November 12, 1953:

There followed a discussion of the functions of labor "representatives" on the Federal Advisory Council and it was agreed that, while thoroughly appropriate and desirable for the AFL to designate officers and staff personnel to serve on the Council, it was not desirable that "representation" be interpreted to require AFL members to serve as instructed delegates. It was recognized by the Committee that in the give and take required for effective participation, the AFL members might well associate themselves with agreement reached by the Council not identical in all respects with official positions of the AFL.

The attitude of employers toward the agreed bill changed during the period under survey. In the 1950 sessions of the council the attitudes expressed by John Lovett and the AFL spokesman were typical of a relationship found in many of the states between old-time managers of state manufacturers' associations and old-time leaders of the state Federations. The position taken by Lovett later in the negotiations under pressure from his advisers back home was typical of the newer, more aggressive employer approach that became evident after the war. It was an approach similar to that of the CIO: it emphasized the making of decisions "on principle" and was therefore relatively uninterested in the framing of agreements, which involved compromise.

One of the CIO's arguments had been that the council was "not the appropriate point for compromises" because the council could not guarantee the legislative action which alone justified making compromises. In appraising the validity of this argument it is helpful to distinguish between the area in which the federal legislature is accustomed to act and the area which it leaves to the state legislatures.

In the first and smaller area—restricted normally to matters of coverage and taxation—agreements have nearly the same value for the federal council as they do for the state councils, and debate on the desirability of reaching agreement turns on issues which are the same for both and which are discussed elsewhere.[34] But in the second and larger area—where Congress is not accustomed to legislate—the issues are somewhat different, and much less reason

[34] See pp. 409–19.

exists for council members to compromise their positions in order to achieve agreement. An agreement usually involves bargaining. But in the second area the effective bargaining is done in each state, and in no two states are the terms of the bargains likely to be identical. Any agreement that the federal council worked out by the bargaining method could be only a kind of "model bargain" offered to the states in the uncertain hope that they would somehow pattern their own—the only effective—bargains on it. It is doubtful whether labor and management on the federal council would consider this achievement worth the effort.

In this area, where the state legislatures are dominant, the chief function of the federal council would seem to be not bargaining so much as "investigation"—using the term in the sense of John R. Commons and meaning all those activities whereby the council members grow in understanding of the program and communicate that understanding to those they represent. If "investigation" is the chief function of the federal council, the chief instrument for performing that function will be not the agreed bill but what might be called the agreed report—a report that is certified by all council members to state the issues without distortion and supply the relevant arguments and data. The function of "investigation" is even more important for the federal council than for the state councils. As the national council, it occupies a central and elevated place. Its connection with the Bureau of Employment Security gives it access to the best technical skills and the most complete collection of data in the country. Its own membership includes the best personnel available in labor, management, and the public. Such a body can exert influence on a nation-wide scale and on long-run trends. Over the years its studies and recommendations tend to create a frame of reference within which issues are discussed—by everybody and almost automatically. This influence is none the less potent for being hard to pinpoint.

It was this function of "investigation" which Secretary Mitchell stressed in the letter quoted earlier.[35] In effect he said, "Let the council give me the issues and the arguments." A question might be raised here. Granted that this is an important function of the

[35] See p. 381.

council members in relation to their own constituents, how valuable a function is it in relation to the secretary? Does not the secretary have the Bureau of Employment Security to do that for him? Yes, he does, but he still needs the council. The secretary is too busy (with the other programs of his department and with politics) to give to this one program the kind of study necessary to formulate an independent judgment on the more controversial issues. He is dependent on his subordinates, especially on the assistant secretary in charge of employment security. But the assistant secretary is in charge of other matters besides employment security, and he also is too busy to develop an independent judgment. He is dependent on the director of the Bureau of Employment Security. Although the director is much closer to the program than the others, even he has too many other duties to become expert; he must depend on his technical staff. Ultimately the secretary of labor is dependent on some technician or small group of technicians in the Bureau. But there is always the danger that the guidance he gets from this source will reflect too much the personal views of some one who is far removed from political responsibilities. The council provides the secretary with the most effective and convenient way of checking on the correctness and political advisability of the guidance he receives from his own technicians.

Granted that this is a valuable function of the council in relation to the secretary—and to the director of the Bureau as well —is it a practicable function? Will these political decision makers, especially the secretary, have the time to read through a fairly lengthy council report? The secretary will read less, of course, than the others; but when the issue is especially important or controversial and he must be especially careful to give the right answer, he will read enough to get guidance. The director of the Bureau will read much more, and besides will have been present at all the council meetings. There is no doubt that even in an immense executive department of the government like the Department of Labor the council's function of "investigation" is highly practicable.

The effectiveness of the council would probably be advanced if it could meet somewhat more frequently than it has in the past.

Quarterly meetings are desirable. They are not strictly necessary, however, so long as the council's committees continue to be as active as they have been. And it is true, of course, that a national council, which draws its members from all parts of the country, must expect to accomplish much of its work through the operation of committees, rather than through meetings of the whole council.

Part Five

SUMMARY AND ANALYSIS

19

THE EXTENT OF EFFECTIVENESS

CHAPTERS 1 and 2 sought to establish the theoretical proposition that advisory councils are desirable and feasible. The proposition is reexamined here in the light of actual experience. Does the experience of eighteen councils over a period of twenty years confirm or weaken the proposition? Did the councils perform in fact the functions expected of them in theory? That is, were they effective? If the councils were effective (according to the norms laid down in Chapter 2), then obviously (according to the assumptions made in Chapter 1) the councils were both desirable and feasible.

The first part of the chapter reviews the positive accomplishments of the councils. This is equivalent to weighing the advantages that have attached to the use of advisory councils. But the relative measure of council effectiveness is net effectiveness; net, that is, after disadvantages have been subtracted from advantages. The second part of the chapter therefore contains the postponed [1] consideration of possible disadvantages attaching to the use of advisory councils.

The chapter is concerned with only the state councils.[2] Since the experience of these councils has been very different with respect to the two divisions of the employment security program—the employment service and unemployment compensation—it will be better to summarize the experience of each division separately, beginning with the employment service, which can be handled more briefly.

[1] See p. 55.
[2] The experience of the federal council is summarized and evaluated in Ch. 18.

EMPLOYMENT SERVICE

The experience of advisory councils in the field of the employment service can be summed up briefly because the councils accomplished so little in that area. Their history follows a standard pattern. Although a few councils had an early origin,[3] most of them began to flourish only after the Wagner-Peyser Act of 1933. Very active and helpful in the early years of the depression, they grew less and less active—as employment improved, as the agencies grew more self-sufficient, and as the interest of their members declined. The advent of unemployment compensation in 1935, although it strengthened the employment service offices in their internal operations, further distracted the attention of labor and management from employment service problems.

During the war, employment service problems came back into the forefront of public consciousness, but the War Manpower Commission was in control of the service then and its labor-management committees supplanted the advisory councils. After the war the councils that were active at all concerned themselves mainly with unemployment insurance problems. This was the case even in states like Rhode Island and Colorado, where the director of the agency was a former director of the employment service division. It was the case even in states which had a council devoted by law entirely to the employment service. These latter councils either did nothing (as in Connecticut) or very little (as in Wisconsin) or, despite the legal limitation, concerned themselves mainly with unemployment compensation (as in California).

Even where councils gave more than the average amount of attention to employment service problems (as in California, New York, Ohio), the attention they gave was somewhat passive and consisted chiefly of receiving and approving reports from the agency. The problems posed by migrant farm workers commanded some interest, but in states where these problems were most important, special advisory councils took over (as in California and Colorado). Where councils theoretically should make a major contribution

[3] For example, those of Illinois, Minnesota, Ohio, and Wisconsin.

—in persuading industrial employers to make more use of the service—the councils accomplished nothing significant.

The local advisory councils that are provided for in most state laws have not materialized. Only two were encountered in this survey, those of Milwaukee and Cleveland. The Milwaukee council was the only one investigated, and it had clearly been in decline for some years at the time of the investigation.

Some of the states were successful in the use of *ad hoc* committees to work on specialized problems,[4] and a few councils on occasion interested themselves effectively in a current, pressing problem of the service,[5] but not a single state had a record of continuing success in the use of the regular standing advisory council.

The main causes of this situation seem to have been four.[6] They are given here in the order of their probable importance. First, the work of the employment service is not as highly controversial as that of unemployment compensation. The work of the employment service has more of the character of a service industry, like that of supplying light and water, and as such its functions command more general agreement. The affected parties are therefore more willing to allow government to decide policy and do not demand as active a share in the process as they do when the program is more controversial. Second, to a much greater extent than in unemployment compensation, policy in the employment service is set outside the council, and even outside the state. Major policies are largely determined by the Bureau of Employment Security in Washington, and relatively few important matters can be settled by a council vote at a council meeting, as can be done in unemployment compensation. Third, the work which is left to the council, the work of effectuating policies, is hard work. It frequently requires more time than unpaid advisers are willing to give on a continuing basis. A fourth cause is the competition of unemployment compensation for the attention of the council members. This is probably a minor factor. The experience of states

[4] For example, see New Hampshire, p. 106.

[5] For example, see New York, p. 202.

[6] The discussion of causes properly belongs in the following chapter but is more conveniently treated here. It keeps the entire discussion of the employment service program together, and it avoids further complicating an already elaborate arrangement of topics in the next chapter.

that had a separate council for the employment service was as poor as that of states in which the same council handled both programs.

The experience of all the councils in the sample leads to the conclusion that the director of the employment service cannot expect much help from a standing advisory council. He probably should plan to supplement (or supplant) the standing advisory council with specialized, *ad hoc* committees suited to cope with temporary, urgent problems. He could well make use, also, of another supplementary technique, which consists in periodically inviting representative employers of a given locality to visit the local employment office and spend half a day with the office staff discussing the employment problems of the area.[7]

The history of councils in the employment service offers the paradox that the branch of employment security in which advisory councils originated and whose law alone contains the specifications for advisory councils is the branch with no record of success in the use of such councils. The paradox raises the question, discussed later, whether these specifications should continue to control advisory councils in the entire employment security program.

UNEMPLOYMENT INSURANCE

In this review of council history it will be convenient to follow the order that was used in the treatment of council functions and to consider the influence of the councils on, first, legislation and then administration. Influence is a subtle element, difficult to measure and easily missed. The councils may well have exerted more influence than could be detected by an outside observer. The estimate offered here may safely be taken as minimal; if it errs, it is as an underestimate.

LEGISLATION

Did the councils influence legislation? When they achieved agreed bills, they certainly did; of that there can be no doubt.

---

[7] For a description of this technique, see Walter E. Parker and Charles C. Rand, "State Office Conference Program," *Employment Security Review*, XXIII (August, 1956), 16, 17.

What a council agreed upon unanimously was nearly always enacted into law, so that for all practical purposes the council functioned as its own legislature.

In the matter of agreed bills, four states had records distinctively better than the rest—Wisconsin, New Hampshire, Utah, and Illinois. Of these, Wisconsin is in a class by itself. For twelve consecutive legislative sessions (1933 through 1955) the Wisconsin advisory council produced a strict and full agreed bill.[8] Practically all the major provisions currently in the law were enacted on the recommendation of the advisory council,[9] and no major provision was enacted which the council opposed. Of the Wisconsin law it may truly be said that it is made in the image of the advisory council. It is possible that the future of the Wisconsin council will be somewhat different, for in 1957 it failed for the first time to produce an agreed bill.

The New Hampshire council has the next most perfect record, but a very much shorter one, having begun only with the 1947 legislative session. In all the six sessions falling within the decade 1947–1957, the council produced an agreed bill. In one session the agreed bill was strict but not full; in all the others it was both strict and full.

The Illinois and Utah councils produced a number of agreed bills, some strict and full, but not all of the agreements were reached by or within the advisory council. In Illinois agreed bills covering controversial matters were achieved in eight of the eleven sessions between 1937 and 1957, and another very extensive one covering so-called noncontroversial items in 1953. Most of these were not strict in type and until 1951 were put together outside the council. However, one or two council members were always active in these outside negotiations. The most recent agreed bills, those in 1955 and 1957, were both strict and full and were produced entirely in and by the council.

In Utah agreed bills were achieved in eleven of thirteen sessions (1935–1957). Even in the two remaining sessions (1943 and 1947) a kind of agreement was reached, namely, an agreement to observe

---

[8] For the definition of these terms, see pp. 49–50.

[9] The single exception: the council's repeated recommendation to extend coverage was not followed.

a legislative truce. Not all of these agreements were strict and full in type, and from 1939 through 1957 they were fashioned with the help of persons outside the advisory council and not all of the council members played an active part. Since 1951, however, all the labor and management representatives on the council have been fully active agents in making the agreement.

The norm of the agreed bill fails us rapidly after we leave these four states. Nebraska can point to six agreed bills in ten sessions (1937–1955), but two of these were agreed truces and nearly all of them consisted of little more than employers saying, "This is what we will support," and labor saying, "We will have to take it." Moreover, the chief decision maker on labor's side was not a member of the council. The council's low meeting average (about two meetings yearly) is a better index of its general vitality than its record of agreed bills.

The councils of Connecticut (begun in 1936) and Colorado (begun in 1941) were roughly similar to that of Nebraska in vitality. They produced some agreed bills, but met infrequently. The Connecticut council regularly produced agreed bills—strict and full—through the period 1936–1943, but the key negotiations were carried on outside the council meetings (as in the case of Illinois and Utah) and involved only two of the council members. The Colorado council produced only a few agreed bills, and they were not strict and full. The Connecticut council averaged less than two meetings a year over its lifetime; the Colorado council averaged less than three.

In point of activity, the councils of New York (begun in 1935), Massachusetts (begun in 1936), and Ohio (begun in 1937) are at the other end of the spectrum. The Massachusetts council averaged over seventy-five meetings yearly, the Ohio council over sixteen, and the New York council over ten. They also held frequent committee meetings. The Massachusetts council produced a strict and full agreed bill in 1939, but thereafter any agreements it achieved were limited to noncontroversial matters. Because of its continuous activity and close cooperation with the agency, it seems to have been a real influence until about 1945, and in the early years of the program had the kind of vigor which produced the "Boston tea party." [10] In the decade 1945–1955 the council, despite its numerous meetings, seems to have been a minor influence. After 1955 it began to grow in influence again. The New York council was clearly a major influence until 1940. It produced strict and full agreed bills in 1937 and 1939. Although the influence of the council diminished with the years, it always remained significant, for the council always had some influential members and always maintained its activities. The trend line of its influence turned up again after 1955. The Ohio council never produced agreed bills and seems never to have been a major direct influence on legislation; but it probably exerted a significant degree of indirect influence because of the ability and activity of its individual members. The findings of this investigation are less conclusive in regard to the Ohio council than in regard to any other. This is a particularly unfortunate circumstance because the Ohio council is the leading example of what might be called the public type of council—one that is characterized by an emphasis on the role of the public members and on the duty of the council to promote the public welfare. If we had an accurate measure of its effectiveness, we would know the maximum potentialities of this type of council; for it is unlikely that any other council built on this model would be any more effective than the long-lived, well-staffed, hard-working Ohio council.

The Minnesota and Rhode Island councils began with strict and full agreed bills (Minnesota in 1938 and Rhode Island in 1948), but neither was ever able to accomplish the feat again, although in Minnesota two agreed bills were put together by labor and management working outside the council.

The late-starting Michigan and Pennsylvania councils were conflict-ridden to an unusual degree, but both had strong and fairly active memberships. Although they never achieved an agreed bill in controversial matters, they did produce some important agreed bills covering administrative and noncontroversial matters. At least potentially they were always very influential councils.

[10] See p. 214.

On the whole the record of these fifteen advisory councils in exerting direct, measurable influence on legislation is not impressive. It seems safe to say that they exercised such influence in less than a third of the legislative sessions during which they were operative. Since these councils were among the most active and influential councils in the country, the record of the rest is presumably no better.

Did the councils exert influence on legislation in any other way than through agreed bills? Undoubtedly they did, but without the use of the agreed bill as a norm, influence is difficult to measure. The best that can be done is to instance council activities which by their nature were designed to have some eventual impact on legislation. The studies which councils conducted, the reports they made, and the objections they registered to legislation originating outside the council are three such activities.

One expectation of theory was that council studies would contribute to the education of the council members and would thus (on the assumption that the members were decision makers) influence the program, even when the council acting as a unit could not exert influence through an agreed bill. It is not possible to trace and to prove this flow of influence from council meetings through the individual activities of council members to provisions of the law, but it is certain that the councils provided the opportunity for this kind of influence by proving themselves to be efficient instruments of education.

The effectiveness of a council in the performance of this function was revealed most clearly on those occasions when a council embarked on some large project that required the agency to do considerable research and the council to absorb and evaluate the results of the agency's work. The experience of the California study group in 1952–1953 is typical of this kind of activity. All the more active councils had similar experiences repeatedly. A "solvency study" was probably the commonest occasion for such an experience in the life of a council.

Most council members testified to the value of the education they received through the council. This value was usually greatest in the case of the labor members, who only infrequently had technical training in the employment security program.[11] Members representing management were more likely to have such skill because it happened more often that their regular full-time work was closely connected with unemployment compensation. The technical competence of some of the management representatives matched even that of the agency staff. Even these members, however, reported that they derived much profit from the council meetings. Of both labor and management it may safely be said that without the council they would have found it more difficult to stay abreast of developments in the program. How difficult that could be even for council members is demonstrated by the experience of the New York council, whose members complained repeatedly that they did not know what was happening in the agency.[12]

Wherever the council meetings were genuine study sessions, everybody involved agreed that the study of the facts had made a difference in the attitudes of the participants. If it did not eliminate differences—and it usually did not—it at least narrowed them. The "conversion" of the Utah employer was a not untypical result of council activities. There were several instances of belligerent labor representatives turning "reasonable" as their understanding of the program widened and deepened.

A number of the councils produced readable and reliable reports both annual and special. How much influence these exerted it is impossible to say. The special reports were more influential than the others, and some, like the reports coming out of the solvency studies, probably exerted considerable influence. The reports which the councils made annually certainly were not read regularly by the governor or the legislators. The reports were read, if at all, only by those few legislators who possessed a workable understanding of the program.[13] However, the few persons—in or

[11] In several states the agency complained that the necessity of educating and helping labor hindered the agency from maintaining the neutral position it preferred. In two states public members who were skilled in unemployment compensation voiced this same complaint.

[12] See, for example, p. 193.

[13] In one large state, it happened that no one in the entire legislature had a satisfactory grasp of the program—if one may believe the unanimous opinion of labor, management, and the agency.

out of the legislature—who may have read the reports would be precisely the ones who were most active in the program and exercised the most influence.

Even when councils were unable to agree on what they wanted, they were often able to agree on what they did not want and were able to achieve a united front of opposition to bills originating outside the council. Such unanimity was achieved more often by the councils that regularly produced agreed bills, but it was by no means restricted to them. All the more active councils had the experience of closing ranks *against* certain kinds of proposed legislation. Usually this was either extreme legislation (inimical to the fundamentals of the program) or particular legislation (designed to favor a small group at the expense of the rest). Where such legislation was defeated there was no way of establishing a clear causal connection between the defeat and the council's action. But the probability is high that the council's unanimous opposition carried considerable weight with the governor and the legislators.

The expectation of theory that effective councils are desirable finds support in the instances when advisory councils *could* have functioned with profit to the program, even if they did not. There were numerous instances of legislation being enacted with less deliberation than would have marked its birth if an advisory council had been the midwife. Among such instances were the way in which the level of benefits was decided in New York in 1942 and the way in which two states made the important decision to add family allowances to unemployment compensation benefits.[14] The gubernatorial veto in Illinois in 1953 was a striking example of the constant danger of unplanned and irrational occurrences in the legislative process. Some other instances that were encountered during this survey are not narrated in the text. For example, in one large state a legislator who was serving his last term and wanted to leave with a final important bill to his name and credit picked up a bill in unemployment compensation, about which he knew very little, and began some vigorous logrolling. When labor, with whom he was usually identified, pointed out to

[14] See Connecticut (p. 229) and Michigan (p. 319, n. 11).

him that the bill was a bad one from its viewpoint, he pleaded ignorance but asked labor to back it anyway because of what it meant to him personally. Although in the end he lost his bill, it was only after a protracted legislative battle and only by two votes.

ADMINISTRATION

The influence of the advisory council on administration is even more difficult to measure than its influence on legislation. Administration is a continuous process made up of a multitude of separate decisions, most of them small, and the advisory council members can be related to this decision stream in many different ways, some as informal as a telephone call between a council member and the director of the agency.

It will be useful here, as in the discussion of council functions, to distinguish between administrative law and "pure" administration.[15] The influence of the councils on administrative law generally paralleled their influence on legislation. That is, the councils which exercised the greatest influence on the enactment of legislation also exercised the greatest influence on its interpretation.

Exceptions to this generalization, however, existed in both directions. A few councils exercised less influence on administrative law than on legislation. There were at least five of these, including two of the most influential councils. The reason in each case was that the director did not want to use the council for this purpose. The more common exception was in the other direction. Many councils which were unable to exert much direct influence on legislation were able to influence administrative law. This is understandable. Council influence is always greater when its members are in agreement, and the council—like labor and management in the case of industrial contracts—found it easier to agree on the interpretation than on the negotiation of a contract.

Most directors were glad to use the council in the formulation of administrative law. They found that the council members could help both in foreseeing difficulties in proposed decisions and in selling final decisions to their constituents. Directors generally

[15] See p. 42.

were in agreement with the New York director that administrative interpretations and rules "stood up better" when they had been worked out beforehand with the parties at interest.[16] California was unique in having a sizable group of labor and management representatives separate from the advisory council and specifically set up to advise on administrative rules and procedures only.[17]

Of the many ways in which the councils influenced "pure" administration, the following are selected as the more important. There was abundant evidence that the councils served as efficient channels for bringing the complaints of individual workers and employers to the agency and to the legislature. The minutes of the council meetings contained many examples of this.[18] Numerous instances, also, were encountered where the advisory council served as an escape valve for dissatisfactions that were building up, and there were other instances where a council, if it had been active, could have performed this function.[19]

Only a few instances were encountered where the council served as a watchdog for the legislature with respect to the administrator and his program,[20] but the few sufficed to prove that councils are competent to perform this important function when need arises.

A few situations were encountered where a council came to the assistance of an administrator who was under pressure to grant benefits to a particular claimant, or to make a favorable tax ruling for a particular employer, or to put a "deserving worker" (political) on the payroll. A more frequent situation was one in which the council was able to assist the administrator in getting appropriations or other administrative aids from the federal Bureau of Employment Security or from the state legislature.

There was no instance in which the advisory council either

[16] See p. 202.

[17] See pp. 357–58. See also the Rhode Island group established for a similar purpose in the employment service program (p. 289).

[18] Several instances were encountered even in the relatively few council meetings which the author himself attended.

[19] For an example of the latter, see the situation in Colorado in 1954, p. 342.

[20] For example, the New York council helped reorganize the agency (p. 179), and the Pennsylvania council called attention to a dangerous situation involving delinquent taxes (p. 304).

prevented the dismissal of an administrator [21] or exercised any crucial influence in his selection. There were three occasions, however, not mentioned in the text, when the advisory council actively intervened to protect the administrator from attacks motivated by politics in the narrow sense, and there were several other occasions when participation by the council in the selection of an administrator would probably have resulted in a better selection.

The councils were most active in "pure" administration at the very beginning of the program—when there were so many things to be done and so few people with any experience to do them. It was natural for the council to assume many administrative responsibilities which the agency later took over.[22] However, even in later years the councils continued to participate in the administrative process in many more ways than can be indicated in this brief summary.[23]

DISADVANTAGES OF ADVISORY COUNCILS

Advisory councils are desirable if their advantages outweigh their disadvantages. To be able to make the comparison it is necessary to balance the survey of advantages just concluded with a survey of possible disadvantages. The principal disadvantages are ten in number and fall into two groups according as they are seen to be disadvantages from the viewpoint of the governed (two) or of the government (eight).[24] Of the ten, the first seven have significance only in the case of an agreed bill, and probably only in the case of a full agreed bill. That is, they are objections against

[21] It is worth noting as a curiosity that the Hatch Act makes an administrator vulnerable to removal for political reasons. Since he is prevented by the Hatch Act from working actively for the governor's election, he is not in line for favors after the governor wins, and he may find himself replaced by someone to whom the governor is politically obliged.

[22] See, for example, the councils of Illinois, New York, Ohio, and Minnesota. The Minnesota council operated almost like an administrative commission for the first year.

[23] The New York council, for example, initiated a revision in the appeals procedure of the agency, and the New Hampshire and Utah councils brought the problem of a budget deficiency to the attention of their respective state representatives in Washington.

[24] Of the eight "government" disadvantages, the last two relate specifically to the administrative agency.

the agreed bills of advisory councils rather than against the institution of the advisory council as such.

1. Unrepresentative. This objection states that an advisory council, necessarily limited in the number of its members, may be unrepresentative, and as a result the interests of certain groups may be neglected.

On management's side, underrepresentation was most frequent in the case of small business, but it also occurred in the case of industries whose interests in unemployment compensation were opposed to those represented on the council.[25] On labor's side, the CIO was unrepresented at various times in some states, and of course unorganized labor could not, strictly speaking, be represented at all. In the states whose councils produced agreed bills, there were usually some employers and employees who expressed dissatisfaction with the procedure. In Wisconsin the criticism was strong enough to evoke a legislative investigation.

The favorable verdict returned in the case of Wisconsin [26] would seem to be applicable generally. The councils have not abused their influence nor been unreasonably unrepresentative. All representation is, to some extent, imperfect. The alternative to an agreed bill is arbitration by the legislature, which is also less than perfectly representative and takes action on the basis of simple majority vote.

Moreover, the final decision *is* made by the legislature; an advisory council is only advisory. The legislature can always change an agreed bill, if it wants to, and on occasion has actually done so. There were occasions, for example, when a council unanimously recommended an extension in coverage and the legislature ignored the recommendation because the extension would have affected smaller employers chiefly, for whom the council did not speak adequately.[27]

Furthermore, representatives of employer organizations were not unmindful of the smaller employers, even when they themselves were connected with large firms. For example, the employer

[25] For examples, see the chapters on California, Illinois, Utah, Wisconsin.

[26] See p. 74.

[27] See, for example, the Illinois council (pp. 150–51) and the Wisconsin council (p. 69, n. 14).

representing retailers on the Illinois council objected on several occasions to proposed council action on the score that while it posed no difficulty for his firm, a very large department store, it would work hardship on smaller stores. The Wisconsin employer quoted previously [28] objected to council action on at least three occasions for the same reason. He himself came from a very large manufacturing firm.

In all the instances encountered in this study where the council acted to beat down amendments requested by individuals it was either because the amendments represented illogical exceptions accorded to individuals at the expense of the whole program (for example, exemptions from coverage requested by certain employers or exceptions from eligibility requirements requested by employees) or because the proposed amendment, although desirable in itself, was deemed unobtainable and perhaps had already been bargained away in exchange for lesser but more certain gains.

2. *A Poor Bargain.* This objection states that advisory councils and their agreed bills result in a worse bargain (for the side making the objection) than could be obtained by calling on the legislature for a decision. The objection was heard from both labor and management; it was heard more frequently from the CIO and the state chambers of commerce than from the AFL and the state associations of manufacturers.[29]

Those who voiced this objection supported their position by two principal arguments. First, the political strength of their side was underestimated. Second, the intrinsic merit of their case was such that quite apart from any consideration of political strength the legislature, the guardian of the common good, was bound to support their side. Both labor and management used both arguments, but the first argument was heard somewhat more often from management and the second somewhat more often from labor.[30] The CIO in its use of the second argument stressed the

[28] See p. 82.

[29] But see Colorado (p. 334), New Hampshire (p. 96), and the Federal Advisory Council (p. 369, n. 15) for instances when this objection was voiced by the AFL.

[30] This usual pattern was reversed in Rhode Island, where it was management which resigned from the council and appealed to the public conscience. (See p. 286.) The situation on the Federal Advisory Council resembled that of Rhode Island. (See pp. 378–81.) The more usual situation is exemplified by Pennsylvania. (See p. 301.)

educative value of repeated legislative struggles, with their committee hearings and floor debates.[31]

How much validity did this objection have? Here more than anywhere else there is room for differing opinions, and here more than anywhere else the opinion of an "outsider" is at a discount. The relevant variables, besides being numerous and complex, are qualitative. Gains in unemployment compensation have to be balanced against gains in other programs, personal gains against group gains, economic against political gains. The proper judges of the net value of the total bargain are the contracting parties themselves, who are intimately acquainted with the details of their own situation and who must live with the results of their bargain.

To this outsider there were no clear indications that either labor or management suffered any important disadvantages from the agreed bills they negotiated. It is not likely that labor lost by the agreed bills. In the particular states in which the agreed bills were negotiated during the years 1937–1957, it is not likely that labor could have gained more against the opposition of employers than it did with employer support.[32] It would seem much more likely that labor profited from the agreed bills, at least in a short-run financial sense. The converse of this proposition is that employers probably suffered some short-run financial disadvantage. That is probably so; but they obtained in exchange the other advantages of agreed bills. It is worth noting how even in Nebraska, where labor was able to count on, at most, one third of the votes in the legislature, employers felt it safer to use the device of the agreed bill.

[31] On the whole, CIO state councils faithfully followed the instruction issued by national headquarters: "CIO members should not try to reach unanimous council agreement on unemployment compensation bills, at the expense of the needs of our members as expressed in the CIO legislative program. While CIO's program may not be adopted immediately, bills embodying the CIO's proposals should be introduced anyway, even if only for educational and publicity value this year. This is not to imply that compromises cannot or should not be made on the final form of legislation. But unless CIO pushes its own bills vigorously, the legislative compromises may be made on the already watered-down bill agreed to by the advisory council rather than on a more adequate bill." *Guidebook No. 2: Unemployment Insurance*, CIO Publication No. 210 (September, 1952), p. 76.

[32] The experience of Wisconsin and Utah furnishes especially clear evidence in support of this proposition. The experience of New Hampshire (p. 96) with "right-to-work" legislation also constitutes some evidence of the practical wisdom of a labor policy that emphasized the "reasonable" approach.

The states whose councils utilized agreed bills most were among the most progressive states in the development of the employment security program. Wisconsin pioneered in developing a counter-cyclical tax system; Utah in developing a benefit system which adjusts automatically to changing wage levels; while Illinois was one of the early states to experiment with the device of a variable maximum benefit. In New Hampshire in both 1953 and 1955 it was the council which succeeded in warding off amendments which would have made the law less effective.

It is even harder to judge the validity of this objection in those instances when the objection prevailed and the advisory council did not achieve an agreed bill. It is always more difficult to know what would have happened if something had been done which, as a matter of fact, was not done. There are a few cases where it is reasonably clear that labor would have lost by an agreed bill: in Rhode Island generally, in Michigan in 1953 and 1955, in Pennsylvania in 1955. In probably more cases it advantaged management not to have negotiated an agreed bill, some of the clearest cases being the reform measures that were inaugurated in Michigan (1947) and in Massachusetts, New York, and Ohio (all in 1951). But there were a number of instances, also, where if labor and management had accepted the agreed bill that was under discussion, they would have fared about as well as they did by taking their differences to the legislature.[33] They would have had, in addition, the advantages that come from self-government.

3. Obscures Responsibility. When an advisory council operates by means of an agreed bill, which the legislature rubber-stamps, the responsibility of government is obscured and it becomes difficult to hold legislators accountable for the resulting program. This objection was usually phrased in terms of the government "dodging responsibility."

There is no doubt that an agreed bill does enable an individual legislator to evade full responsibility for his voting record. At election time the candidate can always answer an objector, whether from the side of labor or management, by saying, "But all I did

---

[33] See, for example, New York (1947), Pennsylvania (1951), California (1953), and Wisconsin (1957). In the first two, labor, and in the last two, management, overestimated their political strength.

was vote for what your own leaders agreed upon; they share the responsibility."

Whether this sharing of responsibility is judged to be good or bad depends very much on how the first objection is evaluated, for this objection is frequently just a corollary of the first. If a group feels that it is not fully represented in the negotiations that lead to agreed bills, it is likely to feel that the only proper decision maker in the program is the legislature. This is probably one reason why the objection was heard most frequently from the CIO, for in most states it was the AFL which took the lead in bargaining with management. In Michigan, where the roles of the CIO and AFL were reversed, it was the AFL legislative representative who voiced this objection and discoursed at length on why it was necessary for individual legislators to "stand up and be counted."

4. Substitutes Expediency for Principle. According to this objection, the agreed bills of advisory councils reduced the governmental process to collective bargaining. But government may not be conducted by collective bargaining. Government may not decide between the conflicting demands of pressure groups according to the simple norm of which group can exert the most pressure, or simply allow competitive forces to work themselves out. Among other reasons, one of the competing groups may be notably weaker than the other, and it is the duty of government to protect the weak. Governmental decisions must be made in accord with the needs of the common good, as that good is established by an investigation of the facts in each case.

This objection was heard most often from persons in government; next often from labor representatives; and only occasionally from employers.[34]

We may grant that the distinction between might and right has meaning and that the government must protect the rights of the weak. We may also grant that the government should make use of investigation and should base its decisions on the facts. We may also grant that government has broader responsibilities than has

[34] It was heard from some employers in Rhode Island and from representatives of retailer organizations in several states who felt that their interests were being sacrificed to the stronger interests of manufacturers' organizations.

any private group and at times may be called upon to make unpleasant decisions for which no private group can be expected to
assume the responsibility.[35] But, even granting these propositions,
we are not forced to conclude that agreed bills are bad.

First of all, the agreed bill of an advisory council represents
only advice. The legislature retains the power to reject agreed
bills in whole or in part, and legislatures have in fact done so.
Secondly, collective bargaining is not identical with sacrificing
right to might. The advisory council members who engage in
collective bargaining should be and normally are influenced by
what they consider to be right.[36] Thirdly, although the legislature
must try to find the "facts" and the "intrinsic merits" in each case,
it cannot always be sure that it has found them. Without taking
the position of philosophical relativism, we may admit that the
powers of the human intellect are not always adequate for foreseeing all the results of a contemplated decision, nor for perceiv-
ing how these results are related to the ultimate norm of human
perfection. The process of governing a complex society necessarily
includes a great deal of guess work as to "facts" and "merits." In
a democratic, pluralistic society the process must therefore include a great many compromises between those who see the facts
and the merits differently. Government consists of a web of compromises that are intended to do no more than achieve a rough
balance between opposing interests.

If the opposing interests can themselves come to an agreement,
this usually represents as good a guess as to where "merit" lies as
if the legislature had made the decision.[37] In this connection it is
worth noting that the states with the most effective councils
avoided the violent swings in legislation, accompanied by embittered relations between labor and management, that marked some
other states.[38]

[35] For a statement to this effect by a California legislator, see p. 354.

[36] As, for example, the Wisconsin employer who gave as his first reason that "it was
the decent thing to do" (p. 82).

[37] On this point see Avery Leiserson, *Administrative Regulation* (Chicago: University of Chicago Press, 1942), pp. 173–74; also see Donald C. Blaisdell's bibliographi-
cal note in his *American Democracy under Pressure* (New York: Ronald Press Co.,
1957), p. 311, n. 11.

[38] For example, Michigan (1947) and New York (1951).

As a matter of fact, the legislature typically made a less thorough and dispassionate search for the facts than did the advisory council. When the legislature came to make a decision—for example, on what the level of benefits ought to be—it was very likely to follow the simple procedure of selecting a figure somewhere between the demands of the two parties, or one where the political pressures seemed to be equal.[39] Often, also, the legislature used the simple norm of what other states were doing.[40] When, on occasion, the legislature did plunge into the technical aspects of the problems before it, it relied largely on the administrator of the agency and on labor and management technicians—that is to say, on what is normally the core of an advisory council.

Fourthly, the "weakness" which is the concern of this objection is precisely the weakness of one party in the legislature, a condition which obviously would not be remedied by substituting a struggle in the legislature for an agreed bill. In the case of an agreed bill the weaker party *prefers* bargaining with its adversary to asking the legislature for a decision. Whether the preference is wise or not is the same problem as that posed by objection No. 2.

Sometimes the legislature put pressure on the contending parties to arrive at an agreement.[41] Whether such legislative insistence on agreement hurt or helped the weaker party depended upon circumstances. If no legislation at that time represented a victory for the weaker party, then the legislature's action favored the weaker party, since it gave, in effect, the power of veto to the weaker party. The opposite was the case when the *status quo* was preferred by the stronger party.

5. *Diminishes the Competence of Government.* If an advisory council regularly produces an agreed bill, the legislature comes

[39] I was in the office of the executive secretary of an employer organization in one large state when he received a telephone call from the chairman of the legislative committee that handled unemployment compensation bills. The legislator wanted to know, confidentially, what increase in the benefit amount employers would accept without feeling too aggrieved. This information would be the chairman's main guide. The executive secretary was not on this state's advisory council, which was active but not very influential.

[40] Logically, this could be a case of the blind leading the blind, but it is a very common practice.

[41] See, for example, California (pp. 352, 353), Illinois (pp. 156, 158), Utah (p. 125). See also the procedure of the Ives Committee in New York (p. 189).

to rely on the council to such an extent that it does not develop competence of its own. When the legislative committee charged with unemployment compensation is not forced to make the actual decisions in that program, it neglects to give to the program the clock-hours of study necessary to understand it. Eventually the legislature comes to lack the normal handful of legislators who understand at least the essentials of unemployment compensation. Likewise the administrator of the program, relieved of the responsibility for many difficult decisions, especially in the field of "administrative law," abdicates his proper position of informed leadership. So runs the objection as put by students of government.

This danger seems to have remained only a danger. In states which had a tradition of agreed bills neither the legislature nor the administrator showed less activity or competence than in other states. Vigorous (not to use a stronger word) debates continued to mark the passage of unemployment compensation bills in the legislatures of such states as Illinois, New Hampshire, and Wisconsin. In none of the states which had a tradition of agreed bills was the administrator a weak man, anxious to dodge responsibilities. On the contrary, these administrators ranked among the most active and influential in the country. Advisory-council agreed bills did not make weak administrators, but came from strong ones.

6. Isolates Unemployment Compensation. This objection states that a tradition of agreed bills builds a wall around the unemployment compensation program and isolates it from the rest of the areas for which government is responsible. Within this protecting wall decisions affecting unemployment compensation are made with a view to the interests of that program alone, independently of what might be the competing needs of others interests. Since the interests of all the parts converge only at the political level, to allow independent decisions to be made below this level is to invite uneven and inequitable development of the various parts. A part can grow at the expense of the whole. Furthermore, within its protecting wall unemployment compensation escapes from its share of the cost of politics. Political life requires the machinery of political parties, and each part of the political whole must expect to bear its share of the costs of that machinery. Unemployment compensation must be willing to provide its share of patronage jobs and must on occasion be willing to modify its aims sufficiently to fit them into a platform on which the party can win an election. The agreed bill of the advisory council has the effect of freeing unemployment compensation from these two political "taxes," especially from the second.

This objection is closely linked with the three previous ones (Nos. 3, 4, 5). Together they amount to a protest against removing unemployment compensation from the political process. But this is a matter of degree, and in point of fact, unemployment compensation was not completely isolated from the political process. The representatives of labor and management who made the decisions regarding unemployment compensation were, generally, the same who made the decisions regarding other interests of labor and management. They themselves, therefore, took account of the importance of unemployment compensation relative to their other interests.[42] On occasion, also, they made concessions to the needs of the political party within which they chiefly worked.[43] Besides, as pointed out before, it is not true (as seems to be implied by this objection) that the decision of the legislature is always more general and more adjusted to the requirements of the universal good than is that of the administrator and his advisory council.[44]

The phraseology of most state laws contains a kind of denial of the validity of this objection. In describing the function of an advisory council the laws typically speak of "assuring impartiality and freedom from political influence." Although in none of the laws is the phrase "political influence" explained, it clearly implies some degree of isolation from what is ordinarily understood as politics (the winning and the keeping of public office). The problem of how much politics to have in unemployment compensation is similar to the problem of how much competition to have

[42] See, for example, Nebraska (p. 257), New Hampshire (p. 96), Pennsylvania (pp. 303–4). There were other instances, not narrated in the text.

[43] Employers in New York, for example, felt obliged to make concessions to labor in order to help Dewey win for the Republican Party in New York and nationally.

[44] See p. 46.

in the economy. It is possible to have too much and too little. But in this case the danger of an excess is almost certainly greater than the danger of a deficiency. Politics is not an end, but only a means to an end. While the cost of politics is a necessary cost, it should, like all costs, be kept to a minimum.

7. *Invites Collusion.* The device of the agreed bill is an invitation to collusion. By means of it labor and management can make agreements for their own gain at the expense of others. Collusion may take various forms. It may simply be an agreement to raise benefits "unduly" and pass the costs along to the public in the form of higher prices. Or it may take the form of the labor representative selling out to management and not pressing for sufficiently high benefits. Or it may follow more complicated patterns. The following two examples, actually encountered in the survey, are only two of many possible forms.

(1) A union persuaded an employer to change two weeks of vacation to one week of vacation and one week of layoff, with double pay during the week labeled vacation. During the other week the employees drew unemployment benefits. The arrangement entailed no additional expense for the employer because he was already paying the maximum unemployment insurance tax rate. (2) After a four-week strike against a large bakery chain the union and the employer reached a settlement which included a promise by the employer not to dispute the payment of unemployment benefits during the first two weeks of the strike, which would be called a period of layoff. Again the employer was one who would not suffer financially by the arrangement.

The danger of collusion by an advisory council is negligible. In the first place, the government is at hand to regulate any possible collusive agreements. An advisory council is only advisory. It has no authority. It is not an administrative board. Its agreed bill does not automatically become law but must pass the scrutiny of the legislature, and the legislature has the administrator available as an independent source of advice. Where the advisory council has public members, these also serve as a check on any collusive agreements.

In the second place, government can depend on the self-regulation of adversary interests. In many activities which government regulates there is only one organized interest—such as the railroads, the investment companies, the military service—but in industrial relations there are two well-organized adversary interests, labor and management.

As a matter of fact, in unemployment insurance there are adversary interests within as well as between labor and management organizations. For example, at one council meeting the representative of a miners' union strongly reprimanded the representative of another union because certain collusive practices of the latter union were draining the fund, which was already weak and which might not be adequate to protect the miners, among whom there was a great deal of unemployment. More often it was an employer who objected to a collusive practice. Since each employer's tax rate is determined not only by his own experience but also by the general level of the state fund, an employer whose tax rate was less than the maximum—and this included the great majority of employers—refused to countenance any practice which, even though it did not directly affect his own experience rate, tended to lower the general fund. It should be noted that in the two examples of collusion given above the collusion was between an individual employer and a particular union. This represents an entirely different situation than collusion between members of an advisory council. There were no cases of collusion by an entire advisory council, and it is most unlikely that there will ever be any.

8. Impedes Final Settlement. The objection is sometimes raised that an advisory council tends to impede the final settlement of the differences between labor and management because it formalizes the process of negotiation.[45] The appointment of an official advisory council focuses public attention upon the members of the council. The labor and management members must negotiate in the full light of this attention and as a result tend to adopt positions of "principle" from which they find it difficult to recede for the sake of bargaining.

[45] This is probably one reason that the reorganized (1955) California advisory council was limited by law to administrative matters.

Experience indicates that this is an objection not against advisory councils, as such, but rather against certain procedures an advisory council might use. Some difficulty, in some councils, was experienced because the council allowed its negotiations to become too public too early. Sometimes this was the fault of the agency, sometimes the fault of the council members.[46] But the difficulty is not inherent in the use of the advisory council, as is amply proved by the success of such councils as those of Illinois, New Hampshire, Utah, and Wisconsin. No state which was free of the "impediment" of an advisory council managed to bring labor and management together in an agreement as often as these states did by means of a council.

9. Invites Meddling. It is possible for an advisory council to be too active. An advisory council is not intended to take the place of the administrator. There is, therefore, a line beyond which advisory councils may not properly go in attempting to influence the administrator of a program. The line cannot be drawn with exactness, and it will vary with the personal relationships that exist between the administrator and the council.

The fear that a council would meddle seems certainly to have been one of the reasons that administrators have not made more use of advisory councils. But experience thus far indicates that the fear does not have a solid foundation. Among the states of the sample only three administrators criticized their advisory councils for meddling, and in only one case was the dissatisfaction expressed acute. The criticism was not voiced in any of the states which had the most active and effective councils.

10. Time Consuming. An advisory council can consume a significant amount of time on the part of the administrator and his staff. The objection states that the amount of time involved is excessive. This was the objection that was voiced most frequently by administrators. If it was not just a rationalization of the desire to be free of council influence (in which case it was simply another form of objection No. 9) it was the chief reason why more administrators were not more interested in advisory councils.

The meaning of the objection obviously depends on the norm

[46] See New York, p. 178, n. 5; and Rhode Island, pp. 285–86.

of worth-whileness which the objector has in mind when he says that the accomplishments of a council are not worth the time they involve. He may mean that even the most effective councils are not worth while. In that case the objection amounts to a denial of the entire thesis of this study—of the theoretical arguments developed in Chapters 1 and 2 and of the supporting materials supplied in the rest of the work—and there is nothing more to be said.

Or, the objector may grant the worth-whileness of only the most effective councils—those that produced agreed bills—and deny the worth-whileness of all less effective councils, even active ones like those of Massachusetts, Michigan, New York, Ohio, Rhode Island. . . . One answer is that there was no sentiment for abandoning the council even in the states with the less effective councils. Both the government and the governed were convinced on the basis of their experience that the advantages of the councils outweighed any disadvantages associated with them. Another answer is that the less effective councils might be made more effective by putting into practice some of the recommendations offered in the following chapters.

SUMMARY

While it cannot properly be claimed for any advisory council that it was strictly necessary, it can safely be said of nearly all of them that they were worth while; and although it must be admitted that effective councils are not easy to achieve, it is safe to say that they are possible.

Not Necessary. Advisory councils are not strictly necessary for either economic or political democracy. That they are not necessary for economic democracy follows from the fact that although employment security has had to get along without the aid of effective advisory councils in most of the states, the program has developed in a reasonably satisfactory way. Certainly its condition is not such as to constitute an emergency or to call for an investigation. It follows also from the fact that there are no notable substantive differences between the states which had and those which did not have effective councils.

Neither are advisory councils strictly necessary for political democracy. All that is strictly necessary is that private groups exist and be active, that their representatives have the requisite expertise, and that government give due consideration to what these representatives have to say. All these conditions have been regularly fulfilled even in the states which have not had an effective advisory council.

But Desirable. But the private groups are more likely to be active, their representatives are more likely to be expert, and government is more likely to give them due consideration if they are represented on a formal advisory body. The findings of the investigation clearly support that conclusion. Most important of all, the findings definitely support the conclusion that when the groups are members of a formal advisory council they are likely to perform their representative functions in a more responsible fashion.

Difficult. Peak council effectiveness is achieved in the fashioning of agreed bills. Since relatively few of the councils (less than half a dozen) produced agreed bills with any regularity, this peak of effectiveness is obviously very difficult to attain.

Although most councils achieved a moderate level of effectiveness, the details of their experiences show that even this level was not easily maintained. Since the sample councils were chosen because they seemed to be the most successful ones, it is probable that the other councils in the country resemble the less successful councils in the sample more closely than they do the more successful ones. Advisory councils seem to be like rosebushes—subject to a large number of debilitating diseases and needing unremitting and skillful care to preserve them in health.

But Possible. Since some councils achieved an impressive record of effectiveness, there is no doubt that councils *can* be effective. Although relatively few of the councils achieved the peak of effectiveness represented by agreed bills, nearly all achieved a moderate level of effectiveness which both the governed and the government considered worth the effort expended. Only a couple of councils, and those only for limited periods, seemed scarcely worth the work put into them.

Some of the circumstances which limited the effectiveness of the councils were external and largely uncontrollable (Chapter 20);

some were internal and largely controllable (Chapter 21). In no
state were the external, uncontrollable limitations absolutely determining.[47] A very low level of council effectiveness was caused
in every case by factors which were and are controllable. The
optimistic conclusion seems justified that reasonably effective
councils are possible if they make use of the lessons of experience
and follow principles which have been established as successful.
The following two chapters distill some of the more important of
these lessons of successful experience.

[47] See Ch. 20, p. 436.

20

EXTERNAL FACTORS OF EFFECTIVENESS

THE preceding chapter reviewed the "what" of council experience. This chapter and the next analyze the "why" of that experience in order to identify the factors of effectiveness in the past and make recommendations for greater effectiveness in the future. The factors of effectiveness fall into two main categories, those external and those internal to the council. This chapter deals with the external factors, of which some were general—that is, were nation-wide in scope and affected nearly all the councils—and some were particular—that is, affected only particular councils.

GENERAL FACTORS

The operation of the general factors can best be seen by considering them chronologically, according as they operated before and after the war.

Conditions before the war made it easier for councils to be effective: opportunities were greater and competition was less. As a result, some councils were very effective before the war which were less so after. This was the case, for example, in Utah, New York, Massachusetts, Connecticut, Ohio, and Minnesota.[1] Opportunities were greater in the sense that there were more things to be done, especially more precedent-making decisions to be made. Competition was less in the sense that there were fewer persons with competence in the program, and those few were likely to be

[1] The Missouri council (not treated in the text) was very active and effective in the period 1937–1939 but almost ceased to exist thereafter.

on the advisory council, which was usually composed of the persons who had been most active in bringing the law into existence.

Another condition that contributed to the effectiveness of the early councils was the New Deal, which was in full tide during the prewar period. The New Deal brought the program of unemployment insurance into existence and for some years continued to sweep the program along in the direction of greater liberality. Employer representatives on the council, recognizing the necessity of making concessions, more easily reached agreed bills. The sweep of the social tide made it easier for public members, also, to contribute more to council effectiveness; in that period, when a public member was technically competent he could be very influential.[2]

In the postwar period different conditions prevailed. Opportunities were fewer and competition was greater. The program was well established, and so there was less to do; the state agencies had become more experienced, and they were therefore less inclined to call on the council for help in what there was to do. Both labor and management were better organized in relation to unemployment compensation than they had been in the 1930's, and their decision makers not only were more technically competent but also were more sharply identified. As a result, whenever these decision makers were not on the council, the council faced formidable competition for leadership, and whether they were on the council or not, the public members of the council generally experienced a loss of influence to these labor and management leaders.

By the end of the war the sweep of the New Deal had slackened and an undercurrent of conservatism set in. The Taft-Hartley Act became federal law, and eighteen state legislatures enacted right-to-work laws. The impact of this conservative swing was intensified in the unemployment insurance program by the charges of abuse which marked the payment of benefits during the reconversion period.[3] Employers demanded a tightening of both eligibility and disqualification provisions. They also demanded the

[2] As were, for example, the first chairmen of the Connecticut and New York councils, and the early chairmen of the Massachusetts, Ohio, and Minnesota councils.

[3] See Joseph M. Becker, *The Problem of Abuse in Unemployment Benefits* (New York: Columbia University Press, 1953), Ch. 2.

kind of experience-rating system which would most effectively enlist the employer as a policing agent. But labor leaders would have found it politically impossible to make such concessions to employers, even were they inclined to do so. This situation constituted a major obstacle to the reaching of agreed bills.

Postwar developments created other obstacles, among them changes in the employer power pattern. An increase in the influence of state chambers of commerce relative to state associations of manufacturers was one such change. Another was the growth of new industries, like aircraft, during the war. Both had the effect, in some states, of making the "old" employer members on the council less representative than they had been under the former power pattern. The effect was clearly manifested in the postwar experiences of the councils of Utah, Illinois, New York, California, and Massachusetts. In some states these "old" employer representatives were further discredited in the eyes of their fellow employers by their connection with the prewar pattern of concessions to labor.

Other postwar developments which hindered agreed bills occurred on labor's side. One was the increased recognition accorded to the CIO in state labor circles as the CIO rid itself of its Communist taint and the AFL resigned itself to the CIO's permanent existence. As was pointed out before, the CIO is less inclined than the AFL to see possibilities in the agreed bill technique. This development had a measurable impact on the unemployment insurance program, however, in only a few states.[4] A more important development was the trend in the AFL toward relinquishing some degree of its former reliance on economic means in favor of a greater reliance on political means.[5] The general effect was to emphasize lobbying in the legislature over bargaining in the advisory council.

PARTICULAR FACTORS

Some factors were particular in the sense that they were less general in scope and affected some councils much more than

[4] For example, in Illinois, New York, Ohio, Michigan.
[5] There was also an observable trend in labor as a whole toward identifying political

others. These factors can be classified roughly as economic and political.

ECONOMIC FACTORS

By far the most important economic factor was the level of unemployment. Councils in states which had a low unemployment rate and therefore low costs for unemployment benefits found it easier to reach agreed bills. They could work out bills that gave something to both labor and management—higher benefits to the one and lower (or at least not higher) taxes to the other. Of the four most effective councils only New Hampshire had an average tax rate higher than the national average, and it was not greatly higher. Generally speaking, councils in states which had a very high level of unemployment and were under pressure to restrict the program found it extremely difficult to arrive at agreed bills. Rhode Island is the outstanding example of a council laboring under such a difficulty. The New Hampshire experience, however, serves as a reminder that a moderately high level of unemployment is no insuperable obstacle to agreed bills.[6]

Another important factor was the general tenor of labor-management relations in a given state. A tradition of good relations was favorable to council effectiveness and increased the likelihood of agreed bills. Where the tradition was one of bitterness and conflict, the council was almost certain to be affected by the general atmosphere and to be less effective. This is one of the reasons that the councils of Wisconsin and Michigan, although so close to each other geographically and almost identical in council structure, differed greatly in effectiveness.[7]

---

means with the Democratic Party and substituting an alliance with that party for the former policy of supporting political friends and opposing political enemies in all parties.

[6] California, with an average unemployment rate nearly as high as New Hampshire's, came very close to an agreed bill in 1951.

[7] A Wisconsin-Michigan contrast is a good way to see a number of factors at work.

Factor	Wisconsin	Michigan
Unemployment	Low	High
Size of state	Small	Large
Dominant labor organization	AFL	CIO
"Abuses" during reconversion	Below average	Above average
Postwar conservative swing	Moderate	Strong

A closely related factor was the practice whereby labor and management lobbyists talked matters over outside the legislature and attempted to arrive at some understanding among themselves. Where this practice prevailed in most matters affecting labor and management, it tended to carry over into unemployment insurance and to influence procedure in the advisory council. The practice varied considerably from state to state. It was much less common in Ohio and Pennsylvania, for example, than in New Hampshire and Illinois. It was also much less common among the CIO lobbyists than among the AFL lobbyists—to some extent because the CIO did not care to have such relationships but more because the employer lobbyists preferred to work with the AFL lobbyists.

Still another factor in council effectiveness was the degree of organization among labor and management groups. To the extent that labor and management were organized with respect to unemployment insurance, their representatives could speak authoritatively for the respective groups and commit them to bargains made in the advisory council. An agreed bill was influential with the legislature only if its negotiators represented substantially all of labor and management, and this in turn depended on the extent to which labor and management were organized in relation to this program.

The problem of organization was typically more difficult for management than for labor. Employers are by the nature of a free-enterprise economy more inclined to work as individuals and to be in competition with one another.[8] Most of the issues that divided employers were economic. Employers with high unemployment and those with low had different preferences with regard to both tax and benefit provisions in unemployment insurance.[9] High-cost employers wanted a tax system that would have a maximum pooling effect; low-cost employers wanted a system that would make each employer stand his own cost. High-cost employers in seasonal industries tended to favor lower eligibility condi-

[8] The statement was made several times, by owners of individual firms as well as by professional representatives of employer organizations, that employers spent much more of their resources fighting each other than fighting either labor or government.

[9] For examples, see Utah, New York, Pennsylvania, California, and others.

tions if the tax system was a pooled one, but stiffer eligibility
conditions if they had to meet their own costs. Some of these
economic differences were reflected in differences between employer organizations. Thus there were at times serious differences
of view between the state associations of manufacturers and the
state chambers of commerce.[10]

A result of employer individualism was that employer organizations were less tightly organized—as compared with labor organizations—and had less control over their members. This in turn
meant that employer representatives on a council were generally
less able than labor representatives to negotiate "with power" and
to commit their groups. The difficulty of committing employers
to a given policy is underlined by the several instances of employer repudiations of agreements made by their representatives.[11]

Despite the difficulties in their way, employer organizations
have grown in size and effectiveness. They had to grow—not only
because of the increasing complexity of the economy, but also
because of the growth in governmental and labor organizations.
The most common form of employer organization was the social
security committee—one in the state manufacturers' association
and another in the state chamber of commerce.[12] Illinois had the
most elaborate overall organization, Utah the simplest, and Michigan the most compact.[13] Michigan may have set the style for the
rather similar overall organizations of Massachusetts and New
York.[14]

Labor experienced somewhat less difficulty than management
in achieving adequate organization. The very nature of a labor
union favors oneness of action; its strength lies in the close union
of its many but individually weak members. As compared with

[10] See Illinois, for example (p. 152). A striking instance of this difference occurred
in Missouri in the 1955 legislative session. A major group of employers under the
leadership of the Associated Industries of Missouri came to agreement with labor on
a bill and it passed both houses; then the Missouri State Chamber of Commerce
went to the governor and persuaded him to veto it.

[11] Examples: Illinois (1937, 1949, 1951), Nebraska (1947), New York (1940, 1950),
Rhode Island (1950), California (1953), Federal Advisory Council (1950).

[12] Although the latter usually antedated the former, it was usually less influential.
In a few states, however, the committee of the chamber of commerce was equally
influential with that of the manufacturers' association.

[13] See pp. 144–46, 138–39, and 326–27.   [14] See pp. 222 and 205, n. 53.

the members of employer organizations, workers were more under the control of their officers, with the result that the officers of the state labor organizations could set policy with less fear that they would encounter influential labor opposition when they appeared at legislative hearings to state what "labor" wanted.

This is not to say that the labor representatives on the advisory council could always speak with assurance for their constituents or commit them firmly to an agreed bill.[15] Labor also had its organizational difficulties. Different sections of labor assigned different values to various unemployment insurance provisions. Faced with the choice, for example, of retaining low eligibility requirements or increasing the benefit amount, unions in seasonal industries chose the first and unions with steadier employment chose the other.[16] Between the AFL and the CIO there ran a regular pattern of differences. Where the AFL, for example, tended to emphasize the extension of coverage to small firms, the CIO was relatively unconcerned about this objective (although favoring it) because nearly all its members worked in large firms. Again, where the AFL deemphasized and sometimes even opposed special benefits for workers with families (because this might obscure the concept of wages as earned income, a main guidepost for traditional AFL policy) the CIO stressed this goal. Finally, where the AFL tended to emphasize the use of economic over political means, the CIO was characterized by the opposite emphasis. This last difference was most manifest in states where old-time leaders of the AFL were still in command; it became less distinct in the postwar period, as the AFL moved toward the CIO position. The difference was always subject, of course, to the variations of local personalities and local circumstances. In New Hampshire, for example, there were two factions within the AFL and two within the CIO divided on the issue of the agreed bill technique. The same was true in Colorado for a time. In Wisconsin there seemed to be a difference between the "intellectual"

[15] Examples of labor retractions or repudiations of agreements are to be found in the experiences of Wisconsin (1949, 1951), Illinois (1955), Rhode Island (1950), Pennsylvania (1953).

[16] For example, Nebraska (1955), Rhode Island (1950), California (1953), among others.

and "worker" types of CIO representatives in their attitude toward the agreed bill.[17]

State labor organizations varied in the degree of freedom which they granted to their representatives on the advisory council to negotiate agreed bills. Some organizations followed a policy of instruction, others a policy of discretion. In some states the labor members of the council were bound, or were supposed to be bound, by the resolutions passed in convention. In other states the convention either did not pass specific resolutions pertaining to a program like employment security in which an advisory council was operative, or the convention agreed that its legislative representatives could modify the convention demands according to the exigencies of the bargaining situation as it developed. There has been a general trend toward delegation of more discretion.[18] The CIO has been less inclined than the AFL to grant discretion to its representatives on the advisory council, perhaps because of the CIO preference for "principle" over compromise. The merger between the AFL and the CIO on the state level will presumably remove or lessen this and other organizational differences in the future.

It is noteworthy that of the four most effective councils—in Wisconsin, Utah, New Hampshire, Illinois—three were in small states.[19] It may be that in a small state the solution of labor-management problems is less difficult. In a small state the leaders of labor and management not only know each other better through direct, personal dealings, but because their organizations are smaller and tighter, they can more easily commit their respective groups to an agreed bill.

POLITICAL FACTORS

The effectiveness of advisory councils was partly determined by political factors, executive and legislative. On the executive side

[17] See p. 72, n. 15.

[18] In 1953, for example, both the Colorado and the California state federations of labor granted their representatives more freedom in exercising discretion.

[19] If Nebraska is included in this group, because of its numerous agreed bills, the proportion is four out of five.

both the governor and the administrator always could and usually did exert a decisive influence on the council. Where the governor worked as a mediator to bring about agreement between labor and management, the council was likely to be more successful in achieving an agreed bill than in states where the governor did not make such efforts.[20] Where the governor did not want an advisory council, the council worked under a great disadvantage or even ceased to exist.[21] Sometimes the governor made appointments for political reasons rather than to build a more effective council.[22] Political appointments of this sort were particularly harmful to the council when the governor's party was not the controlling party in the legislature. Then the advice of the council carried very little weight with the legislature.

The administrator of the employment security agency was a uniquely important factor. No council was better than the administrator.[23] In all the states which had the more effective councils, the administrator was an outstanding personality. He possessed technical competence and experience;[24] he also possessed a reputation for impartiality;[25] but principally he possessed the subtle but unmistakable quality of leadership by virtue of which he could make the council members proud, or at least willing, to work with him. When an administrator had these qualities, he was always the most important external factor.[26]

[20] Illinois exemplifies the first situation, Ohio the second.

[21] For example, in Pennsylvania. The same situation prevailed in Missouri for many years.

[22] See, for example, New York (p. 208) and Connecticut (p. 232).

[23] There was only one temporary exception to this general proposition, and it occurred in an unusual set of circumstances: the administrator was an incompetent political appointee; the council was well established before his appointment; the council's constitution allowed it to run independently of the administrator and still have an adequate supply of technical help.

[24] In the case of the New Hampshire council the administrator at first lacked experience but quickly gained it and in the meantime had the help of a very competent director of the unemployment compensation division of the agency.

[25] When he did not, as was the case for a time in Utah, Massachusetts, and Michigan, the effectiveness of the council was clearly impaired.

[26] Is the administrator properly classed as a factor external to the council? Although the distinction between the council and the administrator is real enough (as some councils proved by meeting independently of the administrator), still the administrator is normally so close to the council in all its operations that he is almost as much an internal factor as the council members themselves. Perhaps the administrator should be thought of as belonging to both sets of factors.

Where the employment security agency was headed by a commission, an advisory council was less likely to be effective or even to exist because the commission considered itself able to perform all the functions of an advisory council.[27] In the case of Michigan, however, the advisory council was as strong as the commission.

Political factors of a legislative nature also affected council effectiveness. Where a legislative committee showed as much initiative as did the Ives and Hughes committees in New York, the influence of a council as a council was likely to be less. In New York both labor and management tended to regard the legislative committee rather than the advisory council as the place where they would finally settle their differences. Where, on the contrary, a legislative committee almost insisted that labor and management go off by themselves and reach an agreement, the negotiations between labor and management on the council tended to take on more importance.[28]

The negotiations between labor and management on the council were affected by the relative power of these groups in the legislature. There was, however, no simple correlation between their relative power in the legislature and the likelihood of their negotiating an agreement on the council. They might reach agreement in a very unbalanced situation—like that of Nebraska—because labor thought it could not get less from management than from an unsympathetic legislature; or in a more balanced situation—like that of Illinois—because both sides were uncertain of the outcome of a legislative struggle and preferred to keep control within the council. In general, however, situations of more balanced power were conducive to greater council vigor. The very existence of two powerful groups, with the implied danger of conflict, stimulated council activity.

In some states to get a bill passed it was necessary to secure the affirmative vote of the majority of all, not merely the voting, legislators. In such states it was much easier to block legislation than to enact it. This was a political factor favoring agreed bills, since

---

[27] See, for example, Massachusetts (p. 210), Rhode Island (p. 279), and California (p. 344).
[28] As, for example, in Utah and Illinois.

there were times when the only way to secure the enactment of any legislation was to win the support of both parties.

One political factor that cannot strictly be classified as either executive or legislative but cuts across both is of unique importance. It is simply this: Unemployment compensation is a program of government, and a failure by labor and management to reach agreement in the advisory council results not in a strike and a stalemate but in compulsory arbitration by government. But when compulsory arbitration stands ready as an alternative to agreement, voluntary agreement is thereby inhibited.[29] Since the agreed bill is the advisory council's most effective tool, this obstacle to agreement is always potentially a serious limitation on council effectiveness.

There is a final factor which is not exclusively economic or political but partakes of the nature of both. The tendency toward specialization which is inherent in modern, complex society worked in the councils' favor. In unemployment insurance a relatively small group of specialists inside and outside of government normally determined the course of the program, and having once become a member of that small group a council grew more effective the longer it continued in operation. The council became one of the few repositories of knowledge and experience and therefore one of the few working parts in a specialized arrangement. The working parts were four in number: the agency (by definition specialized) and the specialized representatives respectively of labor, management, and the legislature. These four small groups developed relationships of mutual reliance. Any one of the four was reluctant to cooperate with an "outsider" against the wishes of the other three, because each realized that the other three must be its normal working partners and that it would need their cooperation on other occasions. Inevitably labor and management leaders outside the council found it a practical necessity to work through their representatives on the council. If they tried to work independently and introduced bills of their own in the

[29] This is the general, though not universal, opinion of those who have had extensive experience in the field of labor-management relations. See R. W. Fleming, "The Search for a Formula," in *Emergency Disputes and National Policy*, eds. I. Bernstein, H. Enarson, and R. Fleming (New York: Harper & Brothers, 1955), pp. 207–17.

legislature, the bills went to the customary committee chairmen, who in turn went to their customary working partners—the agency and the labor and management members of the advisory council. The pattern of a regular working arrangement is a powerful force in a specialized society.

SUMMARY

External circumstances, which are largely uncontrollable, could diminish council effectiveness, but not to the point where the council was useless. There were instances of councils achieving moderate and even high levels of effectiveness despite every kind of unfavorable external circumstance: a higher-than-average rate of unemployment, a history of embittered industrial relations, factions within labor and management organizations, anti-union prejudice in the state, even a hostile administrator. Hence it cannot be said of any single external factor (as it can of some internal factors) that it is universally necessary. All the external factors together, however, are highly important. Unless most of them are favorable, a council is very unlikely to function at the highest level of effectiveness and may fail to achieve even moderate effectiveness.

The ideal situation, in which all major external factors favored the council, would look like this: (1) There is a low unemployment rate. (2) Labor and management are sufficiently well organized to permit their representatives on the council to speak authoritatively in the name of all covered employers and employees in the state. (3) There is a general tradition of good labor-management relations. (4) Political power is about equally divided between labor and management. (5) The governor and the legislature are favorable to agreed bills, almost to the point of insistence on them. (6) The traditional AFL philosophy is dominant in state labor circles.—The listing is roughly in the order of decreasing importance.

21

INTERNAL FACTORS OF EFFECTIVENESS

INTERNAL factors of effectiveness are identical with what were called council methods in Chapter 2. Internal factors comprise council structure and council procedures—the council sitting and the council on the wing. Eight factors of structure and seven of procedures are selected for discussion here. With respect to each factor a choice must be made among alternatives, some of which were indicated in Chapter 2. This chapter, basing its recommendations on the experience of the sample councils, offers guidance for choosing among the alternatives.

STRUCTURE
MEMBERSHIP

A council member in one of the states was a professor of government. While being interviewed he discoursed at length on what he called the four essential requirements of a successful advisory council. When he had finished, the interviewer said to him, "As you were talking, Professor, I was checking your four requirements against councils that I have seen in action, and I could think of two of them that have all four requirements, but are not at all effective, and two others that have none of the four, but are very effective." After a moment of silence, the professor nodded and said, "Well, I suppose it really all depends on who is on the council."

And he was correct. Experience has shown that the factor which chiefly determines a council's effectiveness is the quality of its membership. A council with the right members can be effective even in unfavorable circumstances, while a council without the right members cannot be effective in any circumstances.

Labor and Management Members

The right members are primarily the right labor and management members. The above proposition can be restated more exactly to read: A council with the right labor and management members has the possibility of being effective no matter how unfavorable all other factors are, but a council without the right labor and management members cannot be effective no matter how favorable all other factors are. The right labor and management members are those who are capable and reasonable. The first is an essential characteristic, the second is nearly so.

The capable labor and management members are those who can make effective decisions. In every state there was a small group of persons who were the decision makers in the program. In addition to the administrator and a couple of legislators, this small group normally comprised two or three labor representatives and an equal or slightly larger number of management representatives. In some cases the effective decision was made actually if not formally by a single individual on each side.[1] On extraordinary occasions others might enter the decision-making group and even dominate it, but normally, year after year, the same group continued to make the decisions that determined the character of the program in any given state.

Although these decision makers were not a sufficient condition for peak effectiveness (Michigan, for example, had them as members and yet could not achieve agreed bills), they were clearly a necessary condition. No council which lacked them was highly effective. They were a necessary condition also for even moderate effectiveness. All the councils which had these decision makers were more effective than any of the councils which lacked them, and the councils which lacked them altogether were so ineffectual as to call into question the worth-whileness of a council's existence. The clearest finding of the whole study was the close cor-

---

[1] For example, in Illinois during the early years of the program. This is not a rare situation in labor-management relations. For years the final decisions in the coal industry, for example, were made by John L. Lewis and Harry Moses.

relation between the presence of the decision makers on a council and the degree of council effectiveness. It may be taken as a rule that an advisory council with decision makers, even working at its worst, is more effective than a council without them, even working at its best. The first step, therefore, toward making an advisory council effective is to put the decision makers on it. Their presence will not guarantee an effective council, but their absence rules out even the possibility of effectiveness.

The decision makers drew their authority from one or more of three sources. If an individual possessed all three, he was that much more valuable as a council member, but he needed to possess at least one.

The first and by far the most important source of authority was to represent a constituency. The council members who could speak officially for organized labor or management were by far the most important members. These were the persons who commanded the attention of the legislature, made the agreed bill a possibility, and in general constituted the council an important institution. The proposition restated above can be made even more exact by substituting for the phrase "right labor and management members" the phrase "representative labor and management members."

The second source of authority for council members was to have technical competence. The decisions which had to be made in the course of negotiations in unemployment insurance required considerable technical knowledge. The members who possessed this competence were very influential within the council. Even the "representative" members depended on them for guidance—unless of course the "representative" members were themselves technically competent.

Labor and management each needed to have at least one council member who possessed considerable technical competence. Labor occasionally lacked such a member. When this was the case the labor members of the council had to rely on the agency or on the public members for guidance.[2] Sometimes a large international was able to supply a state council with a technician drawn

---

[2] This sometimes put a strain on the agency's neutrality.

from its own staff—as the I.L.G.W.U. did for the New York council and the U.A.W. for the Michigan council. On management's side competent technicians were more plentiful. They came either from the staffs of the state-wide employer organizations or more often from the staffs of the larger firms. Some were former employees of the agency and completely at home in the program.

Occasionally the labor representatives were better equipped technically than the management representatives. This occurred when management was not allowed a voice in the selection of its representatives and the appointing authority chose "genuine employers," who were comparatively innocent of technical competence." [3] In several states the professional representatives of labor expressed a preference for having "genuine employers" on the council. This was probably just the converse of the preference sometimes expressed by employers for dealing with the "genuine employees" of their own plants rather than with the professional representatives of the international union. Amateurs at the art of negotiating are "easy pickings" when separated from their professional advisers.[4]

The third source of authority is that of the professional lobbyist. It combines some of the qualities of the other two sources but is sufficiently different from both to warrant separate treatment. It is a form both of technical competence and of representation, but in the area of politics. It is the competence and the representative character of one who, engaging directly and continuously in the political process, attends the legislative sessions and the hearings, keeps in contact with individual legislators and with other lobbyists, and builds a structure of mutual favors given and received.

This third source of authority must be clearly distinguished

---

[3] Neil W. Chamberlain notes how the same situation is sometimes encountered in industrial negotiations because the union representatives (the professional representatives of the international) are engaged in a "continuous performance," while many company representatives make only "one night stands." *Collective Bargaining* (New York: McGraw-Hill Book Co., Inc., 1951), p. 81.

[4] The reason for some repudiations of agreements made at council meetings was the lack of technical knowledge on the part of one or another of the parties to the agreement. See, for example, California (pp. 347–48), Pennsylvania (p. 302), Rhode Island (p. 284), Federal Advisory Council (pp. 375–76).

from that of politics as such. The competence spoken of here is the competence attaching to private persons in their capacity as representatives of private interests before the government. It is not the competence of professional politicians, who hold political office and work for political parties, nor even of private individuals with political "connections." An individual who is appointed to a council may also be a politician or have "connections," but that in itself does not qualify him for council membership, and may conceivably disqualify him.[5] The function of advisory councils is to supplement political action with private action. The councils cannot do that if they themselves become political.[6]

When the key lobbyists of labor and management were on the council the efficiency of the council was notably increased. The lobbyists were very useful in seeing through the legislature any agreed bill that was produced. Their presence on the council also increased the likelihood of an agreed bill in so far as it decreased the likelihood of divisions within the ranks of labor and management. When the lobbyists participated in forming the agreed bill, there was no danger that they would later introduce other and conflicting bills. Furthermore, the lobbyists were useful to the administrator in meeting whatever legislative emergencies arose between the meetings of the council. The emergency might consist of an attack on the advisory council's agreed bill or the introduction of other, conflicting bills which needed to be opposed promptly. In such emergencies lobbyist members of the council were useful to the administrator not only because they were on hand at the capital but also because they were freer than the administrator to buttonhole individual legislators and urge the position of the council. In some states the administrator was expected not to lobby, that is, not to take the initiative in urging his position on the individual legislators.

All three sources of authority should be found in the member-

[5] The worth of political connections depends on the particular party in power. When a change of governors occurred, council members with political connections sometimes became a liability to the council rather than a help. The professional lobbyist continues to have a function to perform no matter what party is in power.

[6] The councils are always in danger of becoming politicized. The danger was most marked in the case of the Massachusetts council, at least during some periods of its existence.

ship of the ideal council. If all three do not exist in each individual member, they should exist at least in all the members taken together. The ideal was approached very closely by the Wisconsin council throughout its life. The membership of the Wisconsin council as it stood in 1955 was typical. Its four management members included: the two chairmen of the respective social security committees in the Wisconsin Manufacturers Association and the Wisconsin Chamber of Commerce, of whom one was a very competent technician employed by the largest firm in the state; the full-time professional representative and lobbyist of the Wisconsin Manufacturers Association; and the owner of a small business, who was a former president of the Wisconsin Manufacturers Association. Its four labor representatives included: the president of the Wisconsin State Federation of Labor; the secretary of the largest city central in the state; the state president of a very large international union; and the regional representative of the state's largest CIO union. Two of these four were lobbyists, and one was a very competent technician.

Some would object to this description of the ideal council membership on two grounds: (1) It does not include rank-and-file representatives of labor,[7] and (2) it should not include the professional representatives of management.

Rank-and-file representatives of labor do not make effective council members. They possess none of the three sources of authority, and on the few councils where such representatives were members, they appeared lost and were certainly ineffectual. The function of an advisory council member is to represent others. Persons having the qualities fitting them to represent others prob-

[7] Professor Eveline Burns comments on the desirability of such representation in *National Policies for Education, Health, and Social Services*, ed. James E. Russell (Garden City, N.Y.: Doubleday & Co., Inc., 1955), p. 408. Two British authors, R. D. V. Roberts and H. Sallis, mention the expected advantages of having rank-and-file representatives on the advisory councils in the nationalized electricity supply industry of Great Britain: "Labor-Management Cooperative Committees in Britain's Electricity Supply Industry," *Industrial and Labor Relations Review*, XII (Oct., 1958), 91–92. But these rank-and-file representatives were *added* (in 1957) to previously existing (since 1949) and successfully functioning committees—whose functions, in any case, differ significantly from those of state advisory councils in employment security.

ably will not be merely rank-and-file employees; they will likely hold some office, either in their union or, as was the case with the two Wisconsin CIO workers, in the legislature. A council composed totally of rank-and-file employees (and, say, of the owners of small businesses) could function only as good pupils for their government teachers, good followers for their government leaders. Such a council, instead of limiting the sphere of political government, would extend it by giving it an added instrument through which to control its subjects. Such a council compared to the Wisconsin council would be like a company union compared to a genuine union.

The professional representatives of management do make effective council members and should be appointed to the council. To be fully effective a council must have either these professionals themselves or persons who are in contact with and can speak for these professionals, for they are always among the decision makers.

This answer runs counter to a widely held principle which was heard frequently in interviews with university professors, government administrators, and labor leaders. The principle states that the professional representative of an employer organization is too narrow in his viewpoint and too insecure in his position to be a suitable council member. His job depends on his being able to show his employers that he has saved them money, and this is the only norm he uses to come to his decisions. A man in his position cannot possibly exercise the broad statesmanship required for a public program.

This objection has some foundation in fact, but it does not lead to the conclusion that the professional representatives of employers should be excluded from the council. First of all, the objection applies equally to the professional representatives of labor. Holding elective office as they do, labor representatives are limited in their ability to practice broad statesmanship. In the course of this investigation several situations were encountered in which labor representatives were demanding what was not feasible or desirable at the time—as they admitted privately— because union politics left them no alternative. If the professional representatives of employers are properly excluded on these grounds, the professional representatives of labor should also be excluded—which is not only undesirable but impossible.

Secondly, the objection is not true universally of the professional representatives of either labor or management. Where an individual combined qualities of leadership with long tenure in his post, he acquired a strong, independent position in the organization he represented. He became something like the manager of a giant corporation who, in one sense a hired hand, is in another sense an industrial statesman. Individuals of this sort were encountered in the employ of both labor and management.[8]

Whether the preceding two considerations are valid or not, there is a third which is compelling. It is simply this: To be effective a council must have the decision makers among its members, and the professional representatives of employer organizations are always among the decision makers. Employer leadership in employment security is normally supplied by the full-time professional representatives of employer organizations, and it is futile to expect that other employers appointed to the council either will have the competence to oppose the regular employer leadership, or if they have the competence will be willing to exercise it at the cost of rejection by their own group.[9] It may be taken as a general principle that the state organizations of employers (and of labor [10]) should not be by-passed in the selection of council members.

The membership of more than half of the councils in the sample lacked the decision makers among either labor or management or both. The reason for the lack was either unwillingness on the part of the decision makers to serve on the council or, much more often, unwillingness on the part of the government to invite them to serve. In the few cases where decision makers were unwilling to serve, their reasons were one or more of the following:

[8] See n. 11.

[9] The situation in Illinois in 1951 was unusual and lasted for only the one legislative session.

[10] In several instances where the governor appointed other than the genuine leaders of labor organizations, the total effect of the maneuver was to render the council innocuous.

they were too busy; or they feared that the "public" responsibility of being a council member would hamper their freedom to fight; or the exigencies of union politics (in the case of the labor representative) dictated that the honor and remuneration connected with council membership be channeled by the decision maker to some individual other than himself.

More frequently the decision makers would have accepted an invitation to serve on the council but the invitation was not forthcoming. Sometimes the governor was the cause, sometimes the administrator. The governor had been offended by one or another of the decision makers, or he needed the council places to pay a political debt, or he was just cautious and did not like anybody of the opposite political party to hold even a semi-official position in his administration, or he simply rejected the whole idea of private participation in governmental decision making (the thesis developed in Chapters 1 and 2) and wanted a council—if there had to be one—only for the purpose of helping government carry out government's decisions. When it was the administrator who kept the decision makers off the council, it was usually for the last-named reason. Working on the theory that the administrator knows best, he chose his advisory council so as to exclude all potential troublemakers. The exclusions more often affected management, but in at least five of the sample councils labor was affected also.

In addition to being capable, an advisory council member ought to be reasonable. The experience of every council demonstrated that this was a distinct factor determining council effectiveness. Difficult to define, impossible to measure, the quality of reasonableness, or its contrary, was unmistakable in its impact. The early agreed bills of Illinois were attributable as much to the personalities of the two men who negotiated them as to anything else. New Hampshire's council would not have got off to such a good start, or got started at all, had it not been for two men, one an employer and one a union leader, who possessed "reasonable" personalities. In Utah there was a marked difference in "reasonableness" between the earlier and the later administrators of the program, between the CIO and the AFL leaders, and between

some employers and others.[11] In the course of making this study
I attended a number of council meetings in various states. Several
of these councils had members whose very manner, quite apart
from what they said, tended to arouse antagonism, even in an
observer. Such a personality was obviously a hindrance to arriving
at agreement.[12]

Edwin Witte called the attention of the Federal Advisory Council to the importance of this factor when he warned the antagonists against pushing through "legislation which the other side
violently objects to." [13] On some of the more successful state councils labor and management members explained that they tried to
avoid "ramming things down the other man's throat." As a
description of the spirit of reasonableness this homely phrase,
which recurred repeatedly, has a close affinity to Judge Hand's
more eloquent description of the spirit of liberty:

The spirit of liberty is the spirit which is not too sure that it is right;
the spirit of liberty is the spirit which seeks to understand the minds
of other men and women; the spirit of liberty is the spirit which
weighs their interests alongside its own without bias; the spirit of
liberty remembers that not even a sparrow falls to earth unheeded;
the spirit of liberty is the spirit of Him who, near two thousand years
ago, taught mankind that lesson it has never learned, but has never
quite forgotten; that there may be a kingdom where the least shall be
heard and considered side by side with the greatest.[14]

A search for the causes of the spirit of reasonableness would
take us into the depths of human nature and far beyond the
scope of this study; [15] but two incidental observations can be made
which are based on the findings of this investigation. First, in the
case of several employer members who unmistakably possessed

[11] For a reference to one eminently "reasonable" Utah employer representative, see
p. 118, n. 5.
[12] One council which I studied but did not include in this report had two employer
members who were both executive secretaries of employer organizations but whose
personalities in respect to reasonableness differed markedly. The difference in their
impact on the council, despite the similarity of their positions, was unmistakable.
[13] See p. 372.
[14] An address by Judge Learned Hand delivered in Central Park, New York, on
"I Am an American Day," May 21, 1944 (in *The Spirit of Liberty*, ed. Irving Dilliard
[New York: Alfred A. Knopf, 1952], p. 190). Quotation used by permission of Alfred
A. Knopf, Inc.
[15] The ultimate moral basis of the spirit is clear in Judge Hand's description.

this spirit, there was an early background of manual work and near-poverty. They themselves offered this as a reason for their sympathy with the aims of labor. Second, as mentioned in Chapter 19, there was evidence that the education conferred by the council had the effect of smoothing down the more extreme prejudices which some members on both sides brought to the council.

If advisory council members are reasonable as well as capable, the council will have a much better chance of operating effectively. On this point there can be no doubt. Nevertheless, if a choice has to be made between appointing a capable or a reasonable man, the choice must fall on the former.[16] There is at least the chance that the capable man can be educated out of his unreasonableness by the experience of council membership, but nothing can be done to make an effective member out of a man who is not capable, that is, who does not possess one of the three sources of authority. Appointment to an advisory council recognizes, but does little to confer, capability.

Public Members

In general the public members played a minor role on the advisory councils, and their influence was always less than that of labor and management. Nevertheless there were at least a few councils on which their influence was clearly significant. There were some influential public chairmen and a few influential public "politicians."

The chairman of the councils of Massachusetts, Connecticut, New York, New Hampshire, Pennsylvania, and Ohio all played active, influential parts at one time or another in the history of their respective councils. All but two of them were university professors, and all owed their influence primarily to the second source of authority, technical competence. The chairman of the New Hampshire council had, of course, a literally unique role to play, and his opportunity for influencing the program was greater than that of other public members on other councils. Some public members had influential political connections. They were per-

[16] Essentially this is the same choice that St. Teresa of Avila, mystic and efficient organizer, said she would make in the matter of spiritual directors, if she had to choose between a learned and a holy man.

sonal acquaintances of the governor, or they were active workers in his political party. On a few occasions they made use of their political connections,[17] but more often they did not.[18]

It is possible that public members exerted more influence than was immediately evident. They may have exerted a subtle kind of influence that was no less important for being difficult to prove.[19] Several administrators declared that the presence of public members on the council raised the level of discussion and sometimes saved it from degenerating into an interchange of personal insults. Further, the reaction of the public members to the respective demands of labor and management in the council meetings probably had some influence on the positions that labor and management took later before the legislative committee. That is, the "public" reaction presaged what the legislative reaction would be and influenced the strategy of the negotiators.

However, after all possible favorable allowances have been made, it seems correct to say that the influence of public members on the council was never decisive. Public members were never a necessary condition for council success, as were the labor and management members. It it significant that the most effective council, Wisconsin's, did not use public members at all; that New Hampshire used only one public member, a nonvoting chairman; that Utah negotiated its agreed bills outside the council at meetings attended only by labor and management members; and that Illinois actually, if not as formally, did much the same thing for many years.

To some extent the contribution of the public members was actually negative. That is, they hindered the council rather than helped. They did so in three principal ways.[20]

---

[17] See, for example, Illinois, p. 171.

[18] For the typical situation, see Nebraska, p. 258.

[19] This is one aspect of a more general situation. See, for example, Avery Leiserson, "Public Opinion as a Factor in Labor Disputes," *Annual Proceedings of the Industrial Relations Research Association*, December, 1952, pp. 26–33. In the discussion which followed Leiserson's paper, opinions advanced by experienced mediators ran from "very important factor" to "no strike was ever prevented because it was unpopular."

[20] They can be a hindrance in one additional way, which probably does not occur frequently enough to be of importance. The public members can be too aggressive. This occurred only once among the councils of the sample. The cure is for the public members to remember John R. Commons's principle, that decisions should be left to those who have to bear the results of their decisions (p. 441).

First of all, the presence of public members emphasized voting on the council and diverted the labor and management members from the important task of working out an agreement between themselves to the less meaningful task of trying to win the vote of the public members. In practice this was only a minor hindrance, because most of the time the labor and management members remained chiefly interested in each other.

Second, when the public members were less technically competent than the labor and management members—as was usually the case—they slowed progress. Discussion had to halt while their questions were answered, and explanations of technical points had to be given at greater length and in more elementary form than would have been the case if the public members had been absent. Sometimes they were ignorant, not only of the technicalities of unemployment compensation, but also of the procedures of collective bargaining. When such members awkwardly attempted to mediate between labor and management, they hindered more than they helped. I was present at one such bungling attempt during a council meeting. The council was beginning negotiations which it hoped would lead to an agreed bill. Labor and management had just presented to the council lengthy, detailed statements of the amendments they would like to see enacted. Mostly these were "asking prices" but they represented a great deal of previous technical work. At this point one of the public members, a woman, spoke up blithely: "Well, are only labor and management allowed to present suggestions for amendments? Aren't the public members going to do anything?"

There was a moment's complete silence. Then the chairman said: "Why, of course, the public members are welcome to submit suggestions for amendments. The council will gladly entertain whatever suggestions they have."

The lady member then turned to the other public members and said: "Well, come ahead then, public members, and let's make our suggestions."

Again there was a silence, longer than the first, and growing more embarrassed. The chairman finally broke it to say: "Well, in that case, we will go ahead and consider the recommendations made by the labor and management members." The lady evidently did not understand that proposals made at a council meeting were normally preceded by much work—technical and political—done outside the council meeting.

Third, since the size of the council must be limited for efficiency, the addition of public members deprives potential labor and management members of places on the council. Wisconsin was able to give four places each to labor and management and still not have an unduly large council because no council places were taken by public members. Ohio and Minnesota, on the other hand, had to limit labor and management to two places each because they gave so many places to the public.

The labor and management members generally did not speak favorably of the public members and many expressed a preference for a bipartite council. However, there were several exceptions to this generalization, Utah among them. The labor and management members of the Utah council spoke highly of their public members and were unanimous in favor of a tripartite council— the more so, perhaps, because the agency had devised a unique system whereby the public members, although present at most meetings, did not intrude on the critical negotiating sessions between labor and management.

Labor more often than management expressed a preference for having public members on the council, but further discussion always revealed that the preference was conditioned on having public members who would always vote with labor. The president of the state CIO in one large industrial state enunciated the above proposition and added that the ideal public panel would consist of a doctor, a clergyman, and a housewife. But when the interviewer asked: "Suppose there was a divided vote on the council, and the public members voted with labor against management, would that have an important influence on the legislature?" the interviewee responded: "No, it would have very little influence; probably none."

So many of the public members lacked influence because so many did not possess any of the three sources of authority. Normally public members were not lobbyists. Some had political connections, but that is not the same thing.[21] Obviously they did not

[21] See pp. 440–41.

represent labor or management constituencies. Occasionally they represented other constituencies—the Urban League or a women's club—but the interest of these constituencies in unemployment insurance was not active enough to endow their representatives on the council with importance, and it was a rare exception when a member was able to use such organizations to exert any direct influence on or through the council. Although some of the public members, chiefly university professors, were technically competent, the majority were not. Moreover, whatever competence they possessed, while useful to the council, was scarcely vital. The technical staff of the administrative agency, not to mention the labor and management members, provided all the technical assistance the council could use.

An additional, but less common, reason that public members lacked influence was that they did not always enjoy a reputation for impartiality. Public members were sometimes linked too closely to labor or to management, or to one of the political parties, to be acceptable as neutrals in the council debates. As in the case of the Minnesota legislators,[22] public members were identifiable as "labor," "management," and "public" public members.[23] To the extent that public members were committed to one side or the other, they provided either labor or management with grounds for complaint that the council was "stacked" and caused the aggrieved party to adopt a combative rather than a cooperative approach to the work of the council.

To some extent the emphasis on public members reflects a bygone era. Whatever importance the public members once had has been diminished by changes which have occurred during the past twenty years in the employment service, in unemployment insurance, and in organized labor.

The advisory councils were born under the auspices of the

[22] See p. 264.
[23] Professor William Haber, in discussing the appointment of public members (*Proceedings of the Twentieth Annual Meeting of the Interstate Conference of Employment Security Agencies* [Washington, D.C.: U.S. Department of Labor, 1956], p. 21), mentions only the first alternative facing the appointing authority: to select ignorant persons without views, or informed persons who necessarily have views. This is not the crucial alternative. The crucial alternative is an unmentioned one: to appoint persons with views that favor labor, or persons with views that favor management.

employment service, and their first task was to assist the service to attain respectability. For years, before the coming of unemployment compensation, the employment service literally lived a life of the back streets. It needed the help of persons with prestige to gain community standing. For this purpose public members were very useful. But times changed. The employment service gradually achieved a secure place in the community, and the need for public members of prestige dwindled proportionately.[24]

The advent of unemployment compensation enlarged the scope of the advisory councils, but it did not improve the position of the public members. Unemployment compensation quickly monopolized the attention of the councils. But the public members had less of a role to play in unemployment compensation than they did even in the employment service. Unemployment compensation is so controversial that none of the decision makers (neither of labor nor of management nor of government) were inclined to grant an influential role to the public members—individuals who had no organizations back of them, who had no personal stake in the matters under dispute, and whose views, therefore, had only the weight of private opinion.[25] Moreover, the program of unemployment compensation has undergone a great deal of development over the years. The large, basic decisions that had to be made in the early years have given way in some degree to more detailed, more technical, and more disputable decisions.[26] In this area public members have a smaller role to play.

The final change tending to limit the scope of the public members has been the shift in the balance of power between labor and management. When the employment security program began, labor was a struggling youngster needing considerable public support—from clergymen, university professors, women's clubs —to attain even its minimum goals. But during the intervening two decades organized labor has grown into one of the most powerful groups in our society and is much more capable than formerly of achieving its objectives by its own efforts. This is not

[24] See Pennsylvania, p. 309.   [25] See New York, pp. 206–7.

[26] It was more certain in 1935, for example, that some system of unemployment benefits should be established than it was in 1957 that the duration of benefits should be twenty-six weeks—or more or less, or uniform or variable.

to say that there is no role left for the public to play, but only that the public's role is much less clear and decisive than it used to be.

If the experience of the most effective councils is any guide, it would seem that the role of the public members on the council should be deemphasized—either by doing without them entirely (Wisconsin) or doing without them during the process of negotiations (Utah) or having (like New Hampshire) a single public member acceptable to both labor and management and acting as a nonvoting chairman whose principal function is to mediate between labor and management so as to bring them, if possible, to an agreed bill. The experience of the sample states seems to indicate that the best structure for most states would be that of New Hampshire.[27]

The Wagner-Peyser Act should probably be amended to allow the states more discretion in appointing the members of their councils. Until the act is amended, a state which does not wish to have the kind of council specified therein may avoid its prescriptions by following one of two procedures. (1) It may set up a separate council for unemployment compensation. Since the Wagner-Peyser Act refers only to the employment service, the state will have complete freedom in selecting the members of this council. (2) It may follow the New Hampshire device of appointing to the unemployment compensation council additional special members, who are called upon only when employment service matters are treated.

SCOPE

There are two parts to the question of scope, one pertaining to the extension, the other to the comprehension, of a council's scope. To what areas should the council's responsibility extend? Within each area what should the council's responsibility comprehend?

[27] The above discussion of public members does not necessarily apply to those who were members of the legislature. They are in quite a different situation. There are advantages and disadvantages to having legislators as council members, but it is not clear which outweighs the other. Rhode Island and Minnesota have had some experience with such members, but their experience is not broad enough to form the basis of reliable conclusions. (The councils of Wisconsin and Colorado invited legislators to meet with them, but the invitation elicited very little response.)

There are five areas to which the council might extend its responsibilities: unemployment compensation; the regular employment service; two special forms of employment service activities, namely, farm placement and employment stabilization; and temporary disability insurance. The law should probably state the council's scope as being simply "employment security" without further specification. This should be understood to include the first four areas, at least permissively, and to exclude positively only temporary disability insurance.

In Rhode Island the advisory councils for temporary disability insurance and employment security were merged because several of the same labor representatives were on both councils. It was probably not an adequate reason. In Wisconsin the same labor and management representatives were on both the unemployment compensation and the workmen's compensation councils, but they found it more efficient to keep the councils separate. A council for workmen's compensation must handle specialized problems for which it needs specialized members, especially from medicine and insurance, and the problems can be handled in a few meetings held every couple of years. Temporary disability insurance is somewhat like workmen's compensation in both these respects.

Although the council's scope may include all four areas according to the law, in practice unemployment compensation will probably absorb almost all of the council's attention. This practical fact should be considered when making other decisions regarding the council's structure and procedures. It should also lead to the expectation that more than one council will be needed within the area of employment security. As a matter of fact, when a state embarks on a program of "employment stabilization" it usually establishes a special commission for that purpose,[28] since much more is involved than is ordinarily handled by the administrator of employment security. The problems of farm placement also tend to become the concern of a specialized body. As to the regular employment service, it is best serviced in one of the several ways already suggested.[29]

The council's responsibilities should comprehend both legisla-

[28] See, for example, p. 347.   [29] See pp. 399, 400.

tion and administration. This was the general practice among the councils of the sample. The New York council belatedly raised the question as to whether its scope was restricted to administration, but answered the question in the negative. The California council since 1955 has interpreted its scope as being restricted to administration, but this may be merely a form of the Utah device, whereby negotiations in the field of legislation, although conducted outside the council, are conducted mainly by council members.

With respect to legislation the law should specify that the council is to make recommendations to the legislature as well as to the administrator and the governor. This will give the council a necessary degree of independence of the administrator. Moreover, the legislature is the department of government which must finally pass on the council's recommendations, and the legislature is more likely to regard the council favorably if the law explicitly recognizes this relationship and does not make the council entirely a creature of the executive department. The law should also state the council's responsibility to pass judgment on recommendations made by others than the council. "Report its views on" is the prudent expression used in the Wisconsin law. The Wisconsin council has found this provision of the law quite useful.[30]

With respect to administration the council's responsibility should not be unlimited—otherwise there is meddling—but it is not practicable to spell out in the law what the limitations are. Here it is necessary to depend on the good sense of the council and the administrator.

The laws of Massachusetts and Ohio provide good models for statements of scope that are both broad and detailed. But the very broad interpretation which the New York council once attempted to put on its law [31] and which the Michigan council succeeded in putting on its law [32] in the matter of scope is too extreme. By such an interpretation an advisory council becomes an administrative commission.

John R. Commons, writing in 1915, advised giving the council a voice in the appointment of the administrator. That is still good advice, and if restricted to a consultative voice may be

[30] See p. 64.   [31] See p. 185.   [32] See p. 321.

feasible. A provision to this effect should normally result in the appointment of an administrator who is not only competent but also genuinely nonpartisan and therefore acceptable to both labor and management—and therefore more capable of building a genuinely effective advisory council.[33]

SIZE

A council should be small enough to be a working group, yet large enough to be representative of all the major interests. Adequate representation will require fewer members in states which are small, or in which labor and management are organized compactly. The average council should have about eight or nine members. The eleven of Utah and Colorado were almost too many; the nineteen of Rhode Island and the seventeen of Minnesota certainly were.

It is perhaps better not to specify the number of council members in the law but to leave room for some flexibility. It is enough if the law specifies that the numbers of labor and management members are to be equal and that the number of public members is to be limited to one or, alternatively, left to the discretion of the appointing power.

In some states labor and management had only two representatives each.[34] The experience of these states indicates that more representation for labor and management is preferable. If the "public" does not use up more than one place on the council, labor and management may each be given four places, but they should be given at least three. If the public is given equal representation with labor and management, the council should probably have at least nine members.

TERMS

Council members may be appointed for terms which are indefinite ("at the pleasure of the Governor") or for a specified

[33] The Michigan law, since 1953, has contained a provision which equivalently has the same effect. The administrator is appointed by a four-man commission, which is composed of two representatives each of labor and management.

[34] Connecticut, Massachusetts, Minnesota, Nebraska, Ohio.

number of years. In the latter case the terms of all members may be simultaneous (begin and end together) or they may be staggered.

If labor and management are well organized and are permitted to nominate their own representatives to the council, the specifications regarding terms do not much matter.[35] Still, some principles may be laid down. Other things being equal, the less turnover there is on the council, the better, and therefore it is advisable to provide longer rather than shorter terms. But council members, for various reasons, can lose their value to a council.[36] It is therefore also advisable to provide some regular opportunity for making changes in the council membership. One New York employer suggested that members be ineligible for reappointment until they had been separated from the council for at least one term. This would help to overcome the obstacles to change presented by the internal politics of labor and management organizations, but the occasional gain achieved would probably not be worth the regular enforced losses of good council members.

The main choice is between provisions which result in each newly elected governor appointing a new council and provisions which do not have this effect. Indefinite terms, and simultaneous terms which coincide with the governor's term, belong in the first category. Such provisions can result in an excessive number of "new" councils [37] or even in the discontinuance of the council.[38]

It is probably best to provide for staggered terms and to make them short enough to permit replacement of any council member within three to five years, yet long enough to prevent more than one third of the council members from coming up for reappointment in any one year. It is probably wise, also, to include the provision of the Massachusetts law: "All members shall serve until

[35] See Wisconsin, p. 87.

[36] As is illustrated by the histories of the New York, Illinois, and Utah councils, among others.

[37] The Louisiana council, not described in the text, is the best illustration of this result. Between 1941 and 1955 it had five new councils and fifty-seven different members.

[38] As happened in the case of the Pennsylvania council. The Missouri council, not treated in the text, had a similar experience. Although active and effective in its two brief periods of existence (1937–1940, 1949–1952), it was allowed to go out of existence in all the other years. Its members served "at the pleasure of the Governor."

qualification of their respective successors," [39] in order to prevent the dissolution of the council by the mere inaction of the appointing authority.

REMUNERATION

All states reimburse council members for expenses incurred in attending council meetings, but only twenty provide remuneration beyond expenses—the remuneration varying from five dollars per day in five states to the forty dollars per day paid by New York. Of the fifteen states in the sample, eight provided remuneration: Massachusetts, Minnesota, Nebraska, New Hampshire, New York, Ohio, Utah, and Wisconsin.

Two principal advantages attach to providing remuneration. First, it makes council membership possible for persons who need all their time to earn their living. This applies chiefly to the hourly-paid worker, but includes at times the professor, the professional man, and the small businessman. The value of this advantage is limited by the fact that these people do not constitute important council members. The important council members, the decision makers among labor and management, are typically professional representatives of organizations or technicians in the employ of large companies and unions and hence suffer no personal financial loss by serving on the council.

Second, remuneration encourages attendance at meetings. In the states which provided remuneration, there was general agreement that this was so. Available data on attendance do not contradict the proposition; the councils with the best attendance records were in states that provided remuneration.[40] But many other factors influenced attendance, and available data were inadequate to measure separately the force of this one factor. Illinois, which did not provide remuneration, had as good a record of attendance as some of the states which did (for example, New York, Minnesota, Ohio).

[39] Sec. 9N(a), Ch. 610, Acts of 1947.
[40] For example, Nebraska, New Hampshire, Utah, Wisconsin. In Louisiana (not treated in the text) attendance improved from 51 percent to 69 percent after 1947, when remuneration began to be provided.

The principal disadvantages of providing remuneration are also two. First, it attracts the wrong sort of person.[41] This danger comes chiefly from the side of labor. It comes occasionally from the side of the public, and practically never from the side of management. If the council meetings are well remunerated and frequent, they become a kind of patronage plum suitable for use in union politics. There was some evidence in three states that competition for council "jobs" complicated the task of getting the most effective labor members on the council. But in no state was there clear evidence that this factor seriously impaired the council's efficiency.

Second, it diminishes the influence of the council. A council which is paid for its work does not have the prestige of one which contributes its services. There were several instances of individual legislators remarking that their respect for the council was the less because its members were "on the payroll of the Agency." In several states which did not provide remuneration the council members themselves, especially employers, opposed the idea of remuneration mainly because they feared this loss of prestige. In several states which did provide remuneration, a few employer and public members refused to accept their stipends, and some full-time professional CIO representatives turned their stipends over to the union.

It is true that the prestige of the council, like the prestige of the professions, is partly founded on the fact that it renders service which is not remunerated by a strict *quid pro quo*. It is also true that this prestige is somewhat weakened by the acceptance of remuneration. But in none of the sample states was there evidence that this weakening was of significant proportions. The influence of a council member stems primarily from his having one of the three sources of authority [42] and not from the purity of his motives. Besides, in most states the stipend provided was so small as to be obviously less than the worth of the services contributed. Also, some members, instead of applying to be reimbursed for

---

[41] The ideal council member is someone who, like Plato's philosopher-king, answers the call of duty somewhat reluctantly because he has other things to do which are more to his personal advantage.

[42] See pp. 439–41.

their expenses, accepted the stipend as a simpler way of achieving the same end.

The advantages and disadvantages of remuneration come close to balancing each other, and there is probably no one best way for all states. It may be that the effect of remuneration is not so much directional as accelerative. It will not make a bad council good or a good council bad, but it will tend to make a good council better and a bad council worse.

The following recommendations were suggested rather than established by the results of the survey:

1. Reimburse members for all expenses incurred in council work, including the work of one-man committees authorized by the council. Include wage loss in the definition of expenses.[43]

2. Where the council is organized like that in New Hampshire, with a single, mediating, nonvoting chairman, provide remuneration at least for the chairman. If he is a professor, the definition of his expenses might well include hiring a substitute to take his classes.

3. If all members are remunerated, impose an annual ceiling of twelve to fifteen times the per diem amount.

4. As an alternative: do not reimburse for expenses incurred, but do provide a flat sum for all council members large enough to cover all normal expenses. This will free council members of the bother of filling out forms (to some this was so annoying that they waived reimbursement) and if the allotment is generous will leave them with a slight "profit." It would be desirable to call this an expense allowance, but the laws of most states do not permit the payment of claimed expenses except on the presentation of detailed proof.

APPOINTIVE POWER

Two decisions must be made with regard to the appointive power, namely, how it shall be exercised and who shall exercise it.

Shall the appointive power be exercised with or without par-

---

[43] As is done by New Mexico and Oklahoma (states not included in the sample).

ticipation by the interest groups represented on the council? This is by far the more important of the two decisions. If it is made correctly, the second decision becomes relatively unimportant. Participation may be granted in three degrees. The interest groups may be authorized to submit a panel of names which the appointing authority is free to ignore, or a panel of names from among which the appointing authority must choose, or a single name which the appointing authority must accept.

All the evidence of the survey goes to indicate that some participation is desirable. Since the third degree of participation is probably not feasible, the choice is between the first and the second, with the preference going to the second. The law should provide [44] that appointments be made from a small panel of names (three at the most) submitted by the "major state-wide organizations of labor and management." Of course, if labor and management in the state are not sufficiently organized to make such a provision meaningful, then it cannot be observed. Whatever provision for participation is adopted probably should apply uniformly to both labor and management.

Who should exercise the appointive power? There are three choices: the governor,[45] the administrator of an overall agency,[46] or the administrator of the employment security agency. If the governor makes the appointments they are invested with greater prestige than if made by some lower official. As an inducement to council members to accept appointment this probably is not an important value. The decision makers of labor and management, at least those encountered in the sample states, would not have been decided by this factor in their acceptance of appointment to

[44] Legal provisions are not necessarily carried out (witness the absence of councils in states whose laws specify a council), but if participation is provided for by law, it is more likely to exist in practice.

[45] Among the forty-nine "states" which have or provide for having an advisory council, the council is appointed by the employment security administrator in fourteen, by the overall administrator in nine, and by the governor in twenty-six. (*Comparison of State Unemployment Insurance Laws as of August 1954*, published by the United States Department of Labor.) Among the sample states, the council was appointed by the overall administrator in three and by the governor in the remaining fifteen.

[46] Usually styled a department of labor or an industrial commission. Only eighteen of the fifty-one employment security agencies are within a larger agency. The rest are independent departments or commissions.

them. It was only in the case of public members that some individuals were encountered who sought appointment primarily because they wanted the prestige.[47]

The chief disadvantage of appointment by the governor is that it links the council too closely to politics in the narrow sense. Many instances were encountered among the sample states where the governor appointed members—labor, management, and public —primarily because they were active, working members of his political party, or refused to reappoint key members of the council because they belonged to the opposite party.[48] In one state the governor had appointed an entire new council just previous to being interviewed. He had made the appointments without consulting the administrator of the agency on any of them.[49] When asked whether that might not make the administrator's task more difficult, he replied: "His duty is to get along with whomever I appoint." When asked what he expected from the new council, he replied: "Nothing." When asked: "Why then appoint a council?" he replied: "Because the law requires it." All of his answers were consistent. Together they described an attitude which explains why many councils produced no more than this governor expected.

There is another, although minor, disadvantage attaching to appointment by the governor. The governor has so many appointments to make that he cannot make them as promptly or as wisely as the administrator of the agency. Appointments were sometimes delayed for months and years because the governor was busy.[50] And in two cases the wrong person was appointed because of a similarity in names.

Appointment by the overall administrative agency is the second method. It falls between the other two, sharing the advantages and disadvantages of both, but is closer to the third than to the first. It worked well in the three sample states (Nebraska, Utah, and Wis-

[47] In one such case the governor answered the protest of the administrator by telling him frankly: "The man worked hard for me in the last election, and the only reward he has asked is this appointment. What can I do?" He appointed him.

[48] For the most dramatic instance, see New York, p. 199.

[49] He had secured and accepted nominees from the labor organizations, but not from the employer organizations.

[50] See, for example, New York, p. 198.

consin) that used it. In two of these (Utah and Wisconsin) the administrator of the employment security agency was allowed to exercise a predominant influence in the selection of council members, and this accounted in large part for the success of the system.

Appointment by the administrator of the employment security agency is the third method. The administrator is the one with whom the council must work most intimately and on whom its success chiefly depends.

The task of handling a useful advisory committee calls for an administrator who has the ability, the personality, and the imagination to attract men of vision among influential groups, to impart a sense of urgency in solving his problems, and to give them a sense of pride in being associated with his work.[51]

This cardinal fact would be emphasized unmistakably if the law provided for the administrator to select his own advisory council. It would place the responsibility for an effective council precisely where it belonged. It would also be some bar against council meddling. In one of the few councils which did begin to meddle, the members answered the administrator's protest by reminding him: "We are the governor's council, not yours." [52]

One disadvantage of appointment by the administrator is the diminution of council prestige. But, as remarked above, this would probably not deter the decision makers of labor and management from accepting appointment. The diminished prestige could even be an advantage, in so far as it kept away those who merely sought the honor. Several administrators said that they would not want the appointive power because it would expose them to the charge of "packing" the council. But the administrator could render the charge of "packing" almost harmless by allowing the major interest groups to nominate their own representatives. In fact, he would be almost compelled in self-defense to seek such nominations. This would be an additional advantage to putting appointive responsibility on the shoulders of the administrator. The chief disadvan-

[51] Avery Leiserson, *Administrative Regulation* (Chicago: University of Chicago Press, 1942), pp. 167–68.
[52] See California, p. 356.

tage of appointment by the administrator is that it may make it more difficult for the council to function as adviser to the legislature. To the extent that this possible disadvantage became actual, it would justify appointment by some other method.

No clear pattern for the "best" method of appointment emerges from the experience of the councils in the sample. For most states the most practicable provision may be one that specifies appointment by the governor but requires him to receive nominations from labor and management organizations and to consult with the administrator. However, the final word must be that the particular method of appointment does not matter greatly if the first condition of all good appointments is observed and the organized interest groups, labor and management, are granted effective participation in the choice of their representatives.[53]

STAFF

Whether the advisory council should have a special staff of its own was discussed in the New York chapter.[54] The conclusion reached there with regard to New York seems applicable generally. The council should not have a special technical staff of its own independent of the control of the agency. The situation is too likely to produce bad relations with the agency.

In 1955 the California law was amended to provide for an executive secretary to be selected by the council and to be completely dependent on the council. There has not been enough experience under this provision to justify a firm judgment of its worth. It seems probable, however, that this moderate degree of independence will not cause difficulties sufficient to outweigh its advantages. The same judgment applies to such provisions as that

[53] Arthur Altmeyer made this observation in substance two decades earlier, when he was chairman of the Social Security Commission. In a letter dated March 8, 1937, he wrote to Merrill Murray, currently the executive secretary of the Federal Advisory Council, to say: "I do not think it makes much difference whether the governor or the state unemployment compensation authority makes the appointments. It all depends on the way they go about it, and how they use the council after it is organized." Arthur Altmeyer, it is interesting to recall, was the first chairman, if only for a brief time, of the most successful advisory council in employment security, that of Wisconsin.

[54] See pp. 181, 182.

of Ohio, whereby the advisory council has a veto on the dismissal
of its executive secretary.

It seems to be a workable arrangement to designate in the law
certain personnel of the agency who will have the advisory council
as their special responsibility. Two should be sufficient—an executive secretary and a clerical secretary. New York was the only advisory council which provided both. Ohio and Pennsylvania each
provided an executive secretary and Massachusetts a clerical secretary. In New York the council's executive secretary was the
agency's actuary and in Ohio the agency's head of research; in
Pennsylvania he was the agency's research and public-relations
man. Designation of agency staff for the service of the council,
even though the staff is primarily under the control of the agency,
will normally result in the agency's receiving more administrative funds from the Bureau of Employment Security than if the
law did not specify such service. The additional funds should
normally result in the administrator's being more willing to give
the advisory council the time and attention it needs.

PROCEDURES

The procedures of a council are among the less important factors
which determine effectiveness. Nevertheless they are not without
influence, and the experience of the sample states in respect to
seven procedures is worth noting briefly.

WRITTEN RULES

Written rules of procedure are not essential. Most of the councils, including the very effective Wisconsin council,[55] did not have
them, and the few councils which did have them referred to them
but seldom.

Although not necessary, written rules can be useful, at least to
settle disputes, and it is probably better to have them than not to
have them. The New York council produced the earliest (1935)

---

[55] This was consistent for the Wisconsin council, which had no set times for meetings,
kept no minutes, used no committees, and made no reports.

and fullest set of formal rules. Other councils with full sets were those of Illinois and Pennsylvania and the Federal Advisory Council. Anyone interested in drawing up a set of rules will find adequate models in these four.[56]

MEETINGS

Meetings should be called only when there is something substantial for the council to do or to learn. They should normally, therefore, be all-day meetings—from ten in the morning, say, to three or four in the afternoon. The number of meetings needed to conduct the council's business will vary with circumstances. The council should probably meet at least half a dozen times a year, and oftener when necessary. The number of meetings needed will vary not only with new projects but also with new members. The same project can be handled with fewer meetings if there has been less turnover among the council members. There will normally be more meetings in legislative years than in others, and the meetings will usually cluster somewhat around the sessions of the legislature.[57] The Massachusetts *average* of seventy-six meetings yearly is clearly excessive, and even the Ohio average of sixteen seems somewhat high. But the Colorado, Connecticut, and Nebraska averages of less than three are clearly too low. Utah's average of seven is a bit on the low side, but since the work of negotiating an agreed bill was done outside the council proper, fewer council meetings sufficed.

Ordinarily the administrator of the agency will determine when the council is to meet and will arrange the agenda. He will call meetings or put items on the agenda at the request of the majority of any interest group on the council (labor, management, or public). The agenda should reach advisory council members a week before the meeting. On numerous occasions council members protested because they were asked to take a position on matters which they had not had time to study.

[56] The rules of the New York state council are given in Appendix B.
[57] The clustering effect will be less marked in states which, like New York, have annual legislative sessions.

Who should be present at the council meetings? The general public, as is permitted in some councils? Probably not. The top staff of the agency? Probably yes. Alternates for council members? Yes, but without voting power. Technical assistants to council members, like the "second row" of the Illinois and federal councils? Yes.

At a day-long meeting there will be a lunch period. The labor and management members lunched separately in Wisconsin, but together in Illinois and New Hampshire and most other states. The Wisconsin procedure is probably more efficient, if perhaps less pleasant. The members of the respective interest groups very often have not been in contact with each other between meetings to discuss their common interest in unemployment insurance. Lunching together gives them that opportunity. They come back to the meeting better prepared to conduct their business. This is probably a greater gain than the increased sociability that may result from lunching together, though that also is valuable.

Some councils have called and conducted their meetings independently of the administrator—for example, those of Michigan, Ohio, New York (in its earlier years), and California (briefly). At one time the New Hampshire council considered adopting this procedure. It is probably an unwise procedure. Even apart from the danger that it will produce hostility between the council and the administrator, it impedes both the advisory and the bargaining functions of the council. The administrator will understand the mind of the council much better if he is present at its meetings than if he merely gets a digest of the council's conclusions. More importantly, the council needs the mediating services of the administrator in order to arrive at its agreed bill.[58]

MINUTES

New York and Wisconsin exemplify the two extremes in keeping minutes. The New York council has kept verbatim minutes of all its meetings, while the Wisconsin council has kept no minutes at all. In the case of New York the verbatim minutes

[58] See Wisconsin, pp. 67, 88.

did not seem to hinder free discussion [59] but neither did they prove particularly useful. In the case of Wisconsin the lack of all minutes certainly did not prevent the council from operating effectively, but there were times when some written record would have been useful, especially to settle disputes as to what had been said and agreed upon at a previous meeting.[60] Something between these two extremes, that is, some form of condensed minutes, would probably be best for most states.

A requirement that copies of all minutes be transmitted to the Bureau of Employment Security [61] is indifferently observed by the states and (wisely) not pressed by the Bureau. Just as some states object to any attempt by the Bureau to establish direct contact with their advisory councils, so do some council members strongly object to reporting to a federal bureau on their private (as they see it) activities.

COMMITTEES

Committees did not play an important part in the work of the councils. Even when committees were appointed, they generally did not function. Committees were most useful when they were set up for limited periods to perform temporary tasks,[62] and experience has supported the early advice of the Bureau of Employment Security against having standing committees.[63] When standing committees were appointed, they did either nothing (the usual case) or too much (leaving the full council with too little to do [64]). The Federal Advisory Council, which cannot assemble its full membership easily or frequently, has understandably made greater use of committees.

[59] But see the Federal Advisory Council, p. 368.

[60] The council members sometimes kept records of their own for reference purposes.

[61] *State Operations Bulletin No. 13,* issued by the Bureau of Employment Security, January, 1941.

[62] For example, in New York, Ohio, Pennsylvania.

[63] *State Operations Bulletin No. 13,* issued January, 1941.

[64] As in Minnesota, p. 275.

REPORTS

The issuing of reports has been an important function of some councils—for example, those of Massachusetts, New York, Ohio, Pennsylvania, and, of course, the Federal Advisory Council. Reports were likely to take on importance where the council's public nature was stressed and its collective bargaining function minimized (as in Ohio), and were likely to be neglected where the contrary emphasis obtained (as in Wisconsin, New Hampshire, and Utah).[65]

It is probably best not to require reports by law but to leave them to the discretion of the council. The preparation of a report can be a difficult, time-consuming task, and where the council can produce an agreed bill, as in Wisconsin, there is little need to impose the additional task on the council of getting out a report.[66] The administrator usually makes an annual report, and this should satisfy the need of the legislature and the governor for information and guidance. Where the council cannot produce an agreed bill, it should probably make at least a report.[67] In the case of the Federal Advisory Council, an annual report could be one of its more important functions.

AGREED BILL PROCEDURE

In their attempts to produce agreed bills, council members will do well to observe four rules: (1) To respect concessions made provisionally during negotiations and not to use them for propaganda purposes later if negotiations fail to produce a final agreement. (2) To agree to oppose all legislation other than the agreed bill, even though the other legislation is more favorable to one's own side than the agreed bill. (3) To extend the agreement to include the exact language of the bill, so that there will be no room

[65] The Wisconsin custom of annotating its agreed bill with explanations constituted a kind of council report to the legislature.

[66] A report generally includes a statement with supporting arguments, covering the areas in which the council members do not agree. This public controversy could conceivably interfere with the agreed bill procedure.

[67] To have its maximum effect a council report should be issued early, preferably before the governor delivers his message to the legislature.

for misunderstanding and recriminations. (4) To appear at the legislative hearing to speak for the agreed bill. This shows respect for the legislators and in turn wins respect from them.[68]

COUNCIL RELATIONS TO OUTSIDE LABOR AND MANAGEMENT

All councils follow the procedure of allowing "outsiders" to come before the council and state their views. Some councils regularly invite labor and management to make such appearances, usually when the council begins to prepare recommendations for the legislature.

If the council membership does not include the decision makers among labor and management, this procedure is likely to be useless. In several instances, the decision makers did not bother to attend the council meeting to which they were invited, for they saw little point in presenting their case to members of their own group who had less influence than themselves. Where they did attend, as a precautionary measure, not much was accomplished. The council, after it had heard both sides, still could not make a decision that would be binding on both sides. And neither could it, by means of the meeting, bring the two sides to an agreement. Mediation cannot be exercised in one, formal, semi-public meeting.[69]

If the council membership does include the decision makers among labor and management, the council hearing makes much more sense, but it is not strictly necessary. Since the council members are the genuine representatives of the labor and management organizations, particular unions or employers will normally make their desires known to the representatives on the council through their own organizations.

The peripatetic hearings which the Wisconsin council conducted in 1952 and 1954 were exceptional procedures necessitated

[68] The Wisconsin procedure of supplying the legislators with an explanation of the agreed provisions is an excellent one.

[69] The French mediation system seems to have been relatively unsuccessful partly because it has operated through the media of such formal meetings. See William H. McPherson, "European Variations on the Mediation Theme," *Labor Law Journal*, August 1955, p. 527.

by the strong hint of the legislature. They were productive of some very good results, but because of their cost in terms of time and money they are probably not to be imitated generally.

SUMMARY

With one exception, internal factors taken as a whole proved to be less important than external factors taken as a whole. But the one exception proved to have more relevance for council effectiveness than all the other factors, external and internal, combined. The internal factor of council membership proved to be the prime determinant of council effectiveness. This is a conclusion of optimism in so far as internal factors are controllable factors. It means that the most important factor determining council effectiveness is within a state's control.

22

THE FUTURE OF ADVISORY COUNCILS

SINCE the prospects of effective councils vary greatly from state to state, and since within any one state the prospects can change literally overnight—as when, for example, a new governor assumes office or a new administrator is appointed—it is almost impossible to predict the future of an advisory council in a particular place at a particular time. It is quite possible, however, to foresee on what factors the future of all councils in all states will mainly depend.

Experience has shown that of all the external and internal factors affecting advisory councils, only one is in the strict sense a necessary condition for success—the factor of personalities. The members of the council, as also the governor and the administrator, must be the "right" persons.

The "right" council members are those who are capable and reasonable. They are capable if between them they possess the three sources of authority [1] and if, especially, the labor and management members are able to speak authoritatively for their respective groups.[2] They are reasonable if they have, in the phrase of Learned Hand, "the spirit that is not too sure it is right" and if they are dedicated to the democratic premise that through the processes of investigation, discussion, and compromise men of good will can come to a working agreement.

If the governor is opposed to the idea of an advisory council, as some governors have been, there will be no advisory council, no

[1] See pp. 439–41.
[2] For this it is obviously necessary that labor and management be organized; but they are sufficiently organized in all the industrial states and in nearly all the others.

matter what the law states. If the governor wants a council, but makes council appointments to satisfy his political obligations rather than to obtain capable members, there will be no effective council.[3] The governor need not give the council much, or any, positive assistance. It is enough if he simply makes appointments according to the recommendations of his administrator and then does nothing to impede the operation of the council. But if the future is at all like the past, there will be some governors who will prove an insurmountable obstacle to council effectiveness.

The personality of the administrator is the most important factor determining the effectiveness of a council. An administrator who is opposed to the idea of an advisory council can usually prevent one from being appointed or, if one is appointed, can easily prevent its being effective. It is not enough that the administrator be not opposed to the council; unlike the governor, he must make a positive contribution to the council. To make his contribution, he must have both the ability and the willingness to work with a council. The ability required involves something in addition to the ability to administer the routine operations of the agency. Some aspects of a job can be handled by anyone who can meet the minimum requirements of a given office—be the office one of policeman, general, clergyman, or administrator of employment security. But there are other aspects which demand more than that minimum of ability. There are tasks for which the prestige of mere office is not enough, but which require the prestige of the natural leader. The task of building an effective advisory council is of this sort, and it requires the ability to lead men. Most, though not all, administrators of employment security may be expected to possess the requisite ability.

But even ability is not enough. The administrator must also have willingness. He must welcome the conclusion reached by the Minnesota study commission: "Whatever we do, one

[3] There is a long history of such political appointments, and an early remark of John R. Commons still applies: "The idea of such an 'advisory committee' is usually misunderstood as something that has been tried and 'would not work.' This is because advisory committees were usually appointed by the political administration itself and did not represent the actual corporations and unions, but represented the dominant political interests." *The Economics of Collective Action* (New York: Macmillan Co., 1950), p. 257.

of our concerns should be to encourage rather than discourage the working out of their own problems by employers and employees." The administrator must be a man of imagination who can see the challenge and satisfaction in the task of so governing his agency as to help the governed govern themselves. He must be able to appreciate the point in the saying: "He who governs leads the blind; he who teaches gives sight."

Among the Mother Carey stories that belong to the folklore of the sea there is one that can be used to test whether an administrator possesses the requisite imagination. If he can appreciate the profound truth in the story, there is at least a chance that an effective advisory council will flourish in his agency. It seems that Mother Carey had just made a seagull out of clay. As the graceful bird flew off, a fairy who was passing by exclaimed with admiration at Mother Carey's talent. "Tush, my child," said Mother Carey, "making things is not very remarkable. Anybody can make things. But only God can make things make themselves."

Appendixes

A

COMPARATIVE STATISTICS OF EMPLOYMENT SECURITY ADVISORY COUNCILS [a] IN SELECTED STATES FOR VARIOUS PERIODS [b]

State [c]	Starting Date	MEMBERSHIP [d,e] L M P			Term [d] (Years)	Remuneration [d]	Appointing Authority [d]	Meetings Held (Average per year)	Attendance Record (Percent)
California (8.9)	1947	4	4	4	Indefinite	None	Governor	7 (1947–1953)	69 (1947–1953)
		3	3	1					
Colorado (0.7)	1941	4	4	3	4	None	Governor	2.3	59
Connecticut (1.9) [f]	1936 [f]	2	2	2	3	None	Governor	1.4	84
Illinois (6.8)	1938	3	3	3	2	None	Governor	4.8	79
Massachusetts (3.9)	1936	3	3	3	6	None	Governor	75.7 (1939–1957)	n.a. [g]
		2	2	2		$25			
Michigan (4.8)	1947	4	4	0	6	None	Governor	7.0 (1948–1955)	n.a.
Minnesota (1.6)	1938	[1	1	1]	Indefinite	$10	Industrial Commissioner	2.1 (1940–1957)	78 (1947–1955)
		[3	3	5]		$25	Governor		

State (percent)[c]	Year				Term	Amount	Appointing authority	Percent covered[b]	Percent[b]
Nebraska (0.5)	1937	2 2 3 / 2 2 2			Indefinite 4	None $20	Commissioner of Labor	2.0	96
New Hampshire (0.4)	1948	3 3 1			3	None $20	Governor	8.8 (1948–1956)	90 (1948–1956)
New York (12.2)	1935	3 3 3			6	None $40	Governor	10.4	75
Ohio (6.5)	1937	2 2 3			7	$20	Governor	15.5	76
Pennsylvania (8.0)	1938	[3 3 3]			Indefinite	None	Governor	4.5 (1950–1953)	83 (1950–1953)
Rhode Island (0.6)	1949[h]	8 8 3 / 3 3 3			Indefinite	None	Governor	9.0 (1949–1953)	67 (1949–1953)
Utah (0.4)	1936	[2 2 1] / 4[i] 4[i] 3			Indefinite 2	$10 $15	Industrial Commissioner	5.8	81
Wisconsin (2.1)	1932[f]	[3 3 0] / 4 4 0			Indefinite	None $25	Industrial Commissioner	9.5 (1941–1957)	83 (1941–1957)

[a] Exclusive of early councils limited to employment service.

[b] Where no period is specified, the data apply from the starting date through 1957. Where less than the full period is shown, the usual reasons are changes in council structure or lack of data; see the appropriate chapters for details of structural changes.

[c] Figures in parentheses indicate the percentage of the national covered employment in each state. All the states in the appendix together comprise 59.3 percent of the national covered employment. Data relate to 1956 and are from the Bureau of Employment Security, U.S. Department of Labor.

[d] If changed more than once, only the earliest and the latest data are shown; see the appropriate chapters for details.

[e] Square brackets indicate that representation of the group is required but that the number of representatives is not specified.

[f] Limited to the unemployment insurance program.

[g] n.a. = information not available.

[h] Includes the temporary disability program.

[i] The number specified is the minimum.

B

RULES OF PROCEDURE OF THE NEW YORK STATE ADVISORY COUNCIL ON EMPLOYMENT AND UNEMPLOYMENT INSURANCE [1]

1. The Chairman shall preside at all meetings. In his absence the Council shall select another member to preside.

2. (a) Unless the Council shall direct otherwise, the Chairman shall appoint all committees created by the Council and shall designate the chairman of each.

(b) All committees shall be composed of an equal number of representatives of the public, the employers and the employees.

3. (a) The Council shall regularly meet at such times and places as it may fix from time to time.

(b) The Chairman may call special meetings to be held either in the City of Albany or the City of New York at such times as he may fix.

(c) On the written request of not less than three members of the Council, the Chairman shall call a special meeting, for the purposes designated in the request, to be held not later than seven days after the receipt thereof by the Chairman either in the City of Albany or the City of New York as he may fix. In the event the Chairman fails to call a special meeting within four days after his receipt of a request therefor, the three or more members who made the request may themselves call a special meeting, for the purposes designated in their request, to be held not later than fourteen days after the receipt thereof by the Chairman, either in the City of Albany or the City of New York as they may fix.

(d) Written notice of every meeting shall be given to each member of the Council not less than three days before the day of meeting.

[1] Rules 1 through 10 adopted November 14, 1935; Rule 11, April 21, 1938; Rule 12, November 23, 1938; Rule 13, March 7, 1940; Rule 14, June 20, 1940.

4. (a) The minutes of the meetings shall be sent to each member of the Council together with the notice of the meeting at which they are to be presented for approval.

(b) Final action shall not be taken by the Council on any report or recommendation to the Governor, the Legislature, the Industrial Commissioner, the Director of Unemployment Insurance, or any public officer or public body, nor on any administrative, procedural or interpretive rule, regulation or ruling unless the substance of such report, recommendation, rule, regulation or ruling, together with any committee's report thereon, shall have been sent to each member of the Council not less than seven days before the day of the meeting at which such action is taken and unless, further, the notice of such meeting shall have specified that such action is to be taken thereat.

5. (a) Not less than five members of the Council shall constitute a quorum at all meetings.

(b) Except as provided by paragraph #8 hereof, the Council shall take no action unless the concurrence therein is had of no less than five members.

6. The Council shall designate a Secretary who, with the consent and approval of the Industrial Commissioner may be a member of the staff of the Labor Department. The Secretary shall keep a correct record of the actions and business of the Council.

7. (a) Unless the Council shall direct otherwise no stenographic notes shall be made of its discussions.

(b) Voting at meetings shall be by roll call and a record of each member's vote shall be made and kept as part of the minutes.

8. (a) Additions may be made to these rules of procedure and they may be repealed, modified or amended, in whole or in part, at any time, provided the substance of the proposed addition, repeal, modification or amendment shall have been sent to each member not less than seven days before the day of the meeting at which action thereon is to be taken and provided further that the notice of such meeting shall have specified that such action is to be taken thereat.

(b) No addition, repeal, modification or amendment shall become effective unless it is approved by a vote of no less than seven members of the Council.

(c) Any provision of the rules of procedure may be suspended at any time if all the members of the Council concur therein either in writing or by vote at a meeting. At any meeting at which all of the members of the Council are not present, any provision of the rules of procedure may be suspended if all those present concur therein, provided that written ratification both of the suspension and of any action that may have been taken by reason of or under the suspended rule or rules shall be obtained from all of the absentees within seven days thereafter. Written consents to suspend and ratifications of suspensions shall be kept as part of the records of the Council.

9. No publicity on behalf of the Advisory Council shall be released unless the Council has authorized it or unless it refers to official action taken by the Council based on a recorded vote.

Where publicity is given to any action of the Council based on a divided vote the majority and the minority shall be given the opportunity to include statements of the reasons for their vote and of any comments upon the vote before the publicity is released. Upon the occurrence of a divided vote the chairman shall ask the majority and the minority whether the majority and the minority wish to include a statement with the publicity release. If either side wishes so to do at least 4 hours shall elapse following the termination of the meeting before publicity shall be released and statements not received within four hours after the termination of any such meeting shall not be included in the publicity release. No member of the Council shall orally or in writing quote the views of the Council except to the extent that the same reflect action actually taken at a meeting of the Council.

10. Interpretative rulings which the Unemployment Insurance Division wishes to submit to the Council shall be mailed to the nine members of the Council. The Committee of the Council on Interpretative rulings shall not meet until at least eight days after such proposed rulings are mailed out. During such period of eight days the members of the Council shall be expected to read the proposed rulings and communicate their criticisms and suggestions to the Chairman of the Committee of the Council on Rulings. After eight days the Committee of the Council on Rulings shall meet and is empowered finally to pass upon rulings and make any corrections, alterations or suggestions that the Committee deems advisable subject only to the obligation to bring up for discussion at a full meeting of the Council any proposed ruling which any member of the Council requests be discussed at a full meeting. The Committee of the Council on Rulings may report its findings direct to the Industrial Commissioner and the Director of Unemployment Insurance and shall submit a copy of its report to the full Council.

11. At every meeting of the Council there be held [sic] an Executive Session before the meeting adjourns.

12. The secretary to [sic] send administrative reports to the members of the Council for their study and information at least three days before a meeting of the Council.

13. The Industrial Commissioner may, as a matter of course and without the need of any special invitation attend all executive ses-

sions of the Council; and the Council may, by special affirmative action only, arrange to meet by itself should the occasion ever arise when it wishes to do so.

14. The attendance by one member of a committee of the Advisory Council shall constitute a quorum sufficient for a meeting of such committee; provided that advance notice of such meeting shall have been given to all the members of the committee by the Executive Secretary of the Council. Minutes of the meeting shall be sent to all members of the Council.

A meeting of a committee attended by a quorum or the performance by any member of the Council of any duty or task on behalf of the Council in accordance with authority delegated to such member by the Council shall be deemed a formal meeting of a committee of the Council.

C

AMENDMENTS TO THE WISCONSIN UNEMPLOYMENT COMPENSATION LAW ENACTED ON THE UNANIMOUS RECOMMENDATION OF THE ADVISORY COUNCIL, 1933–1955

1933: The date the law began to apply was postponed from July 1, 1933, until "business recovery is well under way"; this ultimately became July 1, 1934.

A "probationary period" of four weeks was provided during which a new employee earned no benefit credits. The provision was necessary because the law contained no qualifying requirement for benefits.

1935: The maximum benefit was increased from $10 to $15 and maximum duration from 10 to 13 weeks. The waiting period was increased from 2 to 3 weeks (applicable as before to each employer, so a claimant might serve several waiting periods each of three weeks). The maximum tax rate was increased from 2 percent to 4 percent. To prevent rapid rises in tax rates in bad years, rate increases above the standard (2.7 percent) were limited to ½ percent per year. The definition of "employee" was broadened beyond the common law definition by the introduction of the "ABC" test.

A number of changes were made to permit the law to meet the standards of the Social Security Act. Most noteworthy were the expansion of coverage from employers of 10 to employers of 8 employees, and the change in the experience-rating system from a "reserve-per-employee" to the present "reserve-percentage" basis.

1937: Coverage was broadened to employers of 6 employees. Because there was no qualifying requirement, seasonal canning employees were limited in their benefits. Weekly benefit rates were based on average weekly wages instead of the former (unsatisfactory) full-time weekly wages. Participation in the Interstate Benefit System was authorized. More protection was given a claimant whose employer's account was exhausted by making available the fund's interest earnings. (As a result, no claimant was ever denied benefits because of an exhausted employer account.)

1939: This last provision was further strengthened by providing possible extra taxes from employers if needed. Maximum duration was increased from 13 to 17⅓ weeks and the duration ratio was increased from 25 percent to 33 percent. (One week of benefits could be earned by three instead of four weeks of work.) The waiting period was set at not more than two weeks at the first layoff and not more than three weeks for each employer. Benefit rights as to new employers began to accrue during, not after, the second year of taxes. Coverage for most government units was made optional instead of compulsory; so most of them ceased to be covered. Refusal of suitable work, even if for good cause, resulted in the cancellation of one to four weeks of benefit rights.

1941: Unlimited protection was given a claimant whose employer's account was exhausted by making available the entire fund, if needed. Thus Wisconsin then had a "pooled fund" in fact, though not in name. The maximum benefit was increased from $15 to $17 and maximum duration from 17⅓ to 20 weeks, while the duration ratio was increased from 33 percent to 50 percent. The waiting period was set at two weeks once in a year—*not* per employer. A fourteen-week qualifying requirement to measure attachment to the labor market was substituted for the probationary period. An administrative penalty for fraud was introduced to supplement court prosecutions. Separation from employment due to marriage canceled all wage credits.

1943: The maximum benefit was increased from $17 to $20. Benefit rights as to new employers began to accrue a year earlier, that is, employees began to build up benefit rights as soon as their employer began to pay taxes. Further interstate cooperation was permitted by combining multistate credits of interstate workers. Experience rates were adjusted temporarily by introducing "war-risk" rates to build up reserves to meet increased liabilities brought by war time expansion. Unemployment due to an "Act of God" became compensable. Salaried workers who had been employed ten out of twelve months at an average of $200 per month were no longer disqualified from receiving benefits when unemployed. The legislature, with the unanimous approval of the advisory council, instructed the commission to "oppose federalization" [Chapter 108 (14) 14].

1945: Maximum duration was increased from 20 to 23 weeks. No benefit rate (except the maximum) was to be below 50 percent of the average weekly wage. Voluntary quits were not disqualified if they left for "a compelling personal reason" or to take another job.

Quitting to get married no longer canceled wage credits, but only suspended them until the claimant had worked again "for a substantial period." Refusal of suitable work no longer canceled wage credits, but merely suspended them until the claimant had earned four times his benefit rate. The name of the experience-rating system was changed to "pooled." Further changes were made for the better adjustment of rates to changing economic conditions (e.g., the most recent year's reserve percentage was substituted for the three-year average).

1947: The maximum benefit was increased from $20 to $24, maximum duration from 23 to 24 weeks, the duration ratio from 50 percent to 60 percent, and the minimum qualifying average weekly wage from $7.50 to $10. To prevent unduly sharp increases in tax rates in bad years, the schedule of experience rates was changed to provide smaller rate intervals and a 1 percent limit on all increases in one year in place of the former ½ percent limit on only "above-standard-rate" increases.

1949: The maximum benefit was increased from $24 to $26, maximum duration from 24 to 26½ weeks, the duration ratio from 60 percent to 67 percent, and the minimum qualifying average weekly wage from $10 to $12. Waiting period weeks might be fulfilled by partial unemployment. The penalty for fraudulent claims was increased. Flexible authorization was given to require claimants to make an independent search for work.

1951: The maximum benefit was increased from $26 to $30 and the duration ratio from 67 percent to 70 percent, but maximum duration was unchanged. The waiting period was reduced from two weeks to one week. Benefits paid to workers who quit for a "compelling personal reason" or to take another job were no longer charged to the employer's experience. Benefit overpayments might be recovered for six years after discovery. The experience-rating system was again adjusted to provide a lower schedule of tax rates in bad years, thus further extending the long history of making experience rating build reserves in "good" years, and limiting rate increases in "bad" years.

1953: The maximum benefit was increased from $30 to $33, and the minimum qualifying average weekly wage from $12 to $13. More government employees were covered and reserve accumulation was changed to pay-as-you-go financing for government units.

1955: The maximum benefit was increased from $33 to $36. Coverage was extended from employers of 6 to employers of 4 employees. Several minor amendments were made in the disqualification provisions. Another adjustment was made in the tax structure to provide a further counter-cyclical effect.

D

WORKMEN'S COMPENSATION

Workmen's compensation is sufficiently like unemployment compensation to make the differences in their histories instructive. One difference is that workmen's compensation has not been quite so controversial an issue as unemployment compensation. The disputes between labor and management have been somewhat less intense, less continuous, and have been settled much more often by agreed bills. Some states, like Ohio, which rarely or never managed to achieve an agreed bill in unemployment compensation had a long tradition of agreed bills in workmen's compensation.

One reason for this difference may be that workmen's compensation antedates unemployment compensation, and its negotiating pattern was set when the state manufacturers' associations and the AFL were alone as negotiators, before the state chambers of commerce and the CIO came into the picture so prominently.[1] As remarked before, the legislative representatives of the manufacturers and of the AFL, especially those of the older generation, were inclined to favor the voluntaristic method of collective bargaining over the compulsory method of legislation.

The above reason is probably less important than another—the difference in the character of the two programs. Legislators are more sympathetic to workmen's compensation than to unemployment compensation. They understand and grant the need of an injured man more readily than they do that of an unemployed man, and they are less apprehensive of abuse in the payment of benefits to the former. Employers have been aware of this attitude on the part of the legisla-

---

[1] The chambers of commerce and the CIO are still not quite as interested as are the other two organizations in workmen's compensation and yield an informal leadership to them more readily in this program than in unemployment compensation. The reason for this attitude in the case of the chambers of commerce is that their membership is not predominantly in manufacturing, where workmen's compensation plays its main role; the reason in the case of the CIO is that its membership is predominantly in large firms which have programs of sick benefits more liberal than the state programs of workmen's compensation.

tures, and as a result they have been less inclined to risk a legislative battle with labor and more willing to negotiate an agreed bill. Moreover, employers themselves share the legislators' more favorable attitude toward workmen's compensation—not only for humanitarian reasons but also because workmen's compensation protects the employer from the danger of lawsuits.

Another difference between the two programs is that the advisory council has had almost no place in the program of workmen's compensation. With the exception of Wisconsin and Colorado, none of the states in the sample made any use of an advisory council for workmen's compensation.[2] In several states labor leaders said that they would welcome one if it were weighted with public members who could be used to put pressure on employers, but generally neither labor nor management nor the government expressed any interest in such a council—not even in states where labor and management customarily produced agreed bills in workmen's compensation or where the leaders of labor and management were already members of an advisory council in unemployment compensation.[3]

Everyone considered that there was little for an advisory council to do in workmen's compensation other than to negotiate, or attempt to negotiate, an agreed bill in each legislative session, which in most states occurred only every two years. For that purpose they considered it sufficient to assemble an *ad hoc* group composed of leaders of labor and management, some representatives of the insurance companies and of the administering agency, along with the chairmen of the appropriate legislative committees.

[2] Ohio began such a council too recently to be included in this survey.
[3] See, for example, pp. 91–92 (Wisconsin), 140 (Utah), 358 (California).

Index

INDEX